THE RENAISSANCE IN FRANCE 1488–1559

THE RENAISSANCE IN FRANCE
1488-1559

ANNE DENIEUL-CORMIER

Translated by
Anne and Christopher Fremantle

London
GEORGE ALLEN AND UNWIN LTD
RUSKIN HOUSE · MUSEUM STREET

FIRST PUBLISHED IN GREAT BRITAIN 1969
This book is copyright under the Berne Convention. Apart from any fair dealing for the purpose of private study, research, criticism or review, as permitted under the Copyright Act, 1956, no portion may be reproduced by any process without written permission. Enquiries should be addressed to the Publishers.

SBN 04 901018 2

© *1968 by Doubleday & Company, Inc.*

La France de la Renaissance, by Anne Denieul-Cormier, published in France by B. Arthaud © B. Arthaud, 1962.

Excerpts from *The Book of the Courtier*, by Baldesar Castiglione, translated by Charles S. Singleton. Copyright © 1959 by Charles S. Singleton and Edgar de N. Mayhew. Reprinted by permission of Doubleday & Company, Inc.

PRINTED IN GREAT BRITAIN
BY PHOTOLITHOGRAPHY
UNWIN BROTHERS LIMITED
LONDON AND WOKING

Contents

Illustrations	9
Foreword	11

PART ONE SUBSTANCE AND SHADOW

I	The Land of France	15
II	Adventure and Illusion	22

PART TWO THE MONARCH OF THE RENAISSANCE

III	Francis, First of His Name	65
IV	A Time of Scandal	80
V	The Court of the King	100
VI	At the King's Court	118

PART THREE OF HIS MAJESTY, THE MOST LOYAL SUBJECTS

VII	The Gentleman of the Renaissance	143
VIII	Masters and Workmen of the Renaissance	165
IX	Travelers of the Renaissance	176

PART FOUR REVOLUTIONS OF THE RENAISSANCE

X	An Age of Discovery	205
XI	Schools and Scholars	236
XII	The Renaissance of the Soul	267
	Epilogue	316
	Genealogical Table	318
	Index	321

Illustrations

1 Francis I on horseback.	*facing page* 32
2 Knights in combat.	
An early sixteenth-century street.	
3 Francis I. Oval intaglio on chalcedony.	
The Emperor Maximilian I.	
The Chevalier Bayard.	
Ferdinand of Aragon and Isabella of Castile.	
4 Louis XII and Reason.	33
5 Louise of Savoy.	64
Claude of France with her three daughters and daughter-in-law.	
Gaston de Foix, Duke de Nemours.	
6 Louis XII's official entry into Genoa.	
Warriors of the Royal Army preparing for war.	
7 Birth of the Dauphin Francis, son of Francis I.	
Francis I offering his heart to Eleanor of Austria.	
Francis I and Marguerite d'Alençon playing chess.	
8 Queen Eleanor.	
Diane de Poitiers	
The Dauphin Francis, son of Francis I.	65
9 Catherine de Médicis.	96
Henry II, son of Francis I.	
Charles, Constable de Bourbon, as a fugitive.	
10 Salt cellar of gold, decorated with enamel.	
Vase of green jasper in the form of a dragon.	
11 Vase with griffin handles.	
Boat-shaped crystal cup with siren handles.	
12 Hunting the stag.	97
13 Charles V, as a youth, entering Bruges in 1515.	128
14 Mass with music.	
The judgement of heretics.	
15 A nobleman and his lady at the end of the fifteenth century.	
16 Rustic life.	
Threshing the grain and stacking the sheaves.	129
17 Taking out the flock in the morning.	160
Haymaking and woodcutting.	
18 A tourney.	
19 Springtime: weeding, hoeing and planting out.	
Peasant dance.	
20 A good inn.	
Printing shop.	161

ILLUSTRATIONS

21 A bathing establishment. *facing page* 192
    A thermal station.
    Ladies at their toilet.
22 Arab merchant.
    Egyptian woman carrying her child.
    Moorish water carrier.
    Jewish merchant.
23 Picking mulberries and raising silkworms.
    A sixteenth-century navigator at work.
24 A sixteenth-century seaman.
    A caravel caught in a storm at sea.
    A caravel. 193

25 A family of Topinambous. 224
    A visitor is welcomed to a Topinambou household.
    Brazilian cannibals cutting up and smoking their victims.
26 Oronce Fine, Regius Professor of Mathematics.
    J. Toussaint, Regius Professor of Greek.
    Guillaume Postel, Regius Professor of Greek.
    Erasmus of Rotterdam. 225

27 Architect instructing a novice. 256
28 An armoire of the French Renaissance.
    A table of the French Renaissance.
    Armchair of the French Renaissance. 257

29 Pierre de Ronsard. 304
    John Calvin in his study.
    Lefèvre d'Etaples.
30 Ambroise Paré, Surgeon to the King.
    Sixteenth century physician visiting a patient.
31 An open-air preacher.
    A sixteenth-century Bible.
32 Francis I in a procession. 305

Foreword

IN A work dealing with a subject as many-faceted as that of the Renaissance in France, and particularly one in which contemporary writers have been allowed, to a large extent, to speak for themselves, it is obviously not possible to cover every aspect of the subject. The reader, therefore, may find that some personality or some event of special interest to him has not been mentioned. The author, however, while regretting that circumstance, hopes that the reader will find, on closing the book, that he has abstracted from the material that is present the essential themes of the Renaissance in France—the basic events, the dominant personalities, the over-all richness of language and accomplishment.

The first part of *A Time of Glory* is devoted to a description of the land of France and its inhabitants. The stage is set by means of an explanation of the interminable Italian Wars of the period; for, while it is true that while the net result of those transalpine adventures was one of disaster for France, the fact remains that without them the Italian Renaissance would not have been so successfully transplanted to France. There would have been no châteaux of the Loire, no College de France, no Fontainebleau. War, at that time, was almost the sole means of international communication on a large scale.

The second part recalls the nature of French society in the sixteenth century. It was a society that found life at the touch of the great Francis I, the king who was the very symbol of the French Renaissance. He marked, molded, and fashioned his times as had no other monarch before him. New ideas abounded, it is true; but without the royal nod nothing could have been achieved. He lent an attentive ear to the bold suggestions of explorers, of intellectuals, of artists, and he gave at every level the crucial impulse necessary to move them from plan to execution. And the century lived from what he had approved. He was, in a word, the splendid idealized prince of whom those times dreamed.

Given the glory of the king, one may be surprised to discover in the third part that the nobility of the Renaissance preferred the country to the court; but the fact was that the vast majority of the French nobility was composed of what another age would call "country squires." With their tradition of residence on the soil, their ancestral houses, their lands, their tenants, their dovecotes, paddocks, courtyards and orchards and gardens, they were fully content and satisfied to leave the more elegant —and expensive—life of the court to those great lords whose ambition or wealth allowed for it.

Traditionally, one thinks of the peasants of that age as sunk in misery and groaning, "In the sweat of my brow I have labored, and I am dying of hunger." Indeed, it is a view borne out not only by statistical studies but also by contemporary texts and by the standard works on the subject. Yet, it is a powerful temptation today, in the middle of the modern "rat race," to forget for a moment that cry of distress and to recall the delights of country life, for nobleman and peasant alike, described in the works of such contemporaries as Du Fail, Bouchet, and Gauchet. And it is a temptation to which we have succumbed in this work.

The next section of this third part covers an event of maximum importance for a world in which the conditions of labor had remained unchanged since the thirteenth century: the arrival on the scene of one of the first industries of capitalism, printing. Its inevitable consequences were the appearance of a proletariat, strikes, and social unrest. Even viewed from a distance of several centuries, all these have a familiar look.

There was one factor which united all classes of society in the sixteenth century, from the prince to the peasant: a love for travel. Furthermore, it was a predilection for which one could always find an excuse to indulge by pleading the needs of business, illness, or piety. Everyone tried to exchange the monotony of daily life for new horizons, and, fortunately for posterity, they were horizons the charms of which they were eager to record. Thus, we have ample contemporary documents describing not only Europe but also the Middle East, during the sixteenth century.

Finally, the last part of the book is intended for the reader who cares more for the general "feel" of an era than for detailed knowledge. There the author has tried to highlight the important aspects of the century as a time of revolution, of profound upheaval, of metamorphosis, as a time when the heritage of the past in culture, economics, and the spiritual life was rebuilt on a new foundation. It was, as are all historical "eras," a time of transition, the crucible in which a new civilization was being synthesized, and the men of the time exulted in the conviction that they were privileged to live in a time of glory, in a new Age of Heroes.

PART ONE

SUBSTANCE AND SHADOW

I · The Land of France

RENAISSANCE France stretched from Picardy to the Pyrenees and from the Alps to the shores of the Atlantic. In order to resemble the France of today, only Artois was needed, and part of Flanders to the north; Alsace, Lorraine, and Franche-Comté to the east; Savoy to the southeast; and Nice and Roussillon on the Mediterranean coast. The timeless patience of the French kings, exercised over six centuries with intelligence and tenacity, had caused France to expand from the minute Ile-de-France, ruled by a minor feudal lord distinguished only by his crown, to a magnificent realm, sea-girt and watered by gold-banked rivers, furrowed by rich valleys and peaceful streams, where vast wheat fields adjoined game-rich forests.

It is true that many of the great nobles of France devoted their energies to making their king's life difficult; but in the end he had overcome them. He had eliminated them, had worn them down slowly, one by one and bit by bit. He had ground them down by endless stratagems—by war, naturally; but also by law, by the Salic law of primogeniture; and he had given them the *coup de grâce* by contracting immensely profitable royal marriages which created great inheritances. The English had been driven out of the country. To the east, the Burgundian estates of Charles the Bold had been dismembered to the king's advantage. To the west, Brittany had been annexed to the royal domain as the result of a successful courtship of the heiress, Duchess Anne, who, though offered other brilliant matches, succumbed to the glitter of a royal diadem.

By 1500 the Dukes of Anjou, of Burgundy, or of Brittany were no longer mentioned. The only survivors of such great feudatories were the Duke of Bourbon, whose treason would benefit the crown to the extent of all his vast possessions, and the King of Navarre, who would by a genealogical quirk unite his kingdom to that of France. A united France! What a power in a still disunited Europe would be this country, whose frontiers seemed as though by the hand of providence to be protected by great natural barriers. Such an exceptional situation did not fail to attract the notice of foreigners.

"The Kingdom of France," wrote the Venetian Ambassador Michael Suriano, "situated practically at the center of Christendom, is in a very convenient position to unite or divide at will the power of the most potent princes and most warlike peoples. It has Italy before it, England behind, Spain to its right, Germany to its left; on one side are the Swiss, on another the Flemish; it is between two seas, the Mediterranean and the Ocean. Thus by water as well as by land, it can either support or prevent every enterprise undertaken by other States. Nature and art protect France on every side; the mountains separate it from Italy and Spain; the sea divides it from England and more distant States; from Germany, deep rivers; at every important passage there are fortresses; arms and munitions are not lacking, both on the frontiers and in the Kingdom, nor men well able to use them and to practice intelligently everything relating to the art of war."[1]

United in heart no less than in territory, this country—a monarchy, and one in which everything is subordinate to that form—remains entirely submissive to its king:

"No country is as united, as easy to manipulate, as France. Herein, I think, lies her strength: in unity and obedience. Liberty, no doubt, is the highest of earthly benefits; but men are not all worthy of it . . . And the French, who perhaps feel themselves ill-qualified to govern themselves, have placed their liberty and their will in their king's hands. He has only to say: 'I wish for such and such a sum, I command, I "grant it," ' and the execution is as prompt as though the whole nation by their own motion had decided on it. This has already gone so far that some few of the French who see more clearly than others say: 'Our kings were formerly called *reges Francorum* [kings of the Franks]; now they could be called *reges servorum* [kings of slaves].' They pay to the king whatever he asks, then whatever is left over is also at his mercy."[2]

Within reason, the French could afford to indulge their king, for the French soil is rich. The combination of peace, hard work, and a rising population had raised France from the ruin it had suffered in the Hundred Years' War; the deserted countryside was repopulated, agriculture and commerce came to life again. The good times began again in the reign of Louis XII, who had the luck to ascend the throne at a moment when fifty years of ceaseless toil were bearing their fruit and ushering in an era of economic prosperity so great that it is still remembered in France as a golden age. It was a situation well calculated to impress the commerce-oriented Venetians:

"This country, owing to its extent, possesses a great variety of soils and of produce. These are of excellent quality and so abundant that there are enough not only for France herself but also for other nations. For example, the French ship wheat to Spain, Portugal, England and sometimes, too, to Switzerland and to Genoa, if wars do not prevent them. Although the French like their wine, they still have enough to supply the

English, the Scots and the Flemish, Luxembourg, Lorraine, and Switzerland. They profit by its sale every year to the tune of a million and a half crowns, and they sell it dearer than the wines of Spain or Cyprus; although it is not so strong, it is more delicate. France has all kinds of meat: fresh and salt fish are abundant—they are even exported to neighboring countries.

"Another advantage France possesses is a great abundance of salt in Gascony, Provence and Brittany. This salt preserves meat and fish better than do the German salts; and the English get the salt they require from Brittany. If the King of France had ministers as intelligent and as careful as those of the Signoria of Venice, he could buy the salt from private persons and sell it to foreigners at a profit and make a considerable annual revenue. . . .

"Wood for construction and wood for burning are plentiful everywhere in France. Oak and beech . . .

"Ordinary wools are plentiful. Fine cloths are woven with English and Spanish wools. It is true that lower Normandy and Picardy give a rather finer type of wool used for certain cloths, and for one in particular, called camelot. They make also much linen of every quality, but it is not as fine as Dutch linen. The silk trade is substantial. Thus, in Tours they work the silk which comes from Italy and Spain, and this industry is growing all the time. There are eight thousand looms there. Many Venetian weavers have settled there with their families, and a still larger number of Genoese; then there are some from Lucca, not to mention the French themselves who have learned the art of weaving. They have even begun planting mulberry trees for raising silkworms, to profit from them in so far as the climate allows. They try to succeed by their hard work."[3]

How good life seemed in such a flourishing country, and how much foreigners enjoyed traveling there and satisfying their natural curiosity with its happy sights, is a matter of record. The ambassadors of Venice, Machiavelli, the Cardinal of Aragon, and a young Swiss medical student, Thomas Platter, to mention only the principal ones, found it so absorbing that they wrote down their recollections. We owe to them our knowledge of the face of France during the century of the Renaissance.

"The town [Paris] is divided into four parts: the City, the University, the Town, and the suburbs. The city is surrounded on all sides by the Seine, and is joined with the University by three bridges, and with the big Town by two bridges. These bridges, edged on both sides with rows of houses, resemble streets more than bridges. Two splendid great buildings rise over the City; one is the church dedicated to Notre Dame, the other the Palace where suits are judged . . .

"In front of the latter there is a great courtyard closed off by a grille; in this court wait the horses and carriages of those who have business at the Palace. . . . The Great Hall of the Palace is considered by the French to be the finest in all Christendom. . . . All around are the shops of the silk merchants and of the vendors of velvets, precious stones, hats, books, pictures and other goods. It is quite difficult to pass these stalls without buying something, because the vendors, both male and female, call to the passers-by with such affability, and explain what a bargain everything is, and one may look around without any obligation to buy. The women who sell white cloth for blouses, collars, handkerchiefs and other articles of lingerie especially have an attractive way of talking and know how to convince you that nowhere else can anything be found as good; and they are very sly and quick to know who has money and who has not; they observe what you do not have and if there is something worn among your clothes they offer you what you would never have thought of buying from them. If anyone goes by dressed in new clothes, they ask him if he would not like to buy something for his mistress. And those who go there accompanied by their women generally regret the visit! Ask to see something and you are sure to leave your money there; in fact, they first make a very high price but if you bargain you are sure to get it for a half or even a quarter. Alongside these merchants' shops there are very fine galleries where a great number of lawyers and attorneys parade; they carry under their arms their linen portfolios stuffed with papers, in which they note down all their business."[4]

Leaving the city, and coming to the university, by the Pont St. Michel or the Petit Pont:

"It is located on the south, in Hurepoix, and is bounded on one side by the fortifications and on the other by the Seine . . . It has gradually come to be what it is today, one of the most distinguished schools in Christendom. There are fifty to sixty colleges there, of which the principal ones are the following: the Sorbonne, where the discussions are very subtle and eloquent; the College of Navarre, where the pupils are the sons of princes; that of the Bernardins; that of Cluny; that of the Premonstratensians; that of Cardinal Lemoine; the college of Cambrai, where the royal professors lecture in public. . . . The Rector, as head of the University, has precedence over all the most important people when the king comes with his whole retinue, because it is he who comes to ask confirmation of privileges; he alone has the right to do this.

"The students of the city of Paris are divided into four nations—the French, the Picards, the Normans and the Germans—with whom are included students from the north and among them the English. . . . Thirty to fifty thousand students have taken up residence in Paris; they could find convenient lodgings in the colleges, but many take board and lodging with bourgeois families in the town. Anyone who has lived in Paris knows what noise they make there. . . .

"In addition this quarter has twenty-four libraries, seventeen churches, three chapels, four hospitals, and everything necessary for the priests and men of learning."

The residential quarters extend north of the Seine, in what Thomas Platter calls "the Town"[5]:

"Here are the fine private houses, and the most important buildings and streets of all Paris, which can compete with the greatest towns of France. One sees first, quite near the Seine and not far from the new Gate, the King's palace, known as the Louvre.

"It is there that he lives when he is in Paris. The building is very old, but was restored by Francis I in 1529; it was enlarged and finished by King Henry II. These facts are carved above the gates in gold letters on black marble."[6]

Fourth and last there are the suburbs, of which there are nine:

"The first suburb is that of St. Germain; it is very extensive and as populous as a big town; it has its own fairs and churches, numerous streets, fine private houses, as well as tennis courts. Many Germans, both gentlefolk and students, lodge in this suburb with well-to-do people.

"The second suburb is that of St. Michel, where the monastery of the Carthusians can be seen. The third suburb is that of St. Jacques, where there are many churches and hospitals; a windmill has been built in the neighborhood like many that are all around Paris. The fourth suburb, that of St. Marceau, is very big and very populous, with many churches. The others are those of St. Victor, St. Martin, St. Denis, Montmartre and St. Honoré . . . in these too one finds many streets, many churches, palaces, houses with pleasure gardens, and a large number of monasteries."[7]

But travelers did not confine themselves to the capital. They headed for Rouen, a stopping place on the way to Mont St. Michel:

"Rouen lies in a valley; it is a very large and populous town, there is much trade there and there are many different industries. . . . The houses in Rouen are wooden, decorated like those of Germany, and are large and very well planned. The town has fine quarters, although the streets are rather narrow and dirty. There are many fountains and several canals run through the city. On the left, coming from Paris, alongside part of the walls, runs a river called the Seine; it is very wide and navigable from Paris through which it flows. . . .

"The town of Rouen, though rich in various fruits, has no melons, figs or grapes, because the climate is cold. There is plenty of fish, both fresh-water fish—trout, salmon and sturgeon—and sea food of which there are all kinds, particularly shellfish, oysters and little black and white cockles.

"The cathedral is big, with a splendid façade decorated with sculptured figures. It has two very tall towers of which one is still unfinished; they are made of soft stone, which nevertheless has been carved with great art . . . the Archbishop's palace, which was put up by the Cardinal of Amboise, is very fine and all carved in stone; the halls are sumptuous, the rooms richly ornamented, the apartments very convenient. It has a lovely square garden, but without trees, as is the custom in this country. In the center there is a marble fountain, heavily decorated, which sends water up to a great height. . . . Lodging is very good at Rouen, and they drink good red wines, though there are no vineyards."[8]

Rouen's title as "second city of the kingdom" was closely disputed by Lyons, an international city and the capital of fairs and the center for bills of exchange:

"Lyons is a well-peopled and rather well-built town. The majority of the inhabitants are foreigners, especially Italians, on account of the fairs which are held there, and of the trade and exchange which takes place. The greatest number of merchants are Florentines or Genoese. There are four fairs a year, and the sums of money from all the countries that change hands are immense. Lyons is the cornerstone of trade with Italy and of a great part of the Spanish and Flemish trade. I refer to the money markets; that is the most profitable part of the trade.

"Workers in all kinds of trades are plentiful in Lyons, and shops are no less so; they are full of a variety of merchandise which is abundant there because of the fairs. That is why food is not in very great supply there."[9]

These three great cities, to which must be added Bordeaux and Toulouse, remarkable for their parliaments and universities, and a number of towns of lesser importance, of villages and of inhabited castles, constitute the framework in which unfolds the most crowded century of French history.

NOTES

I · The Land of France

1. Tommaseo, N., *Relations des ambassadeurs vénitiens sur les affaires de France au XVIᵉ siècle*. Collection des documents inédits de l'histoire de France, t. I, pp. 475–77. Paris, 1838.
2. *Ibid.*, p. 271–73.
3. *Ibid.*, p. 253–59.
4. Platter, Thomas. *Description de Paris par Thomas Platter le jeune, de Bâle*. Extrait des Mémoires de la Société d'Histoire de Paris et de l'Ile-de-France, t. XXIII. Paris, 1896.
5. *Ibid.*
6. *Ibid.*
7. *Ibid.*
8. Béatis, A. de, *Voyage du Cardinal d'Aragon en Allemagne, Hollande, Belgique, France et Italie (1517–1518)*. Paris, 1913. pp. 139–41.
9. Tommaseo, N., *op. cit.*, t. I, pp. 35–37.

II · Adventure and Illusion

THE most important fact of sixteenth-century life was that of war—wars of expansion, Italian wars, balance-of-power wars, religious wars, civil wars. It was, in a word, a century of blood. Of these wars, we shall linger over those fought for the possession of Italy. Even the battles, intrigues, and policies associated with them have given the entire episode a bad name—"The glory and stink of Italy," as one author wrote about the first Italian war. Specifically, we are concerned with the Italian wars undertaken by the royal house of France in the persons of Charles VIII, Louis XII, and Francis I between 1492 and 1518. These kings, and that span of time, ushered in a critical period of approximately sixty years in which Italy became at once the prize and the battlefield of Europe. The great powers of the age—France, Austria, Spain—fought each other there until, exhausted, they were ready for peace at any price, any peace which would allow them to regather their strength for a common offensive against the new enemy menacing them all: religious heresy.

It was France who set fire to the powder keg; and, like the sorcerer's apprentice, she could not, even had she so wished, extinguish the conflagration. The reasons for the beginnings of the Italian wars are many, and they are as obscure, complex, and controversial as the wars themselves. Alliances? They came and went in crowds. Contestants? They were never the same from one battle to the next. Negotiations? They were endless. Treaties? Innumerable. What was the result of the wars? None—apart from a few profitable marriages; it has even been said that the reigns of Charles VIII and Louis XII could be expunged from history without having France take a single backward step. Was France fighting, then, only to obtain advantageous marriages for her princes? No one knew, any more than anyone ever really knows why he is fighting; for slogans and jingoes were as common and as meaningless then as they are now.

Whatever the immediate provocation, however, it is a fact of history that, for the first time since the Crusades, a king of France, Charles VIII, left his own soil at the head of an army and crossed the Alps. Charles's intention was to conquer the Kingdom of Naples, which he claimed as his own. It did not occur to him that he would have done better to fortify his frontiers. He had forgotten what his avaricious neighbors, alive and bitter, had not forgotten—how much his father, Louis XI, had taken from them, and how well they might profit from his absence to get it all back. So he left his kingdom leaderless and virtually defenseless to go adventuring. What motives could have persuaded him to plunge into the Italian hornets' nest? There seems to be no reasonable explanation. Political ambition? Unquestionably. Love of the dazzling game of war? Perhaps. Pressures of the young nobles? Surely. For fights were hard to come by under a rich and powerful king. Idle, buried in their somber domains, the nobles were bored. Life was so dreary, and the stories of chivalry, with which their heads were stuffed, were so exciting. War, of course, was the traditional outlet for martial instincts. But where to make war? There was only one direction where one could be sure of meeting no one: to the southeast. There, across the mountains, lay Italy, "that lovely country which Apennines divide, which sea and Alps surround" that could be conquered and occupied, where one could quarrel at leisure and taste the divine delights of victory. And in all tranquillity! For the peninsula was incapable of offering the smallest resistance to anyone, least of all to a powerful French king.

A congenital incapacity for being ruled had reduced Italy to what may be called a purely geographic entity. It was composed of a sprinkling of small towns, principalities, and republics, all rivals, and all a prey to internal strife and torn apart by factions. What little real power there was had become concentrated in the hands of a few great families, often of foreign origin. First, and sparkling with all its lamps alight, was the Most Serene Republic of Venice. She was feared and hated both for the wealth piled in her spacious storerooms and for dreams of world conquest rightly or wrongly attributed to her. Then there was the Papacy, a temporal power more than a spiritual one, greedy for this world's goods. The presence on St. Peter's throne of the monstrous Alexander VI Borgia had accomplished its total discredit. The remaining three states—the Duchy of Milan, the Republic of Florence, and the Kingdom of Naples—were grappling with internal problems and with factions ready to call on outside help.

In these states there were nothing but intrigues, conspiracies, traitors, plots, and strange disappearances. They gave, as Barrès has said, "an education to courtesans and schemers," showed "the apotheosis of connivance and diplomacy" and revealed "all that humanity can offer in the way of seduction and busybody activity." In that divided and corrupt country, vice and passion went side by side with the most refined manners, the most exquisite art of living. In splendid palaces great patrons and distinguished women lived to the full their troubled days. It was a brilliant civilization, but an insecure one. Its fate was dependent on badly equipped or nonexistent armies led by lawless and faithless *condottieri*, and on a changeable and ungovernable race who had not forgotten that their ancestors cried both "*Viva la nostra vita, viva la nostra morte.*"

What inflamed covetousness, what opportunities there were for interference by well-heeled neighbors whose vast financial resources and docile populations gave scope to their expansionist dreams. To the west was France; to the south, Spanish Naples; to the north, the Germans and their emperor; to the east, the Turks—everywhere barbarians ready to pounce on the defenseless prey. Italy, still at liberty, was preparing to become, as Machiavelli, the witness of her suffering, wrote, "a country more cruelly ill-treated than Persia, more disunited than Athens, without leaders, without laws, despised, torn, pillaged and enthralled by foreigners."[1]

Three of the kings of France, Charles VIII, Louis XII, Francis I, all flung themselves with the same enthusiasm into the Italian venture, claiming rights of like validity over the coveted lands of the Kingdom of Naples and the Duchy of Milan. For the space of twenty-five years they won Naples and lost it, conquered and reconquered, set up temporary administrations, won and lost again the Milanese state, won resounding victories, suffered bloody setbacks, knew defeat and suffered invasion. The history books say that they were victors at Fornua, at Cerisola, at Agnadela, and losers at Cerignola, Seminara, and Novara; that such-and-such a treaty was signed between such-and-such partners, and such a league formed against this or that king. The stages of a policy still in its infancy must be left at that, and an effort must be made to discover just how men lived during those twenty-five war-torn years, whether they wore the crown or the tiara, the soldier's sword or civilian attire. Their contemporaries tell of their exploits, their difficulties, their joys, and the daily round of a life outside the normal lived under the banner of adventure and danger.

※ ※ ※

When the princes decided on war in Italy, the protagonists were, for France, the Valois king, Charles VIII; for Spain, Ferdinand the Catholic; for Austria, Maximilian of Habsburg, Emperor of the Germans; for Italy, the popes.

Charles VIII, the son of Louis XI and Charlotte of Savoy, brother of Anne de Beaujeu, husband of Anne of Brittany, was not distinguished by any exceptional personality or any acute sense of political reality. He has not had a good press from the historians. His mediocre mind did nothing to help people forget his sickly constitution or his weak body. His contemporaries have left numerous portraits of him. It is doubtful if they can be trusted, since their authors have darkened or enhanced him as they thought fit. The Italians who did not like him have described him unmercifully. Brantôme, on the basis of his grandmother's stories and without ever having known him, has drawn a touching picture. Perhaps the testimony of a specialist, the physiognomist Barthélemy Coclès, may be less partial:

"He had," he writes, "a great head and an exceedingly large aquiline nose, rather flat lips, a rounded and slightly cleft chin, large, prominent eyes, a short and flabby neck, a broad chest and back, rather full, quite wide hips, a fleshy stomach and an ample seat, but his thighs and legs were slender although long. . . . Finally, he was short. This is why his nickname 'little King' stayed with him through subsequent reigns. The Italians, who had reason to detest him for stirring up a war which left them under foreign domination, called him scornfully *Cabezzucco*, that is to say, pigheaded, in allusion to his big head, and they reproached him with stubbornness, as though he had embarked on this journey against all sorts of advice and good sense. But those who wished to praise him gave him this motto: "*Major in exiguo regnabat corpore virtus* [Greater courage resided in a small body."[2]

A minor at his father's death, such he remained through his short life, even when no longer one in years. He sought for and submitted to protective influences—excellent in a few cases but more often questionable, as in the case of Guillaume Briçonnet, Bishop of St. Malo, and Etienne de Vesc, Seneschal of Beaucaire—not to mention other second-rate people whom he liked to gather around him.

Overshadowed by a father who was not anxious to see his son renew the gestures of independence he himself had made when he was dauphin, and deliberately deprived of the instruction necessary for his future task, he is perhaps not entirely to blame for cutting a poor political figure. His was the initiative of the Italian venture; he threw himself into it hotheadedly, even agreeing to the most absurd concessions to get away unhindered. Roussillon, Cerdagne, and Franche-Comté, which had become French territories thanks to the able and persistent maneuvers of Louis XI, he gave back to the interested parties, in a naïve hope that Spain and Austria would make no move during his absence. It has even been suggested that conscientious scruples of conscience were behind this ill-considered action:

"Some churchmen persuaded him that his father had charged them on his deathbed to make restitution, and the Spanish Ambassador found a way of access to his confessor. For, knowing the latter was fond of Spanish wine, he sent him two barrels, one full of wine, the other of gold, both of which he found most agreeable, and these pleaded well in favor of King Ferdinand."[3]

His head stuffed with tales of chivalry, the reading of which filled his ample leisure, Charles fled from reality into idle fancy. Naples was the objective of his expedition across the mountains. After that, why not Jerusalem? What a glorious dream, to attack the Turks and renew the medieval Crusades in which so many deeds of derring-do were accomplished. What an honor to set oneself up as the Defender of Christendom against the perfidious infidel, especially if one could thereby add to one's title of king that of Emperor of Constantinople.

Luck smiled on the young king; his folly did not end in the failure it deserved. Moreover, his Italian war, which lasted six months, was a real military picnic, quite enchanting. From Asti to Naples, all Italy turned out to greet the "Liberator," and there were numerous receptions, feasts, and tourneys in his honor.

As is known, he died soon after, the *Cabezzucco*, knocking his big head on the gate of the Château of Amboise. An accident or a coincidence? An attack, or poisoning from the oranges which his good friend Ludovic Le More sent him? No one really knows. One would hardly dare speak of providence coming to the rescue. But the enemies which any journey over the mountains would not fail to make, they were of another caliber. What then would happen to the kingdom over which this child held sway?

The most dangerous of these was a remarkable person and wily political schemer, Ferdinand of Aragon, King of Spain. At the end of the fifteenth century Spain had drawn everywhere perilously close to France: on the Pyreneean frontier, since the English had quit Guyenne; on the southeast, where Provence had again become a royal domain; and now on the Mediterranean, where the Aragonese royal family held the Balearic Islands, Sardinia, Sicily, and the Kingdom of Naples. Between the two ambitious nations conflict was almost inevitable.

The German Empire, France's eastern neighbor, was a chaotic mixture of free towns, ecclesiastical principalities, and princely domains. It would have been less to be feared had not one of Germany's princely families in full expansion become aligned against France: the Austrian house of Habsburg, whose representative, Maximilian, held the imperial crown. His territorial power and boundless ambitions constituted a direct menace. He coveted both the no-man's-land that separated him from France —the Low Countries, Lorraine, Alsace, Franche-Comté, Savoy attached by loose ties to the empire, and the north Italian cities (Mantua, Modena and Parma; Verona, Vicenza, and Padua), where he and his descendants would try to revive imperial claims. As luck would have it, the emperor, poetic, fantastic, and chivalrous, was always looking for money; "penniless Maximilian," the Italians called him; "Don Quixote without his naïveté," Michelet adds. He was less to be feared than his Spanish brother. Witness the eloquent portrait drawn of him by Machiavelli:

"I will confine myself to adding, as regards the emperor's character, that he is, of all his contemporaries and forebears, the greatest spendthrift of his goods, and as a result he is always short of money; however great his fortune might be, it would never be enough. He is changeable, one day wanting something and the next not wanting it; he takes nobody's advice but believes everyone; he wants what he cannot have, turning aside from what he may have, and for this reason takes all his decisions in reverse. Apart from that he is the most martial of men, well capable of holding an army and leading it with judgment and discipline. He bears all the fatigues of war as bravely as the toughest, and is so brave in the face of danger as to be inferior to none of his captains. When he grants an audience he is human—but he never grants one except at his own wish; he refuses to be courted by ambassadors except when he expressly summons them. He is the most secretive of men, incessantly agitated, both in mind and body, but often undoing in the evening what he had accomplished in the morning. It is this that renders missions to him so difficult." Machiavelli's final judgment on Maximilian sums up the situation exactly: "The power of Germany is great, but it is such that one can make no use of it."[4]

Such were the men with whom the successor of Charles VIII would have to contend. Since Charles died childless, he was succeeded by his nearest male relative, Louis d'Orléans, who took the style of Louis XII. He took Charles's place, first, on the throne, and then in the royal bed, obtaining the dissolution of his marriage in order to marry Charles's queen, Anne of Brittany, lest her immensely valuable duchy fall into hands other than his own.

Louis XII was not an outstanding king. Although superior to his predecessor in both mind and body, he was without political acumen and, like Charles, fell under the influence of his entourage. In that way, the imperious Queen Anne, and his favorite, George d'Amboise, Cardinal-Archbishop of Rouen, held chief place both in the palace and in the nation.

Italy had always fascinated Louis. As Duke d'Orléans, he had used every means available to incite Charles VIII to go to that fabled land:

"Every day he arranged fresh jousts, tourneys, and tournaments. At every street corner in Lyons there were bleachers and scaffolding for the fights. There, one saw only horsemen dressed as Greeks, Romans, Moors, or Turks, with splendid coats of arms. The poets sang only of war; the ladies spoke of nothing else. So, by these feigned combats, their magnificence and the fanfares of trumpets, by the songs of poets and by the enchantment of the ladies, he roused the heart of the young king to noble undertaking and so enflamed his desire for glory that he could not rest until the Italian journey had been decided."[5]

Once on the throne, Louis threw himself wholeheartedly into the Italian affair. This was to overshadow his reign and end in failure. He had less luck than his predecessor, whose promissory notes he was obliged to meet, and he himself committed grave errors. His incoherent policies made him the pawn of popes and the laughingstock of his adversaries. Under Louis XII, the Italian wars took on a new aspect: yesterday's golden dreams became reality and turned into nightmares. The military picnic was over; this time it was war. Throughout the reign there was fighting: pitched battles won for fickle friends, victories without a future, surrender and defeat, sieges and captures of towns, encounters at sea. Agnadela, Ravenna, Gaeta; the taking of Alexandria, of Genoa, of Brescia; the crusade against the Turks; the bravery of Hervé Primauguet. Left behind were men and money, the fine flower of the nobility, the good coin of French cities; and all for nothing. When the king died, the Milanese lands occupied for over twelve years were lost and France was invaded. And already the war had become European, presaging those of the following reign. Started for Milan and against the Italians, it ended in a four-pronged attack—English, German, Swiss, and Spanish—on France's northern and eastern frontiers. The Italians, left to quarrels among themselves, were no longer involved.

The "Father of the People," as Louis came to be called, died from the effects of his third marriage. After the death of Anne of Brittany he had married, despite his age and indifferent health, a beautiful young girl from across the Channel, Mary of England, sister of Henry VIII. She wore him out:

"Where he used to dine at eight, he now agreed to dine at noon; where he was used to go to bed at six in the evening, he often went to bed at midnight. . . . He wished to be an agreeable companion for his wife, but he overdid it. . . . He was already ill and had lived according to a very strict diet, which he interrupted when he was with his wife. The doctors warned him that he would die from it if he continued. Jokingly, in Parisian legal circles it was said that the King of England had sent a fine nag to the King of France, to carry him, soon and softly, to hell or paradise."[6]

The determinant role of the Papacy during all this period is without doubt one of its essential characteristics. From the throne of St. Peter, Alexander VI Borgia, and Julian II della Rovere, changed the course of events to suit their personal ambitions: Alexander's was the establishment in power of his children; Julian II's was his dream of dominating the Italian Peninsula. It was with the alliance of Alexander VI, eager to push forward his son Caesar Borgia, that in two successive campaigns Louis XII conquered the territory of Milan, sent dangerous Ludovico Sforza to end his days at Loches, and filled the King of Naples with such fear that the latter preferred to avoid possible invasion and probable defeat by sharing his lands with Louis. But if this whirlwind beginning did not have its expected outcome, it was because of Julian II, who was to be the principal architect of the French defeat. More soldier than pontiff, and passionate politician, "he took it into his head," says Machiavelli, "to possess Bologna, to ruin the Venetians and to drive the French out of Italy." He dreamed of assuring the ascendancy of a powerful pontifical state—seized from the *condottieri* and the princelings, who shared the scraps—over a pacified Italy, from which the "barbarians" would be driven out. In order to realize this vast design, first he made use of Louis XII, who played his game with extraordinary naïveté, and then, once his enemies had been conquered through the French king's efforts, turned against him. By a series of well-conducted intrigues, he flung the imperial and Spanish forces against the French, drove them out of Italy, and pursued them into France.

When Francis I, cousin and son-in-law of Louis XII, who also had died without a male heir, in his turn ascended the throne, the situation was not very promising. Even if the coalition existing at the end of the reign were dispersed, peace could not be made either with the pope or with the Swiss. These failures did not rouse the new monarch to greater caution. Carried away by transalpine reveries, he became in his turn the dupe of fantasy. His portrait cannot be drawn here, as it will fit better in the context of the brilliant court which was his creation. But it is necessary, for the sake of clarity, to indicate his role in these wars. A chivalrous king cannot accept defeat, even when he is not directly responsible. So he began again, and this decision colored his whole reign. Setting out to reconquer the territory of Milan, he won the crushing victory of Marignano. This brought a change of heart to his enemies of yesterday. The Milanese duchy was occupied; the "Perpetual Peace of Fribourg," which reserved for French service the best market of soldiers in Europe, was concluded with the Swiss; the Concordat of Bologna was signed with the pope. All Europe bowed before the young sovereign. But for how long? The entry on the scene of a new protagonist about his own age, the King of Spain—soon to be emperor under the title of Charles V—cast doubts on the future of peace. Events were not slow to confirm the most perspicacious fears; wars for the maintenance of the balance of power in Europe were in the offing. Before embarking on them, however, let us hear how contemporaries described those that had just taken place.

THE CONQUERORS

For his transalpine conquests of the Duchy of Milan and of the Kingdom of Naples, the King of France had available powerful and numerous forces ready to die for him. For more than twenty-five years, the people of the peninsula were to watch, with mixed feelings, his march through their cities to the strident sound of martial music. Footmen and horsemen; mercenaries of all shades, in bizarre costumes; valiant men at arms mounted on their frisky chargers; fearsome artillery still mainly psychological in impact, which would become effective only when its heavy cannon were replaced by the more manageable musket and harquebus. This army, still medieval, advanced amid the tumult of clanking armor, rattling swords, the martial tramp of foot soldiers, and the whinnying of steeds:

"The gentlemen of the King's household, all on horseback, battle-axes in hand, were followed by Jacques de Vendôme, the viceroy of Chartres, and by Messire Guyon d'Amboise, the lord of Ravel, their captains; then by Jacques Stuart, Duke of Albany, Francis of Orléans, Count of Dunois, the Seigneur de Laigle and Guillaume de la Marche, captain of the king's hundred Germans who, all plumed, halberd in hand and hallecret [a corselet formed of two pieces of forged iron] in front, marched in good order; the Scots archers of the bodyguard, halberd in hand, arms at the ready; the archers of the guard, all on horseback armed with brigandines and curved swords, with their bows strung; and behind them their captains, Messire Jacques de Cressol, Messire Gabriel de la Châtre, Messire Georges Cocquebourne, captain of the Scots, in short, all the flower of the chivalry and nobility of France, with so great a company of Normans, Picards, Swiss, Gascons, Savoyards and other nations of Gaul, that if one tried to enumerate them one would be weary before it was done.

"And anyone who had seen their arms glint in the rays of the sun, their standards billowing in the wind, the great battle horses leaping, and so many lances, pikes, halberds and other ensigns of war on the road, so many men at arms, footmen, artillery and wagons on the march, could surely have thought that here was enough force to conquer the whole world."[7]

At that time the second class of soldier was the French, and more especially the foreign, mercenaries. They were recruited with hard cash in Germany and Switzerland, and sometimes in the Orient. They were undisciplined and greedy, quick to pillage, and perfectly heartless. Their misdoings gave the captains much trouble. Their basic characteristic was their belief that they were always underpaid, and they never hesitated to use the most outrageous blackmail—refusing to fight or threatening to leave in mid-campaign—in order to secure double pay. The chronicles constantly mention such incidents, among them the following, which is typical: a contingent of three thousand five hundred Swiss who had arrived to join the French army, declared they would not move out of the place they were to leave: "Messire Charles d'Amboise, lieutenant of the king, and several other captains tried by every means to get them to march; and with this intention gave their leaders gold and silver and many silken garments . . . and at the same time many persuasive arguments. Still they would not budge. The king was very incensed, and deliberated whether to have them all put to death. The lords of the leagues and cantons were warned of this by the guard. Speedily they gave orders to their troops to march for dear life and to serve the king against everyone else; which they did."[8]

Aggressive, quarrelsome, and overweening, the foreign mercenaries constantly found fault with their colleagues, the French mercenaries, who were no better. "They are always offended, especially after hard drinking." They pulled knives on one another and the captains found it hard to separate them even by force with their halberds except when it all ended in wine and reconciliation.

There is a story of how in a tavern one of these Germans "picked a quarrel with a young French footman who had a mug in his hand wanting wine. The German in spite of coming in after him wished to be served first, thinking himself the finer fellow. The footman, who was thirsty, said: 'Look, I was here before you and will be served first—first come, first served.' And, saying this, he tried to have his mug filled. But the German, who had his mug in one hand and his halberd in the other, which he set down against the wall, shouted in bad French: 'Ha! Villain, villain, do you have the right to be served before me?' And so saying, he took the footman by the collar and tried to push him back. But the footman was tough and held his ground. Seeing that the German would pin him down, he let go his mug and seized him too by the collar, and it went from collar to wig so that they began to scrap and to knock each other about the head and face.

"A number of others, Germans and French lackeys, formed a circle about them and seeing that this was only a fist fight about the wine, began to laugh and let them fight it out, until the German, whose nose was bleeding, wanted to take his halberd and the footman his sword, which was prevented by the onlookers. They asked whose was the blame and laid it on the German . . . Then they made the two comrades drink together and reconciled them."[9]

The mercenaries held booty as sacred, and when that was in question no cruelty was beyond them. Their instinct for pillage, as well as their habit of arson, was given free rein when circumstances were favorable. Everything seemed good to take home. The mercenaries were seen taking home to Germany "oxen and cows, beds, silks for spinning, and other utensils stolen in the sack of Padua, so that the damage there was reckoned at two million crowns, as much for furniture as for houses and palaces burned and destroyed."

Why, then, have recourse to their services? The French needed foot soldiers, since the national infantry did not then exist, and it was necessary to smile in the face of bad luck. Too, in spite of their faults, the Swiss and Germans possessed undeniable abilities as soldiers. These must truly have been outstanding, as the French themselves recognized it and overcame the antipathy which these brutes constantly inspired:

"The Germans despised the French foot soldiers, saying that, without the help of their leagues, the mounted men at arms of the French would not have been able to count on infantry support, because they could hardly keep battle order, were easily dispersed and hard to rally again. In fact, although there were many foot soldiers in France who were good fighters and bold and nimble in warfare, the Germans nevertheless generally kept better order, were more difficult to break up and smarter in rallying; but they were troublesome about payment, often difficult to get going, and always prompt to pillage."[10]

The Albanians, or *estradiots* (scouts), added a further picturesque note to the highly colored scene. These were not foot soldiers but horsemen. They came from the East. Their wild appearance sowed terror in the enemy ranks: "for they are dressed like Turks," notes the Loyal Servitor, "except for the head, where they have something like a girl's bonnet decked with five or six coarse papers stuck together in such a way that a sword does no more harm than it would to a helmet." "They are tough men," Commynes adds, "they sleep out all the year round, both men and horses." They were as cruel as their comrades from across the Rhine, and their captain, the famous seigneur Mercure, was a leader who suited them. This man, in the course of a skirmish, took prisoner his worst enemy, his first cousin who had dispossessed him in his native Croatia:

"On seeing him all the wrongs he had done him came to mind. 'Now is come the moment to take my revenge,' he cried. The other said that was so, but as he had been taken in open warfare he had the right to his liberty, on paying the ransom due to his rank; he offered six thousand ducats and six magnificent and excellent Turkish horses.

"'... Let us speak of that another time,' said the seigneur Mercure, 'but by your faith, if you held me, as I am holding you, what would you do with me?'

"'Since you adjure me by my faith,' replied his cousin, 'I tell you that if you were at my mercy as I am at yours, all the gold in the world would not save you; I would have you cut to pieces.'

"'Indeed,' said the seigneur Mercure, 'I shall not do worse to you.'

"Then he commanded his Albanians in their language to make play with their knives and they suddenly set their scimitars to work and there was not a captain who did not have ten thrusts after he was dead; then they cut off their heads and speared them on pikes, giving as the reason that they were not Christians."[11]

Opposed to this undisciplined and heterogeneous mass was the horse-

1. Francis I on horseback. Anonymous, water colour on vellum, sixteenth century. Musée Condé, Chantilly. Photographed by H. Adant

Knights in combat. Bas-relief from the tomb of Louis XII by Jean Juste, Abbey of St Denis. Photograph by Archives Photographiques

An early sixteenth-century street: apothecary, barber, furriers and tailors. Bibliothèque de l'Arsénal, Paris

Francis I. Oval intaglio on chalcedony, by Matteo de Nassaro. Cabinet des Médailles, Bibliothèque Nationale, Paris

The Emperor Maximilian I, by A. de Predis (1502). Kunsthistorisches Museum, Vienna

Ferdinand of Aragon and Isabella of Castile, the Catholic Kings of Spain. Cabinet des Médailles. Bibliothèque Nationale, Paris

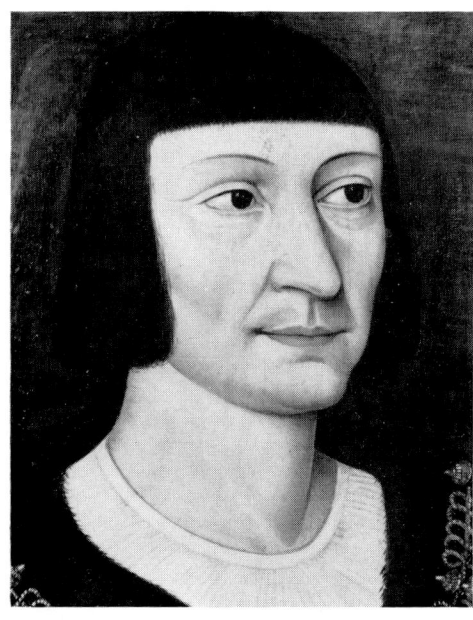

The Chevalier Bayard, "the knight without fear and without reproach." Anonymous painting on wood of the sixteenth century. Musée Stendhal, Grenoble. Photography by Rambaud, Grenoble

4. Louis XII and Reason; in the foreground, Anne of Brittany holds Claude of France on her knees. From Louis XII's copy of the translation into French of Petrarch's *Remedies for One and the Other Fortune* (1503). Bibliothèque Nationale, Paris

man, the man at arms who was always a gentleman. Taught from childhood the profession, honorable above all others, of arms, and nourished with heroic tales, he dreamed only of glory and adventure. When the King of France called on him to cross the Alps, he hastened to obey with enthusiasm, resolved to make himself a name in battle. He, the very soul of the French army, played the decisive role in every military engagement.

The great names of the wars in Italy, whose exploits fill the chronicles, were lieutenant generals of the king in Italy: La Trémoille, Trivulce, Stuart d'Aubigny; valorous captains Louis de Luxembourg, Count de Ligny, Jacques de Chabannes; the lord of la Palice, Pierre d'Urfé, the master of the French horse, Pierre de Pocquières, seigneur de Bellabre, Louis d'Ars, Yves d'Alègre, and the most celebrated of all, Pierre de Bayard. At a time when individual courage was the fashion, their acts of bravery were met with everywhere.

Among so many others who might be cited was that brave Monsieur de la Palice, who, at the start of Louis XII's reign, defended the fortress of Rouvria (Rivo di Puglia) in the Kingdom of Naples like a lion against the superior forces of the renowned Spaniard Gonzalvo of Cordova. Although he was unable to hold the town, honor at least was saved by his desperate resistance:

"Seigneur de la Palice, who was below the ramparts, climbed up by a ladder and, like a madman, snatched a lance from the first of his soldiers whom he met. Like a wild boar he joined the defenders. . . . After a bloody combat, the Spaniards, seeing that they could not gain any advantage and that, as long as he was there, they could not enter, went to look for a fused keg of gunpowder. They succeeded in getting close enough to him to throw it on his head, and with such force that he and the keg, powder and fire, slid all together down to the bottom of the rampart where he was completely crushed.

"The fire and powder had penetrated through the visor of his helmet, the upper part of his cuirasse, and all the uncovered parts of his armor, while it was obvious from the smoke which came out from inside his armor that there was fire inside of it. As indeed there was, the fire of virtue, which by good fortune could not be put out, and the sulfurous fire which his men, by pouring bottles of wine and water over him, just managed to extinguish. . . .

"When he could again see after the liberal washing which his eyes had received, he saw that the Spaniards were getting into the town on every side. Since he could no longer harm them or help his own people, injured and tired as he was, he leaned on two Frenchmen and, tottering, sword in hand, under the gaze of the Spaniards who did not dare to approach him, he went to the front of the castle, picked up a halberd and set his back against the rampart. There, once more, like a wild boar at bay, he so defended himself that so long as his blade flashed only dead and shattered men were to be seen." After this valorous defense, he was obliged in the end to surrender, but to a gentleman, not to a foot soldier, throwing away his sword with these proud words: "Neither thou nor any man shall ever take it from my hand."[12]

His adversary was the first to render homage to such bravery:

"Captain Gonzalvo, seeing his virtuous courage, had him led gently to Baletta, and there furnished him doctors and surgeons: they treated his wounds and took eleven small bones from his head; they tended him so well that they finally made him completely well and whole."

These brawling gentlemen, who only loved sword thrusts and adventures, were bored when battles were scarce. The Treaty of Granada, which divided the Kingdom of Naples between Spaniards and French, begot—instead of the hoped-for peace—a state of latent hostility in which inaction weighed more heavily on them than they would have liked to admit. The following anecdote about Bayard might have been told of any of his companions:

"The good knight, in a garrison where the valiant Louis d'Ars had lodged him, which was called Monervyne [Minervino], with some of his comrades, was bored with being so long caged up without going out into the fields, so said to them one evening: 'Gentlemen, it seems to me we are putrefying in this place without going out to see our enemies; and that two disadvantages could arise from staying here too long, we might all become effeminate, and also our enemies might take heart if they thought we dare not leave our fortress because of the fear which they inspire in us. So I have decided tomorrow to take a turn between here, Andria, and Barletta. Perhaps we shall find some runners from their side, than which I should like nothing better, for we could then do a little hand-to-hand fighting and whoever God honors will win.' To these words none answered but that he wished it so.

"The next day these heroes, some thirty of them, all young gentlemen, were riding toward the enemy garrisons and met on their way a little troop of Spanish men at arms, also longing for a skirmish. Scarcely had Bayard incited his comrades to go into action when they answered in a single voice: 'Let's go at them, captain; don't let us wait for them to have the honor of beginning.' Then, shouting, 'France, France,' they charged the enemy at full gallop. These, with assurance and a haughty look, received them at the charge gaily at the lance's point, shouting 'Spain and St. James.' "[13] Add to these characteristics that the French gentleman at war on the far side of the Alps was foulmouthed and hotheaded, that he was above all touchy about his honor, and there he was in profile.

The French, however, had no monopoly of such dynamism. In this respect their neighbors across the Pyrenees could easily give them points.

Their courage and aggressiveness have often been sung, and even by the French chroniclers, and all of France's brilliant qualities were needed to face that enemy, against whom they constantly battled both in the north and south of the peninsula. The unparalleled cruelty of the Spaniards is the only point on which they might have taught the French something.

In April 1503, after the defeat of Cerignola, in Apulia, the French were recovering their dead on the field of battle, strewn with corpses:

"The Viceroy of Naples, Louis d'Armagnac, Duke of Nemours, was found among the dead and recognized, they say, by the king at arms Champagne. He, seeing him naked among the rest, began to weep, and to curse and swear at the Spaniards, reproaching them for so treating the royal blood of France, which they had no right to touch, much less to insult by leaving him quite naked.

"The Spaniards answered him that if he pitied him naked, he should cover him with his robe. So he took off his coat of arms covered with fleur de lys and threw it over him. At which the Spaniards, seeing that he was disarmed of the lilies, killed him, arguing that he was no longer privileged; in which they acted cruelly, while he was acting foolishly."[14]

※　　※　　※

Of all the heroes of the Italian wars, the Chevalier Bayard is without question the most popular and celebrated for his high deeds of arms and outstanding virtues. He has become legendary, at a price. The soldier of flesh and blood has become the plaster saint, distorted, sweetened, bowdlerized. Helmeted, visor down, lance in hand, haloed, and on his pedestal, he has lost, through the centuries, bit by bit, all his attractive qualities to become just a "knight without fear and without reproach." Poor Bayard! Was he really as he is pictured? Or are we the victims, as the centuries recede, of an optical illusion? To set the record straight, we must turn to his contemporaries, who spoke freely and well about him. One of them, Jacques de Mailles, was his secretary during some of his campaigns and later managed his affairs, was eyewitness to part of his story, and remained in contact with him. For this reason he is better informed, or less to be wary of, than some others. It is to be hoped that he did not idealize his master too much and that he has given a relatively accurate picture. The Loyal Servitor, the pseudonym used by this author, speaks of "the gentle Seigneur de Bayard" whose "very pleasant and lively story" he tells, not that of a "knight without fear and without reproach." It will be seen whether this legend stands up to textual examination.

Pierre Terrail, Seigneur de Bayard, was born about the year 1476 in Dauphiné, "where there are many excellent and large houses of gentlefolk, and whence have emerged so many virtuous and noble knights that their fame has spread through Christendom: so that, as scarlet surpasses in color every other dye for cloth, so without blaming the nobility of any other region, the Dauphiné men are called, by everyone who knows them, the scarlet of the gentlemen of France."[15]

Coming from a family of minor gentry, quite old but impoverished, he belonged to a race of warriors who fought well and left their dead on the field at Poitiers, at Agincourt, and at Montlhéry, or who were gravely wounded like his father, Guinegatte, "who thenceforth could not leave his house where he died fully eighty years of age." He was to remain faithful to that tradition. Leaving home at the age of thirteen to learn the profession of arms, from seventeen years on he traversed the roads of Italy and he too died just before the age of fifty on the field of battle.

During those thirty years of campaigning, he took part in every engagement and fought on every front in Italy, France, and Navarre. He was a born fighter. He loved his profession and knew it backward. Trained to arms, an excellent fencer and an outstanding horseman, "he has in war three excellent things which are most befitting a perfect knight: he assaults like a greyhound, he defends like a boar, and he flees like a wolf."[16] He could charge bare-headed and fight like a lion, as at Fornevo, where he had two horses killed under him, at Garigliano, where he defended the bridge singlehanded for half an hour against two hundred Spaniards, and at Melegnano and many other places. He also knew when not to attack, when not to be implacable, when it was necessary to flee or to use a ruse, as at Mezières. He showed himself, too, as a great leader of men and an able tactician. Gaston de Foix won the victory of Ravenna, thanks to taking his advice, and Melegnano was also his doing. Bayard was, beyond a doubt, a remarkable captain.

In the realm of courage and military qualities, legend often rings true. It is probably less true, however, when it adds chastity to irreproachable courage. That virtue hardly seems a characteristic with the fiery captain who fought through most of Europe under conditions hardly favorable to that state, and who, moreover, had an illegitimate daughter in the process. It is also difficult to picture him as a doughty gallant or a fine courtier, yet he was both. Just as he loved war, he loved society and was loved by it. With women he had great success. His magnificent bearing at tourneys, his gaiety and dash at feasts and dances, made him the cynosure of all eyes, and, had he wished it, of all hearts. But his heart had been given once and for all, and all his life he remained faithful, in spite of a few unimportant incidents.

As a real gentleman, Bayard showed himself so discreet regarding his illicit loves that only the existence of his daughter, Jeanne Terrail, gives him away. It is necessary to read between the lines, as Ballaguy has done. Here is his theory:

Bayard's lady was Blanche Paléologus, the daughter of William VI Paléologus, Marquis of Montferrat, and of Elizabeth Sforza. She was the widow of Charles, Duke of Savoy, Bayard's first master when he was a page. Newly widowed, Blanche left the gloomy ducal residence in Chambéry and went to live in her dower house, at Carignano, in Piedmont. There she held brilliant court as soon as her condition permitted her to do so.

Bayard had been in garrison in the district for a little over a year, when a tourney took place at Carignano. In order to understand the story, it is necessary to know something of the customs of the time. There were still certain survivals from the medieval "courts of love." A discreet lover, careful not to compromise his lady yet burning with a desire to declare himself, portrayed her with the features of someone in his circle. The poet Bembo, for example, in love with Lucrezia Borgia, extolled one of her suite. Bayard, for his part, could not hide the violent passion which he felt for Bernardine de Fluxas, lady-in-waiting to Blanche—though it was the latter to whom he actually was addressing himself. And that is all that is necessary to put the record straight; Bayard was simply laying a false trail.

The following is the only text which lifts the veil from the private life of our pure knight. About April 1500, Bayard went to Carignano to present his duty to Blanche of Savoy as widow of his former master. He found with her one of his earlier loves, now married, whom he himself would have liked to marry, a certain Bernardine de Fluxas, lady-in-waiting and confidant of the duchess. "She [Bernardine] wishing to convey to the good knight that she still felt the honest love she had for him when young, gave him a warm welcome. This gentle lady de Fluxas was as accomplished a beauty, sweet and gracious in speech, as might be found. No one could have praised the good knight more highly than she. She recalled his good deeds, when he measured himself against Messire Claude de Vaudray, the tourney he won at Aire in Picardy, and the honor he received on the day of Fornua, all so renowned in France and Italy. She so lauded and heralded him that the poor gentleman was blushing with shame.

"'Madame,' suddenly exclaimed the good knight, 'you well know that I have loved, prized and honored you from my youth . . . tell me please what I should do to give pleasure to madame my good mistress, to you, above all, and the others of this gay and gallant company?'

"The dame de Fluxas then said to him: 'It seems to me, Monseigneur de Bayard, if you will pardon me, that you would do very well to make a tourney in this town in Madame's honor, who will be very grateful to you. You have here round you many of your companions, French gentlemen and others of this country, who would be very pleased to do it, and I am sure of it.'

"'In truth,' said the good knight, 'since you wish it, it shall be done. You are the first lady in the world to have won my heart to her service by your graciousness, I am sure I will never have anything but your lips and your hands, for to ask you for anything more would be wasting my time; also, on my heart, I would rather die than press you to dishonor. But I beg you to give me one of your muffs, for I have need of it.' The lady, who did not know what he would do with it, lent it to him, and he put it in the sleeve of his doublet without another word. . . .

"The next morning he sent a trumpeter to all the towns round, where there were garrisons, to let all the gentlemen know that if they wished to come to the town of Carignano four days later, which was a Sunday, accoutered with arms, he would offer a prize. This would be his lady's muff from which hung a ruby worth an estimated hundred ducats, to go to who ever would be found best in three lance charges without lists, and in twelve sword thrusts. The trumpeter did his duty and brought back the written word of fifteen gentlemen who promised to be there. This came to the knowledge of the lady Blanche, who was very pleased and had scaffolding put up where the races and combats would take place."[17]

The tourney took place, and Bayard fought brilliantly with lance and sword against opponents of stature. The jousts ended very late, and then everyone hurried to the castle, where the duchess had invited a numerous company to supper: "After supper the hautbois and fiddlers began to play. But before the dancing began the prize must be given to him adjudged the winner. The seigneurs de Granmont and de Fluxas, who were the judges, took counsel with all those present, gentlemen, ladies and the combattants themselves, and all were of the opinion that the good knight [Bayard] had, by right of arms, won the prize. The said judges came to him to present it; but, blushing with shame, he refused it, saying . . . that Madame de Fluxas was responsible because she had lent him her muff and that it belonged to her, in his view, to give the prize where she thought fit. . . . She very humbly thanked the good knight for the honor he did her with these words; 'As Monseigneur de Bayard has done me this favor to say that my muff has made him win the prize, I will keep it all my life for love of him; but the ruby, since the best man will not accept it, in my opinion it should be given to Monseigneur de Mondragon; for it is agreed that he was the best after him.' . . . The prize being given, the dancing began and lasted till after midnight, when everyone retired. The French gentlemen spent another five or six days at Carignano in joyous diversion and feasting, then they went back to their garrisons. The good knight took leave of Madame his good mistress, to whom he said that there was no prince or princess in the world, after his sovereign lord, who had more commandment now over him than she, for which he was greatly thanked. . . . Their true love endured till death; never a year passed without their sending presents to one another."[18]

Where is then the knight without reproach, the monk in armor, offered us today? Vanished, metamorphosed into an amorous page, fallen to the petty pleasures of a refined court, "as much sought after and beloved as though he would be heir to it," whose "prowess, honor, gentleness and courtesy" were, for a month, the chief topic of conversation in the castle. The liaison between Blanche and Bayard can hardly be doubted if it is remembered that the next year little Jeanne was born. There has even been the supposition of a secret marriage. Bayard never married and firmly refused every offer of marriage, even when it came from the Queen of France. What to say of the embarrassed reply of his uncle, a bishop, refusing the proffered hand of Anne of Brittany on behalf of his nephew? "He is too badly off to marry, and has as yet no idea of what it means." This is perhaps going too far. Nonetheless, Bayard's love, licit or not, was faithful "and endured till death," a love full of the idealism of the Middle Ages, that of the lowly knight serving the lady of such high birth that almost superhuman exploits could alone render him worthy of her. Still, the legend remains. If it has distorted the facts, in leaving obscure some aspects of our hero, it remains not less true that his goodness was exceptional. It was that more than anything else which has given him his place in history.

In conditions in which everyone habitually thought of nothing but plunder, robbery, and self-enrichment, Bayard refused to profit by the multitude of opportunities offered by war, but practiced in those turbulent times the virtues of peace. Honorable toward his adversaries, he never used the rights of conquest against civil enemies and he always bore himself like a gentleman, even during the sack of a city, such as that of Brescia. The taking of this city and its memorable sack, in which the booty was estimated at three million crowns, is a noteworthy incident of the campaign of 1512, conducted brilliantly by the Duke of Nemours. Bayard was playing his accustomed valorous role when, during the attack, he was seriously injured and obliged to stop. As soon as the town had fallen, two of his archers put him on a door and carried him in haste, and with great precautions, to the handsomest house they could find:

"It was the home of a very rich gentleman, but he had taken refuge in a monastery and his wife had remained in their house in the protection of Our Lord, with her two beautiful daughters, who were hidden in a loft under some hay. When they came knocking on her door, always trustful of God's mercy, she opened it. She saw the good knight, whom they were carrying thus wounded; he had the door shut forthwith and set two archers by it, saying to them: 'Guard it on your lives and let nobody in who is not of my company.' The archers did as they were bidden, and he was carried into a fine room into which the lady of the house led him. Throwing herself on her knees before him, she spoke in this fashion: 'Noble lord, I give you this house and all that is in it, for I know well that it is yours in right of war; but may it please you to save my honor and my life and those of the two daughters of my husband and myself who are of marriageable age.'

"The good knight, who never thought evil, answered her: 'Madame, I do not know if I will be able to escape the wound I have, but as long as I live nothing unpleasant shall happen to you or your daughters any more than to myself. Only keep them in your rooms so they are never seen, and I assure you that there is not a man in my house who will dare to enter any place which you do not permit; and I assure you, too, that you have here a gentleman who will not plunder you but will accord you all the courtesy he is able.' "[19]

Reassured, the woman sent for a surgeon. He dressed the injuries of the wounded man, said that his life was not in danger but that care and a long rest were needed. And Bayard, tended with devotion by his hostess and her daughters, passed five weeks there, recovering his health little by little. But his new friends learned that in such circumstances the French considered their hosts as their prisoners and before leaving demanded from them a large ransom. Bayard would doubtless not act differently. They thought they could avoid the worst by giving him some money, hoping that he would not ask for more. The day of his departure the mother came to see him, thanked him for all his kindness, and begged him in veiled terms to free them without taking too great advantage of the situation: " 'Here is a little present which we are giving you, if you will please to accept it.' Then she took the box that the servant was holding and opened it before the good knight and he saw that it was full of fine ducats. The gentle seigneur who never in his life troubled about money, began to laugh and then said: 'Madame, how many ducats are there in this box?' The poor woman was afraid that he was cross at seeing so few, and said: 'Monseigneur, there are only two thousand five hundred ducats, but if you are not satisfied we will find you a more ample sum!' Then he said: 'By my faith, madame, if you would give me a hundred thousand ducats, you would not do me as much good as the good fare I have had here and the good care you have taken of me, so that wherever I may be if God spare me, you will have a gentleman at your command. As to your ducats I do not wish for a single one of them and I thank you. Take them back. All my life I liked people better than crowns.'

"The good woman was very astonished to find herself denied. 'Monseigneur,' she said, 'I shall always feel myself the most unfortunate woman in the world if you take so little of the present I make you, which is nothing compared with the courtesy you have shown me till now, and still show me, by your great kindness.' When the good knight saw that she was so firm and that she gave the present with such bold courage, he said: 'Well, then, madame, I take it for love of you, but go and find your two daughters, because I wish to bid them good-by.' The poor woman, who was in heaven that her present had finally been accepted, went to get her daughters, who were very beautiful, good and well brought up, and had done much to amuse the knight during his sickness, because they knew very well how to sing and play the lute and spinet, and were good at needlework. They were brought to the good knight, who, while they made . . . , themselves ready, had had the ducats divided into three parts, two of one thousand and the third of five hundred. When they arrived, they threw themselves on their knees, but they were quickly made to stand up, then the elder of the two began to say: 'Monseigneur, these two poor little maidens, whom you have done so great honor in guarding from all harm, have come to say good-by to you and to thank Your Lordship humbly for the grace they have received.'"

The good knight, moved to tears, thanked them in his turn for their charming company and, taking the ducats which their mother had given him, gave a thousand to each of them and charged them to distribute the five hundred to nuns who had been victims of the soldiery. Then he took leave of them: "So he shook hands with them all, as the custom is in Italy. They knelt, crying so much that it seemed they were being led to execution. The lady said: 'Incomparable flower of chivalry, may the Lord our Saviour and Redeemer Jesus Christ bless you, who suffered death and passion for all sinners, may he recompense you, here in this world and in the next.'

"So as he went out of the room to mount his horse, the two beautiful daughters of the house went down and each gave him a present they had worked during his illness; one was a pair of little bracelets made of fine hair and gold and silver threads, marvelously well done; the other was a purse of crimson satin, very cunningly worked. He thanked them warmly and said that the present came from such good hands that he thought it worth ten thousand crowns; and, to honor them more, he had the bracelets put on his arms and the purse in his sleeve, assuring them that as long as they lasted he would wear them for love of them."[20]

Thus did Bayard take pity. His heart of gold was moved by the sight of suffering and he, the very personification of strength, never failed to fly to the help of the weak, the widow, and the orphan as often as an opportunity presented itself. It is no wonder that he had such renown and enjoyed such extraordinary popularity with everyone, even in the enemy camp.

An accomplished warrior, a faithful lover, a magnificent lord, charitable in heart, as Bayard appears in the light of texts, he had a personality infinitely richer and more complex than legend has allowed him to appear. It should not be forgotten that the "knight without fear and without reproach" was also a man of the Renaissance, overflowing with talent and life.

※　　※　　※

The greatest military man of the age, however, the man who by his genius overshadowed all his rivals and dominated the century, was not Bayard but Gaston de Foix, Duke of Nemours. Fate did not bestow on Bayard the positions of leadership which his soldierly ability would have justified, and it gave to his companions more courage than brains; yet it heaped on their leader the gifts and advantages refused to others. Gaston de Foix was one of those outstanding individuals whose apparition might well have changed the course of history had he not met death in the hour of his greatest victory. As it was, his unquestioned military genius permitted him to discharge with distinction the high offices to which his birth called him. Nephew and brother-in-law of kings, Gaston had a mother who was a sister to Louis XII of France, and his own sister was the second wife of Ferdinand of Aragon, King of Spain. His name is associated with the brilliant campaign of 1512, and particularly its crowning victory of Ravenna. No one was further ahead of his time than this young prince, whose exceptional quality as a tactician presaged the great French commanders of the seventeenth century and the Revolution—Turenne, Condé, and Napoleon.

At twenty-two Gaston de Foix became lieutenant general of the king within the territory of Milan. France at that time was in a critical situation. Pope Julius II wished to drive the French out of Lombardy, and his clever policies had surrounded them with enemies: on the north were the Swiss, on the northeast the Venetians, on the south the Spaniards and papal troops. In three months Gaston de Foix managed to upset the coalition's plans and to open the gates of Rome. In January the Spanish and papal troops were besieging Bologna; on February 5, in a terrible snowstorm, Gaston took it and the allies retreated. On February 10, Brescia, occupied by the French, fell to the Venetians; on the nineteenth Gaston drove them out. At the news, it is said, the pope tore his beard. Now only the Spaniards, who were playing for time, remained to be crushed. To allow the Venetians to recuperate, they refused battle and withdrew to concentrate under the walls of Ravenna. Gaston pursued them thither and forced them to fight. It was both the apogee and the end of his career. "There have been great battles since God created heaven and earth," said a contemporary, "but never was one seen so cruel, so fierce, or so well fought."[21]

In the French camp, every man had taken the battle station assigned to him the day before. "The twelve thousand infantry formed a single troop and, protected by artillery, took their positions opposite the enemy. The men at arms were to the right; on the left were a thousand archers. The Italian infantry and another hundred men at arms remained behind to protect the baggage and to guard against a possible sortie by the garrison of Ravenna. There were exchanges of cannon fire, and each side waited to see who would be first to leave their positions.

"The German mercenaries came out first. Seeing this, the gentle Seigneur de Molart said to his men: 'How now, comrades, shall we let people reproach us that the German mercenaries engaged the enemy before us? For my part, I would sooner lose an eye.' So he began, as the mercenaries were occupying the bridge, to get into the water all dressed and shod, and his men after him. And it must be known the water was everywhere deep enough to come above their breech; and they set about it so briskly that they had crossed over before the mercenaries. After which, the artillery crossed and was put in front of these foot soldiers, who at once took up their battle order. Then the cavalry vanguard crossed, and then the battle array."[22]

While the preparations were going on rapidly in the two camps, "the gentle Duke of Nemours [Gaston de Foix] left his lodging quite early, fully armed except for his helmet. He had on a magnificent accouterment, embroidered with the arms of Navarre and de Foix, but it was very heavy. In leaving his said lodging, he looked at the sun, which was already up and was very red; he began to say to the comrades who were round him: 'Look, *messeigneurs*, how red the sun is.' There was there a gentleman whom he loved wondrously well, a very agreeable companion called Haubourdin, who answered: 'Do you know what that means, My Lord? That some great prince or great captain will die today; it must be you or the viceroy.' The Duke of Nemours began to laugh at these words because he took nothing Haubourdin said seriously. . . . So he went forward to the bridge to see his army finish crossing while the good knight came to find him and said to him: 'My Lord, let us go and disport ourselves a little along the canal, while we wait till everyone has crossed.' To which the Duke of Nemours agreed and took with him the Seigneur de Lautrec, the Seigneur d'Alègre, and some others, to the number of twenty horse. . . . The Duke of Nemours, going thus to disport himself, began to say to the good Chevalier de Bayard: 'We are here on a very nice little hill; if there were some hackbut [a primitive harquebus] men hidden on this side, they could engage us at their ease.' And at these words there came into view a troop of twenty or thirty Spanish gentlemen, among whom was the Captain Pedro de Paz, chief of all their light horse, and the said gentlemen were on horseback. So the good knight advanced twenty or thirty steps and saluted them, saying:

'My Lords, you are disporting yourselves waiting like we are for the fine game to begin. I ask you not to shoot off your hackbuts on your side and we will not on ours!' So Pedro de Paz noticed that everyone honored the Duke of Nemours, and asked: 'Seigneur de Bayard, who is that seigneur in such a fine setup and whom your men hold in such honor?' The good knight replied to him: 'It is our leader, the Duke of Nemours, nephew of our prince and brother to your queen.' Scarcely had he finished speaking when the Captain Pedro de Paz and all those who were with him dismounted and saluted him humbly. . . . The Duke of Nemours very courteously thanked them and said: 'My Lords, I see clearly that within this day we shall know who will win the campaign, you or we; but this matter cannot be settled without great bloodshed. If your viceroy would settle this difference in his person against mine, I would make sure that all my friends and comrades who are with me would agree to it and, if I am vanquished, would return to the Duchy of Milan and would leave you here in peace; so also if he is vanquished, all of you would return to the Kingdom of Naples.' When he had finished speaking, the reply was speedily given: 'My Lord, I think that your gentle heart would have you gladly do what you say, but in my opinion, our viceroy will never agree, as regards his own person, to your proposal.' 'So then, farewell, My Lords,' said the gentle prince. 'I am going to cross the river and promise to God on my life not to recross it again until the field is yours or ours.' Then he rejoined his troops."

On the Spanish side they also were ready to fight. "Their camp was marvelously strong, for they had a good ditch in front of them. Behind were all their footmen lying prone, and in front of them was all their own artillery to the number of twenty pieces, cannon, long culverins, and about two hundred hackbuts on stands; and between two hackbuts there were, on little wheeled carriages, great pieces of sharpened cutting iron, like scimitars, to roll out among the French infantrymen when they tried to penetrate their ranks."

The men at arms, protected on their flank by the Ronco and in front by the artillery, were on the left: in the center, were the infantry, massed as a single corps; on the right, the light cavalry. Then the battle began:

"The Duke of Nemours, when he had crossed the river, gave the order for everyone to march. The Spaniards thereupon shot at the troop of French foot soldiers and killed, before they could close in to fight, more than two thousand. Notwithstanding all the artillery fire of the Spaniards, the French kept marching. Two pieces of artillery, which the Seigneur d'Alègre and the good knight had had brought back on the near side of the canal, fired continuously on the Spanish men at arms, and did them incredible damage, for three hundred of them were killed. It was known later that a single cannon shot had wiped out thirty-three of them. This very much upset the Spaniards, who saw themselves being killed and did not know by whom. Their captain could not hold them. They said, in their language: 'God's body, we are being slaughtered from the sky, let us go fight men!' They began, in order to escape this artillery fire, to go out of their fort into a fine field to get to the fight. They attacked the French men at arms, among whom was the Duke of Nemours. The Spaniards made a noise and marvelous shout as they attacked: 'Spain, Spain, St. James! At the horses, at the horses.' They came on furiously, but were yet more furiously received by the French, who also cried: 'France, France! At the horses, at the horses.' For the Spaniards did not try to do more than kill the horses, for they have a proverb which says: 'Dead the horse, lost the man at arms.' Since God created heaven and earth, never was seen a more cruel or hard assault than the French and Spaniards made against each other, and this fight lasted well over half an hour. They rested, facing each other, to draw breath, then lowered their visors and began again even more violently. The Spaniards were half as many again as the French. So the Seigneur d'Alègre ran from there right to his vanguard and from afar shouted to the men of Messire Robert de la Marche, who bore a black and white device, and called out to them: 'Black and White, march, march, and the archers of the guard too. . . .' On the arrival of this fresh band there was a stubborn fight, for the Spaniards were strongly attacked. The archers of the guard had small hatchets, with which they set up their camp, hanging from the pommels of their saddles, and they put these to work and dealt great rugged blows to the army of the Spaniards. Never was seen such a furious combat; but finally the Spaniards chose to abandon the camp, upon which between two ditches died three or four hundred men at arms."[23]

This put the enemy cavalry effectively out of action. There still remained the main body of the army, the foot soldiers, dangerous to attack, since, lying prone, they could not be seen. Gaston de Foix, a fine tactician, had the idea of attacking them on the flank with his infantry in spite of the artillery fire: "So it was ordered that the two thousand Gascons should go to the rear to loose their arrows, which would make them get up. Now the French infantrymen were not farther from the Spaniards than two pike's lengths, but the position was too disadvantageous, as they could not see their enemy at all and so did not know where they ought to penetrate. . . . The Gascons let fly their arrows very well and wounded several Spaniards, who were discomfited as they showed, but suddenly they arose in good battle order and from behind came out two arrays of a thousand or twelve hundred men, who came forward to fall on these Gascons."[24]

Surprised, the Gascons fell back, and some even fled, but the German mercenaries returned to the fray and the battle was fiercely pursued on both sides of the ditch. The heroism of one captain of the mercenaries turned the balance in favor of the French: "He took the pike the wrong way around, for he was marvelously big, and, thus holding it by the point, he placed it over the pikes of the Spaniards who were prone, and by his great strength forced their points into the ground. Seeing which, the French pushed forward vigorously and entered the ditch; but in crossing it there was wondrous murder, for never did anyone fight back like the Spaniards, who not having an arm or leg left whole, even bit their enemies. . . . The French thereby received grave hurt, but even more the Spaniards, for the men at arms of the French vanguard came to take them on the flank, which broke them completely, and they were all dead and cut to pieces, except their chief, Count Pedro Navarre, who was taken prisoner, with a few other captains."[25]

Thus the French were victorious. But the Duke of Nemours, on the false alarm of some of the fleeing Gascons, believed his infantry defeated and threw himself desperately against the first enemies he met, who, in fact were fleeing. He pursued them in the direction of Ravenna, on a narrow road with no room to maneuver: "On one side there was a canal into which one could not descend, on the other a big ditch which one could not cross. All those who were with the Duke of Nemours were thrown into the water or fell into the ditch. The good duke had the hocks of his horse cut. So he took his sword in his hand, and never did Roland at Roncevaux such feats of arms as he did there; and likewise his cousin the Seigneur de Lautrec, who, well aware of the great danger he was in, shouted as loud as he could to the Spaniards: 'Don't kill him, it is our viceroy, the brother of your queen.' However it was, the poor duke remained there, after receiving several wounds, for from chin to forehead he had fourteen or fifteen, and thereby showed himself a noble prince who never turned his back."[26]

Gaston de Foix, Duke of Nemours, was mourned by everyone. Of all the memorial homage which his early death inspired, he would doubtless have attached the greatest value to that written by the only gentleman who, the conventions and prejudices of the century aside, may be considered his peer, Bayard. Soberly, in terms charged with emotion, the good knight informed his uncle, the Bishop of Grenoble, of the tragic event:

"Sir, if the king has won the battle, I swear to you that the poor gentlemen have completely lost it; for just as we were giving chase, M. de Nemours had found some footmen who were rallying, so he wished to fall on them, but the gentle prince was so ill-accompanied that he was killed there, for whom all the grief and mourning which was ever done was not equal to that which has been and is still continuing in our camp; for it seems as though we have lost the battle. Sir, I promise you that it is the greatest pity of any prince's death in the last hundred years; if he had lived to man's age he would have accomplished things that no prince ever did, and they who are there can well say that they have lost their father. As for me, sir, I can only live in melancholy, for I have lost so much that I do not know how to write it."[27]

* * *

Whoever speaks of the Italian wars thinks of Melegnano, rather than of Ravenna, as the great victory, and to Melegnano is inevitably linked the name of Francis I.

Francis, wishing to wipe out the dishonor of the preceding king's death, began his reign by a transalpine expedition designed to reconquer the territory of Milan. He ran into the Swiss, still at war with him, near the plain of Melegnano. There was a battle. It was confused and added nothing to the history of military tactics, but it was heroic. It gave a fine beginning to the thirty years of power of the first Angoulême Valois. This twenty-year-old king fought like a lion at the head of his troops: "All the night we stayed seated in the saddle, lance in hand, helmeted, and our German mercenaries in battle order; and as I [i.e., King Francis] was the nearest to our enemies, it fell to me to keep watch, so that they did not surprise us at dawn."

This lightning stroke of Melegnano was to be rich in political consequences, unlike Ravenna; it preserved for the French the territory of Milan for a few more years, led to the Perpetual Peace of Fribourg with the Swiss cantons, which has never been violated since, and to the Concordat of Bologna with the pope. In effect, it was to place Europe at their feet.

Melegnano may then be extolled, but the accounts of it make poor reading, even when they come from the enthusiastic pen of the victor. Only the letter that Francis I wrote to Louise of Savoy on the very evening of victory will be quoted here. It has been said, and justly, that it seems to have been penned on a gun carriage. Still afire with action, Francis I recreated the whole atmosphere in a few lines:

". . . the battle has been long and lasted from three yesterday afternoon until two today, without knowing who had lost or won, without ceasing to fight or to fire the artillery day or night; and I assure you, madame, that I have seen the German mercenaries measure their pikes with the Swiss, their lances with the men at arms; and no one will ever say again that the men at arms are 'armed rabbits,' for, truth to tell, without making a single mistake, five hundred of them at a time made thirty fine charges before the battle was won. And it was well fought. There has not been seen so fierce and cruel a battle in the last 2000 years, as they say who were at Ravenna, even at the cost of a falcon. Madame, the Seneschal d'Armagnac [Galiot de Genouillac, grand master of the artillery] with his artillery, even dares to say that he was, in part, the cause of winning the battle, for never did any man use his artillery better. And thank God everyone is all right; I begin with myself, and with my brother the constable, with M. de Vendôme, M. de Saint-Pol, M. de Guise, Marshal de Chabannes, the grand master, and M. de Longueville. Of men of renown there is dead only Imbercourt, and Bussy is at death's door; it is a great pity about these two persons. There are dead some gentlemen of my household, which you will learn without my having to write it down. The Prince of Talmont is seriously wounded and I wish to reassure you that my brother, the constable, and M. de Saint-Pol broke as fine a lance as any of the company whoever they may be. I say this as one who saw them, for they did not spare themselves any more than wild boars at bay. Meanwhile, madame, have thanks rendered to God throughout the realm for the victory he has been pleased to give us. Madame, you will laugh at MM. de Lautrec and de Lescun, who were not to be found in the battle, and who sneered at the equipment of the Swiss who mocked them; we also have great misgivings about the Count of Sancerre, for we cannot find him.

"Madame, I beg the Creator to give you a good life and long.

"Written at Camp Sainte-Brigide, Friday the fourteenth day of September, 1515."[28]

In the flush of victory, Francis I wished to be knighted by the hand of him who in his eyes was the embodiment of chivalry:

"The king, before dubbing the knights, called the noble knight Bayard and said to him: 'Bayard, my friend, today I wish to be knighted by your hand, because that knight who fought on foot and on horse in several battles is held and reputed the most worthy knight.' Bayard replied to the king's words: 'Sire, he who is crowned, praised, and anointed with sacred oil, and is king of such a noble kingdom, and the eldest son of the Church, is the knight above all knights.' Said the king: 'Bayard, make haste.' So Bayard took his sword and said: 'Sire, it is as much as if it were for Roland or Oliver, Godefroy or Baudouin his brother. You indeed are the first prince I have ever knighted; may God grant that you do not run away in war.' And then as if in jest he cried aloud to the sword in his right hand: 'Lucky thou art today, to have given the order of chivalry to so handsome and powerful a king. In truth, my good sword, you will be well preserved as a relic and honored above all others, and I will never use you but against Turks, Saracens, or Moors.' Then he gave two little skips and put his sword back in its sheath.[29]

※   ※   ※

For more than twenty years after Melegnano the French occupied Italy. Today the French know too well what suffering and horror, what compromise and subtle temptation occupation implies, not to feel a pang of conscience at having themselves played for so long the sorry role of occupiers. Still, it is impossible to measure events four centuries apart with a single yardstick. The essential principles may be different. Contemporary texts must be scrutinized to see how the occupiers and occupied of the sixteenth century differ from, or resemble, those of the twentieth.

At the beginning of the occupation the French appear in all their glory. Charles VIII was welcomed triumphantly at Naples and there received a veritable apotheosis: he was acclaimed by the Angevin party as their sovereign, while his rival, the Duke of Calabria, hastily fled. In gratitude for such a welcome, and doubtless the better to show off his splendor, the king offered the nobles of the country a great banquet. It appears they all came and even returned the compliment, since the very next day the king dined in the house of the Prince of Salerno, a fine and noble place built of diamond shaped stones, and there was a great celebration.

Some ten years later, the Italians—the Genoese, in this case—still prepared sumptuous feasts when Louis XII entered their cities: "They cleared out all their upper rooms, cellars, and useful space so as to lodge men and horses; they laid in provision of wood, flour, meat, wine, and other victuals needed for the king's stay and that of the retinue. Then they brought out twenty thousand measures of oats and more than thirty thousand quintals of hay, apart from the town's reserves. The main street, through which the king was to pass, they had sanded for the safety of the horses. Inside the harbor mole were big carracks, ships, and brigantines loaded with artillery and gun powder, to shoot seaward in salute to the king at his entry."[30]

And the French occupier made ready, thanks to the efforts of the occupied, to enjoy a memorable experience:

"At the sound of the great bell of Genoa all the lords and inhabitants of the town, each according to his rank, went out to greet the king. All the ladies, girls, and beauties of Genoa took their places at the windows, in the galleries and on the balconies of their houses, wherever they could be comfortable, and took up positions two deep all along the main street, all or almost all clothed in silk or in fine white linen.

"Near the bridge of St. Thomas's gate to the left was a showpiece of evergreens decorated with apples, pomegranates, and oranges, and shaped like a chapel, in the middle of which at the top was the shield of France fully emblazoned; on the other side, on the right, the arms of France quartered with those of Brittany; on the left, a little lower, the arms of Messire Philippe de Ravestain, Governor of Genoa for the king, and opposite, on the right, those of the town of Genoa.

"All the way from St. Thomas's gate to the church of St. Lawrence, which is the great Cathedral of Genoa, the streets were hung and adorned with woven tapestries worked with bright images, that is to say, with ladies and young ladies, townswomen and market women, all dressed in white and so beautiful and richly adorned that they resembled nymphs and goddesses more than human women.

"The main street where the king passed was made verdant by a sprinkling of leafy branches, and orange and pomegranate sprays planting the ground, with the fruit hanging on their branches."[31]

The king, accompanied by dignitaries among whom were the Cardinal of Amboise, his beloved councilor, and Caesar Borgia, Duke of Valentinois, made his entry in the midst of his army, which marched proudly along. It was followed by "so many archbishops, bishops, abbots, prothonotaries, and other clerics that there were enough of them to hold a council. . . .

"A number of people and of the populace followed in their train, men, women, and little children, who all cried loudly: 'France, France, France, France,' without stopping and making such merry that there was not a heart that was not stirred. . . .

"When the king was in front of the mole, the big carracks and the ships began to boom and thunder and to fire their artillery so noisily that it seemed as though the winds were unleashed, the waves lashed, the rocks split, the air rent, the earth shaken, and that the whole town of Genoa would be engulfed.

"As soon as the king had entered the town, all the bells began to ring; it was marvelous. So he went the whole length of the main street as far as the cathedral of St. Lawrence to attend a solemn Mass."[32]

After the ceremony the king went back to his palace. He only went out again in the evening to go to a regatta:

"There he saw several new amusements and joyous pastimes; the sailors climbed from the bottom of the ships to the top of the shrouds, coming down head first on their arms to the holds; some threw themselves into the sea from the top of the shrouds, others swam in the water, others under the water for a long time, others fired artillery, played on instruments, had races in skiffs, brigantines, galleons, and gave themselves to a thousand other sallies and games in which the king took much pleasure."[33] King Louis returned to the palace after nightfall through streets lit with innumerable torches, while small children with torches ran ahead crying "France! France!", and the crowd again accompanied him cheering.

The feasting continued uninterruptedly during his stay and when he left, the Genoese "for their lands, and the manors which they held in dependence from his town of Genoa, swore fealty, homage, oaths of fidelity, and solemn promises well and loyally to serve him toward or against all." They then showered him and his train with gifts:

"To the king, four dishes, four goblets, and four ewers all of gold, in value twelve thousand ducats. To the Cardinal of Amboise, one gold dish and one gold ewer, to the value of two thousand five hundred ducats, to M. Pierre de Rohan, Marshal of Gie, a silver service worth four hundred ducats; the same to the bishop of Albi; to Master Florimond Robertet, the king's secretary, three hundred ducats; to the quartermasters a hundred handbreadths of black velvet and twenty-five of scarlet; to the valets a hundred handbreadths or spans of black velvet; to each of the doormen twelve ducats: thus there were very few officers of the king's household who were not enriched by the gifts of those Genoese."[34] The king, however, only half trusted the bearers of these gifts. He thought it prudent "to enjoy the benevolent affection of the local lords and also to hold them in fear, to take a number of their children as his boarders . . . and to keep them all in his house." Precaution on the part of the occupier.

The women of Genoa were not absent from the sumptuous feasting; indeed, they played a leading role. Beautiful, distinguished, and frail, so magnificently turned out in honor of the King of France, they were superb creatures whose unclassical elegance heightened their many attractions:

"They are of middle height and well rounded," adds the chronicler,[35] "with fairly fleshy faces, and fresh, pale complexions; somewhat proud and erect in their carriage; gentle-featured; gracious in their welcome; ardent in their love; constant in their will; eloquent in their speech; conditionally loyal; and with all this, so quick to learn that they need no lessons."

To obtain the good will of the occupier, the occupied were prepared to go to great lengths. One of the most efficacious means to that end was the Genoese woman, and she was used shamelessly. Charles VIII's taste for the fair sex had been well known, and he himself made no secret of it. The occupied had hastened to satisfy it. From that time on, Italian diplomats were always accompanied by their women. As for individuals greedy of the conqueror's largess, they offered him daughters and wives without hesitation, and did everything to embellish their charms. Apparently good King Louis XII appreciated the temptations to which his predecessor's tastes subjected him:

"The Genoese, contrary to custom, brought their wives and daughters with them to banquets, masquerades, new dances in fancy dress, turns, frolics, and other novelties, to provide a joyful pastime for King Louis and his courtiers. Some of them brought the most beautiful women and presented them to the king and themselves kissed them to try them out; then the king gladly kissed them, danced with them, and amused himself honorably with them."[36]

These ladies needed no pushing toward the conqueror's arms. From the highest to the lowest, they threw themselves into them. In the sixteenth century in Italy, when love and its play held so great a place that a woman without a lover felt herself discredited, it is not to be supposed that these beauties would snub the rich and powerful victor, crowned with the laurels of the victorious warrior, and endowed with the more prosaic appeal of wealth. The ladies of Genoa thus made fair game of themselves, and no one will judge the French harshly because they culled the flowers proffered to them in that gracious setting. Quite the contrary. The king himself, subject, it is true, to great temptation, was to set an example:

"It was at Genoa in 1502, in the course of the great banquets and joyous parties, that a lady of that city, named Thomasine Spinola, one of the most lovely in all Italy, turned her look often upon the king, who was marvelously handsome, wise, and very well spoken.... After several glances, unquestionably of love, she was so bold as to speak to him and to say several sweet things, which the king, a most human prince, found to his liking. They often conversed together, most worthily, of many things, so that that lady, finding herself his close acquaintance, when opportunity offered begged him very humbly ... that he would be pleased that she should be his *intendio*, and he hers, which signifies honorable acquaintance and amicable understanding. All which the king granted and the noble lady was more happy than if she had gotten all the gold in the world. This gift was so dear to her, that, just because she felt desired by the king she forgot everything else, even to the point of never wishing to sleep with her husband ... and when the king left, her floods of tears showed how her heart grieved, and she said she would never forget her *intendio*."[37]

Certain ladies went still further and become active allies. One Genoese woman, evidently of modest position, risked reprisal and told the French of their danger from her compatriots:

"The Genoese would have taken the fort and the French would not have known, had not a woman of Genoa informed them, by signs, that the Genoese were mining it.... She put herself at a window, but did not dare to show herself for fear of being seen by her own people; she took a great kerchief in her hand and waved it, then took a pick and made as if digging, then a basket and acted out putting earth in the basket; finally she stooped and doubled herself up, as if to enter a narrow place, low and cramped. Then the French understood their fort was being mined.... So they went off to make a countermine and did it so well that they met their aggressors underground and killed a good number of them."[38]

Is the conclusion to be drawn that all the Italian women were fickle and unfaithful? Hardly, for the chronicle only reports the scandals; traditionally, the virtuous have no history.

The feasting and the smiles, however, often proved to be a mask. In fact, hearts were filled with terror and hate, and these violent passions could no longer be silenced when it became clear that the enemy was there to stay. Attitudes and words betrayed them before the blood began to flow. Already while returning from Naples, the French had felt the hostility of the populace; their soldiers, reaching Fornua hungry on the eve of the battle, looked with suspicion on the food offered them:

"They found there a great quantity of flour, wine, and fodder for the horses. The people brought small and very black loaves which they sold dear, wine diluted with three quarters of water, and a few fruits; they did it to please the army. I had some bought, but had them tested in front of me, for there was a strong suspicion that they had left the victuals there to poison the troops, and nobody touched them at first. Two Swiss died from drinking; they took cold and died in a cellar, which made people even more suspicious."[39]

Some time afterward, the crew of a galley, landing to take on supplies at a small town in the domain of Genoa, saw a sight which was scarcely a friendly omen: "On a scaffold set up at a crossroads, a play was being performed in which the King of France was represented by a king sitting in a chair whose bottom they were setting on fire."[40]

Six years later, while the army was parading across Rome in great pomp, "sounding trumpets and clarions and big Swiss drums," some voices were raised against the intrusion, and some Romans bewailed their country's misfortunes and exchanged bitter complaints:

"O what shame, dishonor, and disgrace it is to all the Italies to let the armed French pass who pillage our goods, covet our women, occupy our manors, are always traveling about our country, and finally try to hold us at their mercy. What can be added but that they make good friends but let them not be our neighbors?"[41]

For the moment, the French had nothing to fear other than "looks of hatred, words of envy, and veiled threats." But soon the occupied acted, and the occupier, attacked, had to defend himself. Occasionally, he showed himself magnanimous.

In the course of one of the conquests of the Duchy of Milan under Louis XII, the town of Vaugayres was given to a valiant captain of the king, Sire de Ligny, as a reward. Vaugayres took advantage of the return under arms of Ludovic le More, its original master, to rebel against the French. Ludovic was beaten, and Ligny regained his property. Then, indignant at this betrayal, Ligny decided to take revenge. He made known his intention of taking terrible reprisals, and of putting the town to the sack. His future victims, distraught, tried to dissuade him from this fearful intention:

"Fifty of the leading people of the town came to the house of the Sire de Ligny and, bareheaded, threw themselves on their knees before him, begging for mercy. One of them at the end of an eloquent supplication asked him to receive, as a mark of their humble submission, a small present, all they could afford, of three hundred silver marks; the acceptance of which would show that his anger toward them was ended. Then he had brought in on two tables basins, cups, goblets, and other kinds of silver plate, which the said Sire de Ligny disdained to look at but replied, in a rare bad humor, proudly: 'Wicked, cowardly, and infamous people, how do you dare to enter my presence when, weak in spirit, you have revolted without reason or means? What faith can I have in you now? If I did my duty, would I not have you hanged and strangled, like disloyal traitors, from the mullions of your windows? Go, and never let me see you again.' "[42]

The matter, however, was settled. The offended ruler showed his clemency—without accepting the smallest gift.

On another, and certainly much more serious, occasion, the French had to reply to hatred by using violence and force of arms, when the same Genoese, whose resounding welcome of five years before was still vividly remembered, massacred the French garrison, and their families who had taken refuge in the citadel, with unparalleled cruelty: "They ripped up the men's bellies, washed their hands in their blood, tore out their hearts and set them on posts; they treated the women in even a more terrible way and they died a death so cruel and strange that the horror of the deed forbids speaking of it."[43]

Blood calls for blood, and the reply was grim. The King of France took the repression of the rebellion upon himself. Having raised fifty thousand men, he marched on Genoa and took it after violent fighting. Once master, he wished to show the populace that he could not be attacked with impunity, and to this end he took those terrible, irrevocable measures of repression which have survived the centuries by their notoriety. First he took simple measures to intimidate the populace—a march-past of the king and his troops, a great deployment of force and firing of artillery: "which burst like a fart from hell's rump,"[44] as the author notes. Then the proclamation of martial law, a curfew, and the confiscation of arms:

"The king had proclaimed in both French and Italian, after three trumpet blasts in the palace square, that all the people of Genoa of every rank should bring before evening the next day all the arms they had in their house and lodging, such as cuirasses, coats of mail, helmets, halberds, pikes, *partisanes*, targets and bucklers, spears, axes, and swords.

"All those who would keep or hide them after the said day are declared to be henceforth rebels disobeying the king, and their persons will be seized and their goods confiscated."[45]

At the same time, the king's justice sought out the ringleaders. The greater part of them had taken refuge outside the town. They were relentlessly tracked down. Their chief, old Paolo de Novi, took refuge in Corsica and was found there by a ship's captain, Prégent de Bidoux, and captured with the complicity of a Genoese sailor, whose conscience was bought for two hundred crowns:

"The Genoese found a means of bringing the said Paolo de Novi, to the shore, where there were several barks, ships, and galleys, from Genoa and elsewhere, and among others that of Prégent, disguised.

"The said Prégent, when he saw him, pointed him out to his men and ordered them to take him by surprise. Which was done. In an instant, with arms under their cloaks, they landed as though going to look for fresh water and other provisions to take aboard their vessels. Little by little they approached him till finally they grasped him by the collar. . . .

"The Duke of Genoa began to weep and to say: 'Alas, I see I am a dead man. For the taking of my body my head will pay ransom; what I have done was not of my own volition, but to please the people and avoid their fury, for had I refused, then they too would have slain me.' "[46]

The guilty who fell into the king's hands were executed without mercy, after a summary trial:

"Some had their heads cut off or were quartered in public places of the town, others were hanged from gallows and at crossroads, others were bound near the gates. So in every street it appeared by these evidences how justice had treated the rebels so harshly, that all of their persuasion, seeing this severity, were trembling with fear, and from hour to hour waited for the executioner's arrival and the cord about their necks."[47]

The chief leader of the rebellion, Dmitri Justiniano, was solemnly executed—despite the forty thousand ducats offered to the king for his life—in a fine square in the port section. At the scaffold he tried to say a few words to the crowd assembled in great numbers, perhaps to recall them to a taste for liberty. But the executioner did not give him time:

" 'Talk to yourself,' he told him. Seeing that he would not be heard, Dmitri Justiniano heaved a great sigh; his face pale and his arms crossed, he stayed still for some time. The executioner bound his eyes; then he himself knelt and put his neck beneath the *chappus*. . . . The executioner pulled the cord and the cutting block fell between his head and shoulders, so that his head rolled one side and his body the other.

"His head was set on the point of a lance and carried to the top of the Tower of the Lantern, the head looking straight out toward the town. The body remained on the scaffold all day, and in the evening it was taken, by permission of the authorities, and buried."[48]

However great was the power and wealth of the French occupier of Italy, the terror he inspired, the attraction of his appearance, or the glory which transfigured him, nothing could prevent the occupied, who were convinced of their race's genius and of its superiority in culture and civilization, from considering him to be a barbarian. Italian authors do not hide the scorn with which the French inspired them. The journal of Burchard, master of ceremonies at the papal court when Charles VIII was living there, may be cited:

"A little before his entry into Rome, the King of France spoke to me about the ceremonial of the pope and his cardinals, of the position and rank of Cardinal Valentinois [Caesar Borgia], pestering me with so many questions that I could scarcely answer them all . . . on the following days, the very reverend cardinals residing in Rome visited the King of France one after another according to custom, excepting the cardinals of Naples and Ursins. . . . I had first informed the king that in receiving the cardinals' visits he should himself go to meet them, and also conduct them to the door on leaving and give them his hand; I had instructed him in such customs. But he acted quite differently, he did not meet or accompany anyone; Even the people of his suite did not render the homage to which they were obliged. The Court of St. Mark's Palace, the nearest of the apartments as well as the first hall, were filled with straw and never cleaned; the candles had been fixed to the doors of the rooms and to the fireplaces, and in the end it looked like a pigsty.

"The French, to billet themselves in their own fashion, forced their way into the houses everywhere and threw out the men, animals, and furniture, burned the wood, ate and drank as they pleased without paying, which caused a great commotion among the people. An order was in consequence made, which the King of France had proclaimed throughout the town, which forbade entering houses by force on pain of death.

"On Monday January 5, after papal vespers, before His Holiness left the chamber called *Papagallo*, several of the French were admitted to the ceremony of the kissing of the feet, . . . As the pope was seated on his throne, a crowd of Frenchmen followed one another precipitately and in disorder for a whole hour to kiss His Holiness's feet. The day following, after Mass, on returning home I found seven Frenchmen had moved in who, contrary to my order, had entered with eight horses, turning out the mules and donkeys which I had in my stable, in order to put their mounts in their place, which were eating my hay. A viscount had taken possession of my bedroom, another lord had the room of one of my friends, who had been living with me for some years past. There was a hall below where my people were lodged, as the rest of the house was filled with the servants of these French lords. Indignant at such violence, I went to the king to complain of his people's conduct . . . and after many protests I obtained that another lodging was assigned to the French and only their horses remained in my place.

"Thursday, January 7, the French laid waste the house of Paolo de Franca, a Roman citizen, and murdered his two sons. There were also some others killed and their homes plundered, notably that of Lady Rosa, the mother of Caesar Borgia."[49]

"The barbarians!" How can they not be so described who installed themselves where they liked, treated the customs of the papal court in the most offhand way, stole, pillaged, and murdered? Did the noble spectacle of the pontifical ceremonies not inspire them with the least respect? Or were they incapable of observing the most elementary decency? Did they not recognize the egregious privilege of being able to look on the masterpieces of a civilization two thousand years old? Did they even see them? Did they see any difference between these marvels and their own land, these superb churches and their own village belfries, between these sumptuous palaces and the somber fortresses deep in their muddy provinces of France from which they had recently stomped in their big boots? Indeed, these rude creatures were not unaware of those splendors. While their behavior remained that of warriors on campaign, it did not exclude a sort of gaping admiration. And these barbarians were dazzled. They often described their first amazement in enthusiastic and charming words. The description of Venice, from the pen of Commynes, is well known. Less known is the eulogy in verse inspired by the country house of Pouge Real near Naples, built by order of the reigning prince, whose gates were opened to Charles VIII as conqueror:

> In this fine pleasure place so well preserved
> There are some singular and curious things
> As houses, timbered and many-windowed
> Great galeries, long, broad and ample;
> Pleasant gardens, flowers filled with sweetness,
> And the most accomplished beauties;
> Little patios, passages and gates,
> Borders, fountains and little streams
> To enjoy and at the same time to make sport in,
> Where are ancient alabaster statues,
> Also of marble white or porphyry.
> A part all fenced, where many good herbs grow,
> Much bigger than the Forest of Vincennes;
> Here olives grow, and orange and pomegranate trees,
> Fig trees, date palms, pear trees and almond trees
> Apple and bay, rosemary, marjolane,
> And over them the sovereign lily flower,
> Noble carnations, pleasant gillyflowers,
> Which may be found there in every time.
> And rose trees also, I well dare say,
> Enough to make nine or ten measures of rose water.

On another side are ditches and pastures
Where wander only great wild animals
Like roebuck, which suddenly course away;
High-antlered stags, great does and bucks
Are also there without a rope or picket.
In pasture fair, great oxen and fat kine,
Horses, mules and many mares.
Donkeys, pigs, sows and porkers.
And at the end of all these meadows
Are situated great farms,
Where are capons and fowl,
All and every kind of game,
Quail, partridges, peacocks, swans and pheasants,
And many most pleasant birds from India.
There is also a stove to incubate eggs,
Where one can raise, without hens, a thousand chicks. . . .
From the said park shoots up a great fountain,
Which is so brim full of running water
That it could supply and serve to wash all Naples,
And water all the animals freely.
There is also an excellent vineyard
With claret and with red and white wine;
Greek and Latin are needed to speak adequately of it,
Not to mention exquisite *muscadets* and fortified wines
Of which are gathered yearly a thousand measures.[50]

In other places the warriors became tourists and dawdlers. They were keenly interested in those curiosities of nature whose renown has crossed the centuries: Philippe de Ravestain, chief of a small fleet headed for the eastern Mediterranean, did not hesitate to halt his whole convoy in order to pay a passing visit to volcanic Stromboli, "this mountain which burns day and night." And everyone climbed the heights solely in order to verify for themselves this extraordinary phenomenon. They were ill-recompensed. At the end of four hours of difficult ascent, in ashes up to their knees, they had to give up because the road proved impassable with the approach of night. Their adventurous natures forbade them to return the same way they had come. No good came of it. They arrived at a wood of tall timber, all burned, "after which they looked like charcoal burners." The sky made its contribution and "they had unceasing rain on their backs."

Others, less bold but more fortunate, visited the equally famous grotto of Posillipo under a cloudless sky:

"This grotto at the entrance is the height of a man on horseback with his lance on his thigh, and even more; and as wide as four to six men at arms facing forward; it goes back a quarter of a league in length. At the entry and exit it is light, in the middle rather dark, and the country people say that no harm comes to anyone there, either at dusk or dawn. . . . It comes out in fine flat country, quite far from the sea and near to the mountains, all full of orange trees, olives, meadows, wheat, trees, pear and apple trees. After a little of this flat country one comes to a small seaside town, not far from another town now lost in the sea. The king went through these caves accompanied by great lords and gentlemen and guards, and went to take wine near that little town.

"Behind it is the place where sulfur is made, in a great mountain which is always burning without fire. The king saw, being made in his presence, many bottles of the sulfur as well as other things which do not serve as medicine for the human body.

"At the foot of the mountain and sulfur works flow two springs; one is hot and black as ink, and bubbles like a big pot on the fire; the other is white and cold and bubbles like the first.

"In this valley can be seen a wondrous hole, from which springs a wind so strong and powerful that it holds up, without burning them, stones, sticks, and anything thrown into it, and is very hot. . . . They say that when one puts eggs in it to cook, however carefully one guards them, it always happens that one is lost.

"The king then went to another place, where they make rock alum, and he saw how the water changes into stone and forms salt.

"Then the king came to another valley where there is a great wide lake, long and deep with cold water, near some hot and dry bath chambers, without any heating other than the heat of the mountain; which is a fine thing to see, for it is done without artificial means.

"After all these things they showed the king a hole, quite round, in one of the mountains near the lake. . . . When anything is put into it, it immediately dies. This was tried before the king, for they threw in a live donkey, which died suddenly, and a cat likewise. And I believe firmly it is a satanic place, or hellhole. After seeing all these things, the king came to sleep in his lodging at Naples, and again passed by the caves."[51]

NOTES

II · Adventure and Illusion

1. Machiavelli, Niccolò. *Il principe*.
2. "Memoire particulier fait par une personne d'esprit et bien instruite des affaires touchant Charles VIII . . . ," in *Archives curieuses de l'histoire de France depuis Louis XI jusqu'à Louis XVIII*. (Ms. of the Bibliothèque Nationale, fonds Saint-Germain No. 209.) Paris, 1834–41. t. I, p. 163.
3. *Ibid.*, pp. 175–76.
4. Machiavelli, Niccolò.
5. "Memoire particulier fait par une personne d'esprit . . ." *loc. cit.*
6. Mailles, J. de. *La très plaisante et récréative histoire du gentil seigneur de Bayard par le Loyal Serviteur*. Ed. J. Roman. Paris, 1878, p. 368.
7. Auton, J. d'. *Chroniques de Louis XII*. Ed. R. de Moulde La Clavière. Paris, 1889–95. t. III, pp. 56–57.
8. *Ibid.*, t. I, pp. 238–39.
9. *Ibid.*, t. IV, p. 239.
10. Mailles, J. de., *op. cit.*, p. 209.
11. *Ibid.*, p. 301.
12. Auton, J. d', *op. cit.*, t. III, p. 177.
13. Mailles, J. de, *op. cit.*, p. 90.
14. Auton, J. d', *op. cit.*, t. III, p. 177.
15. Mailles, J. de, *op. cit.*, p. 20.
16. (Anonymous) *Histoire du Chevalier Bayard et de plusieurs choses memorables advenues sous le regne de Charles VIII, Louis XII, et François Ier*. Grenoble, 1650, p. 411.
17. Mailles, J. de, *op. cit.*, pp. 64–70.
18. *Ibid.*, p. 70.
19. *Ibid.*, pp. 284–87.
20. *Ibid.*, pp. 292–97.
21. *Ibid.*, p. 262.
22. to 26. *Ibid.*, pp. 314–37.
27. *Ibid.*, p. 434.
28. "Lettre de François I à Louise de Savoie," in *Les grands faits de l'histoire de Frances racontés par les contemporains*. Ed. L. E. Dussieux. Paris, 1874. t. III, p. 177.
29. Mailles, J. de, *op. cit.*, p. 386.
30. to 34. Auton, J. d', *op. cit.*, t. III, pp. 44–65.
35. to 37. *Ibid.*, pp. 77–80.
38. "La conquête de Gênes," in Cimber and Danjou, *op. cit.*, t. II, p. 23.
39. Commynes, Philippe de. *Memoires*. Ed. B. de Mandrot. Paris, 1901–03. t. II, p. 262.
40. "Le Vergier d'honneur nouvellement imprimé à Paris," in Cimber and Danjou, *op. cit.*, t. I, p. 406.
41. Auton, J. d', *op. cit.*, t. II, p. 36.
42. Mailles, J. de, *op. cit.*, pp. 83–85.
43. "La conquête de Gênes," *op. cit.*, t. II, p. 14.
44. Auton, J. d', *op. cit.*, t. IV, p. 236.

45. *Ibid.*
46. *Ibid.*, p. 302.
47. *Ibid.*, p. 251.
48. *Ibid.*, pp. 279–80.
49. Burchard, J. "*Journal de Jean Burchard de Strausbourg, maître des cérémonies de la chapelle du Pape Alexandre VI*," in Cimber and Danjou, *op. cit.*, t. I, pp. 269–73.
50. "*Le Vergier d'honneur* . . . ," *op. cit.*, pp. 334–36.
51. *Ibid.*, pp. 357–59.

PART TWO

THE MONARCH OF THE RENAISSANCE

Louise of Savoy. From Catherine de Médicis's Book of Hours, Bibliothèque Nationale, Paris

Claude of France with her three daughters and her daughter-in-law (Catherine de Médicis). Miniature from Catherine de Médicis's Book of Hours, Bibliothèque Nationale, Paris

5.

Gaston de Foix, Duke de Nemours, by Le Bambaïa. A detail from the duke's tomb, Castello Sforzesco, Milan. Photograph by Alinari, Florence

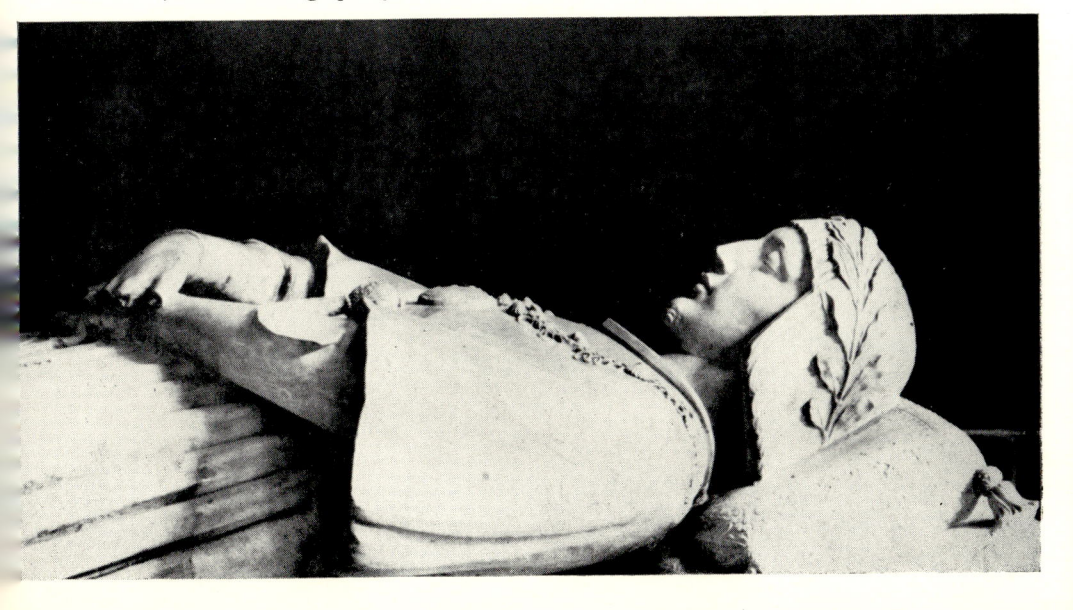

6. Louis XII's official entry into Genoa. Miniature from the *Voyage de Gênes*, by Jean Marot (c. 1510). Bibliothèque Nationale, Paris

Warriors of the Royal Army preparing for war. Detail of miniature from the *Voyage de Gênes*, by Jean Marot (c. 1510). Bibliothèque Nationale, Paris

Birth of the Dauphin Francis, son of Francis I. Bibliothèque Nationale, Paris

Francis I offering his heart to Eleanor of Austria. Contemporary woodcut made at Amiens. Cabinet des Estampes, Bibliothèque Nationale, Paris

Francis I and Marguerite d'Alençon playing chess. Bibliothèque Nationale, Paris

Queen Eleanor, by Joos van Cleve. Kunsthistorisches Museum, Vienna

Diane de Poitier. Enamel by Léonard Limousin. The G. Rothschild Collection, The Louvre, Paris. Photograph from Archives Photographiques

8.

The Dauphin Francis, son of Francis I. Portrait by Corneille de Lyon. Musée Condé, Chantilly. Photograph by H. Adant

III · Francis, First of His Name

Young, brave, tireless, gifted with a brilliant mind, and very much in love with this world's joys, Francis I is the very symbol of the Renaissance, which he seemed to incarnate, since he loved and understood it better than any other French king. Yet in retrospect no king has proved more controversial. For some he is the knightly king, the victor at Melegnano, a patron of arts and letters, a princely hero, a great builder. There are others who regard him as the epitome of vice and ineptitude; one of the few kings of France to undergo shameful captivity; mediocre as a politician; lazy; a spendthrift; an inveterate playboy whose artistic efforts did not rise above setting jokes to music; a puppet manipulated at will by the royal favorites who directed the affairs of France from behind the scenes; the "king who amused himself and died from doing it to excess."

Such judgments, as contradictory as they are extreme, may be understandable when one takes into account that credence has been given to every kind of tale about the king, without considering either the author or the date. Everything has been believed, because it is easy to forget that Francis I had as many flatterers as he did enemies among historians both contemporary with and posterior to his reign, and that the years of his rule, rich as they were in events of great moment, presented an irresistible temptation for such gifted fictionalizers as Victor Hugo. In separating the wheat from the chaff—or, more appropriately in this case, the flowers from the filth—one must find that rare phenomenon, a contemporary observer who is both perceptive and impartial. Happily, there was at the French court such a man in the person of Marino Cavalli, Ambassador of Venice. The ambassador's final duty was to compile, at the end of his mission, a report to his government about the country to which he was accredited. For that task, it would be difficult to find an author more sincere than Cavalli, since he was assured that his report would remain strictly confidential, or more competent, since the nation to which he belonged prided itself upon being the most refined and subtle, and the best informed, of all Europe.

Cavalli has left us a portrait of Francis I in 1546. It is a bit later, perhaps, than one might wish, for that prince could better be described in the flower of his reign and clothed in the attractiveness of youth. But, failing that, one may be content with a representation of Francis in the years of his maturity, in the period of his full development:

"The king is now fifty-four years of age; his aspect is entirely royal, so that if one had never seen his face or his portrait, on first seeing him one would at once say: that is the king! His every movement is so noble and majestic that there is no prince like him. His temperament is robust, in spite of the excesses of fatigue to which he has always been subject and to which he is still subject on his many expeditions and journeys. There are few men who could have stood such adversities. In addition he purges himself of all unhealthy humors which he may have gotten, by a means with which nature furnishes him, once a year: perhaps that is what may make him live long yet. He eats and drinks well, and sleeps even better; what is more, he only thinks of living joyously. He likes to be rather elegant in his dress, which is laced and braided, rich in gems and precious ornaments; even his doublets are finely worked in cloth of gold; his shirt is very fine and shows through the opening of the doublet, as is the French fashion. This way of life, delicate and careful, undoubtedly helps in preserving his health.

"This king, like all the other kings of France, has received the singular gift from God of curing consumptive inflammations by his touch. People even come from Spain to profit by this marvelous property. The ceremony takes place on some solemn day, such as Easter or Christmas, or the feasts of the Virgin. The king first goes to confession and communion, then he makes the sign of the cross over the sick people saying: 'The king touches you, may God heal you.' If these sick people were not cured, they would not come from so far away and would not undertake so costly and tiresome a journey; so, as there are always increasing numbers, it must be believed that it is God who uses this means to deliver the infirm, and at the same time, to increase the dignity of the crown of France."[1]

So much for the physical portrait, to which Marino Cavalli adds a sketch of the royal character:

"While the king bears bodily fatigue well, and never succumbs under its strain, the cares of the mind weigh on him. He unburdens himself almost exclusively to the Cardinal of Tournon and Admiral d'Annebaut. He makes no decisions, and gives no answers, without hearing their counsel; in everything he follows their views; and if ever (which is very rare) a reply is given to some ambassador, or some concession made which is not approved by these two counselors, he revokes or modifies it. But in regard to great affairs of state, and to war and peace, His Majesty, conciliatory in all else, wishes others to obey his will. In these instances there is no one at the court, of however great authority, who dares remonstrate with His Majesty.

"This prince has very sound judgment, and is very erudite; there is nothing in art or learning which he cannot discuss very pertinently, and which he cannot judge with as great assurance as the specialists themselves. His knowledge is not confined to the art of war, how to lead and feed an army and draw up a plan of battle, how to arrange for their lodging, how to assault or to defend a town, and how to direct artillery; he not only also understands all about maritime warfare, but he is very expert in hunting, painting, literature, languages, and the different physical exercises which are necessary to making a good knight. However, despite his knowledge and his brilliant speeches, all his martial adventures have turned out badly, and it is said that all his wisdom is on his tongue and not in his head. But I think that the adversities of this king arise from a lack of men capable of executing his plans. So far as he himself is concerned, he never likes to take part in the execution, or even supervise it in any way; it seems to him that it is quite enough to know one's part, which is that of devising and ordering the plan; he leaves the rest to his subordinates. So what one could wish in him is rather more care and patience, not more knowledge and experience.

"His Majesty pardons faults readily, even as he reconciles himself gladly with those he has offended; he is also by temperament always ready to give, although the necessities of the times have somewhat tempered his generous impulses."[2]

So Francis I appeared at the end of his life. Here already are assembled some of the elements of his personality. Despite this study's brevity, an attempt will be made to define and delineate, with the help of contemporary texts, the majestic silhouette of this king who has been the subject of so much discussion.

※　　※　　※

Francis was not the sort of man to remain a bachelor, nor was his station in life one that would have allowed him to follow such an inclination even had he been so minded. Though he married twice, it was difficult to say which of the two wives was the true queen of Francis' court—Claude of France, daughter of Louis XII, who left Francis a widower in 1524, or Eleanor of Austria, sister to the Emperor Charles V, whom he married as a gesture of reconciliation toward the emperor after his captivity by the latter.

Claude, though homely, short, lame, and shy, was gentle and good and was beloved by those about her. Little known to history, she nevertheless brought her husband the crowns of France and Brittany, and seven royal children in nine years of marriage. Louise, born in 1515, lived only one year; Charlotte, born in 1516, died after her mother in 1524. Her early death caused her prince great grief and among the funeral orations—apparently sincere—which it inspired may be noted the affectionate eulogy of her sister-in-law, Marguerite d'Angoulême, whose sensitive mind pronounced a judgment of apposite sentiment on her brief life[3]:

"God gave us a queen of whom it may be said that she has left splendid gifts to the kingdom: the good renown of those virtues, those graces, and that goodness with which God had endowed her; a figure none could have wished more lovely, perfected by the births of three sons and three [sic] daughters. She gave the Duchy of Brittany to her beloved husband, and after his death to her eldest son, to perpetuate its union with this kingdom. . . . Shriven and clear in her mind and words to the last, she went, it seems to me, in joy, leaving her friends with such a sadness that I am greatly afraid the health of Madame will suffer overmuch from it.

"The king, for his part, seeing the end approaching, made great mourning, saying to Madame: 'If I thought I could buy her back with my life, I would gladly pay. And never would I have thought the bonds of marriage made by God could be so hard and difficult to break.' And we parted in tears, and have no news of how he has taken it, but I am very afraid he can scarcely bear it."

Claude's successor as queen, Eleanor of Austria, found herself in the extremely difficult position of being at the same time Queen of France and sister to Charles V, France's most deadly enemy. After Francis' defeat and capture by the emperor at Pavia in 1525, when the king lost, in his own words, "all save life and honor," the humiliating Treaty of Madrid (1526) had attempted to reconcile the irreconcilable by stipulating that Francis would take Eleanor to wife. And so, Eleanor came to France, where, even though she was forever under a cloud of suspicion, she gave to her husband a tacit love that he was able to accept with tender deference.

It must be admitted that each of these two queens needed every bit of discretion she possessed to survive at court, for they lived in dangerous proximity to other—and far different—women of the royal family. There was Louise of Savoy, the dowager queen; Marguerite of Angoulême, the king's sister; and Renée of France, daughter of Louis XII and future Duchess of Ferrara. The three of them, all ladies of much intelligence and culture, touched off many sparks by their energy and authority.

Louise of Savoy had been married at fourteen, on the orders of Louis XII, to a man of twenty-eight, the fickle and unlucky Duke of Angoulême. After inflicting his mistresses on her, he left her prematurely a widow with two children, Marguerite and Francis. Louise preferred the peaceful towns of Cognac and Romorantin, in her domains, to the ruinous life of the court. There, she was the center of a little world which she succeeded in interesting in the arts and in intellectual pursuits. She led a life both agreeable and difficult, dedicated to defending her children's rights and colored by enduring uncertainties and high hopes. If his cousin Louis XII were to die without male heir, her son would succeed to the throne of France. Yet the then queen, Anne of Brittany, never gave up hoping and brought a succession of children into the world who, thanks to Providence, did not survive; she even gave birth under Louise's very roof. And even when the future seemed assured—after Queen Anne had passed away and Francis was safely married to the eldest royal daughter, Claude, and installed at court—everything was once more thrown into doubt when Louis remarried, this time to the beautiful Mary of England, sister of King Henry VIII. Providence, however, intervened once again, and Louis died before the new marriage could bear fruit.

Louise of Savoy, a firm believer in the destiny of her son, religiously noted all of these events in her journal. Unfortunately, the whole of that document has not been preserved, but it is noteworthy that in what remains almost every entry contains a mention of the son whom she called her "Caesar"[4]:

"Francis, by the grace of God King of France and my peaceful Caesar, had his first experience of the light of this world at Cognac, about ten hours after noon, on the twelfth day of September 1494. . . .

"At Blois, Anne, Queen of France, on Saint Agnes' day, January 21, had a son; but he could not prevent the exaltation of my Caesar, for he lacked life.

"In the year 1507, on May 22, at Plessis near Tours, at two o'clock after noon, was confirmed by the word of those present the marriage between my son and Madame Claude, at present Queen of France.

"August 3, 1508, in the time of King Louis XII, my son set out from Amboise to become a courtier, and left me all alone.

"Anne, Queen of France, passed from life to death on January 9, 1514, and left me the administration of her goods, of her fortune, and of her daughters, including Madame Claude, Queen of France and wife of my son; which I have honorably and amiably discharged; everyone knows it; truth is aware of it; experience shows it, and it is also public knowledge. . . .

"August 28, 1514, I began to predict by celestial revelation that my son would be greatly involved against the Swiss; for as I was in my wood at Romorantin after supper, between seven and eight, a terrible celestial impression having the form of a comet appeared in the sky toward the west, and I was the first of the company to see it; but I was not without great fear, for I cried out so loud that my voice could be heard, and I said nothing but: 'Swiss, the Swiss, the Swiss.' There were with me my women; and of men there were only Regnault de Reffuge and the poor unlucky Rochefort on his gray mule, for he could not go on foot.

"On the first day of January 1515, my son was King of France. The day of the Conversion of St. Paul, 1515, my son was anointed and consecrated in the church of Reims. For this I am much beholden and obliged to the divine mercy, by which I have been amply recompensed for all the hardships and adversities which beset my early years and the flower of my youth. Humility has kept me company, and patience has never abandoned me. September 13, which was Thursday, 1515, my son vanquished and defeated the Swiss near Milan; and began the battle at five in the afternoon, which continued all night and the next day until eleven before noon. And that very day I left Amboise to go on foot to Notre Dame de Fontaines, to recommend to her him whom I hold more dear than myself, my glorious son the triumphant Caesar, subjugator of the Helvetians.

"*Item*, this same September 13, 1515, between seven and eight in the evening, was seen in several places in Flanders a flame of fire as long as a lance; it seemed as if it must fall on the houses; but it was so bright that a hundred torches would not have given such a great light.

"In July 1519, Charles, fifth of this name, son of Philippe, Archduke of Austria, was, after the empire had been vacant for the space of more than five months, elected King of the Romans in the town of Francfort. Would to God the empire had remained vacant longer, or had been well left forever in the hands of Jesus Christ, to whom it belongs, and to no other. . . .

"The seventh of June 1520, which was the feast of Corpus Christi, about six, seven, and eight hours after noon, my son and the King of England [Henry VIII] met in the tent of the said King of England, near Guynes.

"The sixth day of January 1521, the feast of the Epiphany, about four in the afternoon, my son was struck by a rough log of wood on the highest part of his person; for which I was desolate, for if he had died of it, I should have been a lost woman. Innocent was the hand which struck him, but by indiscretion it was in peril with all the other members.

"September 26, 1522, at Saint-Germain-en-Laye, Pierre Piefort, son of Jean Piefort, controller of the salt warehouse at Châteaudun and a relative of several important persons at court, was burned alive, after having, in the dungeon of Saint-Germain, his hand cut off, because he had taken the *Corpus Domini* [the Host] and the ciborium which were in the chapel of the said castle; and, the last day of the month, my son came on foot, bareheaded, a torch in his hand, from Nanterre to that place, to accompany the Host and have it restored to its former place; for the said Piefort had left it in the little chapel of Sainte-Geneviève near this above-mentioned Nanterre. The Cardinal de Vendôme brought it back; and it was such a fine sight then to see my son giving honor and reverence to the Blessed Sacrament that everyone, when they saw him, began to weep for pity and for joy."

Francis responded faithfully to so much love. A grateful son, he surrounded Louise with many attentions and an infinite thoughtfulness, and paid her the highest honors. In a court quite unlike that of Romorantin, he conferred the premier place on her, and, during his captivity, it was she whom he named regent; it was a difficult and heavy burden which Louise took up with energy, like the intelligent woman she was, conscious of her responsibilities and the greatness of her trust. When she died at the age of fifty-seven, her son wrote a long epitaph as a tribute to his dear mother. This was to justify, in the sight of posterity, her memory, which writers in the pay of her worst enemy, the High Constable de Bourbon, made every effort to blacken. In view of the calumnies of the latter, the first stanzas of this homage, inspired by filial love, may be quoted[5]:

> Here lies the corpse, whose soul was glorious
> In the embrace of him to whom she was most precious
> France, what say you in honorable plaint?
> You must regret her who so greatly profited you!
> Nor you alone, who counted her as friend
> But hark the praise bestowed even by enemies!
> Had she not borne with prudence and good sense
> The blows of fortune, coming, France, to you?
> Answer me, weeping. Tell the verity
> Has she not earned a mourning from us all?
> O heart, who owned of woman but the name
> Virtue invincible, worthy of all renown
> Who triumphed over evil, triumphing
> By your high courage and your wise conduct
> Weary, how great your hour, who dwells on high,
> For here below our ills are infinite.

Marguerite of Angoulême, elder sister of Francis I, joined the king in this mourning, and thereafter lavished on him a tenderness which was never to fail. She had been born, according to legend, from a pearl which her mother had swallowed, so she was called "Pearl of the Valois." Married at an early age to the Duke of Alençon, after his death she married Henri d'Albret, King of Navarre, by whom she became the mother of the famous Jeanne d'Albret. She was a woman of broad culture and a lover of the arts; herself a writer, pious and mystical, she became the protector of men of letters. Above all, however, she remained the loving and beloved sister of a king, to whom she tendered complete homage and unlimited affection. In Madrid, she negotiated with Charles

V her brother's release from captivity; she was at the bedside of her dying niece, Charlotte of France, whose sad end she concealed as long as possible from the king, who was away at war; in Flanders, she negotiated, with her mother and Marguerite of Austria, the peace of 1529—which thereupon became known as "The Ladies' Peace."

Always there when needed, always available and eager to listen and to understand, to make allowances, to lend an amused ear to the most hair-raising confidences of an adventurous brother, Marguerite exerted, by means of her devotion and intelligence, a great influence over the king. Undoubtedly, it was she who was the real queen of France, at least during the first half of the reign before her religious views and her compromising friendships with the Huguenots took her to Nérac or Pau in the domains of her husband, the King of Navarre.

Louise of Savoy, Marguerite of Angoulême, and Francis I were known as the Trinity. Poets celebrated them in their songs. Neither bereavement nor absence could disunite them. The ordeal of the captivity in Madrid showed to what point the three remained united. The two following poems, written by his mother and his sister, and both addressed to Francis, share the same rhythm and evoke the same sentiments:

Rondeau of the Duchess of Angoulême [Louise of Savoy][6]

'Tis but one heart, one wish, one thought,
For you and me in love forever caught,
My dearest son and goodly nourishment.
Reason demands, and thus has nature wrought
That which our deed has to fruition brought.

A mother I, who never would do ought
Your pleasure to offend, since every thought
Of ours is of our pure alliancing,
'Tis but one heart!

A love which for love recompense has sought
Can take no joy in pestering or strife,
But makes of everything its care in life,
So loyal love girdles us both about,
Without contrariness in deed or thought.
'Tis but one heart!

Rondeau of Duchess Margaret[7]

'Tis but one heart, and so will never be
I promise it, a heart that's yours or mine;
Whatever may befall or you or me,
Neither our blood nor reason would agree.
And so to this myself I do resign,

I give my will to yours, between your hands
Both words and deeds I place,
Since by this means you shall myself displace.
'Tis but one heart!

While so complete I thus commit, you see,
Myself to you, and so shall henceforth be
Better than formerly, yet please yourself remind
Of our accord, that we shall thereby find
It everlasting, since only in you am I free.
'Tis but one heart!

This familial love, whose excesses some have liked to stress, lasted throughout their lives; and at her royal brother's death in 1547, Marguerite was to sing her despair in verses of painful intensity, before that Death to whom she appealed so loudly carried her, in her turn, to the tomb, only two years later:

Weary and unhappy as I am,
Yet of my misery I cannot speak,
But that it is hopeless.
Despair is already knocking at the door,
To cast me to the bottom of the well,
From where of coming out there is no hope.

So many tears are springing from my eyes,
That they can see neither the earth or heaven,
So great is the abundance of their weeping:
My mouth voices complaints in every place,
Forth from my heart nothing better comes,
Than sighs which render no alleviation.

O Death, who hast overcome my brother,
Come thou then, by thy great bounty,
Pierce through his sister with your lance.
. . . .
Come, then, don't wait;
Run hither with your great strides,
I challenge you!
Since my brother is already in your noose,
Take me also, that a single solace
May render both of us eternal joy.[8]

Though Louise of Savoy was dead by 1531, and Marguerite of Angoulême was away from court, forced by wifely duty to live on the estates of her husband, the King of Navarre, their absence was all but forgotten by King Francis in the delight he took in his children. The personalities and training of these sons (Francis, Henry, and Charles), daughters (Marguerite and Madeleine), and daughter-in-law (Catherine de Médicis) were preparing them to assume the role which Marguerite now played only intermittently.

The king tenderly loved his eldest son, Francis, the dauphin. He even felt a particular preference for him, which he did not attempt to conceal. Indeed, all agreed on the merits of the young prince, as the courtly Brantôme tells us:

"He is of quite a different temperament from his other brothers, for he is cool, temperate, and poised, as was noted by all the great assembly gathered at Marseilles for the wedding of M. d'Orléans and the niece of the pope, Catherine de Médicis.

"I have heard it said that all the foreigners, both high and low, regarded him highly . . . what they liked and admired most was that he was gentle and gracious, very wise and modest. He did not like to dress in colors but wore black, most of the time at least."[9]

By an unkind fate, the dauphin was destined to die unexpectedly in 1536. He was staying at the time with his father in the southeastern part of France. At the end of a game of tennis, when he was very hot, he drank a great quantity of iced water while still sweating. He had to take to his bed, and he died four days later—perhaps of pleurisy. In the general emotion, the hand of crime was suspected, and his young groom, Montecucullo, was said to have been paid by Charles V to poison him:

"This prince was very partial to drinking water, even after meals and when he had taken exercises; and because of this Doña Agnes Pacheco, Queen Eleanor's lady-in-waiting, had presented him with a little vase like those they use in Portugal, made of tawny earthenware very subtle and fine . . . and it has the virtue that whatever cold water you put into it, you see it boil and make little bubbles as though it were on the fire; nevertheless it does not lose its coldness but retains it. . . .

"This prince, then, having played at ball in a field, bade a page of his chamber go and bring him cold water in the little vase which Doña Agnes Pacheco had given him. The page went off and drew water from the well, and while he was watching the bucket in the well and had stood the little vase on the well's edge, the wretched poisoner, constantly on the watch for the opportunity to deal his blow, dropped the poison with two fingers into the little vase; then, looking on, he watched the page pour the water into the little vase, and went off. The page, after filling the vase, carried it to his master, who drank it all without leaving a drop. At once he felt sick and ill, from which afterward he died."[10]

The king had to be told about the fatal accident of which the victim had been his "son so full of hope." Cardinal Jean de Lorraine, "being a very old friend and intimate of the king," accepted this sad mission:

"As soon as the cardinal had set foot in the chamber, both purpose and words failed him, and he could not master his expression. The king could see at first glance from his face that he brought bad news; and, as if his heart had presaged this tragedy, asked him straightaway what news of his son. The cardinal's tongue cleft to his lips and, though naturally facile and eloquent, he chewed the words more than pronounced them and said, stuttering, that he was certainly getting worse, but that it was needful to have hope in God for his cure. 'I can well understand,' said the king then, 'that you do not dare, on first entering, to say he is dead, but only that he will die soon.' To these words the cardinal replied, confessing the truth more by gesture than with his lips. Never were seen such tears, nor heard such sobs and sighs of those present. The king, heaving a great sigh, which was heard in the other rooms, went to the window alone and without saying a word, his heart heavy with grief, and repressing his grief beyond the natural common capacity, until, torn by the conflict between fortitude and nature, he was constrained to heave another sigh; and then, turning his head, and his eyes, hands, and thought to heaven, he said: 'My God, I well know that it would be good to accept with patience and constancy all that comes from Thee; for what can come to me, and for what can I hope, other than such patience and strength of soul? Already Thou has afflicted me with the loss of authority and of the reputation of my armies; now, Thou hast added the loss of my son. What is there left now, but that Thou deprivest me of all? And if this is Thy will, give me a sign, and make Thy will known, so that I do not resist it; confirm me in that patience. Thou alone, aiding and reinforcing natural and human infirmity, art able to do it.'"[11]

The king felt the death of the dauphin Francis even more cruelly for his having no affinity for his younger son, the future Henry II, who the chroniclers say did not possess the exceptional nature of his elder brother. The day after the news of his death, Francis I addressed a short exhortation to the new dauphin, in which he encouraged him to follow the example of his dead brother:

"My son, you have lost your brother, and I my eldest son, whose death brings me, together with a heightened sense of regret and loss, the comfort of the memory and satisfaction which I have from the love and affection and favor which he had already acquired in this kingdom from both high and lowly. Take pains, my son, to imitate and follow him, so that you may surpass him, and may grow so virtuous that those who today are filled with sorrow on his account may find in you that which will allay and obliterate the sorrow they have over him. It is my wish that to this end you address your intention: put your heart, mind, and understanding to work for this. God will not fail to help and succor you."[12]

The king did not want to leave this death unavenged. He accepted the hypothesis of murder as true. On his orders, Montecucullo was tortured and, having admitted everything that they wished him to say, he was declared guilty by the great Council of the king.

"The Council held criminal proceedings in regard to Count Sebastiano de Montecucullo. Interrogations, confessions, re-examinations, confrontations; a certain book on the use of poisons written in the hand of the said Sebastiano; visitation, report and opinion of doctors, surgeons, barbers, and apothecaries, conclusions of the king's procurator-general were all considered. It was concluded that the said Count Sebastiano de Montecucullo is accused and convicted of having poisoned the late Francis, Dauphin of Viennois, Propietary Duke of Brittany, eldest son of the king, with sublimed arsenic powder, put by him in a vase of red earthenware, at Lyons. He is also convicted of having come to France expressly and with the deliberate purpose of poisoning the king, and having made attempts to do it. In reparation of the said case and crimes, the aforesaid Council has condemned him. It condemns him to be dragged on a hurdle from the place where the prison is in Roanne to the square before the church of Saint-Jean, at which place, being in a shirt, his head and feet bare, holding a lighted torch in his hands, he shall cry mercy and pardon to God, to the king, and to justice, and from there shall be dragged on a hurdle as far as the Place de la Grenette, at which place, in his presence, the poisons of arsenic and of Riarga, of which he was in possession, shall be publicly burned with the red vase where he put and threw the poison; and this done he shall be drawn by four horses; and afterward the four parts of his body hung at the four gates of the town of Lyons and his head put on the end of a lance which shall be placed on the bridge over the Rhône."[13]

The people, who loved their prince, felt acutely the horror of such a crime, and gave free rein to their anger and indignation:

"The body was left on a little scaffold for two days there, where the people practically cut it in small pieces; even the little children hardly left a single hair of his beard not plucked out, cut off the nose and pulled the eyes out of their sockets, and with great blows from stones broke the teeth and jaws, with the result that he was so disfigured that he could scarcely have been recognised."[14]

The new dauphin Henry, formerly Duke of Orléans, was born, according to the journal of his grandmother, Louise of Savoy, at seven hours and six minutes in the morning, on March 31, 1519, under the sign of the Ram, a fire sign. His sullen, taciturn appearance belied the fact. Perhaps in that may be seen the imprint left by an unhappy childhood. He lost his mother at the age of five, and he was sensitive, in spite of his early age, to the atmosphere of national mourning which reigned over the court during his father's captivity. In his turn he suffered long months of solitude shut up in the sinister prison of Madrid; somber days, without joy or affection, which left an implacable hatred for Charles V and the Spaniards in his heart. Hitherto he had cut no great figure at the French court, where his position was that of younger brother. He had been recently married, in accordance with the political designs of his father, to the daughter of an unimportant merchant family who happened to be also a niece of the pope: Catherine de Médicis. However, Catherine was young and charming, intelligent, cultivated, and obedient—and she adored him as her sovereign lord. But she had not yet given him an heir.

How could he not have felt lonely, this large, reserved youth, with a father who showed him little or no affection, and a wife whom he did not find at all attractive? Whom did the future King Henry II care for? Diane de Poitiers and the Constable de Montmorency, two deep and lasting attachments which, inexplicable as they appeared, were to remain with him throughout his life.

The Constable de Montmorency, whom the dauphin called his father, was the very influential counselor of Francis I. He was to remain allpowerful when Henry came to the throne, in spite of his advanced age and his impossible character. Diane de Poitiers was twenty years older than Henry. Cold, dry, inscrutable, and grasping, she inspired in him a passion which lasted until death, for which no one could find any justification. What a mystery this improbable liaison is, the scandal of which he so well concealed by his appearance of virtue. The casual observer finally remains perplexed as to the nature of their affair, so inconceivable in its perennial nature! Even the Venetian ambassador Marino Cavalli, sketching the portrait of the dauphin at the age of twenty-eight, was taken in:

"This prince is of quite robust constitution and with a temperament on the melancholy side; he is very adroit in the exercise of arms; he is not very good at repartee, but very firm and clear in his opinions; what he has once said he sticks to. His intelligence is not of the quickest; but it is often such men that succeed the best, like autumn fruits which ripen late but, by that very fact, are better and last longer than those of summer or spring. He believes in having one foot always in Italy; he has never thought that Piedmont should be ceded; for this reason he listens to Italians who are discontented with their country. He spends his money in a wise and honorable manner. He is not at all given to women, his wife is enough for him; to talk to, he likes the wife of the Seneschal of Normandy, who is forty-eight. He has real affection for her, but they say there is nothing lecherous in their relationship, which is like that of mother and son; they affirmed that this woman has undertaken to indoctrinate, correct, and counsel the dauphin and to press him to every worthy action; and her role with him is in fact a marvelous success. From the scoffing, vain youth that he was, caring very little for his wife, he has become quite a different man; and he has corrected a number of other minor faults of his youth. He likes taking part in military exercises; his courage, of which he gave proofs at Perpignan and in Champagne, is generally esteemed."[15]

So at the French court appearances were saved; in place of the eternal triangle, His Excellency of Venice saw only a flame. And if one day, when she was upset, Catherine de Médicis flung in her rival's face the words: "From time to time, in every age, whores have directed the affairs of kings," did many people hear her?

NOTES

III · Francis, First of His Name

1. Tommaseo, N., *op. cit.*, t. I, pp. 279–85.
2. *Ibid.*
3. "*Lettre de Marguerite, duchesse d'Alençon, à l'évêque de Meaux, 31 août 1524.*" In *Les amours des rois de France racontés par leurs contemporains*, ed. G. de La Batut. Paris, 1929, p. 43.
4. Louise de Savoie, *Journal*. Ed. J. A. C. Buchon, in *Choix de chroniques et mémoires sur l'histoire de France*. Paris, 1836, pp. 296–302.
5. "*Epitaphe de Madame d'Angoulême.*" Ed. Aimé Champollion-Figeac, in *Captivité du roi François I*. Paris, 1847, pp. 566–67.
6. *Ibid.*, p. 109.
7. *Ibid.*, p. 105–6.
8. "*Lamentations de Marguerite de Navarre après la mort de François I.*" Ed. G. de La Batut, *op. cit.*, p. 71.
9. Brantôme, Pierre de Bourdeilles, abbé de. *Oeuvres complètes*. Ed. L. Lalande. Paris, 1864–82. t. III, p. 175.
10. *Ibid.*, p. 177.
11. *Les mémoires de Martin et Guillaume Du Bellay*. Ed. V. L. Bourrily and F. Vindry. Paris, 1908–19. t. III, pp. 216–19.
12. *Ibid.*
13. "*Dicton prononcé à la condempnation du comte Sebastiano de Montecucullo*," from *Registres du Grand Conseil du Roy*. Ed. Cimber and Danjou, *op. cit.*, t. III, pp. 17–19.
14. *Ibid.*
15. Tommaseo, N., *op. cit.*, t. I, p. 287.

IV · A Time of Scandal

By 1519, Maximilian of Habsburg and Ferdinand of Aragon disappeared from the worldly scene, leaving in their place their grandson, Charles of Ghent, whom the electors at Frankfurt made Emperor of Germany and acclaimed as Charles V. So were united in the same hands by the chance of inheritance, the lands of Spain, Flanders, the hereditary possessions of the Habsburgs, Germany, and the West Indies—the Old and the New Worlds.

Charles V, son of Philip the Handsome and Juana the Mad, by general agreement the first modern sovereign, nurtured in his positive mind a medieval ideal. He dreamed of the old Carolingian Empire, whose all-powerful master held undivided sway over a boundless Christendom, the temporal head of a world whose spiritual chief was the Sovereign Pontiff. How was this dream of an ecumenical empire, one which had haunted the Middle Ages, to be resuscitated? This question obsessed the mind of this convinced Christian, whose profession of faith, worn on his belt, never left him, and who, weary of the tumult of the world, was finally to leave it and end his days in prayer. That empire had been dismembered, hacked to bits. It must be reconstituted, so that Christendom, united under the banner of its chief, the emperor, who was responsible for it before God and called by Him to this task, might consecrate its strength and energy to accomplishing its supremely important mission. This mission was the crusade against the Infidel, and the propagation of the faith in the pagan lands of the Mediterranean and those beyond the Atlantic.

Now as emperor, that is to say as chief of the German nation, Charles V incontestably possessed rights over the countries which formerly formed part of it and had become detached from it in the course of centuries. His illustrious grandfather, Charles the Bold, sworn enemy of Louis XI, had bequeathed to him with his dominions another fantastic dream, that of resuscitating ancient Lotharingia (Lorraine). This, at the time of the division of Verdun in 843, had separated France from the Holy Roman Empire by a narrow strip running between the Alps and the Central Massif, the English Channel and the Mediterranean: of which he at that time possessed the greater part.

Though Charles the Bold, who by his title of Grand Duke of the West had epitomized all his ambitions, had failed in his crazy enterprises, his great-grandson, now Charles V—and but yesterday the very Flemish Charles of Ghent—raised in the bosom of Flanders' rich plains, revived them on his own account. For he had nostalgia for the Duchy of Burgundy, so dear to his heart as the cradle of his race, which, after the death of Charles the Bold, had been ceded to the eternal adversary. He wished to be buried beside his paternal ancestors in the Chartreuse de Champmol, the mausoleum they had had built at great expense at the gates of Dijon by Flemish artists, among them Claus Sluter.

To this boundless ambition for boundless possession, Charles brought a peerless intelligence, fabulous energy, an inflexible will, excellent soldiery and first-rate military commanders, and finally, the gold which the caravels were to bring from the New World.

But facing him was the enemy, the King of France, who hated him. Francis I was magnificent, brilliant, and versatile; he was twenty-five years old. Charles V was austere and tenacious. Always dressed in black, he had at all times an impassible, severe face; he was nineteen.

The one reigned over a homogenous and submissive kingdom, of which he was the uncontested chief. The other possessed a fragile and dispersed empire, on which the sun never set.

The one, by the victory of Melegnano, had Europe at his feet. But it was a horrified Europe, one which had just refused him the empire. The other, till that moment, had never attracted anybody's attention; but it was he whom the seven electors at Frankfurt had just elected.

The one was Duke of Burgundy and of Milan, and wished to dominate Italy. A fantasy. The other wished to become Duke of Burgundy and of Milan, and to dominate the whole of Christendom. Another fantasy.

They were rivals. They were destined to clash.

It was the unanimous opinion of well-informed onlookers that between the two princes no agreement could ever take place; and the future was to prove them right.

"What I have seen of the King of France during my short stay," wrote the Venetian ambassador Francisco Giustiniano to the Doge, Andrea Gritti, in 1537, "and what I have heard of the emperor at the court or in the Council of Your Signoria, sufficiently proves to me that between these two great princes there will be no union. The Queen of Navarre, sister of the king, a woman of rare talent and wisdom who takes part in all the councils of the Crown, said to me one day that, for these two men to be able to agree, God would have to remodel one on the design of the other. For the most Christian king does not like the business and cares of state, and prefers hunting and pleasures; while the emperor dreams only of his business and the means of augmenting his power. The most Christian king is simple, open, liberal, and docile to the opinions of his councilors; the other is very reserved, very parsimonious, determined in his intentions, and he acts in accordance with his own views rather than in accordance with those of the people about him. The two are, in short, so different in character that the king himself one day said to Ambassador Capello and myself, specifically in reference to the truces about to be signed: 'The emperor tries to do everything the reverse of what I do; if I propose peace, he says peace is impossible, but that a settlement would be better; if I speak of a settlement he proposes a truce. We never agree about anything.'"[1]

This duel between Francis I and Charles V, this vendetta in which personal antinomies interfered with and even overruled dynastic interests, this desperate rivalry between the ruling houses of France and Austria—the one seeking the balance of power in Europe, the other seeking world domination—was to occupy the international scene for forty years. It was an interminable war, interrupted only by truces and attempts at peace which their authors were never quite able to carry through, and it was fought more or less everywhere, in Italy and on France's eastern and southeastern frontiers. Both monarchs were to die without having attained their goals, and they were to leave their sons to conclude the hasty peace of Château-Cambrésis, which allowed them to start yet another war, this time against a common, and still more urgent, enemy: religious heresy.

Since peaceful coexistence was to prove impossible, each prince set to work fabricating alliances. The possibilities in this regard were surprisingly limited, for Charles V in himself ruled almost the whole of Europe. On the European continent, apart from the king, there was nothing left but mere pawns: the Duke of Cleves, the King of Poland, the Voïvode of Transylvania, the Republic of Venice, the pope, and the King of Navarre. Only the support of the Tudor king of England, Henry VIII, could tip the balance, and both sides were determined to win his favor.

Francis, whose luck had already been proved at Melegnano, at first seemed to be in the lead. His relations with Henry were complicated by the fact that the English king still claimed to be (at least theoretically), and—worse yet—still called himself, "King of France." Nonetheless, after the most delicate negotiations by French envoys in London, Henry VIII was received as a friend in the land so long coveted by his precedessors. At the famous Field of the Cloth of Gold, on June 24, 1520, Francis I entertained him with a magnificence that left the parvenu Tudor speechless. Such splendor, however, was self-defeating, for Henry, after parting from his host with protestations of undying friendship, returned to England in a state of furious jealousy. Thereupon, Charles V, with a humility and modesty designed to captivate the English monarch, journeyed to England to solicit an alliance. Henry not only agreed to assist the emperor, but also lent him money, and while Francis' troops were fighting the emperor in Milan, Henry's invaded France by way of Picardy.

The good days of Melegnano were over. A somber future was awaiting the Most Christian King of France, and already in his kingdom the hour of scandal was striking—to the greater glory of the house of Habsburg.

*　　*　　*

While Francis I was allowing himself to be isolated and was suffering his first reverses in Italy, a scandal broke in France which was to be the "Dreyfus affair" of its time: the Constable de Bourbon, one of the principal officers of the kingdom, turned traitor. It had just come to light that he had negotiated with the enemy on a plan for the invasion of France, destined to take place in August 1523, at the moment when the king was to leave Lyons to go to Milan. Charles V, according to the plan, would attack on the southeast; Henry VIII would disembark on the west and would join up ten days later with the Flemish troops coming from the north; Bourbon would go into action with his own troops and with ten thousand German mercenaries who would be sent to him from Germany via Franche-Comté. Francis I was to be seized and shut up in Chantelles, a fortress belonging to the constable. Bourbon would then ride to Paris and have himself crowned, and there await the coming of his future fiancée, the emperor's sister Eleanor.

The affair had been revealed by Pierre de Brézé, Grand Seneschal of Normandy, the husband of Diane de Poitiers. Two Norman gentlemen, approached by Bourbon and furious at such perfidy, had informed the seneschal of it through the intermediary of the Bishop of Lisieux. At once the alarm was sounded, and the accomplices were arrested—in place of the guilty, who had fled. They confirmed the sad truth.

Charles, Duke de Bourbon, was Constable of France, Grand Chamberlain, Governor of Languedoc, cousin to King Francis, and the last representative of that great feudal nobility which the kings, throughout the whole of the Middle Ages, had had to battle so as to secure the royal power. At the dawn of the sixteenth century the rebellious nobles had been almost vanquished, but this last great vassal possessed immense domains in the center of France, a veritable state within the state, whose immense revenues augmented his power and allowed him to keep great style at court. His title of constable, conferred for life and irrevocable, gave him command of the whole army in time of war. If it be remembered that besides this enormous fortune, heaven had richly endowed him with natural talents, and that on several occasions his brilliant military qualities had distinguished him on the battlefields of Italy, it can be understood that such a personality could cause first Louis XII, and then Francis I, no end of anxiety. Perhaps the worst might have been avoided if the latter had been willing to recognize his vassal's worth and had employed him in earnest, instead of preferring mediocrities to him and affronting him publicly. In short, it was in an atmosphere of mistrust on the part of the King of France, and of discontent and rancor on the part of his vassal, that occurred the dispute which brought him in direct opposition to the crown and justified—at least in his eyes—his betrayal of the king.

In 1521, Suzanne de Bourbon, the constable's wife, died without children and left all her goods to her husband. At once the king laid claim to the appanaged lands, and Louise of Savoy, as next of kin of the deceased, claimed those fiefs belonging to the male line of the house of Bourbon. The case was brought before the Parliament, but before a judgment could be pronounced, Francis I took some of the lands to give to his mother and sequestrated the rest. Bourbon, persuaded that the mother of the king could not be beaten in a court of law, saw himself as the loser before the trial began. He could not bear the thought of the scale of life which inevitably awaited him as the result of the consequent loss of income. In an epoch when the notion of loyalty to country was less absolute than it is today, he did not hesitate to redress this injustice by going over to the emperor. Moreover, his peers did not blame him for it: "The Sieur de Bourbon, out of spite, has turned to the side of the emperor" wrote Montluc.[2] "There is nothing a great heart will not undertake in order to obtain revenge." Later, Brantôme, ill content to see himself deprived of favors which he considered due him, was ready to follow Bourbon's precedent and put his sword at the service of the King of Spain: "What would M. de Bourbon have done if he had not done what he did? In the end he would have been imprisoned, as happened to the Constable of Saint-Pol; and he would have been dishonored forever by it, he and his people. Instead of which he died most gloriously, having avenged his injuries and offenses and taken his king (who wished him to die) in battle array. And he was well received and met with those courtesies in foreign lands, which his own had denied him. In this may be seen the truth of the ancient saying: *Omne solum forti patria est, ut piscibus aequor,* that is to say: For a generous man, every land is his land, every country his country, as every ocean is for fish."[3]

Francis I learned of the constable's plans just as he was leaving in haste for Italy. He believed he could bring him into a better frame of mind and went in person to the Château de Moulins:

"The king found the Duke de Bourbon feigning sickness; but the gentle prince, always more inclined to pity than to revenge, hoping to subdue Bourbon and to change his views, went to visit him in his bedroom. There he condoled with him on his sickness, which was wholly feigned, and made known to him the warnings which he had received of the advances which the emperor had made to draw him into his service and divert him from the good affection which he was sure he had for the crown of France. He told him he did not believe that he had paid attention to those propositions out of ill will, either for himself or for the kingdom, being issued from his house to which he was so nearly related; but that despair and the fear of losing his property might have upset the good friendship and affection which he had always had for his prince and lord; and that he should put out of his mind such things as those which troubled him. He promised him that, were he to lose the suit against him and against his mother, he would make restitution of all his goods to him; and that he should hold himself in readiness to accompany him on his journey to Italy."[4]

Francis' generosity came too late. Perhaps Bourbon was already too deeply committed to the emperor to leave him; or perhaps he gave no credence to the king's promises; or perhaps he believed that Charles V would value him and recognize his merits more than had been the case in France. Whatever the reason, he decided to pursue his plan. Instead of rejoining the king at Lyons, as he had promised, he took refuge at Chantelles. Francis then realized that the accusations made against Bourbon were well founded, and sent the Marshal de Chabannes, accompanied by the Grand Master of France, to arrest him.

At this news, "the constable despaired of obtaining pardon from the king, and he began to consider how to save his life" and to flee the kingdom. He left forever his splendid home of Chantelles and set out in the direction of Genoa, in disguise and carrying with him all his gold and jewels. A certain Pompérant went with him, whose servant Bourbon pretended to be. At each stopping place they enquired with great care as to the route of the royal troops. When they were about to cross the Rhône at Vienne:

"The Seigneur de Bourbon remained hidden behind a house, fearing that there would be a guard placed by the king over the river, while Pompérant went for news. He, having come to the bridge of Vienne, found a butcher, to whom he said that he was an archer of the king's guard and asked whether his companions had not come to Vienne to guard the crossing (in case M. de Bourbon would try to cross the river), and he said that his companions had sent word that their standard would be there. The butcher replied that there was nobody there, but that he heard there were a lot of horsemen on the Dauphiné side. Pomérant, having gathered that the passage was not guarded, returned to M. de Bourbon; they decided not to cross the bridge, fearing to be recognized, but to go and cross by a ferry about half a league from there. At that place, being embarked, ten or twelve foot soldiers embarked with them, to the amazement of Bourbon, and just when they were in midstream, Pompérant was recognized by some of the soldiers, at which M. de Bourbon was even more terrified. Nevertheless, he was reassured by Pompérant, who said that if something untoward happened they could cut the rope, making the ferry turn toward the Vivarais country, where they could reach the mountains and put themselves out of reach of danger; but that inconvenient necessity did not arise."[5] Soon, however, because of the danger of capture, Bourbon had to give up his original itinerary and get as quickly as possible into the territories of Charles V, where he would be safe. So he turned toward Franche-Comté and Besançon, where a few faithful friends were awaiting him. With them he crossed Germany and reached Italy. His cousin, the Marquis of Mantua, at whose house he stopped, gave him a retinue befitting his rank. Thus provided, Bourbon offered his services to Charles V, who made him assistant to Lannoy, General of the Imperial Army.

"Meanwhile, the Marshal de Chabannes and the Grand Master of France, having failed to find M. de Bourbon, went to Chantelles, which was handed over to them by the captain when summoned to do so in the name of the king, his sovereign lord. There they found all the furnishings of Bourbon's house, the finest in any prince's house in all Christendom, which they placed in the hands of the king; similarly they placed under obedience to the same prince the castle of Carlat, and generally all the other properties of the house of Bourbon."[6]

The coalition formed by the constable, the imperial forces, and the English attacked, as planned, on the south, the east, and the north. They were driven back without difficulty, except the English, who met with some success and came within twenty-five miles of Paris. They could get no farther, however, and soon retired. Francis seemed to be winning on all fronts. The last representative of feudal opposition to the power of the throne had been eliminated, his lands and wealth confiscated and annexed to the crown. But the king had also lost his best general, and the great traitor vassal had become, in conspiracy with the emperor, a deadly enemy. If Francis had been up to then incapable of estimating Bourbon at his true worth, circumstances were destined to reveal it to him. Two years later, Bourbon was to be one of the generals sharing the command of the imperial troops at Pavia.

※　　※　　※

A scandal greater than that of Bourbon's treason was the utter defeat of the French armies at the battle of Pavia in 1525; the forces of Francis I were routed, and the puissant king himself was taken prisoner there. Incarcerated by the Emperor Charles at first in the fortress of Pizzighettone, and in ignorance of what fate held in store for him, Frances wrote to his mother, who was Regent of France:

Madame,

I write to let you know how goes the rest of my misfortune; of all that I had, there remain to me but my honor and my life, which is safe. And in order that this news should give you a little comfort in your sorrow, I asked that I be allowed to write, which was readily granted. I beg you not to be too downcast by my situation but to use your habitual prudence, for I have hope that, in the end, God will not abandon me. I commend to you your grandchildren, which are mine, and beg you to give safe passage to the bearer to go to Spain and return so that he may learn from the emperor how he wishes me to be treated.

Herewith recommending myself most humbly to Your Grace,
Your very humble and obedient son,
FRANCIS[7]

Francis, in his naïveté, imagined that he would be treated, like a hero of chivalry, with that fine generosity which in tournaments the defeated expects from the victor. Doubtless, he counted on being set at liberty on parole, as was customary. He therefore addressed a most courteous letter to Charles:

If liberty had been accorded me by my cousin the vice-roi, a little sooner, I should not have waited so long to pay you my respects, as the time and place where I am require. Having no comfort in my misfortune other than my estimate of your generosity, which, if it so pleases, will use the effects of victory honorably toward me, and having a firm belief that your virtue would not constrain me to any dishonorable thing, I beg you to judge in your heart what you will be pleased to do with me; for I am certain that the will of such a prince as you can be accompanied only by honor and magnanimity. By virtue of which, if it pleases you to have the honest pity to temper the security which is required in the prison of a King of France whom you wish to render friendly and not desperate, you may be sure of acquiring, in place of a useless prisoner, a king forever your slave.

"So, not to importune you more with my tiresome letter, but ending with humble recommendations to your good grace, he who has no rest while waiting to know that it will please you to name him, instead of prisoner,

Your brother and friend,
FRANCIS.[8]

Charles V made no reply. He wished above all to act in his own best interest. Clearheaded as always, he sought advice. Some wished to take advantage of the occasion to crush forever the conquered enemy. Bourbon, for example, proposed to put into action the 1523 plan of invasion, which had never been effected, and to offer the French crown to Henry VIII of England. Others, wiser or less bitter, judged it useless to seek by war what could be obtained in peace. For what territorial advantages could not be claimed when one held such a captive? Why then place on the throne of France the King of England, already powerful, when one could leave there, to play the noble role, a king whom a well-drafted treaty would render harmless forever?

The latter, more temperate counsel prevailed, and henceforth the emperor was to struggle mightily to obtain from Francis a peace treaty as advantageous to the empire as it should be disastrous for France. He used, without scruple, the innumerable ways of bringing pressure to bear which imprisonment could offer; and the worst of these, to the king's mind, was Charles's unbroken silence with respect to the captive's fate. But Francis resigned himself eventually to enduring with nobility that long captivity of whose end he at times despaired; he was ready, if it were necessary, to sacrifice himself for France's good.

A royal prisoner, however, presents problems for his jailers, and at Pizzighettone they were haunted by fear of the French king's escape. Finally, they decided to move his residence into the heart of the Castilian plateau, where both distance and the assumed hostility of the countryside would obviate such a possibility. Francis gladly agreed to this; once in Spain, he reasoned, it would be easier to obtain the interview with Charles V that he so much desired and that would doubtless set a term to his painful situation.

Spain, oblivious to the jailers' wishes, received Francis with open arms. Valencia gave him an enthusiastic welcome, and the women, particularly, were notable for the warmth of their greetings. It is not surprising that the king, handsome, richly attired, and mounted on a magnificently caparisoned horse, moved them by his bearing. When they had rested a little, the women of the city went to the king's lodging, "dressed in their finest clothing. In masks, and with lutes, viols, rebecks, tambourines, and other instruments, they danced with him in the Castilian style to give him comfort and diversion.

"The good lord, who found himself in such fine and noble company . . . could not keep from heaving some great sighs proceeding from the depths of his noble heart. He thought of the great happiness and joy he had in his kingdom, with so many ladies and young women, so beautiful and modest, who were with his mother; and of his gentlemen to whom he could say, if the fancy took him: 'You there, go and dance with that one,' and: 'Give him a sprightly wench, you will please me if you can tire her out,' and dancing through the hall where the women and girls were, and having a word first with one and then another, joshing one, jostling another, and making many other noble pastimes. And now he was prisoner. . . .

"The king thanked all the ladies and girls of the noble company for the honor, festivity, and comfort which they had given him, and told them he would wish to please them. When he had done speaking there came in a lovely nymph, her hair down her back reaching to her heels, braided and dressed in Castilian style, with her midriff bare and white as alabaster, a smiling face, an attractive nose, a small mouth and coral lips, her neck adorned with a triple collar of pearls and diamonds sparkling like the sun, who had an unbelievably soft and sweet way of speaking. She addressed the king after making three curtsies to him down to the ground. . . . The king sent her and the ladies off very graciously. . . . So, the king stayed in the good town and city of Valencia-the-Great, and was entertained by the ladies mentioned above, who visited him every day one after the other, in great throngs and gatherings, and sent him a variety of beautiful, sumptuous presents and comfits, both aromatic and liquid, and other noble attentions; they offered him pastimes of comedies, dances, parties, and distractions. In brief, the Valencian men and women, gentlemen, gentlewomen, and others, paid their respects as well as they were able, in order to be held in eternal honor and glory by the said seigneur, so that, when he should return to his noble kingdom, he might give some account to their praise and lasting honor."[9]

At Guadalajara, Don Diego de Mendoza, Duke of the Infantado, had prepared a magnificent welcome for him. He placed at his disposal in his palace the suite known as the "Family Apartment," the luxury of which amazed even the king, and treated him splendidly. The few days he stayed there were an endless succession of spectacles, balls, tourneys, games, stick fights, bullfights, combats of wild beasts, tigers, lions, and leopards, which the duke bred in his own menagerie.

The attitude of Charles V was very different from what Francis had anticipated. On hearing the news of his prisoner's arrival, the emperor left Madrid for Toledo and gave orders for the king to be shut up in a tower of the Alcázar in Madrid. Saint-Simon, two centuries later, was to leave in his *Mémoires* an indignant description:

"I considered this horrible cage most carefully and with the liveliest attention, in spite of the pains taken by my guide to distract me and to get me to leave . . . he, embarrassed when I asked to see it, had replied: "O, come, come, My Lord Duke, what are you talking about now?" This room was not big, and had only one door, by which one entered. It was increased by an embrasure on the right as one came in, facing the window. This was big enough to give some daylight, was glazed and could be opened, but had a double iron grill, very strong and stiff, welded into the wall on all four sides. On the room side it was very high, looking out on to the Mançanarez and the countryside beyond. There was room for chairs, coffers, a few tables and a bed . . . from the window of this room to the edge of the Mançanarez, there was a drop of more than a hundred feet and the whole time Francis I was there, two batallions under arms were stationed day and night along the Mançanarez, which runs the whole length of the tower and very close to it."[10]

Such is the place where the foremost monarch of Europe passed seven months of close imprisonment. This man of thirty, accustomed to the pleasures of a brilliant court, to physical exercise, and to the open air, within a few weeks found himself deprived on the emperor's orders of the many visits the Madrid nobility paid him, and restricted to walking around a park under the vigilant eye of his guards. Daily awaiting the visit of an emperor who never came, giving up hope of seeing his troubles at an end, he abandoned himself to despair and fell seriously ill. He was in grave danger when his beloved sister, Marguerite d'Alençon—dressed in white, in royal mourning on account of the recent death of her husband—reached his bedside. Her sweet presence cured him, and the President de Selves hastened to reassure the Parliament of Paris:

"My Lords, considering the great anxiety which you may have conceived on learning of the grave illness of the King, I thought it my duty to write to you about his convalescence and cure, to console the company. I have seen him, in the opinion of two of his doctors and with that of the emperor, beyond hope and with all the signs of death; for he remained some time without speaking, seeing, hearing, or recognizing anyone. It is a week ago today that the duchess had all the gentlemen of the king's household, and her own, and with them her women, pray God, and all received our Creator; and afterward Mass was said in the bedroom of the king. And at the time of the elevation of the sacred Host, the Archbishop of Embrun exhorted the king to look on the Blessed Sacrament and to adore it. And forthwith the king said: 'It is my God who will cure my soul and body, I beg you that I may receive it.' And to one who said that the king could not swallow, Francis replied: 'Yes, he will.' And then the duchess had a part of the holy Host divided, which he received with the greatest compunction and devotion, and there was no one who did not weep. The duchess received the rest of the Blessed Sacrament. And from that hour he has made continual progress; and the fever, which had stayed on him twenty-three days without a break, left him, and he is quite free of it, thank God; and nature has done everything normally, such as the upper and lower evacuations, sleeping, drinking, and eating; so that he is out of danger, which is a miraculous act of God, as the French and Spaniards around him have all judged."[11]

He had been thought dead. Charles V, informed of the alarming state of his prisoner, and greatly fearing to see his hopes for a profitable peace evaporate unexpectedly, rushed to Madrid and to his bedside. At Paris, four mysterious persons, without doubt in Spanish pay, set to work to demoralize opinion:

"On horseback, disguised as postilions, with green bonnets on their heads, four unknown men came rushing through the streets to the palace. They cried aloud and published certain verses, relating that the king, then a prisoner, was dead, that Madame Louise was in misery on account of it, that the wise were concealing it, and that the mad must declare and publish it. They added several other things against the king's honor, against that of Madame and the house of France. The Archchaplain of the Sainte-Chapelle replied to them and they afterwards retired."[12]

The king's illness, however, was not the primary reason of his sister Marguerite's journey; just by a lucky chance she had come to Madrid that week. In fact, she had come to Spain in the hope of speeding, by a personal appeal, the release of her brother. That release depended on the signature of a treaty whose terms were unacceptable and to which Francis had refused his agreement. Charles V, for his part, was opposed to making the smallest concession. Marguerite had the illusion that her intervention might prove helpful, but she was wrong. She had to make up her mind to leave empty-handed, and the king, with an admirable gesture of renunciation, preferred to abdicate than to agree to the dismemberment of his kingdom.

He sent his sister the following act, with the charge to have it registered by the Parliament of Paris:

"Francis, by the Grace of God, King of France, Duke of Milan, and Lord of Genoa . . . , greetings. . . . After having lost a battle, where we had put our person in great danger of death . . . and having had, in that battle, our horse killed under us, and having seen several of our enemies turning their arms against our person, some to kill us, others to make prey and booty of us; and seeing that, since our taking and captivity, we have been put and subdued into the hands of the elected emperor, King of Spain, from whom, as a Christian and Catholic prince, we had till the present hoped for humanity, clemency, and honesty, and even expected it because we were close to him in blood and lineage, and even more we expected humanity, since we have endured a grave malady in prison, such that our health and cure were entirely despaired of; but God, continuing beneficent toward us, has cured and resuscitated us, in which extremity we have not known the heart of the emperor to be the least moved at our deliverance;

"After having shown him that the complaints which he claims to have against us are by no means founded in justice, and having made several large offers to him through our dear sister the Duchess of Alençon . . . nevertheless the said emperor has not wished to accord our deliverance until he has in his hands the Duchy of Burgundy, the County of Mâcon and Auxerre, with several other large and unreasonable demands . . . which conditions we have not been willing to accept . . . but seeing that we are not permitted to leave our prison . . . we make it known that, by good and ripe deliberation of council, we have concluded, ordered, and accepted, and by this perpetual and irrevocable edict we will, ordain, and consent and such is our good pleasure, that our very dear and very beloved eldest son, Francis, Dauphin de Viennois, our true and indubitable successor, shall be from this time declared, proclaimed and reputed Most Christian King, and as King anointed and consecrated, maintaining the requisite and accustomed solemnities, and that he shall govern under the regency and authority of our very dear and most beloved mother the Duchess of Angoulême, until he shall be of age to govern for himself . . . nevertheless retaining, and reserving that if it should please God that the deliverance of our person be accomplished . . . then in this case it is understood that we retain for ourselves the return to our said crown and kingdom for the true continuation of it, just as though we had never been taken and put in captivity."[13]

Francis then asked his captors to grant him a decent house for shelter in his misfortune, and gave order to the plenipotentiaries to break off negotiations.

France, then Europe, came to know of Francis' renunciation. Sympathy was on the side of the underdog, and there were misgivings about the too powerful Charles, and his attitude, so deficient in generosity, was condemned. Erasmus, as reigning prince of the intellectuals, even had the daring to write to his sovereign a moving letter pleading the prisoner's cause:

"If I were the victor I would speak to the vanquished thus: My brother, chance has made you my prisoner; a like misfortune could happen to me, and your defeat shows me the fragility of human affairs. Be free, love me, and let us never have henceforward any rivalry but in virtue. In liberating you, I shall have more glory than had I conquered France; in accepting this act with gratitude, you will gain more than if you had driven me out of Italy."[14]

Under the pressure of adverse public opinion, Charles V began to take fright. He was afraid of being left with a dispossessed—and therefore useless—captive; he was afraid, too, of a Europe which he felt to be increasingly restless and hostile. Francis learned, meanwhile, that the Parliament had refused to ratify his act of abdication on the basis that his act was not that of a free will. Such a consideration opened up new vistas to the king's fertile mind. Since freedom of will was essential to the validity of an abdication, could it not be said that it was equally essential to the validity of a treaty? Without more than token hesitation, Francis sent word to the emperor that he was ready to agree formally to the hitherto unacceptable terms, and, shortly thereafter, he signed the catastrophic Treaty of Madrid (1526). According to the conditions of that document, Francis I ceded to Charles V his cherished Duchy of Burgundy, as well as his rights over Flanders, Artois, Genoa, Milan, and the Kingdom of Naples. Moreover, he undertook to marry Eleanor, the emperor's sister, and to send as hostages to Spain his two eldest children, the Dauphin Francis and Henry, Duke d'Orléans. Thereupon the king was set at liberty.

"On March 15, 1525, My Lords the Dauphin and the Duke d'Orléans took their places in the ferries in which they were to cross the river at Hendaye, the last village in France opposite Fuenterrabia. All the ceremonies were accomplished without a sound; the two barks took them one after the other to midstream. The good king, when he saw his children, had pity for them at the thought that they were going into prison so young, and could find no words but to tell them to take care of themselves, to eat plenty, and that soon he would send to fetch them. As he said this the tears rolled from his eyes, then he made the sign of the cross over them, giving them his paternal benediction. So the two young princes, that is to say the lord dauphin at the age of ten years, and the Duke d'Orléans, aged eight, passed into Spain, and the king, into his most blessed Kingdom of France.

"After he saw that he was on solid ground belonging to him . . . and that he was awaited by his good and loyal servants hereafter named, that is: the principal princes of the kingdom and gentlemen; his two hundred gentlemen pensioners; the four hundred archers of his guard, dressed all in new jackets decorated with gold trimming in the usual manner, who were all well mounted, with their javelins in their hands; and other weapons of war carried by their valets, very well mounted and in order of triumph; the hundred Swiss of his guard, in new dress, velvet tunics in the colors of the said lord, with quartered hose of the same, red caps, bearing plumes of the same colors, carrying their halberds at their shoulder, which made a fine sight; his officers in great number, such as major-domos, grooms, pantlers, cupbearers, and all the rest, which it would take too long to name; and just as the said prince while on the water had wept tenderly to see his beautiful young children pass from his kingdom to be put in his place, that is to say prisoners, so when he saw such an assembly, from the great joy he felt, the tears fell from his eyes in like way. Then he went forward, spurring as brusquely and briskly as he might . . . into his good town and city of Bayonne, where he made no great stay, to go to find his lady mother in the city of Bordeaux, otherwise called Port-de-la-Lune, a very beautiful town, abounding in all goods."[15]

Neither Francis' sorrow at the situation of his children nor his joy at the recovery of his kingdom made him forget his plan to be revenged on the emperor. No sooner was he free than he concluded a treaty with England—whose king had come to feel, with the rest of Europe, that the pendulum of power had swung too far toward the ambitious Charles—as well as with the Republic of Venice, and with Florence, Milan, and Genoa. The alliance, for the sake of respectability, was put under the aegis of Pope Clement VII and—for no other discernible reason—became known as the Holy League. Its stated purpose was to defend the liberties of Italy. Strengthened by the support of the league, and sustained by the patriotic fervor of France, Francis felt that it was time to show his hand. In an address to the Italian ambassadors at Cognac, he solemnly declared that the Treaty of Madrid was invalid because it had been signed under duress, and that it therefore would not be honored:

". . . Was the Holy Father unaware of the manner in which I was treated? With what slyness and knavery they played on my credulity, and with what harshness they insulted my misfortune! King Jean, one of my predecessors, fell, as I did, into his enemies' power, and was taken prisoner to England; but he found there in Edward a generous victor who, far from imprisoning him, lodged him in his palace, admitted him to his table, to his hunting parties, and to all the amusements of the court. Edward had no cause to repent his noble conduct. King Jean was so little tempted to abuse it that several years after having regained his liberty he returned of his own will to England to see his friend there once again. This is by no means the way they treated me. The emperor, forgetting that I am his kinsman, did not deign to honor me with a visit; forgetting that prisons are made for criminals and not for an unfortunate king, he was barbarous enough to make me feel all the horror of them, in threatening to hold me there till the end of my days if he did not extract by despair those conditions which he could not obtain by justice. But his blind cupidity deceived him, and he was not able to make use of me. How many times did I not warn him that it was not in my power to dismember the monarchy of which I was only the tenant; that the laws forbade me to do it, that my subjects would never consent to it. Nothing could make him give up his unjust demands, and he dictated an impracticable treaty. For the rest, his ambitions are not limited to France; they embrace the whole of Europe, and he will never rest until he has crushed all the powers. Italy at this moment is the principal focus of his attention. If your masters aspire to preserve their liberty and independence, they will always find me disposed to join them, not in order to recover any transmontane possessions, but only to succor them and to compel our common enemy to give me back my children under acceptable conditions."[16]

It may be imagined with what fury Charles V was seized when he heard such news:

". . . Forthwith he commanded that all the gentlemen and officers of Messeigneurs the Dauphin and Duke d'Orléans, his prisoners in the place of the King of France, their father, should be put in prison and separated from one another, and certain of them put to the galleys as though they had been thieves, all of which was done. There only remained with the princes Monsieur de Brissac and Madame his wife, their tutors. Thereafter they were served by Spaniards and their way of living changed, which was very strange to them at first, because they were made to eat herbs in the Spanish fashion. And for this reason they were compelled to learn to speak Spanish or Castilian, which they speak like natives born and bred. This lasted the space of two or three months or more, until his fury had passed, but the good gentlemen and poor officers of the said seigneurs, held in great captivity and poverty, here and there, without news either from France or of their good seigneurs and masters, were as though numbed and stricken, of which some died, as apparently did those who were forced to the galleys."[17]

Francis sent his king-at-arms, Guyenne, to protest against such measures. Charles replied by a challenge to settle the quarrel in single combat. The challenge was accepted:

"Francis, by the Grace of God, King of France, Lord of Genoa, to you Charles by the same Grace elected Emperor of the Romans and King of Spain, let it be known that we are advised that in all the replies which you have made to our ambassadors and heralds, sent you for the sake of peace, wishing without cause to excuse yourself, you have accused us by saying that you had our oath, and that on it and, in addition, against our promises we were gone and departed from your hands and power. . . . We say that you have the lie in your throat, and that as many times as you say it you lie; and being determined to defend our honor to the very end of our life, and since, as it is said, you have wished to charge us against truth, from henceforth write us nothing more, but inform us of the field and we will bring you arms. And we say that if, after this declaration is made, you write or say words which are against our honor, that the shame of putting off the combat shall be yours, seeing that by coming to the said combat an end is put to all writing. . . ."[18]

The idea of the two monarchs meeting in personal combat to settle a dispute between their nations is not so farfetched as it may seem to the modern mind; it was a custom hallowed by use throughout the Middle Ages. Nonetheless, the adversaries in this instance were prevented from going further than a rather formal exchange of insults, for war was threatening anew.

Such were the tangible and immediate circumstances and the denouncement of King Francis' captivity by the Emperor Charles V. Humiliating as the entire episode was for both Francis and France, it did serve at least to demonstrate that the kingdom was utterly faithful to the king, that Francis' authority was uncontested and his institutions solid. For a long, and difficult year, under a female regent, the people of France had calmly awaited the return of their prince. The period inspired many a legend and song in which the nation's solidarity—as well as its traditional tenderness and humor—found expression; for that, we may forgive them their historical inaccuracies:

>Alas! La Palice is dead,
>He died before Pavia.
>Alas! Were he not dead,
>He still would be alive.
>
>When the king left France
>He left for ill luck;
>He left on Sunday,
>And Monday he was taken.
>
>Render, render yourself, King of France,
>Render yourself, for you are taken.
>I am no more King of France,
>You don't know who I am.
>
>I am a poor gentleman,
>Traveling through the countryside.
>
>They looked at his casque,
>And saw three fleur-de-lis.
>
>Looking at his sword,
>They saw Francis written there.
>
>They took him and led him
>Straight to the Castle of Madrid.
>
>And put him in a room,
>Where he couldn't be seen, day or night.
>
>Except by a little window
>Which was at his bedside.
>
>Looking out of the window,
>A courrier passed by there.
>
>"Courrier who carries letters,
>What do they say of the king, at Paris?"

Catherine de Médicis. Anonymous. British Museum

Henry II, son of Francis I. Jean Clouet. Musée Condé, Chantilly. Photograph by H. Adant

Charles, Constable de Bourbon, as a fugitive. Pen drawing by Titian. Cabinet des Estampes. Bibliothèque Nationale, Paris

Salt cellar of gold, decorated with enamel. Made for Francis I by Benvenuto Cellini. Kunsthistorisches Museum, Vienna

10.

Vase of green jasper in the form of a dragon. Crown Collections, sixteenth century. The Louvre, Paris. Photograph from Archives Photographiques

Vase with griffin handles. Crown Collections, sixteenth century. The Louvre, Paris. Photograph from Archives Photographiques

II.

Boat-shaped crystal cup with siren handles. Crown Collections, sixteenth century. The Louvre, Paris. Photograph from Archives Photographiques

Hunting the stag. From a tapestry depicting *The Twelve Hunts of the Emperor Maximilian*, by B. van Orley. The Louvre, Paris. Photograph by Bulloz

"By my faith, good gentleman,
They don't know if he is alive or dead."

"Courrier who carries letters,
Return to Paris,

And go and tell my mother
Go tell at Montmorency,

To have them mint money
At the four quarters of Paris,

If there is no gold in France
Let them take it from Saint-Denis

Let them bring the dauphin,
And my little son, Henry.

And say to cousin de Guise,
That he must come here to fetch me."

No sooner said the word—
Than Monsieur de Guise arrived.[19]

❋   ❋   ❋

King Francis, despite his misfortunes, was hardly of a mind to admit defeat. Ten years of adversity had taught him that all is not lost in one battle. Indeed, in this case it seemed that the worst was behind him, for Europe, offended and alarmed at the power of Charles's empire, turned with a smile toward his less fortunate adversary. He did not therefore lose courage, but set out to win allies.

The King of England, unpredictable and more than a little venal, could not be entirely counted on; his friendship depended too much on, among other more tangible things, the "policy of balance" which the Tudor king practiced throughout this reign. Francis I needed far more than this ephemeral friendship. With his armies suffering reverses, he saw that his hope lay in his ability to gain allies who, though less powerful than Henry VIII, compensated for this defect by being strategically situated at the sensitive points of Charles V's too vast empire. Such friends already existed: the Protestant princes of Germany, the papal forces, and the Turks. It remained only to win them over to Francis' plans, and Francis had high hopes in that respect despite the disparity of his expected allies.

Such was the policy adopted by Francis I, then by his heir, Henry II, in the struggle carried on relentlessly against first Charles V and then his son, Philip II. It was the occasion of lengthy and costly wars in the course of which France was invaded from the north, south, and east, in which Marseilles was invested and Paris itself was threatened. But the emperor, exhausted by the fruit of Francis' policies of harassment, could never obtain a decisive advantage. Eventually, he had to accept the fact that his grandiose dream of universal empire was unrealizable; heresy was victorious in Germany and was contaminating the Low Countries; the infidel Turks were infesting the Mediterranean. And, worst of all, the King of France, that fox who hid under an air of chivalry, had proved to be like the reed in the fable: he could be bent but not broken. And thus, Francis I succeeded in substituting, for the ancient ideal of a universal Christian republic, the reality of a European balance of power.

NOTES

IV · A Time of Scandal

1. Tommaseo, N. *op. cit.*, t. I, p. 172.
2. Montluc, Blaise de. *Commentaires.* "Collection des Mémoires relatifs à l'histoire de France." Paris, 1821, t. XX, p. 354.
3. Brantôme, Pierre de Bourdeilles, abbé de. *op. cit.*, t. VII, p. 238.
4. Du Bellay, M. and G. *op. cit.*, t. I, p. 266.
5. *Ibid.*, pp. 272–73.
6. *Ibid.*, pp. 277–78.
7. "Lettre de François I à Louise de Savoie après la défaite de Pavie." Ed. Champollion-Figeac, A. *op. cit.*, p. 129.
8. "Lettre de François I à Charles Quint." *Ibid.*, pp. 130–31.
9. Moreau de Villefranche, Sébastien. *La prinse et délivrance du Roy, venue de la royne, soeur aînée de l'Empereur, et recouvrement des enfants de France.* Paris, Bibliothèque Nationale, ms. fr. No. 9902, ed. Cimber and Danjou, *op. cit.*, t. II, pp. 304–07.
10. Saint-Simon, Louis de Rouvroy, Duke de. *Mémoires.* Paris, 1865. t. XII, p. 314–15.
11. "Lettre du President de Selves au Parlement de Paris." Ed. Champollion-Figeac, A. *op. cit.*, pp. 331–32.
12. Rey, J. *Histoire de la captivité de François I.* Paris, 1837, p. 145.
13. *Actes sur la prise de François I.* Paris, Bibliothèque Nationale, ms. suppl. fr. No. 29.
14. Rey, J. *op. cit.*, p. 153.
15. Moreau de Villefranche, Sébastien. *op. cit.*, pp. 327–28.
16. Rey, J. *op. cit.*, p. 234–36.
17. Moreau de Villefranche, Sébastien. *op. cit.*, pp. 349–50.
18. *Ibid.*, pp. 356–57.
19. Rey, J. *op. cit.*, p. 54.

V · The Court of the King

THERE was an aspect of Francis I's character which perhaps endeared him even less to the austere Charles V than did his political dexterity. Francis was unashamedly in love with the world, and had a lively interest in those pleasures known to the ascetically inclined as "worldly." He loved brilliant company, beautiful women, and agreeable companions; he delighted in organizing festivals and hunts for their pleasure and in meeting them again in the evening at a ball or masquerade. With this natural gregariousness he combined a talent for the joys of brilliant and instructive conversation. Thus, he was naturally fitted and yearned for the opportunity to hold sway over a cultivated assembly devoted to literature and the arts, one whose talents could serve as an example to an admiring nation.

This assembly, unfortunately, did not exist in France. It did, however, sparkle brilliantly in Italy, the place to which natural inclination as well as political ambition so often led Francis, and particularly so in those little princely courts which revealed to the envious French the charms of a world in renaissance. Urbino, a leader among the courts of the peninsula, enjoyed a European reputation. Count Baldesar Castiglione, a citizen of that city, sang the praises of his country in *The Book of the Courtier*—a work in the completion of which Francis' encouragement had played a large part—and it was undoubtedly that work which served as the model of the ideal court that Francis wished to create in France:

"Duke Federico di Montefeltre, among his other laudable deeds, built on the rugged site of Urbino a palace thought by many the most beautiful to be found anywhere in all Italy, and he furnished it so well with every suitable thing that it seemed not a palace but a city in the form of a palace; and furnished it not only with what is customary, such as silver vases, wall hangings of the richest cloth of gold, silk, and other like things, but for ornament he added countless ancient statues of marble and bronze, rare paintings, and musical instruments of every sort; nor did he wish to have anything there that was not most rare and excellent. Then, at great expense, he collected many very excellent and rare books in Greek, Latin, and Hebrew, all of which he adorned with gold and silver, deeming these to be the supreme excellence of his great palace. . . .

"His son Guidobaldo saw to it that his household was filled with very noble and worthy gentlemen, with whom he lived on the most familiar terms, delighting in their company; in which the pleasure he gave others was not less than that which he had from them, being well versed in both Latin and Greek and combining affability and wit with the knowledge of an infinitude of things. Besides this, so much did the greatness of his spirit spur him on that, even though he could not engage personally in chivalric activities as he had once done, he still took the greatest pleasure in seeing others so engaged; and by his words, now criticizing and now praising each man according to his deserts, he showed clearly how much judgment he had in such matters. Wherefore, in jousts and tournaments, in riding, in the handling of every sort of weapon, as well as in revelries, in games, in musical performances, in short, in all exercises befitting noble cavaliers, everyone strove to show himself such as to deserve to be thought worthy of his noble company.

"Thus, all the hours of the day were given over to honorable and pleasant exercises both of the body and of the mind; but because, owing to his infirmity, the duke always retired to sleep very early after supper, everyone usually repaired to the rooms of the duchess, Elisabetta Gonzaga. Here, then, gentle discussions and innocent pleasantries were heard, and on everyone's face a jocund gaiety could be seen depicted, so much so that this house could be called the very abode of joyfulness."[1]

The king set about to implement this ambitious program, and, as history was to prove, the results he obtained surpassed even the dreams of Castiglione.

The first task, obviously, was to provide the proper setting for the brilliant assembly envisaged by Francis. Ever since his return from Spanish captivity, he had been busy building palaces tailored to his stature; these were not in the valley of the Loire, which was the traditional homestead of the kings of France, but in the Ile-de-France. Here, in the midst of forests abounding with game, and at a place not far removed from his dear Paris, the king decided to spend "the greater part of his stay and sojourn."

As an enlightened and informed amateur, Francis had admired the masterpieces of the Roman High Renaissance epitomized by Bramante in architecture and Raphael in painting during the previous decade. Now he wished to introduce this new style into France. The French, however, were not yet ready to assimilate classical art; they were currently addicted to a style, derived from the famous Charterhouse at Pavia, which had been introduced into the country by the artists and architects brought back from Italy by Charles VIII. It was a style which consisted mainly in covering essentially Gothic edifices with arabesque decorations, the exuberance of which matched the luxurious window dressing of flamboyant Gothic. Obviously, it was a form worlds removed from that of Bramante. His work, unfortunately, was almost unknown in France, for the French master masons had never visited Italy and could not—since there were no translations—consult for themselves the architectural manuals where the new rules were codified. As a result, when Francis I was presented with his masons' crude interpretation of the Vatican model for the façade of the rooms at Blois, he was forced to cease trying to impose his own tastes and to entrust to French hands the royal residences he was building—with the single exception of the Château de Madrid. (This palace, which is no longer standing, was wholly Florentine in character, as its architect G. della Robbia, born on the banks of the Arno, was as far removed from the art of Bramante as from that of the Charterhouse of Pavia.)

Of the great royal projects built in the Ile-de-France—Madrid, Villers-Cotterêts, and Fontainebleau—the last was by far both the most magnificent and the dearest to the king's heart.

"His Fontainebleau where he was so happy that, whenever he went there, he would say that he was going home," wrote the architect Androuet du Cerceau. The monarch had left his parents' house at the age of fourteen to live in the house of the King of France; and afterward he had stayed at his wife's home, at Amboise, and at Blois. But nowhere did he feel himself really at home. Once on the throne, he thought of remedying this and had Chambord built; but that palace had scarcely risen from the ground when he decided to move closer to Paris. There already existed at Fontainebleau an ancient hunting lodge, used by the French kings since the twelfth century. He chose to establish himself there "for the pleasure he takes in the said place, and for the diversion of hunting the russet and black game which are in the forest of Bière and the neighborhood," and he confided the construction of the castle to a master mason of Paris, Gilles le Brêton. The specifications, dated April 28, 1528, have come down to us, revealing the full grandeur of the enterprise.

The new palace was to be composed essentially of two blocks. One was raised on the foundations of the ancient house, of which only the dungeon was kept. It comprises the king's apartments, a bedroom, a dining room, and a study; the apartments of the queen, later to become the drawing-room of the king; those of the royal princes, later destroyed; the pavilion of the Golden Gate; the two superimposed chapels; and the great staircase, preceded by a portico long attributed to the Italian architect Serlio. The celebrated ballroom was only undertaken later.

The second block consists of four large sets of rooms placed at right angles, of which the south wing was later to include the famous

Ulysses gallery, decorated by Primaticcio and since destroyed. They surrounded a vast courtyard, known in our days as the White Horse Court because of a statue which Catherine de Médicis had placed there, designed to serve as a setting for tourneys.

The buildings of the Oval Court and the White Horse Court are connected by the gallery of Francis I, which is on three floors, set lengthways and designed to house the steam baths, the banqueting hall, and the library.

From this specification, too long to reproduce as a whole, may be singled out one passage concerning this gallery, the décor of which was to be Fontainebleau's great novelty and one of its finest ornaments:

"This is the specification of the works of masonry which it is agreed to make for our lord, the king, in his castle of Fontainebleau, to make and build anew there the body of the house and the buildings hereinafter declared:

"... *Item*, a gallery must be made of thirty-two *toises*' [about 225 feet] length or thereabout, and of three *toises*' [about 20 feet] width inside the edifice to lead to the hall which shall join the large old tower to the other block of the building; and make the two big wall facings on the two sides of the gallery, the foundations to be of masonry of ashlar, block, quicklime, and sand, each three and a half feet thick up to the ground level, and at the ground level of two feet eleven inches' thickness, and to continue them at the said thickness, diminishing three inches at the first offset, and two inches at the offset at the first architrave, and from there on up, two feet and a half thick up to the entablature; which entablature shall be of the same height and level as the entablature of the main body of the house already declared, and in each of the walls to set three rows of faced limestone ... and to erect also in these two wall faces all the windows and openings necessary at the gallery level, of which the piers and covings shall be of limestone for the facings, and the tracery shall be of Portland stone from Notre-Dame-des-Champs at Paris, carrying an honest molding; and on the ground level ... shall be erected the appropriate bays and windows also in faced stone, and in making this two offices must also be erected on the two sides of the gallery; and the walls must be coated for the inside work, and roughcast outside, with a fine roughcast of lime and sand as befits it.

"*Item*, there must be made and erected all and each of the dormers necessary, above and at the place of the windows of the gallery and offices. . . .

"*Item*, five fireplaces must be made of brick for service both in the gallery and in the above-mentioned offices in the places and locations which will be decided to be most suitable.

"Gilles le Brêton, mason, stonecutter, living in Paris, promises to make and cause to be made well and duly, in the opinion of workmen knowledgeable in this, for our lord the king, in his Castle of Fontainebleau, all and every one of the works of masonry and cut stone."[2]

Gilles le Brêton built Fontainebleau in four years. Although the architecture offered no more than a compromise between the styles of Chambord and Madrid, the interior decoration was renovated in a remarkable fashion, thanks to the talent of the Italian artists, Rosso and Primaticcio, summoned to court by Francis I.

After his accession, the king had attempted without much success to add to the Italian personnel whom Charles VIII had brought from his transalpine jaunt. With this in view, he addressed himself to the principal Italian schools then flourishing. Titian and Raphael had answered his requests with polite but firm refusals; Leonardo da Vinci came and was installed at Clos Lucé near Amboise; but he died soon afterward in the arms of the king, who had rushed to his bedside. Andrea del Sarto came but fled within the year, taking the cashbox with him. To decorate Fontainebleau, the king now made a new bid for the most distinguished artists of the time in Italy, Rosso and Primaticcio; they accepted. With the king's encouragement and support, they were to create that art center which posterity would call the first School of Fontainebleau.

In order that his palace should equal those of Italy, Francis I wanted to replace the tapestries, which until then had covered the roughcast walls, by paintings of classical inspiration in imitation of the admirable frescoes with which Raphael and his pupils had adorned the Vatican. He had luck in that the Italians, instead of slavishly imitating what they had seen done at home, created in his honor an entirely new decorative style, the most characteristic example of which is found in the decoration of the gallery which bears Francis' name. It was executed between 1534 and 1541, under the direction of Rosso, who had conceived the gorgeous decoration after having been initiated into the technique of stucco by Primaticcio. The walls of this gallery are sheathed for half their height by rich paneling, and covered, in their upper part, with great stucco figures in very high relief, which serve as a setting for frescoes of classical inspiration in praise of Francis I. Father Dan, historian of the castle, has left a scintillating description of them:

"The ornaments and embellishment of this gallery consist in a fine great gilded ceiling comprising several compartments, of a floor made of parquet, and of paneling ornamented with scrollwork, where are the arms of France and of Salamanders, with various trophies, low-cut reliefs, and these Latin words: *Franciscus Francorum Rex* [Francis, King of the French].

"Between the paneling and the ceiling are fourteen pictures, each eight feet high and eighteen wide, which represent various historical and symbolic scenes, and poetical inventions. They are all embellished by stucco borders with diverse figures in relief and low relief, which decorate the place marvelously.

"The first picture, on the side of the Fountain Court at the entrance coming from the Great Staircase, is symbolic: several blindfold men and women, some guiding themselves with a cane like blind men, are seemingly going toward a temple, at the entry to which is the great King Francis, crowned with a laurel wreath, a book under his arm, a sword in his hand, indicating by a gesture his wish to open the door of this temple in order to lead and bring these blind people into it. In that symbol may be seen the care which the illustrious monarch had taken to drive forth the blindness of ignorance belonging to his times and to provide entry to the Temple of the Muses in order to cultivate Science and the Arts. . . . The border of this first picture is composed of a golden salamander, which is at the top, in a little architectural theme; below is a hide on which is stenciled a low-relief garland; and at the sides of this border are two great figures of satyrs in relief, with little children, all on a golden background, on which there are also other figures, of women and animals.

"In the second picture, the same armed king is represented standing in the middle of a hall, holding in his hands a pomegranate which a child, kneeling at his feet, is presenting to him. The prince is accompanied by a multitude of people; some are old men, like senators; others represent captains and soldiers. This is also, like the previous picture, symbolic, and by it may be interpreted to mean that no sooner was the king elevated to the crown than he planned not only to drive out the blindness of ignorance from his kingdom but also to establish good order and discipline, both in civil affairs and in the military command; the pomegranate signifies that as long as all his subjects remained at one with His Majesty, like the seeds of the fruit, the whole kingdom would continue to flourish. Its border is like the preceding one and all the others which follow, with ornaments placed on a great golden ground. On the two sides are two great ovals filled with painting and embellished with figures in relief, with lions' heads which support big festoons, and with a golden salamander, just above the border, and some other small embellishments."[3]

The other pictures respectively represent the memorable piety of Cleobis and Biton, the legend of Danae receiving the shower of gold; the death of Adonis; the Fountain of Youth; the Combat of the Lapithal and centaurs; Venus rebuking Love for having abandoned Psyche; the centaur Chiron instructing Achilles; a shipwreck; the ruin of Troy; a triumph symbolized by a stork at the feet of an elephant, which doubtless signifies the victories of Francis I; and finally a sacrifice, which has never been identified.

A general plan governs the iconography of this gallery, Father Dan concludes:

"It is Sieur Rosso who has designed and arranged all the pictures in this gallery. Because he was not only knowledgeable and intelligent as regards the art of painting, but also well versed in the humane sciences, he has tried to represent, by the different stories and subjects of these pictures, the principal events in the life of the great King Francis, his inclination toward the sciences and arts, his piety, courage, skill; his loves and his victories, notably the battle of Cerisola, expressed by the combat of the Lapithal. It is thought that the picture portraying a shipwreck represents his misfortunes. The whole very appositely and with modesty is represented symbolically by means of these inventions of the classical poets."[4]

The ground floor of this gallery was occupied by stoves and baths whose size and sumptuous character prove that the French of former times loved water more than some people have been willing to admit. What is still more surprising is that the king chose this place to house his most precious easel paintings.

Francis I was a devotee of painting, and had purchased pictures throughout Europe, from Italy to Flanders. Raphael painted a St. Michael on his order, to ornament the Hall of the Order. The work pleased the king so much that he doubled the payment agreed to. Not wishing to be in his debt, the painter made him a present of a *Holy Family* which he expressly executed for him. Kings and popes, knowing his tastes, offered him pictures on numerous occasions. In this way he came to possess pictures of every origin, mainly Italian, but also Flemish, as is proved by an extract from the *Comptes des Menus Plaisirs:*

"To Jean Duboys, merchant, living at Antwerp, the sum of seven score and nineteen pounds, eighteen sols of Tours for payment of the following items, that is to say: £73. 16s., for three pictures on canvas, on which are figured, on one, the temptations of St. Anthony, on another, a peasant dance, and on another, a man making a snout of his mouth."

"£28. 14s. for two pictures of the Passion done in oils, £7. 8s. for four other pictures also in oils in one of which are portraits of two children embracing; in another, a child holding a death's-head; and in another, a lady in waiting dressed in Flemish fashion, carrying a candle in one hand and a pot in the other. . . ."[5]

One wonders whether, placed where they were, these pictures were not spoiled. Henry IV had them installed in a pavilion built in the reign of Charles IX, which became known as the Cabinet of Paintings. It is perhaps interesting to read the description of these given by Father Dan in order to identify them in the Louvre today:

"Raphael of Urbino, so famous for his color and for the intelligence and merit he possessed in painting, enriched and rendered this cabinet very important by several of his paintings.

"The first is of Our Lady with the Infant Jesus, accompanied by St. Joseph, St. Elisabeth, St. John, and two angels scattering flowers; it is one of the finest works of this excellent painter, which King Francis I bought for twenty-four thousand francs.

"The second is of St. Michael, made expressly for the said King Francis.

"The third is a great portrait of Joan of Aragon, Queen of Sicily, considered to be the most beautiful princess of her time; which portrait Cardinal Hippolito de Medici presented to Francis I.

"I shall give here second place to the pictures and rich paintings of Leonardo da Vinci . . . of this excellent painter there are five paintings in this cabinet.

"The first is Our Lady with a little Jesus supported by an angel, all in a very charming landscape.

"The second is St. John the Baptist in the desert.

"The third is a half-length Christ.

"The fourth, a portrait of a Duchess of Mantua.

"The fifth in number and first in esteem, as a marvel of painting, is the portrait of a virtuous Italian lady, and not of a courtesan, as certain people believe, called Mona Lisa, commonly known as *La Gioconda*, who was the wife of a gentleman of Ferrara named Francisco Giocondo, an intimate friend of Leonardo, who, having asked his permission to make this portrait of his wife, was granted this. The great King Francis bought this picture for twelve thousand francs.

"Andrea del Sarto here holds third place. This cabinet is enriched by two of his pictures."[6]

The king, in his love of the arts, did not forget sculpture. Aware that minds felt new needs and were aspiring to a direct knowledge of antiquity, he sent Primaticcio to Rome as early as 1540 to look for authentic examples of classical art. The latter brought back 133 cases of marbles and casts of the most distinguished ancient statuary which could be found in the Eternal City, among which were molds of the Laocoön, of the Tiber, of the Venus of Cnidos, and of the Apollo Belvedere, to name only the principal ones. A foundry was installed in the western wing of the White Horse Court, and bronzes were cast there which were destined for the façades and gardens of the castle, which today may be seen in the Louvre.

Benvenuto Cellini, the renowned goldsmith, came to France at Francis' urging and was installed in the House of Petit-Nesles. He lived to see his own work judged to be the equal of the king's famous statues. Cellini relates, in his extraordinary *Autobiography*, an anecdote about this which—though of questionable authenticity—is too amusing to omit.

It seems that Cellini had brought to Fontainebleau a great silver statue of Jupiter which the king had ordered. The Duchess d'Estampes, a favorite of Francis but a bitter enemy to Cellini, maliciously had the statue installed in the Gallery of Francis I along with the statues recently brought back from Italy by Primaticcio:

". . . when I saw this great display of the wonders of art, I said to myself, 'This is like passing between the pikes of the enemy; Heaven protect me from all danger!' Having put the statue into its place, and fixed it in the most advantageous situation I could, I awaited the coming of the great monarch.

"This figure of Jupiter had a thunderbolt in his right hand, and by his attitude seemed to be just going to throw it: in his left I had placed a globe, and among the flames I had with great dexterity put a piece of white torch. Madame d'Estampes had detained the king till night, with a design to make mischief, either by preventing his coming or contriving to make my work appear unfavorably in the night. As God, however, has promised to befriend such of his creatures as put their trust in him, it happened quite contrary to her expectations; for, on the approach of night, I lighted the torch in the hand of Jupiter, and as it was raised somewhat above his head, the light fell upon the statue, and caused it to appear to much greater advantage than it would otherwise have done. The king came, accompanied by Madame d'Estampes, the dauphin his son, now King of France, and the dauphiness, the King of Navarre his cousin, the Princess Margaret his daughter, and several great lords and noblemen, who had all been instructed by Madame d'Estampes to speak against me. When I saw His Majesty enter, I ordered my boy Ascanio to push the statue of Jupiter before him, and this motion being made with admirable contrivance, caused it to appear alive: thus the above-mentioned bronze figures were left somewhat behind, and the eyes of all the beholders were first struck with my performance. The king immediately cried out, 'This is one of the finest productions of art that ever was beheld: I who take pleasure in such things and understand them, could never have conceived a piece of work the hundredth part so beautiful.' The noblemen who had been directed to rail at my performance seemed now to vie with each other in praising it; but Madame d'Estampes said, with the utmost confidence, 'It appears to me that you are very much at a loss for something to commend, when you lavish encomiums upon that statue. Don't you see those beautiful antique figures which stand a little beyond it? In these the utmost perfection of art is displayed, and not in those modern pageants.' The king then advanced, as did the rest likewise, and cast an eye upon the other figures, which appeared to a great disadvantage, the light being placed below them. His Majesty, observing this, said,— 'Those who have endeavored to hurt this man have done him the greatest service imaginable; for, from a comparison with these admirable figures, it is evident this statue is in every respect vastly superior to them. Benvenuto is, therefore, worthy of the highest esteem, since his performances, instead of being barely upon a par with those of the ancients, greatly surpass them.' In answer to this, Madame d'Estampes observed that my statue would not at another time appear a thousandth part so well as it did by night; and that it should be farther taken into consideration that I had thrown a veil over the figure to conceal its blemishes. This was an exceedingly thin drapery, which I had placed so gracefully that it gave additional majesty to the figure. Upon hearing the above words, I took hold of the veil and, pulling it away, discovered the parts it was intended to conceal. The lady thought I had done this out of contempt. The king perceived her resentment; and I, being overcome with passion, was just going to speak when the wise monarch uttered these words deliberately, in his own language: 'Benvenuto, I must interrupt you—therefore be silent—and you shall have a thousand times more treasure than you could wish.' Not being allowed to speak, I discovered my emotion by my contortions: this caused the lady to be more highly incensed than ever, and made her mutter her indignation to herself. The king left the place much sooner than he otherwise would have done, declaring aloud, for my encouragement, that he had brought over from Italy one of the ablest men that the world had ever produced, and one who was endowed with the greatest variety of talents."[7]

Cellini went home quite mad with joy and spent the rest of the night drinking to his good fortune; the celebration ended in a distribution of his entire wardrobe among his friends and servants. The next day, he went back to work with renewed ardor.

Francis I was as addicted to the pleasures of literary art as he was to those of the plastic arts. He installed, on the third floor of the gallery which bears his name, an extensive library which he entrusted to Guillaume Budé, Grand Master of the Library; under Budé's supervision were two assistant keepers of the library and several bookbinders.

An entirely novel measure was the opening of the royal library to the public, even though, to be sure, it was a limited "public" composed of French and foreign scholars. The purpose of this innovation was to assure the diffusion of the treasures of the civilization of the ancient world by duplicating the king's books once these scholars had extracted from these precious works their "substantial marrow" and established critical editions of the texts.

The king's library consisted of almost three thousand volumes; it was, for that time, a treasure house of knowledge. The books had come from various sources; through inheritance, as in the case of the libraries of the families of Orléans and Angoulême, into which the celebrated collection of Charles V had been incorporated when Louis XII and

Francis I ascended the throne. Others were acquired by purchase from private persons, as in the case of the library of Louis de Bruges, a nobleman of Flanders who had devoted a part of his fortune, and most of his life, to the acquisition of exquisitely illuminated fifteenth-century Flemish manuscripts; Louis XII succeeding in purchasing the collection under circumstances which are still unknown. Inevitably, the more or less legal—or, at least, common—practice of plunder and pillage in time of war had also brought some important items into the royal bookshelves, such as the manuscripts brought back from Italy by Charles VIII, and those of the Dukes of Milan which had been pilfered by Louis XII at Pavia. Finally, there were volumes which represented an exercise of the royal prerogative of confiscation, such as the magnificent collection of the Dukes of Bourbon, which had required eight generations to gather.

The role of Francis I, however, was not exclusively that of a keeper of treasures left to him by others. He showed himself an avid collector, with a predilection for the Greek manuscripts which were the great novelty of the time. Jean Lascaris, a scholar and a protégé of the Medici Pope Leo X, had told Francis of a way to obtain such manuscripts. After the fall of Constantinople to the Turks in 1453, many Greeks took refuge in Italy and especially in Venice. One of the most distinguished of these, Cardinal Bessarion, a learned humanist, bequeathed his own library to the republic. It contained the essentials of classical literature and science, and Bessarion's compatriots were allowed to work there freely. Often in need, as is usually the case among exiles, they were not averse to making a little money by copying the manuscripts of the cardinal's library; the king therefore charged his ambassador, Guillaume Pellicier, to make use of their services.

Pellicier was himself a passionate collector; having now to satisfy both his own appetite and that of his sovereign, he set to work with enthusiasm. He took into his service as many as twelve copyists at a time and gathered in his house scholars responsible for revising and correcting the texts of these copies. By a letter dated August 29, 1540, Pellicier informed the king of his activities, and ended with a discreet appeal for money:

"Sire, I think that you have been advised of the delivery of the thousand crowns which it has pleased Your Majesty to command for the gentleman who has presented you his Greek books . . . And because, sire, on account of the age of these books, a number of their leaves are spoiled and eaten by worms, so that one could not read them clearly in those parts, we were of the opinion that, before sending them to you, we should have these leaves reconstituted in the places which have deteriorated. So he and I go every day to search, in both public and private libraries, to try to find copies of these books to correct and complete them. We have already done a good part of them, and we shall not fail to continue, in so far as we can find the complete books, until we have furnished you with all, or at least unless you please to command us otherwise.

"The Greek gentleman is quite resolved to make all the arrangements for going where he can find the rarest manuscripts. At the same time, knowing how much letters of authorization would help him to obtain them, he particularly desires you will please to have them sent to him.

"And, sire, he has given me to understand that you desire me to have copied here all the Greek books which are not printed and which are not in your library. It is something I have a great desire to do, as would be anything which I knew would be agreeable to you, and the more so because it is honorable, profitable, and will be a perpetual memorial . . . At the same time, sire, may it please you to know that since I have been in this town, by your command, I always have had many copyists. I still have eight, of whom one is for Hebrew, who writes for me the best things which I can find in that language here. These cannot be maintained without considerable expense. So I most humbly beg Your Majesty, if it is your good pleasure that I continue to do this, to order that there be delivered some sum of money, to please and satisfy the said copyists, who, being poor and driven out of their country of Greece, cannot wait long for payment . . . of which I have wished to advise you, so that you may let me know your good pleasure, which I will do all in my power to accomplish."[8]

This lack of funds by no means prevented G. Pellecier from writing three days later to the French agent in Turkey, asking him to use his credit with the Grand Turk to widen the area of his prospecting in those countries.

All these manuscripts were deposited at Fontainebleau. To them were added manuscripts from the Latin classics, for which the king had search made in the rich abbey libraries, often to the great displeasure of the abbots.

The scale of the new royal achievement may be judged, and the prestige which went with it, by the eulogy written by a humanist of the time, Pierre Galland:

"One cannot pass in silence over a library more considerable than those of the kings of Pergamon and Egypt, in which Francis I collects the most ancient books that he has been able to acquire at great expense not only in Italy and the neighboring countries, but even in Greece and all Asia. It was to be in the intention of this great prince, an arsenal which should furnish all the arms which might be needed to defend letters against the barbarian invasion. Jealous to shelter this mass of books from dust, damp, and worms, he allotted special funds for the payment of men entrusted with keeping and maintaining them in a good state. By no means did he act from ostentation; his sole motive was the public good. What proves this are the cuts he had engraved and the elegant characters he had cast for the publication of his principal manuscripts; and also the grants by which he persuaded the printers to associate themselves with so noble an enterprise."[9]

Finally, the place of music in this palace dedicated to arts and letters must not be overlooked. This king, so richly gifted, was also a fervent music-lover:

"Music had long since ceased at the courts of our kings of the third dynasty; it was first re-established there by Francis I; I refer to sung music, for organ music was already known there from the time of Louis XII, in whose reign there was an organist with a salary of 120 pounds.

"King Francis, who loved music, instituted that *schola cantorum*, following the court of the year 1543; perhaps that was the year that he sent, they tell, musicians to Suleiman, Emperor of the Turks, thinking to please him; but Sultan Suleiman sent them back to him and had the instruments burned, so that, he said, his people should not lose their courage through their ears. . . .

"The first master of the *schola*, who exercised his office from 1543 to 1547, was Françis, Cardinal of Tournon, Archbishop of Auch, with salary of 1200 pounds a year.

"In addition there were two undermasters, six children, a regular cornet player, another cornet player, two sopranos, eight basses, eight tenors, eight countertenors; eight chaplains, four chapel clerics, and two grammar teachers for the children, which makes in all fifty-one officials."[10]

To all this must be added a tapestry workshop, where were woven a series of hangings, the cartoons for which were inspired by the pictures in the gallery of Francis I; fine gardens; a grotto, called the Pine Grotto, which Primaticcio arranged in the southwest pavilion of the White Horse Court on the model of those which were numerous at that epoch; a Cabinet of Rings, where the king kept his jewels; and a Cabinet of Curiosities, where he collected "everything he could find of curious little objects, such as medals, antiques, silverware, vases, figures, animals, clothes and works from India and foreign countries, and innumerable similar curios. Nor must one forget the hydra, or seven-headed serpent, brought from Turkey and embalmed by the Venetians; it was valued at six thousand ducats and, because of its rarity, the latter made a present of it to the great King Francis de Valois."

The impression made by the magnificence of Fontainebleau may well be imagined. Vasari declared it to be a "new Rome," while dazzled contemporaries vied with each other in their praise:

"In the Gatinais," declared the writer Belleforest,[11] "are the magnificent house, superb castle, and royal palace of Fontainebleau, the seat and pastime of the Kings of France, which from being almost in ruins has been raised up again in our times by this great King Francis, first of his name, who . . . has had this masterpiece made, unique in all Gaul. And this place is in so fine a locality for pleasures, with the verdant woods, as much game as one could wish, streams and lakes, fish and fowl, the air healthy and free there, that no place in France could be found more proper for the retreat of princes. . . ."

※　　※　　※

To this perfect setting King Francis naturally wished to admit only the "perfect courtier." In establishing the measure of such, however, he found himself quite beyond his depth. The customs of France at that time were still crude, and the gentry were given to attempts to affirm their virility by a display of ignorance and by a flood of obscene words. Brantôme tells us, for example, how Lescun, a brother of the king's mistress, Françoise de Chateaubriant, boasted of having learned nothing in the schools of Pavia, "for fear of being effeminate, which does not become gentlemen." As to the women, custom required that they be inconspicuous and submissive, and that they be brought up exclusively in the practice of religion and in retirement from the world.

To refine his circle and to bring it into conformity with that ideal of the "perfect courtier" outlined by the exigent Count Castiglione, Francis first ordered that *The Book of the Courtier* be translated into French. It was his hope that everyone would thus learn, and follow, the models given there and so become polished men of the world.

Castiglione's first requirement for a courtier was that he be of noble birth:

"Thus, I would have our courtier born of a noble and genteel family . . . for noble birth is like a bright lamp that makes manifest and visible deeds both good and bad, kindling and spurring on to virtue as much for fear of dishonor as for hope of praise. And since this luster of nobility does not shine forth in the deeds of the lowly born, they lack that spur, as well as that fear of dishonor, nor do they think themselves obliged to go beyond what was done by their forebears; whereas to the wellborn it seems a reproach not to attain at least to the mark set them by their ancestors."[12]

At the court, more than anywhere else, clothes make the man; so the perfect courtier should take great pains about his person:

"I would have our courtier's face be such, not so soft and feminine as many attempt to have who not only curl their hair and pluck their eyebrows, but preen themselves in all those ways that the most wanton and dissolute women in the world adopt; and in walking, in posture, and in every act, appear so tender and languid that their limbs seem to be on the verge of falling apart; and utter their words so limply that it seems they are about to expire on the spot; and the more they find themselves in the company of men of rank, the more they make a show of such manners. These, since nature did not make them women as they clearly wish to appear and be, should be treated not as good women, but as public harlots, and driven not only from the courts of great lords but from the society of all noble men."[13]

The perfect courtier should have many and diverse talents, without forgetting that he is first of all a man at arms:

"I hold that the principal and true profession of the courtier must be that of arms, which I wish him to exercise with vigor; and let him be known among the others as bold, energetic, and faithful to whomever he serves. . . . Therefore, let the man we are seeking be exceedingly fierce, harsh, and always among the first, wherever the enemy is; and in every other place, humane, modest, reserved, avoiding ostentation above all things as well as that impudent praise of himself by which a man always arouses hatred and disgust in all who hear him."[14]

Though the courtier should know how to handle all kinds of arms, on horse and on foot, though he should know how to fight, run, jump, put the shot, play tennis, and show himself a perfect horseman in all saddles, a perfect jumper, a perfect hunter, he must above all excel in what he undertakes, and even in the most exacting disciplines:

". . . And even as we read that Alcibiades surpassed all those peoples among whom he lived, and each in the respect wherein it claimed greatest excellence, so would I have this courtier of ours excel all others in what is the special profession of each. And as it is the peculiar excellence of the Italians to ride well with the rein, to manage wild horses especially with great skill, to tilt and joust, let him be among the best of the Italians in this. In tourneys, in holding a pass, in attacking a fortified position, let him be among the best of the French. In stick throwing, bullfighting, in casting spears and darts, let him be outstanding among the Spaniards. But, above all, let him temper his every action with a certain good judgment and grace, if he would deserve that universal favor which is so greatly prized."[15]

Nevertheless, the life of the body ought not to take precedence over that of the mind. "I blame the French," writes Castiglione,[16] "for thinking that letters are detrimental to the profession of arms, and I hold that to no one is learning more suited than to a warrior." Fortunately Castiglione, speaking through the mouth of the Magnifico Giuliano, had already hedged his bets: "What you say is true; this error has prevailed among the French for a long time now. But if kind fate will have it that Monseigneur d'Angouleme succeed to the crown, as is hoped, then I think that just as the glory of arms flourishes and shines in France, so must that of letters flourish there also with the greatest splendor."[17]

Thus, the perfect courtier should add, to his physical qualifications, a knowledge of letters. He should be able to handle with equal felicity the pen, the brush, or the lute; and, above all, he must cultivate the art of conversation to the extent that elegance of speech shall have no secrets from him:

"Therefore, our courtier will be judged excellent, and will show grace in all things and particularly in his speech. . . .[18] [He should have] a good voice, not too thin or soft as a woman's, nor yet so stern and rough as to have a boorish quality, but sonorous, clear, gentle, and well constituted, with distinct enunciation and with fitting manner and gestures. The last mentioned, in my opinion, consist in certain movements of the entire body, not affected or violent, but tempered by a seemly expression of the face and a movement of the eyes such as to give grace and be consonant with the words, together with such gestures as shall signify as well as possible the intention and the feeling of the orator. But all this would be empty and of little moment if the thoughts expressed by the words were not fine, witty, acute, elegant, and solemn, according to the need. . . .

"Nor would I have him always speak of grave matters, but of amusing things, of games, jests, and jokes, according to the occasion; but sensibly in everything, with readiness and a lucid fullness; nor must he show vanity or a childish folly in any way. . . . Likewise, when occasion demands, let him know how to speak with dignity and force, and how to stir up those sentiments which are latent within us, kindling and moving them as the need may be; and speak at other times with such simple candor as to make it seem that nature herself is speaking, to soften such sentiments and inebriate them with sweetness, and all this with such ease as to cause the one who listens to believe that with little effort he too could attain to such excellence—but who, when he tries, discovers that he is very far from it."[19]

The French were to prove themselves to be apt pupils. They regarded with interest and respect the model offered to them, and their zeal was all the more lively since they knew that conformity to that model was the surest way to the favor of the prince.

These budding "perfect courtiers," however, did not represent the whole of the French nobility. Many of that class lived upon, and seldom left, their estates. For the most part, only the great families appeared at the king's court—the Montmorencys, the Guises, the Rohans, the Bourbons, the Boissys, the Bonnivets; and even they were "courtiers" only for a few months each year. Their resources, however great, did not allow them to stand the enormous expense entailed by a year-round attendance upon the king.

A large part of that expense was necessary simply to keep up with Francis, for the court, like most of the courts of the time, was nomadic, and the king wandered from castle to castle according to his whim. Whoever wished to be in his favor followed him. And naturally everyone smiled and followed; and while they followed smiling, they grumbled, beginning with the Venetian Ambassador, Marino Giustiniano:

"My mission as ambassador lasted forty-five months, and I was traveling almost the whole time. Shortly after my arrival in Paris, the king left for Marseilles; we traveled, in excessively hot weather, through Bourbonnais, Lyonnais, Auvergne, and Languedoc, until we reached Provence. The interview with the pope was put off so long that everyone thought it would take place in the summer, but it only took place in November. So, the ambassadors, who had brought only summer clothing, had to outfit themselves anew for the winter.

"We payed for all the furs at one-half above their value. In this journey I lost a horse and a mule. From Marseilles, we went through Provence, Dauphiné, Lyonnais, Burgundy, and Champagne, to Lorraine, where the king met with the Landgrave of Hesse, and thence we returned to Paris. I assure you, on the faith which I owe Your Serenity, that this journey of a whole year cost me six hundred crowns more than the pension I receive from the state. The exchange from Lyons to Venice went up 10 per cent, for there was a run on the banks there.

"Shortly after my arrival in Paris, the king wanted to set off again; I was obliged to buy another ten horses, and this just at the moment that His Majesty had summoned his whole body of vassals to pass them in review, armed and mounted, which caused the price of horses to rise tremendously; and as I was waiting in vain for the subsidies to be sent by Your Serenity, I was obliged to sell a part of my silver. Never, during the whole time of my embassy, was the court in the same place for fifteen consecutive days; first it moved to Lorraine, then to Poitou, then to different places in Belgium; then to Normandy, to the Ile-de-France, to Normandy once more, to Picardy, to Champagne, to Burgundy. These trips necessitated excessive expenditures, not only for myself—who, as everyone knows, am but a poor gentlemen, but for the richest lords, who also felt it."[20]

NOTES

V · The Court of the King

1. Castiglione, Baldesar. *The Book of the Courtier.* Translation by Charles S. Singleton. New York, 1959, pp. 13–16.
2. LaBorde, L. de. *Les comptes des bâtiments du roi (1528–1571).* Paris, 1877. t. I, pp. 43–46.
3. Dan, R. P. *Le trésor des merveilles de la maison royale de Fontainebleau.* Paris, 1642, pp. 87–89.
4. *Ibid.*, p. 93.
5. *Comptes des Menus Plaisirs.* Archives Nationales, division historique, vol. 100.
6. Dan, R. P., *op. cit.*, pp. 134–36.
7. Cellini, Benvenuto. *The Autobiography of Benvenuto Cellini.* Translated and edited by Thomas Roscoe. New York, 1904, pp. 406–8.
8. "Lettre de Guillaume Pellicier à François Ier du 29 août 1540," in *Le cabinet des manuscrits de la Bibliothèque Nationale.* Ed. L. Delisle. Paris, 1868–81. t. I, p. 154.
9. *Ibid.*, t. I, p. 167.
10. Du Peyrat, G. *Histoire ecclésiastique de la Cour.* Paris, 1645, p. 479.
11. "*Eloge du palais de Fontainebleau.*" Ed. R. P. Dan, *op. cit.*, p. 23.
12. Castiglione, Baldesar. *op. cit.*, p. 28.
13. *Ibid.*, p. 36.
14. *Ibid.*, pp. 32–34.
15. *Ibid.*, p. 38.
16. *Ibid.*, p. 73.
17. *Ibid.*, p. 67.
18. *Ibid.*, p. 47.
19. *Ibid.*, pp. 54–55.
20. Tommaseo, N. *op. cit.*, t. I, pp. 107–11.

VI · At the King's Court

THE court of Francis I was not governed by an etiquette as strict as that which was later to reign at Versailles under Louis XIV; the formalities of the latter era had not yet been introduced into France by Catherine de Médicis. Francis lived and ruled, nonetheless, in an atmosphere of authority as absolute as that of his Roi-Soleil descendant; but it was an authority the severity of which was tempered by the simplicity of the king's manner and by an affability which extended to the lowliest of his subjects. The ordering of his day, however, had to be arranged so as to make the best possible use of his time, and there is a record of that horarium in a letter of Catherine de Médicis to her son, Charles IX, concerning "the ordering of the court and the government of the state":

"I would desire, sir, that you fix the hour of your arising, so as to content your nobles, as did your father the king. When he took his shirt and his clothes were brought in, all the princes, lords, captains, knights of the orders, gentlemen of the chamber, major-domos and gentlemen-servants entered then, and he saw and spoke with them and this pleased them greatly. That done, he went about his affairs, and they all went out, except for those who had to do with those affairs and four secretaries. If you do the same, it will keep them content, because such was also the custom at all times of your royal father and grandfather. After that, you should devote an hour or two to listening to the reading of dispatches and to affairs which cannot be expedited without your presence.

"Do not let ten o'clock pass without going to Mass, as your royal father and grandfather were accustomed to do. Let all the princes and lords accompany you . . . and on leaving Mass, dine if it is late; or if not, take a stroll for your health; and do not dine after eleven. After dinner, at least twice a week, give audience, which is something that gives infinite pleasure to your subjects; and afterward retire, and come to see me or the queen; so that there may be a habit of the court which gives great pleasure to the French, as they have become accustomed to it. After remaining for half an hour or an hour in public, you may retire to your office or to your own apartments, wherever you think best.

"At three in the afternoon, go for a walk or a ride, so as to show yourself and satisfy the nobility, and pass your time with the young folk in some honest exercise, if not every day at least two or three times a week; this will please them all very much, being accustomed to it from the time of the king your father, who loved them greatly. After that, sup with your family, and after supper, twice a week, give a ball; for I have heard the king your grandfather say that two such days are needed to live in peace with the French, and that they love their king to keep them gay and occupied with some exercise."[1]

The business of government adequately dispatched, then, the king and the gilded youth who surrounded him turned happily to the joys of the outdoors and of physical activity. The monarch had doubtless understood that "the French have become so accustomed, when not actually at war, to taking exercise, that if one does not provide them with it, they pass their time in other and less innocuous avocations." But such a comment, perhaps a trifle obvious, touches only the surface of the deep need of physical exercise felt by the people of those times. Following the example of ancient Greece and Rome, they considered its pursuit indispensable for poise. Sports were regaining popularity in all classes of society; the echo of this has come down to us through the celebrated educational program of Pantagruel—an expression of reality, not merely Rabelaisian fantasy.

The gentleman, a professional soldier, proud and quarrelsome, was like his king, devoted to vigorous amusements, at which he excelled:

"You chiefly delight, sire," wrote the hellenist Guillaume Budé, "in two kinds of exercise; that is hunting deer and boar, and taking part in tourneys fully armed with sharp lances; a spectacle not so dangerous as in appearance bold and rough; showing yourself so adroit at both that all recognize your excellence. . . . I have seen you suddenly, in the presence of King Louis your father-in-law, enter the lists, followed by your troop wearing your colors; then, the tourney ended, going out at the sound of the retreat, make the horse you were riding leap through the air. . . . So mounted on a flying horse, you held your seat as firmly as though your thighs had been glued to the saddle; then I remember having heard some say that you seemed not a man on a horse, but a hippocentaur!"[2]

"Next after arms, hunting is the true pleasure of great lords which best suits the courtier," wrote Baldesar Castiglione,[3] "for it has a certain resemblance to war." It was the favorite pastime of Francis I. This builder-king sought sites for his palaces in deep forests, where he could thus indulge his leisure. There was not a day when he was not seen out riding with his retinue, or in the company of his "little band" —and with his monkey, who knew how to shoot with a bow—led by a baying pack. He rode through the tall forests of the Ile-de-France, Rambouillet or Bière, free enough to lose himself there one winter's evening and, half dead from cold, to take refuge in a grotto where, late at night and after a long search, his servants found him.

Knowing this great passion, Guillaume Budé wrote a treatise on venery for him, which describes the different phases of Francis I's favorite sport:

"The King, dressed for the hunt, followed by lords and ladies of his court, leaves his castle and goes to take up his position in a pleasant glade. There, he decides at leisure about the stag he will hunt that day and sets about locating the place where it is to be found. The beast should be of a good height and size, with at least ten-point antlers; generally it keeps company with another stag, smaller, which is called its groom.

"The company gathers in some fine place, under the trees, and the huntsmen, seated on the grass, spread the cloth on the leaves and greenery, and take their collation near the King's table, where the decision is being made which stag, of those considered worth hunting, should be run.

"It has become the custom to allot different positions to the hunters, so that they do not hinder one another. They look at the movement of the stag and the kind of hoofs it has, its tracks in the leaves and grass, the scratching it has made on the trees. If the place is damp or if it has been raining, or if the soil is scenting, they use a bloodhound for tracking, and so proceed as to discover by certain conjunctions the lair or chamber where the stag has rested. But so that the stag shall not take fright at the approach of the huntsman, or the sound of the bloodhound, or some other reason, as often happens, and does not leave his dwelling (for although such dogs with big ears are mute by nature, in the excitement of the approaching animal they cannot stop themselves yelping and making a noise), so that the stag may not through such an accident leave his morning lair and get away, they have the habit of making an enclosure there and keeping the dog close by the collar and not setting out from thence, until they have made sure the animal is in the place thus marked out."

Duly informed, the trackers report the results of their search to the meet. On this information, they choose one or two of the most suitable stags and go straight to their posts:

"The bloodhound again indicates the signs of the lair; it is held back by the leash on its collar, which greatly excites the animal. Then the hounds are unleashed and, with sound of trumpets to rejoice and encourage them, the signal is given that the hunt is beginning. Relays are unleashed to replace the tired hounds when necessary; and these and other packs entirely reserved for the afternoon. The stag selected is hard pressed by the running hounds, the pikemen, the trumpets' sound, the huntsmen's cries, and the sound of baying.

"When the stags find themselves pressed by the speed and ardor of the hounds, they play various tricks, turning this way and that to escape, by making a change; they go and seek out the does and other stags which share their resting places and mix with the herd in order to deceive the hounds. At times they take some with them and accompany them a distance, then separate suddenly and turn off rather far down another track and stop, so that the hounds, engaged in following the trail of the fawns or does, move away from them. . . . While the hounds are held up in their pursuit by such twists and turns, the stags get well away; meanwhile the hounds, eagerly running, are exhorted and excited by the trumpets. . . . The stags have a habit, it is said, of running away from the windward side for three reasons. First, because when they go against the wind, it enters their mouth and nose, makes their tongue dry and interferes with their exhalation. Secondly, fleeing down the wind, they easily hear the hounds' baying and by it know if they are close or far away . . . Thirdly, that, by this means, they prevent the dogs getting their scent."[4]

The ruses of the hunted stag for getting rid of the hunters are innumerable. The following was recounted to Guillaume Budé by Louis XII's chief huntsman during a hunt he gave, in honor of one of the presidents of the court of Parliament:

"When not long ago I was hunting an old and cunning stag, it happened, in the heat of the chase, which continued quite a time, that we lost it to view, at the same time the dogs did not want to go farther; everyone was wondering and looking this way and that, doing what they could, both the huntsmen and the pikemen. It was marvelous how, as if by magic, the beast apparently had vanished into thin air, or the earth had opened and then closed, swallowing it up. Finally, as happens in such cases, we were looking everywhere and this sly stag was discovered by an extraordinary chance. There was a whitethorn growing in a thickly covered spot the height of a tree, into which the stag after exhausting all its tricks threw itself with a single bound, and there it stayed, up in the air, and having crushed the branches by its leap was so enveloped that it could not get out, or perhaps it was because it was winded. In the end, weary and battered, it was slain there, deserving, for such a marvel, not to die so soon, had Diana been pleased to grant a reprieve."

When the beast, at the end of its strength, sees itself lost, it turns nasty and may fling itself, antlers down, on the first huntsman in its path, if it is not run through immediately; but finally the stag is killed, and the retreat sounded: "which is like a shout of joy after the deed well and truly done." The huntsmen, pikemen, and hounds gather round, and the feeding of the pack takes place:

"This is the hunting dogs' right, just as in falconry the first morsels are due to the birds of prey. It is necessary that whoever makes distribution to the dogs be expert in this and know well how to flay the animal and cut it apart, limb from limb. The skin removed, the head must be cut off, and given to the bloodhound which has led the hunt, it is his right. . . . So that in tearing and gnawing at the head he may receive the fruit of his labor first, and in the future may have the same courage, since his guidance and conduct have brought the rest to the conclusion of their undertaking. . . . The same should be done with the other bloodhounds and less valuable dogs. Then the huntsmen take bits of bread which they dip in the blood of the stag, with which they mix some fat cut in small pieces, and put it on the skin; moreover if the dogs are weak or thin, or have done very well that day, the huntsmen treat them better and add some morsels from the neck and shoulder. Then the dogs begin to feed with yelps of enjoyment; for while this is being prepared they are kept on leash round and about, and the servants prevent them approaching with flicks from a switch. This feeding finished, another one immediately begins—but not in the same place—of the cleaned and washed intestines, which are also offered to Diana and her dogs, not divided into portions or cut up, but whole. So the huntsman who has fed the pack, after lifting them in the air and showing them to the dogs to give them more appetite, throws them whole into their midst."[5]

The court, easily adapting themselves to the prince's tastes, doted also upon exercises of arms, the dangers of which increased the attraction tenfold. It was considered self-evident that it was glorious, and eminently worthy of a gentleman, to risk his life for pleasure and to exhibit his skill before a select company—particularly when that company included the most beautiful women in the world. It mattered hardly at all that blood flowed, and that deaths were not uncommon in these games. Thus, tourneys, defenses of barriers, combats at the gates, all forms of simulated battles were the favorite spectacle in court celebrations. In 1517 took place the baptism of the Dauphin of France, where the pope stood godfather; it was followed by the marriage of the Duke of Urbino, the papal ambassador, to Madeleine de la Tour d'Auvergne, future parents of Catherine de Médicis. This double festivity occasioned a magnificent celebration lasting over a month:

"And for eight whole days there was combat in the lists and outside, on foot and at the gates. The Duke of Urbino took part and did his best before his sweetheart.

"Among other things there was a kind of tourney that I saw nowhere in my life but there: the king had a town built of wood, surrounded by moats, all in the open country and quite large. He had placed there four great pieces of artillery, cannon and double cannon which fired volleys above the said town, as though supposedly a battery. M. d'Alençon with a hundred men at arms on horseback, lance at thigh, was in the said town. L'Aventureux, with four hundred men at arms on foot and well armed, among whom were the hundred Swiss of the guard, went to his help, feigning to rescue M. d'Alençon. M. de Bourbon with a hundred men at arms on horseback, and M. de Vendôme with a hundred men at arms on foot, besieged the town as if l'Aventureux was going to relieve it.

"And as all this was taking place, the king, fully armed, came to throw himself with l'Aventureux into the town. The great cannon, made of wood and bound with iron, fired with powder, and the cannon balls, which were great balls full of air and as big as the back of a wagon, struck the besiegers and knocked them down but did them no harm.

"Then, that pastime ended, M. d'Alençon, the king, and l'Aventureux, with all their armed men, sallied out from the town, and the three pieces of artillery began to fire as if on the battlefield. Elsewhere M. de Bourbon came against M. d'Alençon and M. de Vendôme, against the king and l'Aventureux; and suddenly set upon both the horsemen and footmen. This was the most beautiful combat that had ever been seen and the most nearly approaching the reality of war. But the pastime did not please everyone, for many were killed and badly scarred. That done, it was broken off, but with difficulty; matters would have been worse if the men and horses had not been winded, for as long as their wind lasted they kept on fighting."[6]

※ ※ ※

Francis, nonetheless, ever mindful of Castiglione's "perfect courtier," prided himself upon the fact that the pleasure he derived from things of the mind was equal to that obtained in his elaborate games of war. In the afternoons and evenings, this strapping soldier, this most remarkable jouster in all France, this expert horseman, joined the queen's circle to take part, with zest and wit, in conversations which were both learned and entertaining.

The prince was seconded in this task by his mother, Louise of Savoy, whose court at Angoulême was very cultivated, and above all by his sister Marguerite. Under this aegis was born the great tradition of conversation in France, which was to reach such perfection in the seventeenth and eighteenth centuries. Already in the Middle Ages, lords and ladies gathered to witness tourneys and to hear the troubadours in the great hall of the castle sing poems and ballads, recite epics, or read aloud stories of the Round Table. But they had no notion of conversation in its classic meaning. Around 1520, the art was still in its infancy; Gallic coarseness frequently broke surface, and if it did so amid still barely repressed chortles, it shocked no one; the sentiments were superficial but the tone was lively, and the repartee quick and spirited. A gay and family atmosphere reigned over these gatherings, in which the women were a match for the men. If they did not care to talk for hours on end about the niceties of a sentiment or an idea, as was done a century later, nevertheless they touched on the realms of psychology and feeling, through anecdotes, real or imaginary, in the vein of the dialogues of the *Heptaméron*, in which come to life again, despite the passage of time, those fleeting and somewhat precious conversations of a society which was beginning to civilize itself.

The *Heptaméron*, a collection of stories from the lively pen of Marguerite of Navarre, concerns ten companions, of whom some can be identified with important people at court: Louise of Savoy with Dame Oisille; Anne of Vivonne, the mother of Brantôme, with Ennasuite; Henri d'Albret with Hircan; finally Marguerite herself with Parlamente. They have just finished the cure at Cauterets, and on the way home numerous dangers assail them. Cloudbursts, rivers overflowing their banks, a hostile mountain, bears, and bandits imperiled their lives in turn and prevented them from reaching home. They all met, as luck would have it, a few leagues from Somport, at Notre-Dame de Sarrance in the Aspe Valley, a halt of pilgrims to the Spanish shrine, St. James of Compostela. There they waited a few days before continuing and whiled away the time by each one recounting ten true stories.

Of what did these ten companions speak? Of love, naturally; of the innumerable aspects of love, from the most profane to the most elevated, from adultery to platonic love—and more frequently of the former than the latter. The work is sometimes called "The Story of the Fortunate Lovers."

Dame Oisille, oldest of the gathering, herself tells in the thirty-second story how a French gentleman, Lord de Bernage, entrusted by King Charles VIII with an important mission in Germany, asked hospitality from a lord of that country[7]:

"It was time to dine; the gentleman led him into a beautiful hall hung with fine tapestries. Just as the meat was being brought to the table, he saw a woman come out from behind the tapestry, the loveliest woman imaginable, but her head was all shaven, and she was entirely clothed in black in the German style. . . . She went to sit at the other end of the table without a word to anyone, nor did anyone speak to her. The Lord de Bernage looked closely at her; she seemed to him one of the most beautiful women he had ever seen, but her face was pale and her expression very sad. After she had eaten a little, she asked for something to drink, which the servant brought her there in an amazing vessel--it was a skull which had eyes filled in with silver; and so she drank two or three times. The young woman, after dining and washing her hands, made a reverence to the lord of the house and went out behind the tapestry without speaking to anybody."

The Frenchman could not conceal his astonishment, and the gentleman then told him the truth. While he was on one of his journeys, this woman, whom he loved more than anything in the world, had betrayed him shamefully with a knight of his household. On his return he found them in the act, killed the man with his own hands, and inflicted on his accomplice a punishment worse than death:

"I shut her in the same room to which she had retired to enjoy her greatest delight, in company of him whom she loved too well and more than me; in that place I had put in a cabinet all her friend's bones, displayed like some precious object in a showcase. And so that she would not forget it, when she ate and drank I had her served at table not from a cup, but from the head of this villain; and there right in front of me, so that she should see alive the one whom she had made her mortal enemy by her fault, and the man whose friendship she had preferred to mine, dead through his love for her. . . .

"For the rest I treat her like myself, excepting that she is shaved, for a coiffeur is not for an adultress, nor a veil for the shameless. For this reason she goes shaved, showing that she has forfeited the honor due to virginity and modesty. If you care to see her, I will take you to her."

The Lord de Bernage accepted. Before such a piteous spectacle he could not help revealing his emotions to the young woman, nor on parting from his host, urging him to clemency. These wise words, and the arrival of the painter Jean de Paris (sent by his master the King of France on hearing the gentleman's report to make a portrait of this touching beauty), and finally the humility of the guilty party, touched the heart of the offended husband, who forgave the lady.

The ten companions were not slow to comment on so unusual a story. Their lively repartee and its gay and happy tone give a vivid glimpse of the general trend of French conversation in the Rennaissance:

"'My ladies, if all those who had found themselves in a like situation were to drink from such vessels, I am afraid that many golden goblets would be beaten into skulls. But God preserve us, for if his bounty did not restrain us, not one of us but would not do worse; but he guards those who, trusting in him, confess that they cannot guard themselves; and those who confide in their own strength are in great danger of temptation, to the point of confessing their infirmity. . . .'

"'I find,' said Parlamente, 'that this punishment is the most reasonable possible, for as the offense is worse than death, so the punishment too is worse than death.'

"Said Ennasuite: 'I am not of your opinion, for I would rather, all my life, look at the bones of all my suitors in my cabinet than die for them, since there is no crime for which amends cannot be made, but after death there is no amendment.'

"'How would you make amends for the shame?' said Longarine. 'For as you know, nothing a woman can do, after such a crime, can repair her honor.'

"'I pray you, tell me,' said Ennasuite, 'does not the Magdalen have more honor among men today than her sister, who was a virgin?'

"'I admit,' said Longarine, 'that she is praised among us for the great love she bore to Jesus Christ and for her great penitence; but nevertheless she is still called a sinner.'

"'I am not worried about the names men give me,' said Ennasuite, 'but that God may pardon me and my husband too; there is no reason why I would wish to die.'

"'If that young woman had loved her husband as she should,' said Dagoucin, 'I am surprised that she did not die of grief, looking at the bones of him whom she had killed through her sin.'

"'So, Dagoucin,' said Simonault, 'have you yet to learn that women neither love nor regret?'

"'I have yet to learn,' said Dagoucin, 'because I never dared to try their love for fear to find it less than I would wish.'

"'So then you live by faith and hope,' said Nomerfide, 'like the plover lives on air, easy to nourish.'

"'I am satisfied,' he said, 'with the love I feel in myself, and with the hope that it is in the hearts of women, but if I knew it, as I would hope to, I would have such extreme content that I should die of it.'

"'Mind you don't catch the plague,' said Géburon, 'because of that sickness one really dies, I assure you.'"

*   *   *

The good taste obvious in the *Heptaméron* was not the rule in all the court's pastimes. The professional fools and the dwarfs who were to be met in the palace corridors made one wonder whether even the coarsest jokes from their lips were enough to make men laugh. A relic of the Middle Ages, the king's fool had a definite charge of court:

"The greatest of kings liked them so much," wrote Erasmus,[8] "that many a one would not sit down at table nor make any move without their presence, nor dispense with them for an hour. They prized their fools far more highly than the austere sages whom they have the custom of ostentatiously entertaining. This preference is easy to explain and is not surprising when it is seen that sages bring nothing to princes but sadness.

". . . The buffoons, on the other hand, bring what the princes looked for everywhere and at all costs: amusement, smiles, laughter, pleasure. The fools also must be granted one quality not to be despised: they alone are frank and truthful. . . . All that is in a fool's heart shows on his face, is expressed in his talk; sages, on the contrary, have two tongues: one to tell the truth, and another to say what is expedient."

The great fool of the court of Francis I was not Triboulet, a poor buffoon who has been given a place of honor by the romantics, but Brusquet, who was granted the privilege of posting horses, and was married and endowed by the king. His tricks were innumerable, and he persevered in them even when he proved to be their first victim:

"Once the queen had a great longing to see Brusquet's wife, who M. de Strozzi had described to her as being excessively ugly, which she truly was; and she had told Brusquet she would not love him at all if he did not bring her to see her; which he did. And he brought her to her dressed up, attired, turned out no more and no less than as for her wedding day, with her hair down on her shoulders like a young bride. Seeing which, he told her to retain that look, and, himself taking her hand, he led her thus in the Louvre before everyone, who almost died of laughter, for Brusquet put on the sweet and affected air of a newly-wed."

Brusquet had told the queen in advance that his wife was deaf, and then he ordered his wife to speak out at the top of her voice to the queen, who was hard of hearing:

"So when she was before the queen, after making her a very low reverence, accompanied by a clownish little smirk, as her husband had taught her, she said: 'My Lady Queen, God preserve you from harm.' The queen began to examine her and to ask at the top of her voice how she was. Her husband having left her at the entrance, she began to speak and shout like a crazy woman: and when the queen shouted she shouted even louder; so that the noise resounded even down to the courtyard of the Louvre.

"M. de Strozzi arriving there, wished to join in the conversation with her, but Brusquet had warned his wife that he too was deaf, and even more so than the queen, and that she should never speak to him but right in his ear and as loud as she could. Which she did not fail to do exactly.

"M. de Strozzi, having suspected that there was behind all this some prank of Brusquet's, had a bloodhound handler waiting in the courtyard with his horn hanging round his neck, and he asked him to come up. And having had him come into the chamber he said to the queen: 'Madame, this woman is deaf, I am going to cure her.' And he took her head and bid the valet sound all the stag hunting calls in both her ears; which he did. He blew so loud that she was stunned, head and ears alike, and she remained over a month crippled both in head and hearing, without understanding a word, until the doctors found a remedy for her, which cost a pretty penny. And so Brusquet, who had given the others the trouble of shouting so loudly at the wife he pretended was deaf, suddenly was forced to do the same himself, and his home life was not improved when he asked her for anything."

This M. de Strozzi was no other than Pierre Strozzi, that fascinating personality of Florentine descent, who was Marshal of France and Commander of the Galleys. His birth and high station did not prevent him from engaging in every kind of joke with the court fool, and he and Brusquet plotted practical jokes together like two old cronies.

One day Brusquet begged the marshal to honor him by coming to dine with him, together with a dozen noble lords who were friends of his. He promised to treat them royally. Strozzi accepted the invitation. His host came to meet them, a napkin on his shoulder, and welcomed them to his house:

"'Wash your hands, gentlemen,' he told them; 'make yourselves at home, and I will go and find you something to eat.' Which he did. And for the first course he brought in at least thirty pasties, small, middling, and big, and nothing else. All were hot and smelled delicious, for he had had an excellent and most appropriate sauce made to go in them, and had not spared the spices and cinnamon, nor even musk. After bringing in the first dishes he said to them: 'Now, gentlemen, I am going to fetch the rest, and meanwhile eat up what is in these dishes to make room for more.'"

And, going out of the hall, he took his cape and sword, and went straight off to the Louvre to tell the king about his party.

"Now inside these pasties, in some were old pieces of horses' bits, in others old straps, in others old girth leathers, old cruppers in others, old breast pieces, old bridle ornaments, old head straps, old pummels, old saddle bows; in short, the pasties of these gentlemen were full of all the old remnants from his posting horses. Some had little bits of trash, others had great pieces and were shaped like venison pies.

"When these gentlemen, who were all extremely hungry, sat down at the table expecting to put a square meal in their stomachs, they greedily set about opening the pasties, which smelled so good. I leave you to picture their astonishment when they saw such fine, exquisite meat. It is even said that some of them put pieces in their mouths, thinking that they were delicious morsels, but quickly spat them out again. Finally they all shouted: 'This is Brusquet's work.'"

The guests did not think of leaving the table, in the expectation that after the farce was over they would be regaled with something good. But nothing came. They noticed that the master of the house had vanished, the cupboard was bare, and the kitchen cold. There was nothing left to do at that late hour but go home with empty stomachs.

13. Charles V, as a youth, entering Bruges in 1515. Nationalbibliothek, Vienna

Mass, with music. Engraving by J. Stradanus. Cabinet des Estampes. Bibliothèque Nationale, Paris

14.

The judgement of heretics. Woodcut of 1541. Bibliothèque de Grenoble

15. A nobleman and his lady at the end of the fifteenth century. Detail from a contemporary Flemish tapestry. Musée des Arts Décoratifs, Paris. Photograph by H. Adant

16. Rustic life. Miniature depicting the parable of the sower. Threshing the grain and stacking the sheaves. Pierre de Crescens, Bibliothèque de l'Arsénal, Paris

Meantime, the king and the court, hearing, through Brusquet's good offices, of the prank, laughed heartily at the guests' expense.

Strozzi, good-natured fellow, took no umbrage, but laughed like the rest and saw in it a good opportunity for his revenge. He got hold of a very fine little mule owned by Brusquet, had it made into a pie, and invited its master to the banquet. When he had eaten his fill:

"'Well, Brusquet,' asked the marshal, 'haven't I made you a treat? I haven't cheated you like you did me, who made me die of hunger.' Brusquet replied that he was pleased with him, and had never eaten better. 'So,' answered the marshal, 'would you like to see what you have eaten?' Suddenly he had brought in and set on the table his mule's head served up like a boar's head. 'There Brusquet is the meat you ate,' he said. 'Do you recognize the animal?' Who was surprised now? Brusquet, who 'thereupon vomited so violently that they thought he would die, as much with nausea that seized him as with misery at having thus devoured the poor little mule which he loved so much, and which carried him so gently in the fields and in town, and everywhere.'"[9]

COURT CRONIES GOSSIP

In the small, closed world of the court, there were opposing interests, jealous outbursts, clashing ambitions. In that atmosphere, tongues wagged quite freely, and friendship was rare. Sweet-tongued dukes and countesses gossiped away joyfully and pronounced judgment, without benefit of doubt or right of appeal, on everyone. The year 1539 offered a choice subject for the exercise of such talents. The occasion was the remarriage of the Maréchale de Montéjean, née Philippe de Montespédon. That inveterate talebearer, Vieilleville, tells the story in detail[10]; if he is to be believed, he played a leading part in it.

This unfortunate widow in question was young, beautiful, and virtuous; and she was rich, having sixty thousand pounds in rents in her own right, and being sole heir to M. de Châteaubriand. As a result of these virtues, she was assiduously courted:

"The Marquis Jean-Louis de Saluces was the first who paid court to her, and the lady made pretense of listening, because it offered her a convenient way of returning with him from Piedmont, where she was at the time of her husband's death, to France, whither he was bound by the king's command. In the hope of marrying her, he paid for her journey from Turin to Paris; and also for that of all her retinue, which was very large, for she was accompanied by her late husband's very numerous servants of all ranks as well as her own, with no means of satisfying them but those which the marquis offered. For that reason, he felt quite sure of the marriage, and on the way he joked about it and arranged everything, as though they were already engaged or living together, going so far as to say that she should dismiss and send home all her husband's gentlemen, servants, and officers, and cut down her own by half, and principally so many women; for she had, besides her ladies and young women, fifteen or sixteen chambermaids and others for work. But she was so prudent and wary that not a word escaped her which could or should oblige her, yet so courteous that she made use of this opportunity most dexterously."

They made a stop at Lyons. Envoys of Vieilleville (who was a cousin of the *maréchale*) were waiting there for her, and very secretly gave her a missive from their master. The entire court, he wrote, was talking of nothing but her approaching marriage with the Marquis de Saluces, and the king was very pleased about it, for political reasons which she knew; but he, Vieilleville, could not bring himself to believe in it. The bonds of kinship and friendship which had always linked them made him believe she would have told him of her project, if, despite her recent widowhood, she had resolved on it.

Madame de Montéjean sent him a reply in the same way, that he had been quite right not to give credit to the rumors which were going about. She certainly had no wish to marry the Marquis de Saluces and had no commitment to him. But this did not prevent her keeping company with the marquis, in so far as that was useful for her affairs:

"The marquis spent twelve days at Lyons to make his preparations, intending to arrive at court in great splendor. They had both so much finery that they needed six large boats to carry them and all their suite, for they did their cooking on board, and had all their chests, their trunks, and a great quantity of other baggage with which they had furnished themselves at Lyons. In addition there was a band of fiddlers which the marquis had hired at Lyons to entertain them on the River Loire and also to try to assuage the grief which the *maréchale* still felt for her late husband. And embarking at Roanne, they sent the horses and mules by land, which were at Briare as soon as they."

From there, by short stages, they reached the capital. But the lady secretly let her agent, the Sieur du Plessis-au-Chat, know that when they arrived at the Port de Saint-Marceau they would have to separate her retinue from that of M. de Saluces:

"Having entered the Faubourg Saint-Marceau all together, where they made a splendid great troop, Plessis-au-Chat took one side of the street and moved off down it followed by all his mistress's train . . . seeing which, the marquis, thinking there was some mistake, asked where they were going. At which the *maréchale* stopped and answered: 'My Lord, where they are going is where they should, for your house is at the Hôtel des Ursins, at the Cloister of Notre-Dame, and mine at the Hôtel St.-Denis, near the Augustins. And my honor compels me not to lodge with you, but to leave you. So now I take leave of you, and most humbly thank you, sir, for the good company it has pleased you to keep me; as to your expenses on the journey on my account, I have everything written down. Your major-domo and du Plessis-au-Chat will settle that together so well, that in less than a week we shall be quits. By that I refer only to money, for my obligation will be perpetual and I do not think I shall ever be able to repay it. Begging you will believe that this departure is bodily only, for I leave you my heart, of which be pleased to take good care.' And thereupon she kissed him, saying to him: 'Adieu, My Lord, we shall see each other tomorrow at the king's lodging.'"

The marquis, dumfounded, could not at first utter a single word, but, taking hold of himself, "looking at her with an eye very far from that of love, said to her: 'Madame, your farewell has disheartened me, but your last words and the kiss which you have honored me with have restored me. . . . Tomorrow, as you say, we shall see each other, but remember well the promises you have made me and farewell, madame.'

That very evening the faithless woman dined with her cousin, Vieilleville. He suggested a very good match to her; the Prince de la Roche-sur-Yon, kin to the blood royal of France and the possessor of a vast fortune. She did not find the match unpleasing.

The actual successor of the lady's dead husband as Governor of Piedmont, M. d'Annebaut, Marshal of France, was quick to join the growing list of suitors. Absent from court, he asked the dauphine to plead his cause, and gave her several arguments to substantiate it:[11]

"The first, that Madame de Montéjean would not lower herself in any way, for he possessed estates as great as those of her late husband; the next, that he had done such great and signal services to the king that if there remained any great estates in France to be divided, he fully expected to receive preference, which he also should since he was an admiral; thirdly, that he had lands in Brittany, neighboring on and running with those of the widow, among them the estate of Henodaye, very fine and lordly, which would be a great convenience to both of them; and finally, if this alliance were made, they could, putting together their fortunes, found a house of a hundred thouand pounds' rents, something very rare in the kingdom, except for those with the rank of prince."

The dauphine hastened to press d'Annebaut's suit with the widow, and extolled her protégé's merits at the expense of the man whom she believed was already far ahead in the running:

"'I must confess that the Marquis de Saluces is three times richer,' she said, 'and that he has more than eighty thousand crowns in rents; but these goods are all being held in escrow, and at the least suspicion he will be ruined, and shamefully so for they will call him a traitor.

"'As to the difference in person, the marquis is very unattractive—fat, dirty, black, swarthy and very ungainly. I leave it to you to judge of

M. d'Annebaut, as you have seen him and are not unaware how honorable he is and how presentable in everything.'"

The *maréchale* thanked the dauphine with becoming deference and courtesy "that so great a princess, and the most excellent in all Christendom" had deigned to take the trouble to be concerned for her modest person.

"'Nonetheless, madame,' she continued, 'I have gone so far toward marriage with another, that I could only get out of it with difficulty; and I would scarcely know how to do so without being accused of frivolity and perfidy; at least you will not be displeased that I wish to ally myself with one who will one day have the honor of being the very humble servant and near kin of my lords your children, if by God's grace you are favored with them.

"'In heaven's name, who can that be?' asked the dauphine. 'It is the Prince de la Roche-sur-Yon,' she said. 'My cousin Vieilleville has already gone so far in the matter that I cannot gainsay him.'"

The dauphine was delighted. She immediately gave up pleading the cause of Monsieur d'Annebaut, and counseled the young woman to expedite matters somewhat in the direction where her affections lay, since the king, who would be glad to see her marry the Marquis de Saluces, could easily intervene in the latter's favor.

The Marquis de Saluces, however, did not despair of making his lady relent and overcoming her intransigeance. He visited her daily—but he always met there Prince de la Roche-sur-Yon, "which was a very sore thorn in his flesh." Seeing himself losing ground, he resolved to have his revenge, and summoned the *maréchale* before Parliament. She came there on the appointed day, accompanied by her cousin, Vieilleville, and a few friends. Interrogated by the president, she replied with emotion:

"I swear to God and to the king—to God on my soul, to the king on my honor and my life—that never did I give my oath or my word or my promise of marriage to the Marquis Jean-Louis de Saluces; and, what is more, that I never in my life thought of it. And if there is one who would say the contrary, here (taking M. de Vieilleville by the hand) is my knight, whom I present to guarantee my word, which he knows is completely truthful and pronounced by the lips of a woman of honor."

The president turned toward the marquis:

"Well, monsieur, what do you say about this exchange?"

"I do not wish," he replied, "to have any woman by force; if she does not want me, then neither do I her."

M. de Vieilleville then asked the court if the *maréchale* could remarry as she wished. The reply was in the affirmative.

"Then, messieurs," he said, "if you care to come with me to the Archdeacon of Hardaz, we shall find there the Prince de la Roche-sur-Yon, accompanied by the Dukes d'Etampes, de Rohan, and de Gié; he is waiting to become betrothed to her, and the Bishop of Angers is prepared for this."

The Parliament excused themselves from coming. And so, they took their leave of one another. But someone whispered in a low voice to M. de Vieilleville as he passed: "The trial would have lasted six months if you had not been so direct, for the marquis had a questionnaire of forty articles, to interrogate the *maréchale* on all the intentions she had ever had toward him and his people, and the kisses she had given on the road, and that at the Porte Saint-Marceau; and among other things, that she had promised (something which hurt him very much) to the major-domo of the said marquis a chain worth five hundred crowns to wear at the wedding."

"Well, now," said M. de Vieilleville, "this is a Frenchwoman who has fooled a hundred Italians."

So, three days later Madame de Montéjean was married at the Church of the Augustins—but without much pomp, for after all she was a widow—to the Prince de la Roche-sur-Yon, bringing to a happy ending the enthralling tale which had been the subject of general, and animated, conversation for several months.

※　　※　　※

Such preoccupation with the affairs of others can flourish only where there is ample opportunity for social contact and for a consequent exchange of "confidences." At Fontainebleau, a ball was given twice a week, and there were festivities at every opportunity. Perhaps the most sumptuous of these, and the ones which left a mark on their epoch, were those celebrated on the occasion of Charles V's journey through France in 1539. The previous year the two irreconcilable enemies had finally agreed to meet; they had then greeted one another at Aigues-Mortes, under Queen Eleanor's tender gaze, and vowed eternal peace. Some months later, a serious rebellion broke out at Ghent, which made the presence of the emperor imperative. Faced with a crisis, he asked his brother-in-law to allow him to cross his kingdom, in order to punish the guilty parties before it was too late. Francis I, despite the protests of those around him, not only agreed but decided also to give Charles a reception the magnificence of which would be worthy of the King of France.

In early November 1539, therefore, he sent the dauphin, Henry, and the Duke d'Orleans, accompanied by the Constable de Montmorency, to receive Charles V at Bayonne, and to escort him, by way of Bordeaux, Lusignan, and Poitiers, to Châtellerault, where Francis himself came with all his court to receive Charles. The two princes then set out for Fontainebleau amid general rejoicings, triumphal entries, feasts, jousts, and tourneys. Everywhere their reception was magnificent. Only one untoward incident occurred, an unfortunate fire which broke out in a tower at Amboise and almost asphyxiated the emperor and his suite. (Some have construed this as a plot, but there is no evidence to that effect.)

Fontainebleau, the monarch's favorite residence and the magnificent palace which had all Europe talking, had to live up to its reputation and, as a contemporary writer noted, had set up an unrivaled program of entertainment:

"On the edge of the forest of Bière, a great number of princes, lords and the nobility, in gorgeous robes, awaited the emperor.

"As he entered the forest he was greeted by a troop of people dressed up as woodland gods and goddesses who, at the sound of hautboys, gathered and ran forward to perform a rustic dance, which was not the less agreeable for their strange costume and the order they maintained; who after having danced for a certain time, dispersed hither and thither into the forest, while the emperor, continuing on his way, arrived at the castle.

"His entrance was by way of the great avenue along the causeway. At the gate was a triumphal arch decorated with trophies and adorned with paintings, representing the king and the emperor dressed in classical garb and accompanied by Peace and Concord, to let the emperor see with what benevolence and frankness the king received him. Here, there was another concert of music; after having listened to a number of airs, he was taken into the château, to the sound of trumpets and drums; and, entering the small gallery, he met the king . . . and from there he was conducted to the Pavillon des Poëles, where he was to lodge.

"When supper had been prepared in the ballroom, the king, who had left the emperor time to rest at leisure, went to his room to fetch him, and they came in to supper together, both giving evidence of great rejoicing.

"The next day, and the several days that he stayed here, the king gave him every pleasure that could be devised, such as royal hunts, tourneys, skirmishes, combats on foot and mounted, and in short every kind of diversion."[12]

During this time Paris was feverishly being readied. No less than Fontainebleau, the capital of the kingdom should receive this distinguished guest with suitable magnificence. The king had carefully attended to it, and as early as November 8, on his orders, the aldermen of the city of Paris met with the Constable de Montmorency, who had gone there specially for that purpose. Montmorency let them know "that the desire and intention of his master was that they should think both about making preparations for the entrance and the reception of the emperor, and about the presents which it was appropriate for the city to offer him, which he understood were to be unique and magnificent and of greater value than those they made to him; and that for this purpose they were to find good master painters, and devisers of curiosities; and further that it must be seen what artillery they had in the town for the said lord understood that on the day of the entrance the town should be aflame with the animation of these pieces; and equally, that the streets must be kept neat and clean.

"The aldermen replied that they were ready to accomplish the wishes of the king, and those of the good constable, but that the city was short of money, and that they would like to know what sum was available from the accounts, which had been brought before the council in the last few days.

"To this remonstrance the constable replied that the king had never refused his city of Paris anything that had been asked of him; and that for his part, he was a citizen and a Parisian, and he was always concerned and would continue to be; but it was necessary to go beyond that, for this was the greatest pleasure which the city could give the king, being the most famous in the kingdom, and he intended to show it to the emperor in all magnificence; and therefore, for everything, that had been spoken about, the necessary orders were to be given."[13]

Shortly afterward, the king sent for one of the aldermen in order himself to signify his intentions and to review the current preparations with him:

"After greeting the king on behalf of the city, the alderman showed him the sketch of the eagles which were to be put at the two ends of the sideboard which would be presented to the emperor; these eagles and sideboard the king did not find good, saying that on a previous occasion the emperor had told him that he detested the tapestries of his own country of Flanders, for they always represented some banquet, pots, cups or grapes, which are things to do with eating. . . . It would be appropriate to give him something of a personal nature, which would remain with him as a souvenir. After hearing a number of suggestions, the King decided on a statue of Hercules, covered with a finely gilded lion's skin, holding in his hands two columns, as though planting them in the ground by force. These columns would be designed to hold torches, and would bear the motto of the emperor, *Plus oultre* and the sash of Hercules, *Altera alterior robur*. The king commanded Seigneur de Boissy to write to Master Roux (Rosso), his painter, living at Fontainebleau, to make the design and molds for it. . . .

"Moreover, the king did not agree that there should be, on the canopy which would be carried over the emperor, any armorial bearings other than those of Charles, as everything was entirely designed for that prince. As to the designs for the theaters, the King found them good, but he wished everything concerning the emperor to be on the right;

and also, that since on one of these designs there was a salamander, which might indicate his own person, he wished the salamander removed and replaced by the double-headed eagle of the Habsburgs; and they were to ask if the eagle should be crowned.

"The alderman proposed that some people should recite aloud verses in the emperor's honor when he was passing. The king ordered that the verses should be put on large and legible inscriptions, instead of being recited, for that would be comical he said, and the emperor would not stop to listen to them."[14]

The alderman executed every detail of what had been prescribed. He had all the streets paved on which the official procession would pass, and had the paving removed from the street of St.-Antoine for the arrangement there of the lists, then again hurriedly repaved, as they had meantime changed their minds and the combats would now take place at the Louvre. For two months, goldsmiths, painters, sculptors, carpenters, cabinetmakers—in short all the artisan guilds—worked night and day to prepare for the solemn entry, which took place the following New Year's Day, on a fine winter morning with the sun shining in special favor, if the stanza composed for the occasion is to be believed:

> When Paris, Caesar, it
>   pleased you to see,
> And the town for you
>   wore its finery,
> The next day before,
>   the rain began,
> But the morrow it
>   was bright again.
> For such a favor,
>   Caesar, to you,
> No special credit to
>   Heaven is due,
> For Heaven, as though
>   by destiny,
> Favorable is wont to be.[15]

"The emperor was mounted on a fine jet black horse, dressed in a little cloak of black cloth and wearing a black felt hat, because he was in mourning for his wife.

"Arrived at the gate of St.-Antoine, he was urged and begged by the gentlemen of the town to take his place under the fine canopy, which he did not wish to agree to, saying that this was a prerogative only of the king; but in the end he accepted. When he was at the Baudoyer Gate, he halted to watch a beautiful play which was taking place there on a large scaffold. There could be seen a fine park, called the French Park, filled with beautiful lilies and other lovely flowers, where a fountain was playing. At the extremities of this park were two gates, one well closed and locked, called the Gate of War, and the other open, named the Gate of Peace, from out of which came a lovely nymph and celestial lady named Alliance, who entered this French Park; and in the middle of the park was a great sheep with a golden fleece, who carried these words written: 'I will depart in peace, for thou art with me,' and not far from it the noble lord St.-Michel, who also bore in writing: 'I will guard thee in all thy ways.'

"After having viewed all this, the emperor crossed the bridge of Notre-Dame, all covered with ivy leaves, coats of arms, and candelabra. He went to Notre-Dame and from there to the palace, where he was feted."[16]

The banquet was sumptuous, served in the great hall of the palace, which had been hung with silk and gold, with the arms and mottoes of the emperor, and of the king and the queen:

"The emperor was seated at the upper end of the table and the king near him, on his left. And below were seated my lords the dauphin and the Duke d'Orléans, Monseigneur the Papal Legate, the King of Navarre, my lords the Cardinals of Bourbon and Lorraine, the Duke de Vendôme, the Duke de Lorraine, and other princes.

"The Constable and Grand Master of France served as major-domo; my lord of Enghien, brother of my lord of Vendôme, served as carving equerry; the Count of Aumale, son of my lord of Guise, served the bread; my lord Charles de Bourbon, Prince de la Roche-sur-yon, served as cupbearer. And the banquet over, the presentation of a silver-gilt vase, richly made and adorned, weighing seventy marks, was announced by Normandie, French King-at-Arms, for the Most High, Most Puissant, Most Illustrious and Most Magnanimous Prince Charles. . . .

"After the supper came several princes and lords in masks, all dressed in cloth of gold and embroideries, who did Moorish dances and other diversions, the most brilliant imaginable."[17]

The second day of January, the emperor visited the Sainte Chapelle. On the fourth, the town presented to him the famous Hercules. The days following were passed in feasting, jousts, and tourneys. Then, by way of Chantilly where the Constable de Montmorency received him, the emperor went to Flanders without further delay. There, other pastimes, far less agreeable, awaited him. Who better could eulogize the hope of peace brought to the people by this journey, than the court poet Clément Marot, whose post obliged him to put the various happenings of royalty's life into verse?

He composed on this occasion a fine ode:

Caesar it was who once o'ercame the Gauls.
Honored by the world, but he's more honored yet
By these same Gauls, for Caesar's now returned
Surrounded by no warrior legions, but
By love and life itself; bearing for arms
The black crowned eagle; with no sword in hand,
But olive branches. Francis and he come straight
From banks of Loire to Seine, Paris to see,
Leading war captive with them, which was wont
To sow discord between them. Now the one
Passes this way, by need to see this land
Sans fear or fainting; and the other one,
His heart too high to countenance deception,
Gives him the right to hold command in France.
If there is any doubt to be disputed,
It's which of them deserves the greater merit,
Or Caesar for his splendid confidence,
Or Francis for his deep fidelity.
O Kings, by more than kin united,
Happy the man who lived to see this day
Of your firm union, that shall keep the world at rest.
Come then, O Caesar! bring perpetual peace,
Between your men and ours. Paris lift high your gates,
To let the greatest Christian enter in.[18]

NOTES

VI · At the King's Court

1. "*Avis donne par Catherine de Médicis à Charles IX pour la police de sa Cour et pour le gouvernement de son Etat*," Bibliothèque Nationale, collection Dupuy No. 218. Ed. Cimber and Danjou, *op. cit.*, t. V, pp. 246–47.
2. Budé, G. *Traité de la vénerie, traduit de latin en français par Loys le Roy, dit Regius*. . . . Ed. H. Chevreul. Paris, 1861, p. 1.
3. Castiglione, Baldesar, *op. cit.*, p. 38.
4. Budé, G., *op. cit.*, pp. 11–13.
5. *Ibid.*, pp. 18–23.
6. Florange, M. *Mémoires du maréchal de Florange, dit le Jeune Adventureux*. Eds. R. Goubaux and P. Lemoine. Paris, 1913, t. I, pp. 225–26.
7. Marguerite of Navarre. *Heptaméron*. Ed. M. François. Paris, 1950, pp. 242–47.
8. Erasmus, Desiderius. *Eloge de la folie*, translated by P. de Nolhac. Paris, n.d., p. 73.
9. Brantôme, Pierre de Bourdeilles, abbé de, *op. cit.*, t. II, pp. 244 seq.
10. "*Mémoires sur la vie du maréchal de Vieilleville par Vincent Carloix, son secrétaire*," Ed. J. Buchon, *op. cit.*, t. IX, pp. 432–34.
11. *Ibid.*, pp. 435–36.
12. Dan, R. P., *op. cit.*, t. III, p. 219.
13. "Registres du Bureau de l'Hôtel de Ville de Paris," Archives Nationales. Ed. Cimber and Danjou, *op. cit.*, t. III, p. 219.
14. *Ibid.*
15. Corrozet, G., and Dupré, J. *L'ordre tenu et gardé à l'entrée de très haut et très puissant prince Charles, empereur toujours auguste en la ville de Paris, capitale du royaume de France*. Paris, 1539.
16. "Registres du Bureau de L'Hôtel de Ville de Paris," *loc. cit.*
17. Corrozet, G., and Dupré, J., *op. cit.*
18. Marot, Clement. "Sur l'entrée de l'empereur à Paris, 1540," in *Oeuvres complètes*. Paris, 1824, t. II, 14th canticle.

PART THREE

OF HIS MAJESTY, THE MOST LOYAL SUBJECTS

VII · The Gentleman of the Renaissance

NOT all the nobles of Francis I, as has been observed, resided at court. The perfect courtier constituted a minority of his class, and the king's innovations did not reach into the ancient, and unchanging, depths of rustic France.

The greater part of the population of France, whether noble or commoner, lived in the country districts which were the repository of ancient tradition. The sufferings of the Hundred Years' War had long been forgotten; the religious wars and their train of horror were still in the future. The breathing space between the two cataclysms permitted the countryside to benefit from those major developments which resulted from a happy union between regained material prosperity and a harmony between man, his environment, and the conditions of his existence. In the rhythm of sun and seasons, masters and laborers alike led a simple, industrious life, in peace and in profound agreement with nature. After the sowing came the harvest, after the hay came the grapes; laughter echoed in the long evenings and feasting erased the memory of the cold of winter and the cares of yesteryear. Those were, in fact, the proverbial Good Old Days, that happy epoch whose successive delights satisfied the dreams of rising at dawn, the open-air life, a satisfying physical weariness, and the pleasures of the fields.

Such days begin in the sixteenth century, in the shadow of country manor houses, when the hunting horn sounds the chase, and when, on St. Samson's morning, the Master and Pierrot, with a fine spray of roses pinned to his red cap, walk together toward the church; while the wheat winnowers fill the breeze with scents which rival those of violet and lily and, in the midday heat, the mower, stripped to the waist, cuts the ripe ears.

Over that countryside reigned, paternal and all powerful, a nobility no longer wholly feudal but one which the king had not yet domesticated. In this privileged time, a balance was established between the rugged individualism of the Middle Ages and the absolutism of the final stages of the French monarchy, and it was that balance which gave the upper class its particular character. It was certainly a warrior nobility, whose wholehearted devotion to the king, coupled with a lively taste for fighting, made them quick to join the royal colors at every opportunity. It was a landed nobility, too, profoundly attached to the good earth of their fathers, to which they always returned. And it was a nobility which hated the town, that new entity constituted yesterday at their expense, where the bourgeoisie treated them as interlopers or even enemies. Similarly no love was lost between this country nobility and the court, of which they went in awe and which, when their services were called upon, cost them dear.

The nobility was, then, for the most part, composed of that type of man whom later generations were to refer to as the "country gentleman." He was to be found bright-eyed, cheerful-faced, wearing a large felt hat, big boots and a dagger at his belt, striding with assured step over the land which his ancestors had bequeathed to him at the cost of many a sword thrust. Deep affection bound him to his "country house," the only domain where he was unquestioned master, and he was strong in the privilege which his birth had conferred on him: a rich master, whom a farm income and the variety of rents due to his rank had endowed with ample sustenance. Convinced of his rights, as of his duties, he conscientiously administered those lands, which the king's peace allowed him to do profitably, aided by a work force which a recent rise in the population had rendered numerous and therefore cheap. In contemporary texts, his cheerful silhouette may be glimpsed; it is almost always that of a gay, bustling man, content with life, careful of his own goods and of those of his people, always ready for a laugh or a fight. It was, for him, a golden age. But it would last only a few decades. The end of the century would see it away in a storm of war.

THE COUNTRY HOUSE

The country gentleman did not live in the splendor of such houses as Villandry, or Ussé, nor even more modestly in a Montal or a Trécesson. His country house, described so well by Charles Estienne, is to be found —with few variations, with a few different moldings here and there— all over France. It is the Mesnil-au-Val of Gilles de Gouberville, deep in the Cotentin; the Hérissaie of Noël du Fail, near Montfort in Brittany; Ozillac in Saintonge, fief of François de Reilhac; or Romaneaux in Vivarais, the seat of the Lermusières family. Its site was chosen with care, "On the shoulder of a slope, of a small hill or of some bump of land if the country is undulating or mountainous, for by this means, its owner freely enjoys the air and the fine view, is protected from the mists, is not chilled through in winter by the frost, nor overheated in summer, and the foundations of his house are not undermined by torrents and erosion. The principal outlook is on the east, for the east winds of

March and September are dry and warm rather than cold, but very healthy for a man's body and spirit, and the sun's warmth, which comes into the house in the morning, is most beneficent; and in addition the more easterly a house faces, the better it is for a breeze in summer, and the less it suffers from storms and frosts in winter."[1]

The master's house was built at the far side of a large square courtyard, enclosed by walls sufficiently thick and high to protect against marauders:

"Access to it is by a flight of not more than eight steps, which lead to the first floor and give onto a passage of medium width, with access to the garden, where there is an identical flight going down. On the right of this passage are the kitchen, pantry, larder, and rooms for two or three servants. Between the kitchen and pantry is a spiral staircase with its entrance in the kitchen that leads to the attics. Near the kitchen are the presses and laundries. The first floor is carried, both in length and width, on vaulting over the ground floor, supported firmly on pillars, and well ventilated on both sides, so there is a floor of the same length and width below as above, which is part storeroom and part cellar. This, besides protecting the house from earthquakes, serves to house the wines and ciders, without risk of the hoops rotting, the bacon, salt meats, oils, candles, even the wood and fruit during frosts. The dwelling is one story high; above are only garrets and attics, nothing else; so the house is lower and less exposed to the fury of the winds, which is marvelously economical as the tilers do not have to be called in constantly.

"On the left side of the same passage is the entrance to the quarters of the master of the house, from which there is access to his bedroom, and thence to his wardrobe and closet; and at the end, if the house is spacious enough, there is a bedroom for lodging guests, which is entered by a spiral staircase from the side of the courtyard, so that the guests can come and go freely. The gentleman has his principal outlook and windows on the east side overlooking the garden, and keeps only half lights onto the court to be able to see his men and to know who comes and goes from the house. At each extremity is a privy for the needs of each of the two sides of the house. The roof and the part above the passages, hall, bedroom, wardrobe, and guest room are granaries, which serve to house separately the rye, wheat, and fruit, and for storing the dirty linen; they have little windows on the side of the north wind, for this part of the sky is the coldest and the least humid, both of which are excellent for keeping the wheat and preserving it for a long time.

"Beyond the presses and laundries are the chicken houses and cover for other fowl, in the form of a rectangular tower, longer than it is wide, so that the bottom serves for the waterfowl, such as geese, and the upper part for the courtyard poultry, with their roosts and laying baskets; under the henhouse a separate place is made for the Indian cocks and hens, beneath the floor of which are lodged the pheasants in a latticed enclosure. As for the peacocks, they are left to roost where they will."[2]

Not far from the house of the head of the family, and enclosed in this same square courtyard, is the house of the farmer. The stables and various sheds, destined for agricultural equipment, are built at either side of the entrance gate.

The vegetable garden and the orchard, with its nursery, grafting beds and withy beds, are situated behind the house. They lead to a small paddock or pasturage, bordered by a little "verdant brook," its banks planted with willows, where the master of the place can be pictured enjoying himself on fine days in company with his wife and his numerous children, legitimate or not.

Not to be forgotten is the "false door (which is otherwise known as the back door, or field door) at the side of the paddock, for the master's use; it is decorated with two chevrons on an architrave, no more, and four or five crenellations above, and closed by a strong door, for in that way he enters his house and goes out secretly when he sees fit, without his people knowing, and without the bad smell of the stables and the great courtyard."

The man who lived in such a house loved the life that he led, a life of freedom in the open air, and Noël du Fail's lively pen has left many a description of him. A country gentleman himself, and a writer as well, he has sung in his *Propos rustiques* the praises of this rural existence, which his peers held unexpressed deep in their hearts:

"But . . . do you think it a small thing that in the morning, scratching your back and stretching your sinewy and muscled arms, after listening to your clock, which is your rooster—more reliable than those of town—you rise without complaining about your stomach or your head, as anyone would do who was drunk the night before . . . ? Then, binding the yoke on your oxen, so accustomed to it that they almost do it for themselves, you go out into the fields singing at the top of your voice, exercising your healthy stomach, unafraid of waking either your master or madame. And there you have for company a thousand birds; some are in full song, perched on the hedge and others following your plow and showing you their friendly familiarity, by feeding on the worms which come out of the freshly turned earth. Others by flitting here and there show where there is a fox . . . or they show you what the weather will be. Thus the gloomy heron, motionless at the water's edge, signifies the approach of winter; the swallow skimming the water predicts rain; and flying high, fine weather. The jay, going to roost earlier than usual, feels winter's approach. The cranes, flying high, announce fine and serene weather. The green woodpecker never fails to sing before rain. When the little owl hoots during rain it signifies fine clear weather. When the hens do not retreat undercover from the rain, it will surely continue. The geese and ducks diving constantly in the water feel the coming rain; when the frogs croak more than usual it signifies the same, or when old walls exude moisture. A serene autumn foretells winter winds. Thunder in the morning signifies wind; at midday, rain. The sheep running hither and thither feel winter coming.

"On other occasions, to leave this subject which you know all too well, with your pruning hook on your shoulder and billhook bravely tucked into your belt, you make the round of the fields to see that the horses, cows, or pigs have not got in, and immediately to stop quickly a new gap with thorns; and there you pick some apples and pears at your leisure, prodding first one, then another; and those not worth eating you take to sell in town, and with the money they bring you get a fine red cap or a black jacket lined with green. At other times, in the morning, seeing which way the wind is blowing, you go to look over the traps you had set the day before for foxes, who steal your hens or geese, or sometimes —the wicked creatures—the tender lambs, unconcerned by the chill air, the autumn fever or the dog days; but at those times, fraught with danger for others, you go barefooted in the fields, binding a wheat sheaf or cleaning out a ditch, and thus you grow strong, robust, and joyous, doubly so as the townsfolk, who care only for indulgence. . . . That is why a good captain likes an old soldier brought up during his early years in the fields. . . . So if you fall ill with some sickness, as is natural, you do not look for clysters, purgatives, bloodletting, or other such nonsense; for you have the remedy right in your garden, of good herbs, whose virtues are handed down from father to son. What more can I tell you, my children? I think there lacks nothing there for your complete happiness but the love of the Great Shepherd, and may He incite you to acquire it by virtuous deeds which the good and fruitful teachings of our priest suggest. And I shall pray Him, the great keeper of our flocks, that He may accord you the grace not to wander from the path given to us poor travelers, and, recommending myself to your good graces, I beg you to take all this in good part."[3]

The main occupation of the gentleman was making the most of things. A well-planned general cultivation took care of all his needs. Besides the vegetables from his kitchen garden and the fruits from his orchard, there were his fields of cereals, if he was north of the Loire, and if south of it then vineyards and livestock everywhere—horses, and cattle, without counting the big droves of goats and pigs, which, all together, roamed at liberty through the fields and woods. The good management of a domain of average size absorbed the greater part of the landowner's time; directing and supervising a numerous staff, collecting the rents and disposing of surplus production constituted the principal activities of this profession, which he preferred to every other. He agreed with the choice of Eutrapel, the hero of the *Contes* of Noël du Fail, who, when weary of the deceptive attractions of the town, tells his friends he wants to retreat to his country house and sketches out for them the life which awaits him there in a picture where may easily be recognized the life of every noble countryman worthy of the name:

"I take leave of you, said Eutrapel. . . . I am retreating to my country house, which I have prepared over these years, and made of it a true dwelling place of philosophy and rest, at the entrance and front gate of which Janvier, the gentle mason from St.-Erblon, has carved the words: *Inveni portum: spes et fortuna, valete* (I have reached harbor: hope and fortune, farewell). I have built it averagely strong—to hold my own against thieves, vagrants, and the enemy, if God wished to punish me that way—on the strength of some little streams which are around, with the enclosure, woods, garden, and orchard. In the orchard you'll find me at work with my billhook and pruning hook, my sleeves rolled back, cutting, trimming, and pruning my young bushes according as the moon, which works more or less on these lower bodies, dictates. In the garden, creating order according to my plan, straightening up the square of the paths, training this way and that the flowers and roots or, what is better, making extracts from them and turning them into rich liqueur; and getting mad with the moles and voles which do me so much harm, and sowing various and strange seeds; mixing and blending the warm earth with the cold, watering the dry parts, forcing the late fruits, and controlling by knowing tricks, commonly ignored, the effects and results of nature. In the woods, I am deepening my ditches, aligning my walks, and meanwhile listening to a hundred bird songs and getting my workmen to recount a raft of rustic tales. By the streams, amused and solitary on the bank, I fish with a line, often stretching out my arm to ascertain from the line's movement what kind of fish are nibbling at the bait; or setting out nets and traps in those places where the flow of the water gives the best run. Sometimes too, with a leash of greyhounds and eight running dogs, I shall be out hunting foxes, roebuck, or hares, without knocking down or damaging the laborers' wheat, as do some breakers of the law and common justice. I tell you that after such a division and distribution of my time, having first prayed Almighty God that the day may pass without offense to him or my neighbor and having spent the odd hour reading books, at supper, which should be more copious and abundant than dinner, I do not need any Athiac sauces, or the brews of Aeschylus to make me sleep.

"Farewell then, sir; here on this peg I hang my little plumed hat, my big hooded cape, my padded doublet, my sidling and swaggering gait, the hand-kissing, bravado, forced laughter, treacherous greetings, jealousies, envys, thievery of the goods, and advantages and honors of others, quarrels, love, and such constitutions and mortgage interests in which there are dealing and common traffic in court and town alike. I am quite lost; my nature, which was good, is all changed and altered, my conscience too is obliged to a false liberty, which ruins and destroys the greater part of men. I shall make, since the malice of the living would have it so, a present of my pants to great Jupiter Ammon, as the lackey did to Buridan, his master. (Buridan, a gentleman of our part of the world, but a terrible liar if ever there was one, gave a pair of pants to his lackey, on condition that, when called as witness of his tales, he would boldly tell that what his master said was true, and, if need be, swear to it. But on one occasion when Buridan was presiding at the table, and lying like a president, the lackey could not bring himself to acquiesce in these fearful lies, and, taking off his pants very frankly, put them on the end of the table, saying as he burst into tears: 'Sir, take back your pants, I can't bear them any longer.') So, Sir Polygamy, here are the keys; I am wasting away in your courts and towns, where nothing is pure nor anything like it. Your laws, policies, and all that is dealt and done there, are double-faced and tainted, and the good and the wise know nothing of them."[4]

In the profession of landowner described by Noël du Fail there is no improvisation. Much knowledge and even more experience are needed to make the best of it. There are numerous volumes designed for the cultivator, in which he can find precious advice, such as the celebrated work of Charles Estienne and Jean Liébaut entitled *L'Agriculture et la maison rustique*,[5] a veritable encyclopedia of what every agriculturalist should know. The country gentleman will there learn how to make the best use of his farmer's time, according to the months and seasons: "So that his men may not remain idle, and may not lose a moment without being devoted to some useful work, he should have what is to be done in every month and time of year at his fingertips."

The month of January is devoted to woodcutting, trimming the trees and the vines, working the land which was not worked in October, and getting the agricultural equipment into condition.

In February, the laborer prepares the ground to receive the seed, takes a look at the wines, and looks after the livestock: "He will clean out the dovecote, the henhouse, and the shelter of the peacocks and geese, because these birds, at the end of the month, begin to get hot and broody. He will visit the warren to restock and mend the earths. He will buy some bees, clean out their hives carefully, and kill the drones. He will buy some falcons, sparrow hawks, and other birds of prey, which, at the end of this month, he will put in the mews."

In March he sows. With the return of fine weather, he has not a moment to lose if the patient toil of winter is to bear fruit:

"In April, about St. George's day, the farmer will bring out into the open the lemon and orange trees, and all the other trees which have been under cover since Martinmas, and he will dig around the foot of each one, taking out the surface roots and the excess branches, not allowing even one branch to cross another, either sideways or upward. He will plant olive trees, pomegranates, lemons, and myrtles. He will graft the figs, chestnuts, cherry, and orange trees. He will prune the new growth of vines, because at that season it can bear the pruning more easily. He will be careful to feed the pigeons, which at that season find little in the fields. He will mate the horses, the donkeys, and the sheep.

"In May he will water the newly planted trees, he will shear the sheep, will collect a great quantity of butter and make a lot of cheese; he will castrate the calves, and will begin to take care of the bees and the silkworms, of which he will collect a good number. He will weed the wheat, cultivate the vineyards for the second time. He will pollard the excess branches of the trees, and graft the olives which need budding.

"In June he will prepare the threshing floor, and will have it well cleaned of all filth; he will mow the meadows, harvest the barley, clip the vines, and thresh some seed wheat to sow in the sowing season.

"In July he will harvest the wheat and the vegetable seeds, he will pick from the apple and pear trees the bad apples and pears and those which weigh down the tree, will manure the vines for the second time, and root out the bent-grass commonly known as dog-tooth, and will cut wood for heating around the year.

"In August, he will pull the flax and the hemp, will gather the fruit from the tops of the trees to make a reserve, will take off the leaves round the late ripening grapes, so that they will receive more heat from the sun; he will make the verjuice, will dig the ground for a well, or find a spring of water, if he needs one. He will remember to prepare his barrels and other things needed for the vintage.

"In September he will give the final touch to his unsown plowing, and will sow his wheat, rye-wheat mixture, rye, and other, similar grains, he will harvest the grapes, knock down the walnuts, mow the late meadows to have the aftermath, collect the straw for the roof of his stables, and for heating the oven around the year; will cut the twigs of the madder and collect the seed for sowing the following March; he will gather the leaves of the pastel [a plant formerly esteemed for yielding a blue dye] and dress them till they are reduced to a ball and will dry in the sun or by a moderate fire.

"In October, he will make his wine and put it in casks. He will bring in his orange and lemon trees under cover, against danger from the coming cold weather; he will make his honey and beeswax, and chase out the old bees.

"In November, he will put his wine in the cellar, collect acorns for feeding his pigs, will gather chestnuts and sweet chestnuts, and those fruits which will keep from his garden; he will lift the turnips from the ground, taking the leaves off and putting them in sand to protect them from frost; he will wrap his artichokes and cover them well so that the frost does not get to them; he will press the oil; he will make the beehives, baskets, flat baskets and wicker baskets of osiers."

What activities still present themselves for the conscientious farmer during the month of December, but to watch over his fields, exposed to the vicissitudes of the winter? And when the heavy rains, ice, and snow keep him at his fireside, "he will make a myriad little wooden implements such as ladles, trenchers, bobbins, tubs, bowls and other things for the household, also harrows, rakes, and handles for his tools."

The country gentleman, concerned for the best yield from his lands, will take careful account of the time of year and state of the weather before beginning the sowing, for sowing cannot be done at just any time or haphazardly. The vegetable world obeys very stringent rules, which are better not transgressed if good harvests are desired. These are listed in "Tables (pages 152 and 153) for knowing the time when several kinds of seeds may be sown,"[6] to which the gentleman will profitably refer.

* * *

The county gentleman, ranked first in his own domain, was associated with local administration by the sovereign, and was also the first in his village. If he did not abuse this situation, which could rarely be reproached him, he enjoyed general respect. To his farmers and laborers he was "our master," ready to offer, to whoever asked him, judicious advice, small or great services, and medical aid of all kinds. To him were owed, but in a decreasing degree, various duties: rents in cash or kind for the use of the oven, of the press, and of the mill, which he alone possessed, or for the passage of wagons across his lands. Finally, he collected a certain percentage on the sales effected within his fief. It also fell to his lot to check the state of health of the cattle sent for human consumption, to tax commodities when the common interest demanded, and above all to mete out justice. This roster of activities in itself justified the position held by the man who exercised them in his district. In fact, he owed his unquestioned authority to his unique privilege of bearing arms, which resulted in his being considered by the community as their natural protector. This was undoubtedly his greatest claim to glory. The moment the peace was disturbed, all turned to him. Unintellectual and simple in his tastes, living, in close contact with the people of his land, almost the same life as they, the master had no

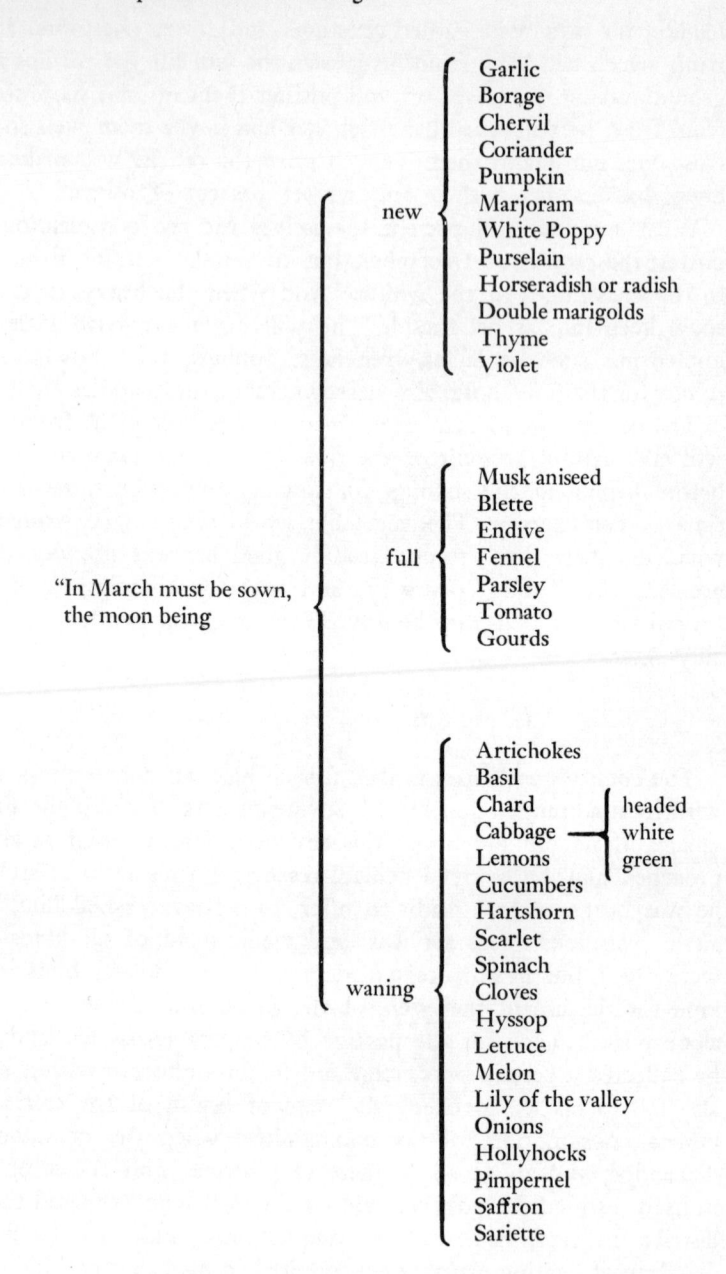

March is the special month for sowing:

"In March must be sown, the moon being

- new:
  - Garlic
  - Borage
  - Chervil
  - Coriander
  - Pumpkin
  - Marjoram
  - White Poppy
  - Purselain
  - Horseradish or radish
  - Double marigolds
  - Thyme
  - Violet

- full:
  - Musk aniseed
  - Blette
  - Endive
  - Fennel
  - Parsley
  - Tomato
  - Gourds

- waning:
  - Artichokes
  - Basil
  - Chard
  - Cabbage — headed / white / green
  - Lemons
  - Cucumbers
  - Hartshorn
  - Scarlet
  - Spinach
  - Cloves
  - Hyssop
  - Lettuce
  - Melon
  - Lily of the valley
  - Onions
  - Hollyhocks
  - Pimpernel
  - Saffron
  - Sariette

March is the special month for sowing:
"The plants coming from the sown seed can be transplanted in any season, excepting spinach, chervil and parsley, which are worth nothing if transplanted, unless the weather be damp or rainy; otherwise they must be watered after being transplanted.

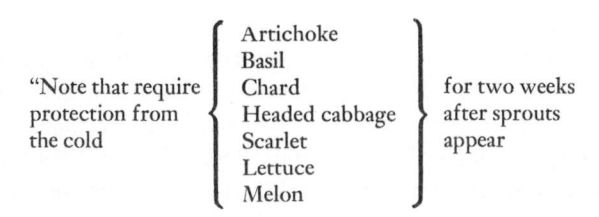

"Note that require protection from the cold { Artichoke, Basil, Chard, Headed cabbage, Scarlet, Lettuce, Melon } for two weeks after sprouts appear

"Note that the seeds do much better when they are sown on warm days which are neither hot nor cold, than on cold, hot or dry days.

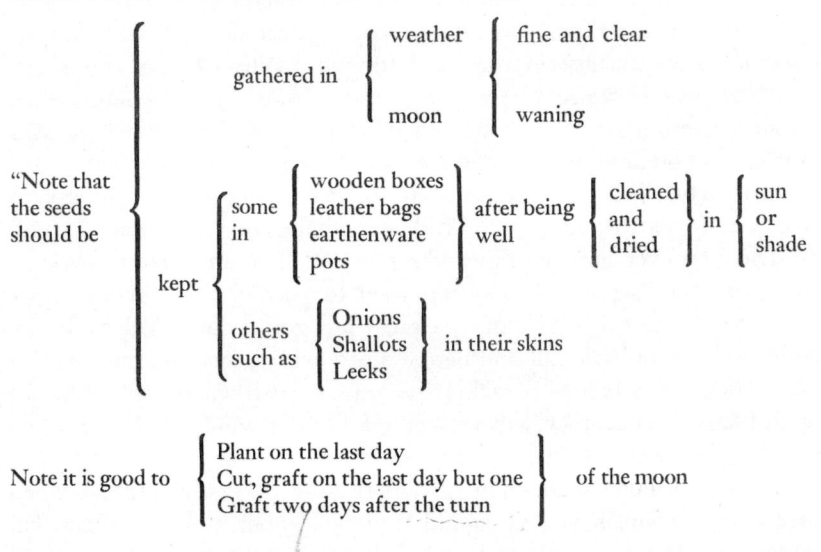

"Note that the seeds should be kept {
 gathered in { weather { fine and clear }, moon { waning } }
 some in { wooden boxes, leather bags, earthenware pots } after being well { cleaned and dried } in { sun or shade }
 others such as { Onions, Shallots, Leeks } in their skins
}

Note it is good to { Plant on the last day, Cut, graft on the last day but one, Graft two days after the turn } of the moon need to go to the town to find diversions which were on his doorstep. He liked to share his leisure with the people of his village, for whom he felt no contempt. If literature depicts the peasant in a somewhat unflattering light, it must be remembered that the portrait often comes from the pen of a townsman, such as Bonaventure des Periers, footman to the Queen of Navarre:

"Take the case where you are on a journey and it is cold and bad weather; in short, you are in a bad temper about something or other and, as luck would have it, you don't know the way; you call out to a Poitevin some distance away, who is working a field; you begin to ask him: 'Ho! there! my friend, which is the road for Parthenay?' The ox goad, although he hears you, does not hurry to reply, but he addresses his oxen: 'Garea, Fremantin, Brichet, Castin, come on after me, you are making a nice clopity-clop!' This he says to his beasts; and he lets you shout two or three times, good and loud. Then, when he sees that you are annoyed and would like to ride straight at him, he whistles at his oxen to stop them, and says to you: 'What do you say?' But he is much more graceful in the local tongue: 'Wha-at d'yo sa-ay?' So you think this is really pleasant, after you have waited a long while and gotten into a sweat, and shouted fit to burst, that this cowherd asks what it was you said; well, so you have to say it again: 'Where is the road for Parthenay? Tell me!' 'Did you say, to Parthenay, sir?' he will say to you. 'Yes, to Parthenay . . . !' 'And, sir, where are you from?' he will say. Did you ever hear anything like that? 'Where am I from!—Which is the road for Parthenay?' 'Do you want to go there, sir? Well; come! come! have patience.' 'Yes, my friend, I am going there. Where is the road?' At that he will call another ox goad who is nearby, and says to him: 'Micha, this fellow is asking the way to Parthenay; isn't it down by this way?' The other will answer (if God is good): 'They tell me it's over that way.' While the two of them are there discussing your road, it's you alone who know if you're sane or crazy. Finally when these two Poitevins have had a good argument about it, one of them will say to you: 'When you come to a big divide, turn to the right and you keep straight ahead; you can't miss it.' And are you any the wiser?"[7]

There is nothing in common between the author of this satire and the country gentleman who loved his folk, took pleasure in their society, and lived with them on a familiar and, surprisingly enough, even an intimate, footing. Their diversions were the same as his, and they were many. First were field sports. Hunting, hawking, and fishing were necessities and at the same time favorite activities. The pursuit of vermin, wolves, foxes, and their cubs often inspired a general call on the village as a whole to organize drives, which always ended in good cheer and festivities. There was also game hunting, according to season and the mood of the day, of stags, boars, and badgers, or hares with greyhounds, and of coneys or rabbits with ferrets. Even feathered game were not exempt: flying for partridges with falcon tiercelets (male falcons which were a third, or a *tierce*, smaller than the female), taking larks with dragnet and mirror, and ringdoves in a very unusual way known as "clattering":

> Having said my piece and feeling quite gay,
> I invite my friends to put sadness away
> "Come! come! friends, I say; this evening,
> If you're ready, I'll take you clattering."
> . . .
> In the kitchen, hither and thither
> Everyone runs to find first whatever
> Will make a noise. One takes a kettle,
> Another a mortar of noisy metal,
> Another a drum, another a boiler,
> Another a fry pan, another runs to the barber
> To borrow a basin; in short, each brings
> To make a great noise, all sorts of things.
> . . .
> Once in the forest we begin to take
> The sounding instruments, forthwith to make
> Such a noise in the fields, the woods, in the sky,
> Which goes forth, that whoever hears it will say
> . . .
> In the woods around, some horrible hell,
> Has broken loose and come to dwell.
> . . .
> With such a clamor we take the road
> Where the ringdoves in the nearby wood
> Of hornbeam, oak, and willows roost,
> The chill night through.
> . . .
> Under the trees we redouble our clatter
> Soon the fire's alight, its bright rays scatter
> To aid the incontinent eye as it reached
> The great flock perching in the branches.
> The ringdoves watch, necks craned, and turning
> Immobile at the noise and bright flames burning,
> Which in an instant suddenly flare.
> Now the harquebus men begin to prepare,
> They attentively look at the tree to take stock
> Of the densest mass of the startled flock.
> Then suddenly sounds a volley of shots

Mixed with the clatter of pans and pots,
Which fill the woods with a horrible blare
While the small-shot ravage in the leafy air
Whatever they meet, and rain on our head
A hail of ringdoves; the rest, full of dread,
Stay still in the tree, or merely change place,
Fluttering about in the bright, clear rays,
Perching more in the light, on the first twig that offers.
Thus, better seen than before by the shooters,
Rest quite at ease, till they start to fall stricken
Tumbling topsy-turvy. One with a wing broken,
Another shot through the neck, another hit in the head,
Another falls stone dead.
Another beats its wings to die far from us
But it beats in vain. . . . While the branches above us
Empty of fat ringdoves. The volleys rage
Through nearby places, nor our bursts assuage.
With smell of powder and dead birds around
And noise, it seems a proud battleground.
So seeing nothing left at which to fire,
And all the damage done one could desire,
The clattering stops; then silence reigns around,
With the noise that's gone do all our ears resound.
We return to Beaujour in the breaking light,
To pass in sweet repose what's left of night.[8]

* * *

The chase, duties, family events, Sundays and feast days, Christmas with its recitals, morality and mystery plays, Shrovetide and Carnival with their masks, and the feasts of patron saints the year round, all offered excellent pretexts for joyous gatherings, in which the festive table and more or less vigorous games like tennis, quoits, bowls, skittles, or wrestling, attracted their partisans. Dancing too had its enthusiasts; indeed at this period it was a real passion.

When the first flowers appeared and the air was balmy and the grass tender, the time of village feasting came around again; and everyone came together, the lord taking the lead in the merrymaking. Contemporary accounts paint an agreeable picture of these gatherings:

"On feast days our fathers would sooner have died than not gathered all their folk at the house of some villager, for rest and recreation after the week's work. After a drink, they began to chatter freely about the state of the crops and to listen to each other's tales. Father Jean, the late priest of our parish, was at the head of the table, to give honor where honor is due, picking up the skirts of his cassock, a trifle pompous, reciting either the Magnificat of the day or giving some good teaching thereon, or conferring with the oldest of the married women, seated near him with her hood thrown back: and gladly they spoke about some herbs for fevers, colic or the grippe; at the lower end there was some Robin Goodfellow, like my crony Lubin there, telling how many late evenings had been spent spinning during the week, how he himself had been the best and had done I don't know how much more, or so he led the company to believe. He also told how his black colt had got away from him near the vineyard and galloped as far as Liboart's land. . . .

". . . The rest of the good fellows talked about the growing season, when it would be advisable to plant the leeks, when was the right season for hoeing the vines, for grafting, for pruning the walnut trees or chestnuts, and for making hoops for the barrels. Then someone of the village would produce a rebeck [a musical instrument with strings and bridge, derived from the oriental *rebab*] from under his coat, or a flute, on which he played with great skill, and so seduced were they by the gentle sound of his instrument, with a hautboy which was there to support him, that they were constrained forthwith, putting off their coats and smocks, to begin a dance. The old, to give example to the young, and to show they were not bored, had the first try, making two or three turns of the dance without kicking up their feet much or leaping about like the Maçonnais, which we could do very well. The young people then did their bit by tap dancing and leading the gallop, and there was not a man there that did not dance with all the girls, except Father Jean, who had to be pressed a little, saying 'Sir, wouldn't you care to dance?' And then, having played at refusing a little, he went to it and outdid them all, for he was fresh, and just a bit flirtatiously he made a turn with his old cronies; and this venerable priest said: 'Tut; tut; we never felt younger, we should take things as they come, and bad luck to anyone who halts.' And when the fumes of the wine began to fuddle the heads, some good Gallic lass would dance on the table, the benches, the boxes, first on one side and then the other. Then everyone did as he pleased. 'What!' asked Anselm then. 'These old folks kept up with the others?' —'Not so,' replied Master Huguet; but these good folk were warming themselves with a faggot of vine clippings, with their backs to the fire, watching and appraising the turns, saying: 'This one dances well; So-and-So's father was the best dancer of the country; such a one in former times used to challenge all the people of Vindelles to dance.' The dance ended, they again began to toast and drink high and wide: then after warming themselves up, if they felt like it, they went to look at some meadow or well-tended field. . . .

"Then they all went home, fresh and lively, and there began to tipple again freely, and when they had got to the point, and they had had it, down to the last notch of the belt, they began to sing louder than you ever heard: *Have you never seen Peronnelle? The wood of mourning. Who can tell? Sooth me, sweet lovely brunette. The little heart. Alas! My father married me off. When the English came. The pretty nightingale of the woods. On the Bridge of Avignon. My God, I come to Thee for succor. Hold my bread. Who wants milk? I feel affection, her reply*, and other songs, more popular than musical. After that, without stopping or pausing, they began to drink toasts again, till all were drunk. Then, as everyone was taking leave, someone invited the gathering for the following Sunday to the same banquet and like ceremonies, where he hoped to give them a good treat even if it cost him not a little. Safely home, the father of the family would inquire diligently, if he could remember to, how the oxen, the cows, the sheep, and the pigs had been tended, and how everyone was. For the rest, after taking off his coat, and already beginning to undress, he gave out the work for next day, as he thought best, and at this point the good fellow fell asleep on his knees."[9]

* * *

But with the winter season, the pleasures of the fields came to an end. What then was left to fill the long evenings? To read *Amadis*, to do the accounts, to write up one's journal? The master did not care for those pastimes. He preferred to gather his friends in his big kitchen, around a good fire of twigs, and stay there until it was time to go to bed, sipping his wine and gaily conversing. That is, if he did not visit Robin, his farmer, who was not one to beget melancholy:

"Gladly after supper, his stomach tight as a drum, Robin, tipsy as Patault, chattered with his back to the fire. . . . Jeanne, his wife, spinning on the other side, kept up the conversation; the rest of the family was each busy with his own work; some getting ready straps for their flails, others making harrow teeth, drying out cords for binding, if it proved possible, the axletree of the cart, broken by being overloaded, or fashioning a whip from medlar wood. And when they were all occupied with their different work, good Robin, having asked for silence, began the story of the stork, in the days when animals could talk, or how the fox stole the fish; how he got the wolf beaten by the washerwoman when he was teaching him to fish; how the dog and the cat went a long journey; about the lion, king of beasts, who made the donkey his lieutenant, and wished to be king of all; about the crow who lost his cheese by singing; about Melusine; about the werewolf; about

Annette's leather strap; about the stuffed monk; about the fairies, and how he often spoke familiarily with them, even in the evening going down the hollow road; and that he saw them dancing a round, near the fountain of Cormier, to the sound of a fine musical instrument covered in red leather as it appeared to him, for he was shortsighted as, since Vichot had beaten him with a trencher on his backside, his eyes had always wept. He said, continuing, that they came to see him, adding that they were tremendous gossips, and he would gladly have told them to shut up if he had dared. And if someone by chance fell asleep when he was telling these tall stories, to which I was audience so many times, Master Robin took a burning hempstalk at one end and blew through the other end into the nose of the sleeper, making a sign with his hand not to waken him. Then he said: 'God bless us! I had so much trouble learning them and here I am breaking my head setting it to work thinking, and now they don't even deign to listen to me!' And if they didn't laugh at this, the brave fellow broke wind three times, which amused them all, and then all laughed fit to bust. The good fellow, weary of storytelling, for he usually forgot where he was in his fables, asked Jeanne, his wife, for a little drink. The good woman, pot in hand, grudgingly in haste to go and get it, saying that he was always thirsty, and that she was convinced he had hot coals in his stomach, and that next time she would not go, and he could die of thirst before she would take a single step. 'I wish I had heard the wife at home answer me back like that,' said Pasquier then. 'I think that Martin my stick would come trotting out!' 'You're right,' said Robin, 'if I gave my wife a whack with a stick every time she swore at me, we would have been more than nineteen years without hearing a word from her.' But listen! As she was telling him that it was always his way to send her to fetch him something to drink, and that he never thought to send anyone else, Robin, not wishing to cross her, said that it mattered little to him, so long as he had a drink, and he tried to soothe her down; he told her that he seldom asked her for a drink, that it was once in a hundred times, and once is not a habit; and if she always wanted to rebuke him, he would rather go and drink down at the stream, praying her with clasped hands that she would not make him beg like that, or that, on his faith, he would go next day to the miller's wife, who kept a tavern at Noyal, and that he'd just as soon be who-knows-where. To which she replied that that did not worry her, and that was what he did anyway; but she begged him at least not to beat her when he was drunk, as he made a habit of doing, and that she was surprised he was not ashamed. 'On my life!' said Robin, seeing he could not by force get the better of her, 'I would rather be in hell, my Jeanne. Whom God would help, his wife dies. Get along, my good girl, and may the best of devils break your neck. I assure you, I would rather eat a cartload of hay and die than suffer like this!' The good woman, looking sour . . . picked up her skirts to go and draw the wine, protesting that she would draw from that next the wall, and she would not pretend to fill it, because Roulet Lambin, having come, asking to borrow a hatchet, would surely drink heartily. Coming back, she gave them the jug as though vexed; and they fell on it so heartily that not a fly could have drunk what was left. Seeing this, she said that if he had been an honest man he would at least have offered her a glass, though she would not have taken it, and that honest folk showed what they were; and that he should remember it, by God. Then, her hands on her hips and weeping, she began to swear like a trooper; at which poor Robin laughed aloud, saying that he well knew the character of this young woman, and that she was a woman through and through; that when she had been given her head, she became a devil in a cap and, worse still, that the devil had made the mold for her head and there was neither rhyme nor reason in anything she did; that to see a man with a horse's head is strange enough, but a woman without malice still more so: also that she wept to order, and that she really had a quarter of the moon in her head. But seeing she was beginning to win at words, he sent everybody to bed."[10]

In Poitou, family quarrels gave way to joyous talk, and the cronies, of whom a few had been to school, talked inexhaustibly of the most diverse subjects, punctuated by bursts of loud laughter. That evening they were discussing the tricks of the Mattois who were the denizens of a famous thieves' quarter of Paris:

"A lad from the Matte spoke not three weeks ago to a gentleman, a man of high rank, who well knew how to play the hautboy. He complained to him about the damage done throughout the country, by thoughtlessly cutting down all the oaks; and if he would believe him, there would be a profit of a hundred thousand crowns for him, by saving him more than half of his great woods which produced more than that, and that it was really a small thing; for, he told him, you make a error in having the female oaks cut as well as the males; the female oaks could bring and produce for you the same quantity again of female oaks, and you would have plenty for cutting. And to make him swallow the story, he asked this grand gentleman whether he had never heard say that there were three sorts of oaks, one called *Robur*, another *Quercus*, and the third *Ilex*, and that Theophrastus said that in each one of the three species there were both males and females, and that the male oaks were called sterile, and the females, fruitful. And so he promised to teach him to distinguish male and female in all these kinds. This gentleman, very happy to perpetuate his forest and to continue making money out of it, by means of the females which would be left standing and which would be fruitful, agreed on a price and firmly promised never to teach anyone else; for, the Mattois said to the gentleman, you would thus

Haymaking and woodcutting, Pierre de Crescens. Bibliothèque de l'Arsènal, Paris

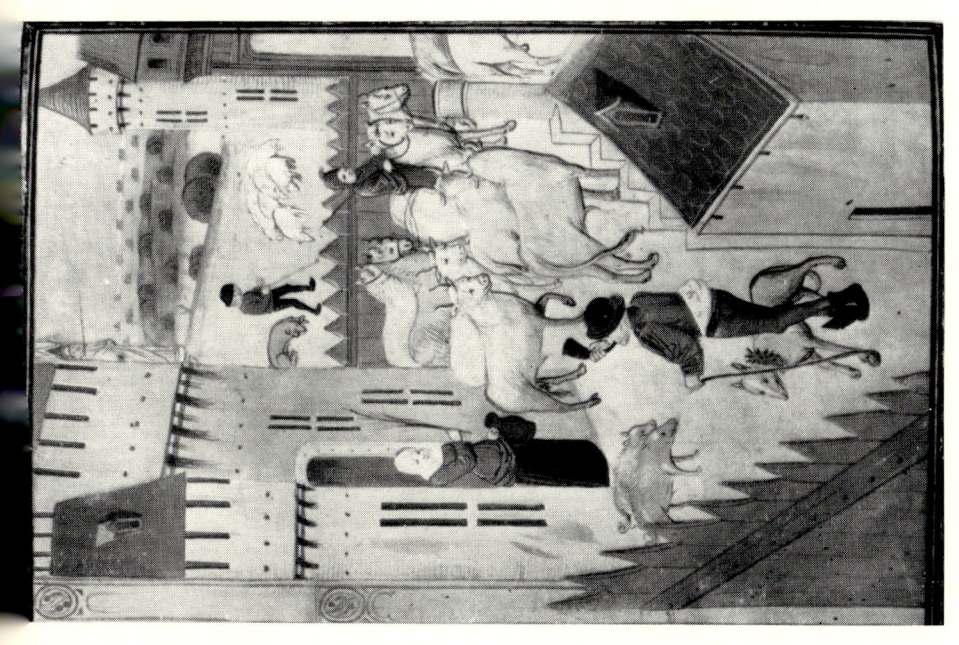

17. Taking out the flock in the morning, Pierre de Crescens. Bibliothèque de l'Arsènal, Paris

18. A tourney. From a sixteenth-century Book of Hours, British Museum

Springtime: weeding, hoeing and planting out. Contemporary engraving. Bibliothèque Nationale, Paris

Peasant dance. Engraving by C. Reverdy. Cabinet des Estampes, Bibliothèque Nationale, Paris

A good inn: in the foreground a woman holds a pot of *concoyotte*, a cheese set to warm under a woman's skirt. Detail from *Hiver* (Winter), after J. Stradanus. Cabinet d[es] Estampes, Bibliothèque Nationale, Paris

20.

Printing shop. Engraving after J. Stradanus. Bibliothèque Nationale, Paris take away my means of livelihood. Having received cash on account, the Mattois mounted the gentleman on his best horse, saying that he himself must go on foot, and that before nightfall they would both be tired out. No sooner had the two of them reached the forest than the Mattois made the gentleman dismount from his horse, and taking it from him, he himself mounted it. Then he showed him an oak tree, and told him: 'Monsieur, embrace that oak as tightly as you can,' which the gentleman did, hugging it with all his might with both arms; then the Mattois asked him: 'Sir did you not feel moved?' 'Absolutely not' answered the gentleman. 'Then it is a male,' said the Mattois. 'Let us leave it there, and mark it; there is nothing to risk in felling it, for it is a male.' 'But I see another there,' said the Mattois, 'with the big base and squat; I would certainly think that is a female; go and couple yourself to it, embrace it as you would your wife, and press it as closely as you can.' The gentleman having done what he had been told was questioned by the Mattois as before, whether he did not feel a tingling sensation in his flesh; and having said no, as before, the Mattois answered him: 'All the same, it is a female, if I am not mistaken; you do not embrace the oak firmly enough, nor long enough.' While the gentleman, paying great attention, was stuck against the thick trunk to find out whether it was male or female, the Mattois, on the opposite side, leaving the gentleman there, makes both himself and the horse disappear.

"Since we are speaking about the Mattois, says another gossip, one of them needed a pair of boots, and being in a hotel, had the idea of sending for a bootmaker, so as to be able to get a pair without money. Having tried them on, the Mattois said to the bootmaker that the boot on the left foot hurt him a little, and asked him to put it on the last for two or three hours. The bootmaker, leaving him with one boot on, took away the other; but the Mattois, having that boot taken off, straight away sent out to find another bootmaker, to whom he said, after trying on his boots, that the right foot seemed a little tighter than the other, and, having made a price, he had that boot taken off so that he could stretch it on the last till after dinner. What more could you want? Having two boots from the two bootmakers, one for the left foot, the other for the right, and giving his old boots to the stable boy, he paid his host, mounted his horse, and departed. Just afterwards, along came the two master bootmakers, each with a boot in his hand; and wondering if they had made a mistake, they looked at each other, and then began to laugh; and made their masters to write in the statutes of their guild that thenceforth it was forbidden to every qualified master bootmaker to leave one boot on a stranger and take away the other, either to dress it, or put it on the last, before being paid, under pain of losing one of the boots and seeing the other, which remained in their hands, confiscated and the money paid and applied to the guild funds. This confidence trick became known, for its author was well known for other offenses which he had done, being a magician, and using a candle made of human tallow, which when lighted rendered people immobile so that he took away their goods right in front of them, without their making any effort to stop him. Which he knew well how to without any candle, as you have heard."[11]

The people of the Matte used slang for the purpose of promoting the successful outcome of their activities. And if, in our own day in the same circles, such elegant expressions as "to have worms in one's sponge," or "sand in one's oysters" have a special meaning, those who use such expressions cannot claim to be innovators: "One of them, in the evening, waking up, will say: To prevent me being cheated by the Mattois who *'matt,'* I would like to understand their jargon and know their language, so that I could understand what the Mattois are saying, and the Bleches, the Contre-Porteurs, and the beggars of the hostelry, who all help one another, using the same jargon among themselves. And to show how that language is by no means a poor one, and that all its words have their meaning and that it can be compared to Hebrew, Greek, or Latin, I will tell you a few words of it:

"They call," he said, "a shirt: a 'file'; stockings: 'laces'; shoes: 'passers'; a cloak: a 'flyer'; straw: 'frisk'; earth: 'hard'; and they say: 'he slept on the frisk' or 'on the hard'; and he was 'lashed', that is hanged 'six feet from the hard'; a pig is a 'grunter'; lard and salt pork are 'squeal'; they call bread, 'burned'; 'burned bleeding' is shit; wine: 'drink'; 'pinky drink' is red wine; 'whitey drink' is white wine; *'pier'* is to drink; a pot is a 'little body'; he has *'pié* a little body' means he has drunk a pot of wine; *'pier ance'*, to drink water; when the wine is good, it is 'gourd'; a cup is a 'crown letter'; a barrel is a 'rusty'; a girl is a 'whirl' and in good slang one says 'plant a kiss on the whirl.' Night is 'the brown'; lashed is 'hanged'; if any of their companions have been hanged, they say he has been 'married,' and 'So-and-So has danced his wedding,' that is to say, he has been whipped; they call a crown a 'red piece'; a teston, a *'testard'*; a dozen: a 'round'; a half-farthing, a *'herpelu'*; a doubloon, a 'burned'; a penny, a 'thin'; change is 'marbles'; counterfeit money is 'shabby marbles'; to cut a purse, is 'to take a rat by the tail'; going to prison, the Mattois say: 'he got a rat by the tail'; if he has killed a man, they just say, 'he cut down an oak'; ears are *'ances'*; *'andré'* is a woman; *'ambier,'* which usually means to go, is 'to turn about,' and they will ask: 'where did the courrier go?' he will answer: 'I'm going around to the shack,' that is to say, to the house; fire is 'twigs,' to 'twig it' is to warm oneself; the 'courrier from the high mountain' is God; the 'curves' are the legs; the 'block,' the head; to 'shave the block' is to cut off the head; the 'saber,' the whip; *'andosse,'* the spine; 'he has had the saber on his *andosse'* is to say he has been flogged; the *'fouil-*

louse' is the bag; to 'sing' is to talk; I have 'sung to his *han*,' I talked to him; '*étrever*' is to understand; a 'bleater' is a sheep; a 'rapier' is a sword; 'flyers' are chickens, hens, and other birds; '*nouans*' are fish; 'to guzzle' is to eat; a hare, young hare or rabbit is a 'leggy'; 'hell' is the mill; the mule is the 'devil'; and they interpret thus when the miller says: 'the devil is taking me to his hell'; to prattle, is 'pavement'; '*andré* who walks on the pavement' is a woman who is going to prattle; '*bezarder*' is to die; 'he is *bezarde*' is to say, 'he is dead.' "[12]

Landed gentlemen laughed and amused themselves while these happy days lasted. But the "good old days" were nearly over. Soon, they would no longer be so happy in their houses, on the fields of their fathers, living at ease and in honor. Soon they would no longer hear, no longer see the lovely contours of their hills, the thick greenery of their woods or the roundabout of swifts in the pure skies of summer's evening. They would become insensible to the pleasures of the field, or to anything which was not of the court. The court was to uproot them and to rob them of the memory of the earth from which their race had sprung, and of the taste for liberty itself.

NOTES

VII · The Gentleman of the Renaissance

1. Estienne, C., and Liébaut, J. *L'Agriculture et la maison rustique de MM. Charles Estienne et Jean Liébaut, docteurs en medecine.* Lyons, 1538. Livre I, ch. V, f. 7.
2. *Ibid.*
3. Du Fail, Noël. *Propos rustiques, baliverneries, contes et discours d'Eutrapel par Noël Du Fail, seigneur de la Herissaye.* Ed. J. M. Guichard. Paris, 1842, pp. 39–41.
4. *Ibid.*, pp. 399–401.
5. Estienne, C., and Liébaut, J., *op. cit.*, livre I, ch. X, ff. 20–21.
6. *Ibid.*, ff. 12–13.
7. Des Périers, B. *Les contes ou les nouvelles récréations et joyeux devis de Bonaventure Des Périers.* Ed. Charles Nodier. Paris, 1841.
8. Gauchet, Claude. *Le plaisir des champs, avec la vénerie, volerie et pêcherie, poème en quatre parties.* Paris, 1869, p. 325.
9. Du Fail, Noël, *op. cit.*, pp. 34–36, 41–42.
10. *Ibid.*, pp. 43–46.
11. Gouchet, G. *Les Sérées de Guillaume Bouchet, sieur de Crocourt.* Ed. C. E. Roybet. Paris, 1873–82. t. III, pp. 124–26.
12. *Ibid.*, pp. 127–29.

VIII · Masters and Workmen of the Renaissance

AT THE time of the Renaissance, workers generally lived at the tempo of the artisan and were held to abide by very strict rules as set out in Etienne Boileau's *Book of Trades*. An exception, however, must be made of the newest of the trades of the Renaissance: printing. This industry of the mind had been born of recent technical advances, and it was the great invention of the century—discovered "by divine inspiration, unlike artillery which was by diabolical suggestion," as Rabelais observed. Its novelty consisted in its being the child of capital, and as such it inaugurated, as Henri Hauser has remarked, the future mechanical and capitalist organization of modern industry.

Printing, indeed, from the very start, required a considerable financial investment. Because of this, the poor apprentice, promoted a journeyman after five years of hard, laborious work and after completing his tour of France, could not, as he could in other trades, open a workshop in a room with the help of his small savings, and maintain it with the help of his wife, his children, and a single workman. A book has to be printed, illustrated, and bound; there must be paper, printing equipment, a press, type, engraved wood, binding materials; there must be considerable work space, and help which must be fed and paid. Five or six workmen were reckoned necessary to keep a press busy, with five or six presses required for a big publisher and three for an average one. Inventories made after death give an idea of the funds necessary for the purchase of materials. One such is that of a Parisian book printer of average size, Didier Maheu.[1] It was drawn up in April 1520, on the death of his wife, and valued 'as is,' that is to say, not new, at 351 Parisian pounds:

"Follows the printing press belonging to the said estate appraised by Jean Adam
– And firstly, the matrices of a missal letter, adorned with flourishes, of one point, with the two molds . . . . 24 l.p.
– The matrices of a gloss of Bourgoys adorned with large and small flourishes and two molds . . . . 20 l.p.
– A final letter, also adorned with flourishes and a mold . . . 8 l.p.

– A set of finial angels . . . .   8 s.p.
– A font of missal letters with gloss weighing two pounds or thereabouts . . . . 11 l.p.
– A font of gloss of Bourgoys weighing 104 pounds or thereabouts . . . . 21 l.p.
– Two old fonts in text and gloss of Bourgoys weighing 360 pounds or thereabouts . . . . 24 l.p.
– Two fonts of letters of Perrot weighing 360 pounds or thereabouts . . . . 24 l.p.
– Two fonts of letters of Perrot weighing 360 pounds . . . 24 l.p.
– A font of finial angel letters weighing 180 pounds or thereabouts . . . . 12 l.p.
– 150 pounds of material for making printed letters . . 10 l.p.
– Three presses furnished with iron frames, screwed, flat beds, screws, and bolts, all serving for the said presses . . . . 60 l.p.
– Twelve type cases, of which two large double and the others medium, with pairs of trestles . . . . 62 s.p.
– A dozen boards for moistening paper . . . . . . 20 s.p.
– Three frames of small vignettes of 16 pages . . . . 20 s.p.
– Sixscore squares and lancets of copper of various sorts and sizes with three alphabets, also in copper . . . . 16 l.p.

A master printer's text of the period gives most interesting information on the structure of the industry, the capitalistic nature of which here clearly appears:

"The art of printing is chiefly exercised by three categories of persons. The first is that of notable and rich merchants who have the means to create a large fund of deniers, which may be ten or even twenty thousand, for printing, at heavy cost, big and difficult works . . . they have always made it a primary duty to help in the advancement of printing . . . and derive honest profit from it.

"The second is the master printers, who possess as capital all sorts of Hebrew, Greek, or other characters, as well as the presses and materials necessary for the practice of printing. It is undeniable that in this kingdom even today there are the most expert master printers, and indeed the most excellent of all Christendom.

"The third category consists of journeymen, so dependent on one another that there have to be four, five, and sometimes six at each press, according whether the letters are big or small, and they can scarcely do anything without one another. Two of them are called printers, for their job is to work the press and to print the paper with that admirable ink which dries as soon as it is applied. The other journeymen necessary to make the press roll are called compositors, because their job consists in composing and collecting the characters into words, the words into lines, the lines into pages, and the pages into complete forms. It is an incredible thing to see that four or five journeymen, thanks to this most excellent art of printing, can do in a day the work of three or four thousand of the best scribes in the world.

"Also, the abovementioned three categories of persons have each done their duty so well that the leading merchants have furnished large sums of money, and the master printers have been so diligent to command, and the journeymen to obey, that this harmony has been the cause of the splendor and dignity of printing in this realm."[2]

In fact, from the historic date 1470, when the Rector Guillaume Fichet had had three German typographers come to Paris—Ulrich Gering of Constance, Michel Friburger of Colmar, and Martin Kranz of Steyn—to work the first printing press installed by his good offices in the Sorbonne, this art had made progress. Around the university and the Petit Pont were many workshops whose signs took on the color of the century: "At King David," "At the Four Elements," "At the Image of St.-Barbara and of the Knight of the Swan," all in the Rue St.-Jacques; "The Golden Sun" was in the Rue St.-Jean de Beauvais; "The Red Rose" in the Rue de la Parcheminerie; "The Silver Flask" in the Rue St.-Victor; "The Wild Woman" in the Rue des Carmes; "The Green Horse" in the Rue des Irlandais. Everyone knew "The Striped Donkey" at the corner of Place Maubert, "The Great Reeds," "The Unexcelled," "The Four Winds," or "The Red Apple" . . . The great dynasties of humanist printers, the Josse Bades, the Petits, the Vascosans, the Gryphes, and the illustrious Estiennes, published the great texts of classical antiquity with complete accuracy, and gave to the public typographic masterpieces which were worthy of the manuscripts, illuminated according to the norms of a centuries' old art, which they replaced. And so, during the first half of the sixteenth century, printing passed through a veritable golden age the echoes of which have reached to modern times:

"Since the great King Francis, first of this name, was declared Protector and Patron of all good letters, sciences, and disciplines, and he offered an outstanding salary to the most excellent men from the whole world, who wished to come to Paris with the most honorable title of Reader to so great a king, and make public profession of Hebrew, Arabic, Greek, and Latin letters, and of the seven liberal arts, it is almost impossible to describe what a great increase took place in the noble art of printing, almost immediately, throughout the kingdom and especially at Paris and Lyons. For, from about 1525 to 1550, there were printed there the great Bibles, and the works of the doctors of the Church such as St. Jerome, St. Ambrose, St. Augustin, St. John Chrysostom, and others, as well as the great lectures on civil and canon law by the doctors of one and the other law, and all the works which were longest in labor and greatest in cost. The Christian nations, even the most distant, beginning with Sweden, and turning toward Scotland and England, then Spain and Italy, and finally Germany and even the Kingdoms of Poland and Bohemia, in brief, all peoples, however distant, who valued good letters highly, came to France to obtain the works which were being printed there. And, according to the report of leading merchants who at that time made a great traffic in books, not a year passed without foreigners bringing into the kingdom a million in gold."[3]

But an economic crisis followed such prosperity. Prices went up, competition grew, and yet production and prices had to be maintained at the same level. How was it to be done? The rule is: let it be at the expense of the weakest. The workers were the cost factor in the operation, so the masters reduced the hired help and replaced the journeymen, whom they paid, by apprentices who cost nothing; they refused to put salaries on a sliding scale and demanded a longer working day. Opposing them there grew up a new race of men fashioned by printing: the typographical worker. Although the typographer was a manual laborer like others, he was also a man of letters to some extent. To compose his forms, he had to know how to read, and he had to be acquainted with elementary Latin. The new ideas which his art diffused awakened his intellect. What subject was more appropriate for the exercise of his reason than his condition, constantly becoming worse owing to the bad times? He was in revolt against the person whom he considered responsible, the master of the shop. To fight him, every means was legitimate, and the most effective means by far was the strike, generally considered a "modern" expedient.

The first such began in 1539 and lasted for three years—with the usual consequences: work stoppage, unemployment, and misery. Despite such inconveniences, strikes remained endemic until the end of the century, and attempts by the crown to re-establish order by ordinance were as numerous as they were ineffectual. In 1571, the king had published the famous Edict of Gaillon, in a tone which called forth the typographers' indignation. They protested before the Court of Parliament in a violent pamphlet entitled: "Complaints and Memoranda for the Journeymen Printers of Paris and Lyons versus the Booksellers, Master Printers of the said places, and their assistants."[4] The masters replied by a "Plea for the Reform of Printing."[5] These pamphlets furnish us with the complaints of both parties.

In the first place the journeymen typographers accused the master printers of enriching themselves at their expense and of demanding oppressive labor from them for a mere pittance:

"If it has ever been seen in any condition or profession that the masters try by innumerable means to subjugate, subordinate, and treat with all harshness and servitude the journeymen and servants who are under their orders, this has been practiced in all times, and is today, in the printing business. The booksellers and master printers—notably those of the town of Lyons—have always done everything, openly and by underhanded means, to oppress and vilely enslave the journeymen, who are nevertheless necessary members of the most great and excellent work of printing; thus they seize an authority that is more than tyrannic, with extreme contempt and the greatest avarice toward the said journeymen. Do they forget that they have brought them and daily bring them great and honorable riches, at the price of their sweat, their admirable zeal, and even their blood? For if these miserable people survive the extreme fatigues of such a hard profession, burdened with their wives and children, they carry forward to their old age for all rent and recompense nothing but poverty, gout, and other sicknesses caused by the incredible work which they are constrained to endure. Anyone has been able to see, both in France and abroad, only too many examples of poor journeymen reduced after long servitude to calamitous and unworthy indigence, and driven to despair after having spent their age, their youth, and their industry in the said conditions. The booksellers, on the contrary, with great repose of body and spirit, make easy fortunes for themselves, sometimes double and triple their money by the end of the year, in selling the printed sheet at three or four deniers or even more. There lies the sole reason for the high price of books, which they by calumny impute to the poor journeymen and which comes, in fact, from their boundless cupidity, and their thirst for gain which is, at the least, one hundred and fifty per cent. That is the reason why at Antwerp, in Germany, and at Geneva, books are cheaper, even though their booksellers are compelled to use our papers, our characters and our fonts, because they are content with an average and honest profit."

To these vehement accusations, the masters replied that if there was anyone who was abused and taken advantage of it was certainly themselves, and entirely through the typographers' fault, who refused to do any accurate work and made exorbitant claims. Their strikes, at the time called "monopolies," were fomented on the least pretext and led them straight to ruin:

"To understand what has brought them up to such a pitch of bold insolence as to league together against their masters in order to reduce them to a form of slavery, it must be known that each printing press is worked by two printers, and by two, three, or four compositors, who, in general terms, are called journeymen printers, and can do nothing one without the others. If one of them stops work the others have to stop. So the master printers are always very afraid of seeing one of their journeymen leave, for they have to deliver an entire form of thirteen of fifteen hundred sheets a day to the merchants who have financed the publication of editions of ten and twenty thousand books. If they do not fulfill their engagements, the merchants have the right to demand interest from them, always high, to be sure, because sometimes for a long labor they have committed seven or eight thousand pounds which remain inactive until the book is completed."

The master printers, careful of their money, always kept a weather eye open. As soon as a ringleader or lazy fellow seemed to want to spread confusion in the workshop, they were quick to dismiss him and replace him by a more docile element. But the workers decided otherwise:

"From the moment when the master printer has received the journeyman at the printing shop, he cannot dismiss him as long as the work begun is not finished; if he does, or if the journeyman leaves in discontent with his master, it is forbidden for any other journeyman to take his place or to finish his work. The journeymen have bound themselves and one another to the observance of their monopolies by innumerable and severe means. They banish from their printing shop and their guild those who do not strictly observe their monopolies; even to cursing them with the word scab, which for them is the worst of insults, and giving them a good beating, or even blows with a sword."

The masters dealt with this by replacing the insubordinate journeymen with apprentices, of whom they always had a few in the shop. The journeymen replied by a second monopoly:

"It is forbidden to any journeyman printer to work with an apprentice under pain of being declared a scab, and being banished from all the printing shops and penalized in the accustomed manner."

To avoid this second conspiracy, the master printers dismissed the journeymen in Lyons and Paris and engaged natives of Rouen, Toulouse, Bordeaux, Poitiers, Angers, or even Germany and other nations in alliance with the crown of France. "The first mutinous and quarrelsome journeymen thus received no other recompense for their mutiny than being a long time in the street with nothing to do and without earning a living."

The journeymen soon announced a third monopoly: "Only the journeymen printers of Paris or Lyons may work in the printing shops of the said towns, and if journeymen coming from elsewhere wish to do some work there, then the old and original journeymen of Paris and Lyons will attack them, to drive out and exterminate them.

"And moreover if in the course of an argument with the master, the irritated journeyman comes to pronounce this syllable: *'tric,'* the journeymen of the same printing shop will be obliged to leave their work immediately and go to the tavern, without returning to their master's house except to demand their portion.

"This monopoly was observed very strictly, even in Lyons. It happened almost every day that one of the journeymen said *'tric'* and left the printing shop. Immediately, after this fine word '*tric*' was uttered, all the others, even if there were thirty or forty of them, followed the author of the dispute, and all went to the back room of a tavern. The printing shop of the unfortunate master thus abandoned, the leading merchant, who perhaps had already advanced six or eight thousand pounds, continued to ask him for a complete form per day, as was his perfect right. There was therefore no way out left to the unfortunate printer than to go along in a fashion both undignified and prejudicial to his authority as master, and implore the workmen to leave the tavern, and himself pay the bill. After having sufficiently implored them he shepherded them back, not without some trouble, to their accustomed lodging, like wild bulls. And what was the worst for the masters was that if they wished to have peace in their house they had to admit that it was they who had been wrong."

To demands for wages were added those for food. The masters at the beginning had fed their workmen—and always badly, the latter complained. Such numerous conflicts resulted that the edict of 1571 was aimed at putting an end to them and doing away with this obligation. But the journeymen demanded its restoration, alleging the following reasons[6]:

"The journeymen are compelled, by an arbitrary demand of the booksellers and masters, to deliver a certain amount of work every day; they can scarcely accomplish it, although they never quit the saddle and do not waste time at work. If they had to go to town four or five times a day to eat, as the hard work compels them to do, they will spend their day in coming and going, or waiting for one of their companions. Add to this that they are not lodged in the big towns and that meals cannot be found there ready at the moment they are wanted, as in Lyons, where the taverns are forbidden them, and where various obstacles arise which can delay them.

"On the other hand, if the master feeds them, he can confer during the meal about their common work, done and still to be done, and speed it and the expense is less. It must also be taken into account that they work in teams of four or five at each press, the absence or tardiness of any one of them immobilises the others; in consequence, they cannot accomplish their quota. They must not be compared to other artisans who do their day's work at their discretion. So, to cut matters short and do away with all frivolous excuses, the journeymen make the following offers:

"In view of the fact that the journeymen of Paris complain with justice at being obliged to deliver 2650 sheets per day, which is impossible if they have to eat, those of Lyons have even more just cause of complaint and despair, being obliged, incredibly, to deliver 3350 sheets per day. They can scarcely do it even being up from two in the morning to eight or nine at night, winter and summer, fed by the masters, and that without any recreations. They will nevertheless be glad to feed themselves provided that the enormous work is diminished which they have to deliver, in proportion to the loss of time which being obliged to take their meals in town necessitates. If not, let them be fed, as was the tradition and custom, continuing their works abovementioned."

At the same time they asked for a just salary, fixed by an equal number of masters and journeymen chosen among the most ancient "who know and really understand the work, and not by booksellers and master printers, who are really their enemies and will be both judge and advocate, for the ruin of the poor journeymen whom they have to pay with their own money."

The masters took up each heading of the accusations point by point and defended themselves vigorously. They first reproached the journeymen with being impossible to feed:

"The quarrels and seditions which have been made in printing under pretext of food are incredible; for to begin with the bread, the journeymen have made this rule among themselves that on Wednesday and Saturday morning they will have fresh bread. Now the mistress of a family cannot make so exact a provision that there is not some little stale bread left over from the previous market. In case there is some left, the journeymen have decided that they will not touch it; and they are insolent enough to make their master, mistress, and the family eat the stale bread while they help themselves to the fresh bread. Even so there are endless sour comments: the bread is black, or underdone, or has not risen enough, or is too dry. The white wine is too sweet, or too fiery, or too weak; the claret is too tart, too deep in color, or too stinted. If they have it three or four days in a row it is flat. In short, everything serves as an excuse for ceaseless complaints. The meat is too lean or badly cooked; one wants greens in his soup, another wants turnips, another leeks. Some complain that they are stinted of salt, and cannot eat without mustard. As to fish, it must be from the last tide; then they want fresh-water fish, and if one gives them two dishes of carp, one must be stewed and the other fried, served with green sauce. A good cook would really be hard put to please so many different palates and various, if not actually incompatible, tastes. On all feast days, plus Tuesday and Thursday, they have to have a roast in the evening, which has to be very tender and well prepared and recently, on Sunday and Thursday evenings, chicken or waterfowl. On feast days in the summer, the journeymen who are normally ten, fifteen, or twenty, according to the number of presses, go for recreation to town, where they sometimes eat. Before leaving they order the most mutinous of them to stay at home, and to have himself served as many dishes for himself alone as for the whole company. Which he never fails to do: he carves all the meats in succession so as to observe another monopoly which has been decided among them, never to accept meat which has been presented or carved at the previous meal. In short, a day hardly goes by without disputes about food. There would be no end to, and the Court would be wearied by, a recital of the thousand and one ways in which the journeyman printers molest their masters and make difficulties for them."[7]

So the latter, desperate at the state of affairs, urgently demanded that the journeymen feed themselves, even if they had to pay them a food allowance. Let the Court not believe that this measure would harm their work:

"They are well nourished in Germany and in Flanders; let those of France do the same. If they were sober and temperate, they would gain considerably by it, for they could live at home and make some saving. But they wish to be free to eat as much, and even more, than nature can bear."[8]

Still graver than questions of pay and food, the abuse of employing apprentices instead of journeymen constituted in their eyes a major complaint against the masters. The apprentice was engaged by the employer to learn his trade according to the terms of a contract drawn up almost invariably in the same form:

"François Estienne, living at Paris, retains for his apprenticeship, receiving him from the Administrators of the Refuge of the St.-Esprit, Jean Becquet, orphan from the said refuge, aged fourteen years, to whom he promises to teach his trade of bookseller. He will maintain him after the said institution has given him a jacket, three shirts, a pair of stockings, and a hat, as it is the custom to do for the children of the said refuge."[9]

In fact, the apprentice constituted free help which the master abused at the expense of the journeymen. The latter, of course, were violently opposed to the article of the edict which permitted the employer as many apprentices as he pleased. Caught between the master, who exploited him, and the journeymen, who accused him of stealing their bread, the poor apprentice's only recourse was to hope for better days.

The king determined to put an end to the argument. He did this by the edict of 1573, which is considered today in France as the Magna Charta of printing. From then on, the conflicts seemed at an end. Masters and journeymen were silent. Was it the calm of peace, or the silence of death? In fact, printing, one of the finest gems of the French crown in the sixteenth century, fell completely into decadence:

"This kind of indignity and conspiracy have ruined the state of printing in this kingdom. For some of the master printers have abandoned their profession or were ruined; others have not been willing to undertake any work other than what they could do without being obliged to deliver to the great merchants a whole form per day, and the notable merchants dared no longer use their money in the printing business, being no longer sure that the works undertaken might not be a long time in completion. We see today that many good books written by various great persons of France are printed outside the kingdom and brought here by foreigners who openly make off with the profit which should be ours. If today we ask for the works of Master Guillaume Budé, in his lifetime Master of Requests to the king, and Plutarch's *Lives*, translated into our French tongue by Master Jacques Amiot, Bishop of Auxerre, who had the honor to be our king's tutor, we have them at a better price from the printers of Germany or Flanders than from the French printers. What is more, if some booksellers in France wish to have printed some work of importance, they can more profitably send it to be printed at Chambéry, Lausanne, Geneva, Lucerne, or elsewhere outside the kingdom, and then have the printed paper brought back to this city to add there only the title page, than have their printing executed at their own doors and in this kingdom."[10]

Thus ended, in the storms of the end of the century, the good days of a "divine invention." Political and religious troubles, economic crises and social conflicts sounded the knell of the great dynasties of humanist printers who had contributed so much to the spread of the new spirit. With them had closed the golden age of this noble art.

NOTES

VIII · Masters and Workmen of the Renaissance

1. Coyecque, E. *Cinq libraires parisiens sous François I.* Paris, 1894, p. 95.
2. *Plaidoyer pour la Réformation de l'imprimerie.* Paris, n.d. (c. 1572), f. 3.
3. *Ibid.*, f. 1.
4. *Remontrances et mémoires pour les compagnons imprimeurs de Paris et de Lyon, contre les libraires et maîtres imprimeurs desdits lieux.* Bibliothèque Nationale, Reserve, fonds Morel de Thoisy, Université. t. XI, ff. 138 and 143.
5. *Plaidoyer pour . . . , loc. cit.*
6. *Remontrances et mémoires . . . , op. cit.,* f. 140.
7. *Plaidoyer pour . . . , op. cit.,* f. 5.
8. *Ibid.,* f. 16.
9. "Contrat d'apprentissage," in *Documents pour servir à l'histoire des libraires de Paris*, ed. Pichon and Vicaire. Paris, 1895, pp. 53–54.
10. *Plaidoyer pour . . . , op. cit.,* f. 11.

IX · Travelers of the Renaissance

THE people of sixteenth-century France were wholeheartedly nomadic, like their kings, who moved their residence according to the season. Despite the uncertainties of the road, potholed and muddy highways, and the probability of robbers waiting around every corner, they were constantly on the move. The love of travel was in their blood, even more than it had been in the Middle Ages. On horseback, in litters, often on foot, noble lords and great ladies, burghers, merchants, and common men all traveled the roads of Europe on business, in search of health or for the salvation of their souls. Whatever the condition of the traveler or the reason for his voyage, one element remained constant: the pleasure of travel, the love of change and of adventure.

An abundant literature was engendered by this taste for travel, and it waxes eloquent particularly on the subject of lodging and shelter. This is not surprising; when the traveler, riding over the roads of Europe astride a good horse, with well-stuffed moneybags, reached a stopping place in the evening, he was weary, jaded, and hungry. As he held his horse's bridle, he wished only to find some comfortable hostelry, one with a big log fire at which to warm himself, a good meal to recover his strength, and a soft bed on which to rest his aching body. At times, he knew of such a place in the vicinity; at others he trusted Providence to provide him with a night's lodging. When he returned home and told the story of his travels, he doubtless spoke of the cities he had seen and of his adventures and encounters, and certainly never failed to mention the good taverns.

The French hostelries generally enjoyed a high reputation. A notable traveler of the times, Erasmus, retained such special memories of an inn at Lyons that he extolled its charms in one of his *Colloquies*. And the author of the *Journey of the Cardinal of Aragon*, Don Antonio de Beatis, extended this appreciative eulogy to include the whole country:

"Generally lodging is good in France, and better than in Germany where one finds as many beds as the rooms will hold; in France in each room there are a feather bed for the master, a little servant's bed, and a good fire.

"The soup is good, and there are pies and cakes of every kind. The veal is generally good, and the mutton better, so that for a shoulder of roast mutton with little onions, as they prepare it all over France, one would gladly forsake the most delicious fare. Partridges, pheasants, young partridges, peacocks, rabbits, hens, and capons are plentiful there, cheap and very well served. The game of all sorts there is bigger than I have ever seen, the custom being to hunt them only in the season which is suited to each species.

"However, of all sections of the country, that which offers the best lodging and where the conversation of the gentry is most refined is the Ile-de-France. In all the provinces, and particularly in that one, they have a habit of lining the apertures of the windows, doors, and particularly the fireplaces with plaster, which gives them a luxurious appearance."[1]

Erasmus too in his *Colloquies* proclaims the inferiority of the German hostelries, of which he had unhappy memories:

". . . When you enter the hostelry, nobody greets you; the innkeeper doesn't want to look as though he was looking out for travelers, for this would be base and servile and altogether unworthy of German dignity. When you have shouted for a long time, you see the window of the stove room, where they stay practically until midsummer's day, open a crack; somebody puts his head out as cautiously as a tortoise out of its shell. It is up to you to ask if they would be good enough to receive you. When they tell you 'no,' you gather there is room for you. You ask where the stable is; they show you with a wave of the hand. There you put up your horse after your own fashion, because none of the house servants do it. . . . When you have cared for your horse, you transport yourself, with your boots, baggage, and mire, to the stove room; there in only one, which is common to all . . . there you take off your gaiters, put on your socks, change your shirt if you wish, you hang up your rain-soaked clothes by the stove; you get near it to dry yourself. There is water all ready to wash your hands, but it is usually of a cleanliness that requires you afterward to look for some more to wash off the first wash. . . . Often then, there assemble in the same stove room eighty or ninety travelers, on horse or on foot; merchants, seamen, carters, peasants, children, and women, sane and sick, one does his hair, another wipes off his sweat, another brushes off his gaiters or his boots, another blows in your face with a pestiferous garlic breath. In short, its the same rumpus, and the same confusion of tongues there was in former times at the Tower of Babel. If they see a stranger whose clothes announce him as being of some distinction, all the company stare at him fixedly, contemplating him like some strange animal recently brought from Africa; even when they are seated at table they turn their heads to gaze at him and they do not let their eyes leave him again; they forget to eat or drink."[2]

But M. de Montaigne, who had also traveled in Germany, held quite another opinion. In the course of his *Travel Diary*,[3] he notes the good places and their respective advantages. At Augsburg, cleanliness was the rule: "The steps of the staircase of our lodging were all covered in linen on which we had to walk so as not to dirty the steps of their staircase which they had just washed and cleaned as they do every Saturday."

At Constance one must stay at the Pike, and not on any account at the Eagle; at Lindau, at the Crown. The food was so good there that he regretted not having brought a French cook with him who could have learned to cook their way, so different from the French way. They served the soup at the end of the meal, and placed among the meat dishes: "a silver or pewter affair with four compartments, where they put several sorts of piled-up spices"; and served them with cooked plums, tarts of apple or pear, or combined with fish, which by the way was excellent. Of trout, they only ate the liver.

At Kempte, at the sign of the Bear, drink was served to the guest in "great silver cups . . . well worked and decorated with the arms of various lords."

At Chonguen, a little town in Bavaria, the hosts of the Star "arranged the salt cellars on a square table cornerwise with the candlesticks in the opposite corners, making a St. Andrew's cross with them."

At Innsbruck, stay at the Rose, a very good house, especially if one liked embroidered sheets. M. de Montaigne had there "sheets which had all round them four fingers of rich work of white trimming."

At Kollmann, the glasses were washed with white salt (a luxury in those days) "and the first service is with a very clean pan which is placed on the table on a little iron instrument to rest on and to raise the handle. In this pan there are eggs poached in butter."

Erasmus' opinion notwithstanding, one left Germany with regret, and doubtless M. de Montaigne voiced the general view when he confided to a friend in Basel "that he had had such pleasure from his visit to Germany that he left with real regret, although he was going on to Italy; that foreigners had to suffer there, as elsewhere, from the exactions of their hosts, but that he thought this could be corrected. His whole visit had seemed to him full of convenience and courtesy, and especially of justice and safety."

So now, arriving on the Italian side, some fifteen miles from Trent on the Adige, at the hostelry of Rovereto, the crayfish served twice a day in Germany were missing; but the snails were to be appreciated, much larger and fatter, if not as flavorous, as their French colleagues, while the truffles, eaten sliced thin with a vinegar sauce, and the first olives and first citrus fruits announced that one was indeed in a Mediterranean land.

At Scarperia, in Tuscany, "they have a custom of sending one of their people to meet the strangers six or seven leagues away, to persuade them to lodge with them. You often find the host himself on horseback, and in various places several well-dressed men on the lookout for you; and all along the road M. de Montaigne, who wished to entertain them, pleasantly discussed the various offers which each made to him, and made no promises. There was one who offered him a hare as a free gift, if he would only come to his house. Their argument and repartee ended at the town gates, and they dared not say another word. In general they offer you a mounted guide at their expense to lead you and take part of your baggage to the lodging where you are going."

At Foligno, one would find marinated fish, peas, and green almonds, as well as almost raw artichokes; but the wine was not worth the drinking. San Lorenzo was to be avoided at all costs, as the traveler was obliged to sleep fully clothed on a table because of the swarms of fleas in the beds. At Fano, on the other hand, "you will find in almost all the hostelries rhymers who make up rhymes on the spur of the moment to amuse those present." A not inconsiderable advantage.

The Italian hostelries were, for the most part, satisfactory. And, M. de Montaigne concludes, "I have always been not merely well, but agreeably, lodged in all the places at which I have stopped in Italy, except Florence and Venice."

※　　※　　※

The traveler met with most frequently in this period was the pilgrim— a survival from the Middle Ages, with his staff, his wallet, his cockleshell necklace, and his even stride—a picturesque brown silhouette against the tender green of the copses and meadows, under the clear sky of a spring morning. When the fine weather came, he, whether cleric or layman, headed for one of the innumerable sanctuaries which flourished owing to popular piety, perhaps to thank his patron saint for protection in difficult moments or to fulfill vows taken either in gratitude or in distraction. Often, his destination was one of the two great Western pilgrimages, Rome or St. James Compostela—for the cruelty of the infidel forbade him Jerusalem.

Recommendations for the road abound. A popular guide for travelers advises: "a staff on which the body leans usefully when climbing and descending, and spectacles of glass or crystal to protect the eyes from the snow; the peddlers sell these glasses cheaply. . . . To cross mountains and glaciers, steel points fixed on iron strips are attached to the soles; they are to be found today for sale almost anywhere. On stony and muddy roads, nothing is as good as the soles [overshoes] used in France; they are hard to wet and dry rapidly; they can be trimmed with oakum so as not to hurt the feet. If rocks have to be traversed, put beneath your shoes thin soles of iron, in Turkish style. For dry and short roads, sandals are preferable because they keep the feet warm."[4]

The flocks of pilgrims created an industry and were good for business. "At Mont-St.-Michel," writes the Italian, Beatis,[5] "men and women have no profession other than painting in all sorts of colors the cockleshells from the sea which are picked up on the beach. They paint them red or yellow or gray, and they sell them to the pilgrims who wear them across their shoulders like a scarf. The inhabitants of the mount also make statuettes of St. Michael of silver and pewter of different kinds. They make large numbers of horns with branches of trees, or colored clay or glass; these horns are much smaller than the trumpets made in Milan. All these objects and others like them are sold in great numbers, for there is not a pilgrim who does not buy some so as to return home decked out in cockleshells, carrying statuettes, and sounding the horn all along the way."

Overseas travel was rare. The Holy Places were in the hands of the infidel. At the beginning of the century they had driven out the Latin monks who lived there, and now they firmly refused access even to the pilgrims who did not hesitate to face the perils of the sea and of passage through enemy territory to pray at the tomb of the Savior. Unshakable faith and undaunted courage were no longer enough; an exceptional reason was necessary, such as was presented to Brother Jean Thénaud, guardian of the monastery of the Franciscan Friars at Angoulême. His protectress, Louise of Savoy, bade him take the road to Bethlehem to place in her name on the cradle of Our Lord the gold, frankincense, and myrrh of the Magi. To limit the dangers of the journey, he was to join the train of the French Ambassador, André le Roy, sent by Louis XII to the court of the Sultan of Egypt to improve French relations with him.

On July 2, 1511, Thénaud left Angoulême and joined the Ambassador at Valance. They embarked at Aigues-Mortes on November 14 and, passing by the Italian coast, the Strait of Messina, Zakynthos, Cerigo, and Crete, arrived at Alexandria on February 29 and at Cairo on March 29. The sultan was expecting them, received them with honor, and installed them in a comfortable house. There were "six or seven fine halls paved with marble, porphyry, serpentine, and other rich stones, the walls being decorated with the same, painted with gold and blue and rich colors; the doors were ornamented with ivory, ebony and other rarities, but the workmanship always outdid the materials. In these halls there were fountains. It was said that this house had cost eighty thousand seraphs of gold to build and that in Cairo there were a hundred thousand of them incomparably more lovely, of which I saw several. This place was surrounded by sumptuous great gardens full of all kinds of fruit trees, such as lemons, limes, gourds, oranges, apricots, black currants and apples *de muse*, also called Adam's apples because they are said to be the fruit by which Adam sinned against the commandment of God; morning and evening these gardens are watered with water from the Nile brought by oxen and horses; on this account there is no garden which costs its proprietor less than at least five hundred thousand seraphs of gold a year. Near Cairo there are more than fifteen hundred such. The mamelukes and admirals who took us there banqueted in our house and all left sodden with wine, for they considered they had not been well entertained if they were not drunk."[6]

Leaving the ambassador and his people to go about their business, Thénaud rested in these pleasant surroundings from the fatigues he had endured, prepared for those he was yet to endure, and gave himself up to the pleasures of tourism. Cairo enchanted him. It can be imagined that the Capuchin from Angoulême looked at the spectacle of this great city in wide-eyed amazement, for he was in the richest and the most commercial city of the Moslem East. Here for centuries spices and silks from Asia, ivory and rare woods from Africa were gathered before being sent on to Alexandria, where the Venetians, Genoese, and Catalans came to fetch them to resell at exorbitant prices in the West. Brother Thénaud fell under the city's spell:

"That city taken as a whole is three times as big as Paris, and has five times the population. I think they burn as much oil there as they drink wine in Orléans, for there are counted twenty thousand mosques in each of which, all told, three hundred lamps normally are burning. Then there is no living room or bedchamber where there is not a lamp burning all night; the same in all the streets, lamps and torches; it is not surprising that they consume so much oil; and never a tallow candle, but only of oil or white wax. They lack wood, therefore they cook their bread and meat with animal dung, palm branches, and earth mixed with straw. They do their cooking in the streets, in public, and so dirtily that we had a horror of it, and they eat there as they come and go. Wine is very dear and costs thirty seraphs a bottle, for they do not grow grapes, the use of wine being forbidden by their law; in spite of that they drink it immoderately when they can find it. In Cairo a hundred thousand men carry around water for sale in goatskins on their shoulders; and fifty thousand camels carry it to the houses and the streets, which are sprinkled morning and evening to freshen the city. Also, the town is not paved. Almost everything is sold by the pound, such as meat, fish, oil, honey, and fruits, which are abundant. In the city and its environs, more than a hundred thousand vultures are to be seen; it is forbidden to hunt or kill them, for they scavenge the city and the filth of the Nile, which by reason of its size cannot be cleaned. Any corpse of an ox, camel, or dead horse is put out in the street, or in some place of their houses where the vultures can have access; they come down in such multitudes that two hours later there is nothing left but bones. . . . Cairo is richer than the other towns, by the fertility of the country and the abundance of merchants who come there daily. There are bazaars and halls appropriate to each particular kind of merchandise such as the hall of gold and silver, the hall of perfumes, of gems, of silks, of cloths, of medicaments, of carpets and so with everything. . . . The cemetery is very great, although there exists more than a hundred private cemeteries; Saracens wish to be buried in virgin soil, where no corpse has been before, and the greatest displeasure one can do them would be to step on the tombs of their dead. . . . Each Friday, the women go to visit their family graves. They scatter a quantity of perfumes there, jasmin, basil, roses, oils, and perfumed water; they think that on that day the souls of the dead feed on these perfumes."[7]

The town having no more secrets for him, Brother Thénaud explored its surroundings:

"We saw outside Cairo two things worthy of note; the ancient tombs of the kings of Egypt, which are called pyramids, situated on the other side of the Nile in Libya, at two leagues from Cairo, and reckoned among the wonders of the world. Not without reason, for that of Cheops —which is the highest and largest, but the least sumptuous, to build which, according to our historians, two hundred thousand men worked for twenty-two years—has so many so large stones and so polished and well set that I think two cities like Paris would not have as many. All the most splendid things in Cairo, such as bridges and arches, have been made with stones taken from them. I was at the top and inside with M. de Soubran, Master François de Bon Jehan, and several others, and when we had visited everything we said that the building was of marvelous and incredible beauty. The two others, of which one was built by the son of Cheops and the other by Rhodopaeus, are not open to the public. Near this was sculpted the statue of Isis, taller than the towers of Notre Dame, of which the head still remains. Other tombs may be visited seven leagues upstream, but we did not go there.

"To the east of Cairo is the village of La Matharée, where the dough never rises nor can bread be fermented, because the women of the place answered the glorious Virgin Mary, whom Herod's persecution had forced to leave Judea, and who asked them for bread, that the dough had not risen. There is a big fig tree which bowed to give her its fruit when she sat beneath its shade. Farther on is the fountain where the most glorious Virgin washed the linen of Our Lord and from which the water is taken to water the garden where grows the best balm in the world. That of India or Arabia Felix is not as good. Its goodness can be recognized as good by several points: if it is strong and cures recent wounds, if a drop put into water goes down whole to the bottom and can be brought up whole with the aid of a pin, and if chicken liver or any other flesh greased with it never putrefies."[8]

Alas, all good things come to an end. Two and a half months had already elapsed since Thénaud's arrival in Egypt. He had now to think about the mission which had brought him to that agreeable abode. On investigation, it turned out that a caravan of twelve thousand camels was going to Thor on the Red Sea, to fetch spices coming from India. From Thor, it would be easy to reach Mount Sinai. Taking his courage in both hands, he left the ambassador's suite and, sole Christian amid the Infidels, he set out on the great adventure:

"June 3, 1512, I left Cairo with the caravan of Arabs and Moors to journey as far as Mount Sinai. The next day, we entered the Arabian desert. There are three Arabias: Arabia Petra, Arabia Deserta, and Arabia Felix. We journeyed for three days without finding water; but near a port of the Red Sea called Suez, in a brackish country quite good for camels but not for men, our caravan stopped all day to water the animals, for there would be no water for three days to come, except at Moses' fountain, situated at one day's journey. Water having been drawn for a previous caravan, I bought a pitcher of it for five médins. It was half mud, and stank worse than sulfur. Filtered five times through a cloth, it still smelled so bad that one had to hold one's nose to drink it. . . .

"Then we skirted the Red Sea. Neither this sea nor its banks are red. . . . St. Jerome says the Hebrews called it Mare Suph, which signifies: "sea full of reeds and rushes." I had a pleasant time fishing there for cockles, sea urchins, white coral, and pearl oysters, and in washing in it since our fathers had miraculously crossed it. We followed its banks almost half a day. Then I had to leave the big caravan which was going to Thor and follow ten or twelve camels which took the road for Sinai. When we had journeyed a day and a night in the mountains, we took some rest to give the camels pasture. The Arab who was guiding me then left me in order to allow the others to harm me. As soon as he was gone, two Moors came and said to my interpreter: 'Tell the dog and son of a dog to pay us the seraph he owes us.' He replied he would do nothing of the kind and that they were robbers. The Moors seized me by the beard to make me open my wallet in which were my victuals, which I did immediately, but they found nothing there but biscuit, onions, and cheese so hard and evil-smelling that it would have driven the rats out of a house. I had brought nothing else for fear it would be taken from me. They asked me for meat or eggs. I answered them: 'I do not have any.' 'O stinking old shoe, you say you have none, then give us money,' they replied. I answered: 'I have no money.' As I was speaking I was being beaten all the time, boxed on the ears, and receiving kicks with which they were very generous. Then two other Arabs came who each asked me for six médins for a toll which I had passed without paying, and wished to put me in chains if I did not give it them; I answered them, 'I have no money.' Then they threatened to strip me and tear up my clothes. In order to save them, I undressed, but they wished me to leave everything, stockings and shoes and with beatings they made me run two bow shots beyond that place. There I stayed almost three hours naked on the sand, commending myself to God and several saints to whom I was devoted. At the moment of leaving, my robbers appeared, feigning to repent their outrages. My interpreter took courage and shouted at them: 'You are not worthy of the Moorish race, nor of the holy law of Mahomet, who forbids stealing and breaking faith, for you maltreat this poor fellow, who has come with the sultan's safe-conduct, as though he were a murderer, although his food, his garments in which you found no money, and his gestures prove to you that he is a simple man. His master, whose close friend he is, lives in Cairo where the sultan receives him daily. If he loses him, he will try to find out what has happened to him and you will be flayed alive.' They answered: 'Tell him that he will be free for one seraph.' 'He doesn't have one,' he told them, 'I lent him money twice to buy water and onions and he promised to have me repaid in Cairo. He is a poor holy man who, for his faith, exposes himself to all these dangers. . . .' My interpreter pleaded my cause so well that they gave him back my clothes, which he brought me torn in several places. The next day I suffered similar outrages. The interpreter told me that at one moment they had all decided to kill us, him and myself, to appropriate our things and the cloaks we covered ourselves with in the sand at night. Only one, to whom he had given some wine to drink in Cairo, opposed their projects, and made the undertaking miscarry. . . .

"June 22, in the morning, we arrived at the desert of Pharaoh, which is a paradise among deserts thanks to five fountains forming a stream, which waters a valley a league in length and two bow shots wide, full of palm trees, melons, small roses, watermelons, cucumbers, and other delectable things. There we saw partridges as fat as capons and many Arab dwellings. After we had rested three hours in this agreeable abode, we traveled on our camels about ten hours to pick up the road an hour before dawn. We found on the trees and rocks a manna thick as honey and sticky to the hand; if it stays long in the sun it cracks. The morning air was so perfumed that I could have believed myself in a shop of aromatic herbs."[9]

After ten days on the road, Thénaud saw, at the foot of Mount Sinai, the Monastery of St. Catherine, where he was to make a halt:

"This monastery occupies the place where Our Lord appeared to Moses in the burning bush which was not consumed. Four high walls, thirty or forty fathoms long and twenty high, surround it. To enter, they let down from the top of the walls a rope furnished with a ring in which one puts one's feet, and by a turn one is pulled up. For if there were a door below, the Arabs, who would like nothing better than to destroy the monastery, would always force their way in. I stayed down below more than four hours without their wishing to send me the cable, for the Greek monks hate the Latins and, full of envy and avarice wished to hold me to ransom, although they may be of a very austere life.

"Once I was up there, the master of the monastery led me to the chapel reserved for Latins. To dine, they spread out a mat from which twelve scorpions rushed out. They gave me fresh rye bread, olives, dates, water in some vinegar. Wine I could not get. When I heard vespers sounding, for it was the vigil of St. John, I went to the church to make my devotions. At the side of the great altar, in a tomb of white marble, rests the body of the Glorious Virgin and Martyr, St. Catherine. At the moment of communion, I found myself with some Greek monks. The blessing was given in their Greek manner, on the bread and wine; each one had to drink twice of a wine so delicious, sweet-smelling, special and fragrant of manna that there did not exist, I was sure, in any part of the world, a wine which could be compared to it. The collation finished and complines said, I retired to the hall reserved for Latins. The master of the monastery, who brought walnuts, apples, and pears, asked what I thought of their wine. I answered that if St. Onuphros, St. Hilarios, or St. Macarius, who had made penance in that countryside, had drunk it they were not to be pitied. He added that if I had money he would sell me some. Desire and the need I felt to drink some of it made me trade the Irish cloak with which I covered myself in the deserts against two jars of wine.

". . . I think I never passed such a St. John's day, either for the spiritual delights which I experienced at finding myself in this most holy place, adorned with innumerable sacred objects, or for the delicious wine, which made me forget my past trials. . . .

"The day of St. John early in the morning, the tomb of the most glorious St. Catherine was opened for me by the Greek monks. They had tapers in their hands and made three prostrations before kissing the relics. When prayers had been said, I was permitted, and commanded, to touch and raise the head of the glorious saint, her hand ornamented with a bracelet of gold which Our Lord gave her, and her other holy bones. Then they gave me cotton dipped in the oil which formerly issued from her holy limbs and bones, which had ceased to produce it since the monks had wished to sell it in Simoniacal fashion a good two hundred years ago. They also gave me candles and fragments of the first tomb in which the angels had placed her. I have since deposited these holy relics in our monastery at Angoulême, founded in honor of this blessed person. I also gave some of them to the monastery at Cognac in the best way I was able."[10]

At seven next morning, Thénaud was climbing the slopes of Mount Sinai, where the Eternal had appeared to Moses, dictating His law and establishing His alliance with the people of Israel. When this first pilgrimage was over, he returned to Thor, where he was able to obtain admission to a caravan returning to Cairo. He arrived there on July 16; but two weeks later he again left for the Holy Places.

Wedged between the humps of his camel, physically exhausted, his mouth parched and his beard grown long, Brother Jean, the poor *"roumi"*—as the Arabs called Christians or "Romans"—traversed deserts and oases, did reverence in passing to "the Damascene field where Adam was created and where one is shown an orange red pit from which every year a thousand wagonloads of earth are drawn, used for making crockery"; the place where Cain killed Abel; "the splendid church at Hebron which covers the sepulchers of Adam, Abraham, Isaac, Jacob, and their wives, Eve, Sarah and Rebecca." He reached Bethlehem without incident: "As soon as I came in view of Bethlehem, I was so filled with joy, consolation, and spiritual gladness that I forgot all my past miseries; I seemed to be flying as I recited the hymns of the Holy Nativity, of the Feast of the Kings, and of Our Lady. I arrived at the monastery of Bethlehem on August 21, toward eleven in the morning. I first offered in the holy chapel of the Nativity the gold, frankincense, and myrrh which I had brought and prepared according to the request and desire of my most feared sovereign and illustrious lady and of Monseigneur at present our august and most serene king. My devotion done, I was almost as well received by my brethren as the holy souls in paradise.

"Bethlehem is in ruins today, with the exception of that splendid and solemn church which was once built by St. Helen and enlarged by Godefroy de Bouillon and his successors. There the Virgin and most blessed Mother gave birth to her most holy and precious Child. Two altars have been built there with seven feet between them, one over the place where he was born, the other before his cradle. Although numerous princes and great prelates have taken the trouble to decorate and enrich this august place, nevertheless it remains characterized by such great austerity that no one could fail to have great compassion for the Virgin Mary, who suffered and gave birth there. In this place, the kings adored Our Lord and the star appeared.

"From the gardens one can see three churches, one built at the place where the angel appeared to Joseph to show him the way to Egypt; another where the angel announced the good tidings to the shepherds. This was formerly a convent of virgins, of which St. Eustochia was the first abbess. No stone of it can ever be moved, for men or camels which have tried to take some have gone mad and died within the year. The third church is dedicated to St. Nicholas; the Moors have made a mosque out of it. . . .

"Near the sanctuary of Bethlehem is a little cave where Our Lady hid herself for several days for fear of Herod and where she nursed her son. The women of the country, in order to have children and milk, visit this place and powder the stone of the cave, which is soft, like chalk, and drink it."[11]

But the supreme goal of Thénaud's journey was the Holy City, Jerusalem. His first visit was to the Holy Sepulcher:

"In the church of the Holy Sepulcher is first of all the precious tomb of Our Savior, Jesus Christ; then the place where Our Lord appeared to the Magdalen as the gardener; the chapel where he appeared to his glorious Mother; his prison; the place where his executioners gambled for his clothing; the column near which he was crowned with thorns, which was brought from the house of Pilate; the holy hill of Calvary, which is ascended by thirty steps; there one can see the holes made by the cross and the rock is rent between the place of the cross of Our Lord and that of the cross of the wicked thief; another chapel is that of the angels, the third that of St. John the Baptist, and the fourth that of the Magdalen, then the place where Our Lord was embalmed and placed in a winding sheet."[12]

The Franciscan still had ten pilgrimages to make. The fourth one was in the city itself:

"The place where Our Lord stumbled beneath the weight of the cross, the house of Veronica, the house of the Magdalen in front of which is that of the wicked rich man; the place where the Jews forced Simon the Cyrenean to carry the cross and where Jesus said to the women of Jerusalem: 'Weep not for me, but for yourselves,' in predicting the complete destruction of the city; the place where Our Lady wept on seeing her son carrying the cross and wearing the crown of thorns; the house of Pilate, where Our Lord was interrogated, beaten, crowned with thorns, and condemned to death; the place where Our Lady was born; the pool where the sacrificial victims were washed; the gate of the town near which St. Stephen was stoned; the Golden Gate by which Our Lord entered Jerusalem on Palm Sunday; the splendid temple of Solomon, high, round, very richly painted and situated in the middle of a great place paved with white marble; it is there that the presentation of Our Lord took place, where he argued with the doctors of the law, often preached, and did several miracles; the mosque of the virgins where Our Lady learned to read and where some two thousand lamps burn day and night."[13]

In the course of the other pilgrimages, which had as objectives Mount Sion, the valleys of Josaphat, of Siloam, and of the Jordan,

Nazareth, Lake Tiberias, or even Damascus, the New Testament was recalled with the same simplicity.

Brother Thénaud had fulfilled his vow. He started for home. It took many long, perilous, uncertain months to reach Cairo, in the baggage train of a Persian princess who was fleeing from the persecutions of her nephew "and whose litter, very fine and rich, was carried by two camels. All night long torches burned before her going in front, and a blind man with a marvelous voice spoke and sung the deeds of her ancestors, giving glory to God." From her kitchen Thénaud often collected morsels. So returning was not as hard as going.

He reached France again by way of Damietta and Rhodes; then, traveling up the Loire as far as Amboise, he found there "glory be to God, more pleasure than he had had on the Nile, although it was the second river of the earthly paradise." He gave account to Madame Louise of the successful accomplishment of his mission, and returned to his brethren to finish his days in tranquillity "praising God, His glorious Mother, and the glorious saints Ausonius and Cybart," who had guided him so far and brought him safely back to a safe port.

※ ※ ※

At the other end of the century, a philosopher, the very antithesis of the simple friar of Angoulême, set off on horseback across Europe. It was a Monsieur de Montaigne, a comfortably off bourgeois of liberal views and the future mayor of Bordeaux. Traveling for the sake of his health, in order to treat "the stone" from which he suffered cruelly, he sampled all the waters of Germany and Italy. The most celebrated were those of Plombières, of which he has left a description[14]:

"It is on the borders of Lorraine and Germany, situated on a chasm between divers lofty scarped hills, which close it in on all sides. At the bottom of this valley several springs, cold and hot as well, flow forth. The hot water has neither smell nor taste. . . . Only two of the springs are drunk. One which flows from the eastward and forms the bath, which they call the Queen's Bath, leaves in the mouth a certain sweet taste, not unlike liquorice, and no disagreeable aftertaste. But after very careful attention, M. de Montaigne declared that a slight flavor of iron might be detected therein. The other spring, which rises at the base of the mountain opposite, and of which M. de Montaigne drank only one day, is slightly harsh, and has the flavor of alum. The habit of the place is to take a bath two or three times a day. Some take their meals in the bath, where they are cupped and scarified, and do not drink the waters except after a purge. If they drink at all, they take a glass or two in the bath. . . .

"We saw some men cured of ulcers and others of pimples on the body.

The wonted course is a month at least, and rooms are let most readily in May. Few people frequent the place after the month of August, by reason of the cold, but we found much company there still, because the heat and drought had been abnormally prolonged. . . .

"This bath was formerly used only by Germans, but for several years past the people of Franche-Comté and France have come in great numbers. There are several baths, and the principal one is built oval in shape, after the fashion of an ancient edifice. It is thirty-five paces long and fifteen wide. The hot water rises from several springs, and cold water is made to trickle down into the bath so that the heat may be moderated according to the taste of those who use it. The places in the bath are set out side by side by bars suspended like those in our stables, and planks are laid over the top so as to keep off the heat of the sun and the rain. There are stone steps all around the baths as in a theater, where those who are bathing may sit or recline. The visitors in this place maintain a singular propriety of carriage, and it is reckoned indecent for men to bathe naked or with less clothing than a little jacket, or for women to wear less than a chemise. . . . Every year they write afresh on a tablet, hung up in front of the principal bath, the laws there inscribed in the German and French tongues as follows:

"'Claude de Rynach, knight, lord of St. Balesmont . . . councillor and chamberlain of our sovereign lord monseigneur the Duke &c., and his balli of the Vosges.

"'Let it be known that for securing the comfort and quietude of the many ladies and other persons coming from divers countries to these baths of Plombières, we have, according to the intention of His Highness, decreed and ordained as follows:

"'It is forbidden to all people, of whatever quality, condition, region, or province they may be, to use provocation in insulting language tending to lead to quarrels: to carry arms while at the baths aforesaid: to give the lie: to put hand to arms under pain of severe punishment as breakers of the peace, rebels and disobedient to His Highness.

"'Also it is forbidden to all prostitutes and immodest women to enter the baths, or to be found within five hundred paces of the same under penalty of a whipping at the four corners of the town. And the householders who shall receive or conceal them shall incur the pain of imprisonment and arbitrary fine.

"'The same penalty will fall on those who shall use any lascivious or immodest discourse to any ladies, or damsels, or other women and girls who may be visiting the baths, or touch them in a manner unbecoming, or enter or quit the baths in ribald fashion, contrary to public decency.

"'And because by the boon of the baths aforenamed God and nature have afforded us cure and relief in many cases, and because decent cleanliness and purity are necessary in order to keep off the many contagions and infections which might well engender in such a place, it is expressly commanded to the governor of these baths to take the utmost care, and to inspect the persons of those who frequent the same by day and by night; to make them keep decency and silence during the night, making no noise, nor scandal, nor horseplay. And if any person will not render obedience the governor shall forthwith carry the affair before the magistrate, so that an exemplary punishment may be given.

" 'Beyond this it is prohibited to all persons coming from infected places to repair to Plombières under pain of death. It is expressly laid upon all mayors and officers of justice to have careful watch over the place; and upon all the townsfolk, to furnish us with billets containing the names, surnames, and residence of all the people they may have taken into their lodgings, under pain of imprisonment.' "

Montaigne was also traveling for pleasure. He was, as he said, "like those who are reading some agreeable tale and begin to be afraid it will soon end, or some good book; in the same way, he greatly enjoys traveling at ease. . . ." And he adds "that after having spent an uncomfortable night, in the morning when he remembered what he had to see, whether city or country, he got up with enthusiasm and delight."

The difference, of course, is that Thénaud traveled like a man of the Middle Ages, while Montaigne had the same curiosity and the same critical spirit as a man of today. He wanted to see everything, visit everything, observe all—things, people, places, customs. He was interested in everything, and he considered visiting foreign countries an indispensable part of a man's education:

"It is not only to bring back, as our French nobility do, how many steps there are at Santa Rotonda or the opulence of Signora Livia's pants, nor, as others have done, how much longer or wider is Nero's face on some old ruin there than on some other medal, but rather to bring back the temperaments of these nations and their habits, and to rub and rasp our brain against that of others. . . . From frequenting the world a wonderful clarity of human judgment is acquired. We are all stuck and pinioned within ourselves and our view is limited by the length of our nose. . . . This great world . . . is the mirror where we must look to see ourselves aright. . . . So many humors, sects, judgments, opinions, laws, and customs teach us to judge our own more sanely and teach our judgment to acknowledge its imperfection and its natural weakness; the which is not an unweighty apprenticeship."[15]

The account which Montaigne has left of his stay in Augsburg is testimony enough of such a state of mind. "Augsburg," he wrote, "is considered the most beautiful town of Germany, as Strasburg is reputed the strongest." He had decided to spend a few days there because of its reputation, and he reached the city at the end of a long stage. As soon as he was rested, however, he set eagerly about making the rounds of the town. It was Sunday, and he naturally visited the churches.[16] In Luther's homeland, he lingered in one church with his companions and had the good luck to witness a christening.

"Six of the churches are Lutheran and served by sixteen ministers, two of the churches being taken over from Catholics and four built by the Lutherans themselves." One of the latter was visited by Montaigne on that Sunday morning, and he found it to resemble "the great hall of a college, with neither images nor organs nor cross, but with the walls covered with inscriptions in German taken from the Bible. There were two chairs, one for the minister or for whosoever might preach, and another one placed lower for the leader in singing the psalms. At every verse the people wait for the leader aforesaid, who gives the note. They sing in haphazard fashion, each one according to his humor, and with head bare or covered. After the singing, a minister who had been in the assembly went to the altar, and read from a book several prayers, at certain of which the people stood up and clasped their hands, and made deep reverence at the name of Jesus Christ. After he had finished his reading to the assembly, he put before him on the altar a napkin, a basin, and a saucer, in which was water. A woman, followed by a dozen others, brought to him a child, swaddled and with face bare, whereupon the minister thrice took the water in the saucer and sprinkled it on the child's face and said certain words. This being finished, two men approached and each one of them placed two fingers of the right hand upon the child; the minister then addressed them, and this was all."

M. de Montaigne held a conversation with this minister after he left the church, and was informed that the ministers receive no stipend from the church, their salary being paid by the Senate as a public charge; that there was a greater crowd of worshipers in this one church than in two or three of the Catholic churches together. "We did not see a single handsome woman. The women wear a vast variety of attire, and in the case of the men it is a hard matter to say who is noble and who is not, for as all sorts of men wear bonnets of velvet and carry swords by the side."

In this rich city of merchants, the powerful Fugger family ruled the roost. They were illustrious bankers, brokers to princes, and their florins more than once swayed the course of European politics. Montaigne admiringly visited their sumptuous homes.[17]

"The Fugger family is a very numerous one; they are all very rich, and hold the highest position in this city. We visited two apartments in their house, one high, of grand measurement, and paved with marble, and the other low-ceilinged, enriched with medals, both ancient and modern, and having a small room at the end. These are the most sumptuous rooms I ever beheld. At the gathering after the wedding we saw some dancing, and they danced nothing but allemandes. They constantly stop dancing and lead the ladies back to their seats, which are ranged in double rows against the walls and covered with red cloth; but the gentlemen do not sit there with them. After a slight pause they take their dames out again, kissing their hands, which salutation the ladies accept without returning it; and then, having placed the arm under the ladies' armpits, they embrace them, and the ladies put their right hands on the gentlemen's shoulders. They dance and chat together with heads bare and in sober attire.

"We saw more houses belonging to the Fuggers in other parts of the city, which is beholden to this family for the great outlay of money they spend in its adornment. These houses are summer residences. In one we saw a clock which was worked by the flow of water which serves as a counterpoise. At the same place were two large covered fishponds full of fish, and twenty paces square. Around the brink of each of the ponds are divers small pipes, some straight and others curving upwards, and through each of these water is poured in very pleasant wise into the pond, some delivering it in a direct jet, and others spouting it upward to the height of a pikestaff. Between the ponds is a space some ten paces in width floored with planks, and between these planks are hidden certain little taps of brass. Thus, at any time when ladies may go to divert themselves by seeing the fish play about the pond, it needs only the letting go of a certain spring to make every tap aforesaid send a jet of water straight upward to the height of a man, and drench the petticoats and cool the thighs of the ladies. In another place there is a fountain pipe, contrived to play a merry jest upon the spectator, for, while you look at the same, any one who is so minded may turn on the water in tiny hidden jets, which will throw in your face a hundred little threads of water; and there is set up a Latin inscription: *Quaesisti nugas, nugis gaudeto repertis* [You wished to be amused, rejoice that you succeeded in being so]. Near thereto is a large cage, twenty paces square and twelve or fifteen feet high, which is enclosed all around with copper wire, well knit and fastened, and inside are ten or twelve fir trees and a fountain. This cage is full of birds, among others Polish pigeons, which they call *d'inde*, and which I have seen elsewhere: these are large birds beaked like partridges.

"We saw also the handiwork of a certain gardener who, foreseeing cold, inclement weather, had transported into a little shed a great quantity of artichokes, cabbages, lettuces, spinach, chicory, and other vegetables, which he had gathered as if to consume them at once, but in lieu thereof had set them by the root in soil, and hoped to keep them good and fresh three or four months; and indeed he had there a hundred artichokes, not the least withered, though they had been plucked more than six weeks.

"We went to see certain men who were conveying from Venice two ostriches to the Duke of Saxony. The male was the blacker of the two,

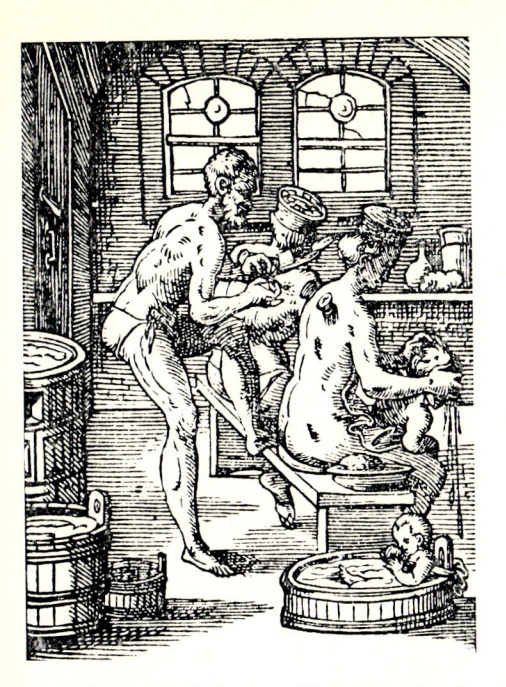

A bathing establishment. Engraving by J. Amman. Bibliothèque de Grenoble

A thermal station (1553). Cabinet des Estampes, Bibliothèque de Grenoble

21.

Ladies at their toilet. Sixteenth-century miniature. Bibliothèque Nationale, Paris

Arab merchant. Sixteenth-century engraving. Bibliothèque de Grenoble

Egyptian woman carrying her child. Sixteenth-century engraving. Bibliothèque de Grenoble

22.

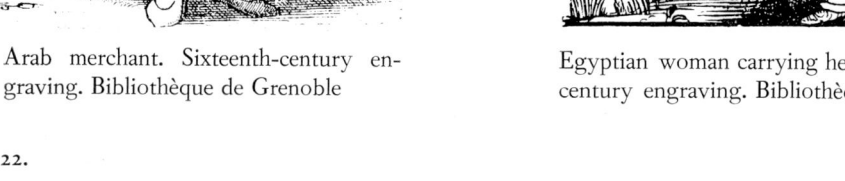

Moorish water carrier. Sixteenth-century engraving. Bibliothèque de Grenoble

Jewish merchant. Sixteenth-century engraving. Bibliothèque de Grenoble

Picking mulberries and raising silkworms. Contemporary engraving after
J. Stradamus. Cabinet des Estampes, Bibliothèque Nationale, Paris

A sixteenth-century navigator at work. Engraving after J. Stradanus. Cabinet des Estampes, Bibliothèque Nationale, Paris

A sixteenth-century seaman. Engraving by J. Amman. Bibliothèque de Grenoble

A caravel caught in a storm at sea. Illustration Psalm 107. Bibliothèque de Grenoble

24.

A caravel. Sixteenth-century miniature. Bibliothèque Nationale, Paris

and had a red neck; the female was of a gray color and laid a great number of eggs. The men said that these beasts felt less fatigue than they themselves, and constantly contrived to escape, but they kept them in hand by means of a band which girt them around the back above the thighs, and another one above the shoulders. These bands held them in all around, and the guards had caused to be fastened thereto long reins by means of which they could stop them."

Augsburg possessed other attractions. Prodigies, the result of centuries of ingenuity, had endowed the humblest villages with clocks and automatic figures perched high on their belfries roofed with shining tiles, and had given the citizens running water, a mark of progress that no town in France could boast of at that time. . . . "At the city gate by which we had entered, we observed a copious stream of water which was brought into the city from outside . . . This current in its course turns a number of waterwheels attached to pumps which, by means of two leaden pipes, raise the water of a spring, which rises in a hollow, to the top of a tower some fifty feet in height. On the top of this tower the water is poured into a great stone cistern, and from this cistern it runs down through divers pipes and is distributed all over the city, which in consequence is abundantly supplied with fountains. Private persons, if it be their wish, may have a right of water for their own use on payment of an annual rent of ten florins to the city, or for two hundred florins paid down. The city was enriched by this magnificent work about forty years ago."

But the time came to leave Augsburg. After Germany and Austria came Italy. Going by way of Venice and Padua, Ferrara, luxuriant Bologna, Florence, and Siena, M. de Montaigne set out for Rome for a five months' stay. His first interest, and for him the chief attraction of Rome, was the papal city. Soon after his arrival, he was received by the sovereign pontiff[18]:.

"On December 29, M. d'Abain, who was then our ambassador, a learned gentleman and a long-standing friend of M. de Montaigne, advised him to go and kiss the feet of the pope. M. de Montaigne and M. d'Estissac went in the coach of the ambassador, who, after he had been granted an audience, caused them to be called by the pope's chamberlain. According to custom, only the ambassador was with the pope, who had by his side a bell which he would ring when he might wish anyone to be introduced. The ambassador was seated, uncovered, at his left hand; the pope himself never uncovers before any one, nor can any ambassador remain covered in his presence. M. d'Estissac entered first, then M. de Montaigne, then M. de Mattecoulon, and last M. d'Hautoy. After taking a step or two into the chamber, in a corner of which sits the pope, the incomer, whoever he may be, kneels and waits for the pope to give him benediction. This done, he will rise and advance to the middle of the room, but a stranger rarely approaches the pope by going directly across the floor, the more ordinary practice being to turn to the left on entering, and then, after making a detour along the wall, to approach his chair. But when the stranger has gone half the distance he must kneel again on one knee, and, having received a second benediction, next advances as far as the thick carpet spread out some seven or eight feet in front of the pope. Here he must kneel on both knees, while the ambassador who presents him kneels on one, and moves back the pope's robe from his right foot, which is shod in a red shoe with a white cross thereupon. The kneeling stranger must keep himself in the same posture until he is close to the pope's foot, and then bend down to kiss it. M. de Montaigne declared that the pope raised the point of his foot a little. They all kissed it one after the other, making room for each other after the ceremony was done. Then the ambassador covered the pope's foot, and, having risen to his seat, said what seemed necessary on behalf of M. d'Estissac and M. de Montaigne. The pope, with courteous expression of face, admonished M. d'Estissac to cultivate learning and virtue, and M. de Montaigne to maintain the devotion he had always exhibited toward the Church and the interests of the most Christian king: whatever service he could do them they might depend on, this being an Italian figure of speech. They said nothing, but, having been blessed again before rising as a sign of dismissal, they went back in the same order. Each one retreats as it seems best, but the ordinary custom is to go backward, or at least sideways, so as always to look the pope in the face. As in entering, each one kneels halfway on one knee for another benediction, and again at the door for the last."

Some time afterward M. de Montaigne visited the Vatican Library. "On March 6 I went to see the library of the Vatican, which is contained in five or six rooms all communicating one with the other. There are many rows of desks, each desk having a great number of books chained thereto. Also, in the chests, which were all opened for my inspection, I saw many manuscripts, of which I chiefly remarked a Seneca and the *Opuscula* of Plutarch. Among the noteworthy sights I saw was the statue of the good Aristides, with a fine head, bald and thickly bearded, a grand forehead, and an expression full of sweetness and majesty. The base is very ancient, and has his name written thereupon. I saw likewise a Chinese book written in strange characters, on leaves made of a certain stuff much more tender and transparent than the paper we use, and because this fabric is not thick enough to bear the stain of ink, they write on only one side of the sheet, and the sheets are all doubled and folded at the outside edges by which they are held together. It is said that these sheets are the bark of a certain tree, as is a fragment of ancient papyrus which I saw covered with unknown characters. I saw also the Breviary of St. Gregory in manuscript, which has no date, but the account they give of it states that it has come down from one hand to another from St. Gregory's time. It is a missal not unlike our own, and it was taken to the recent Council at Trent as an authority for the ceremonies of our church. Next, a book by St. Thomas Aquinas, containing corrections made by the author himself, who wrote badly, using a small character worse even than my own. Next, a Bible printed on parchment, one of those which Plantin has recently printed in four languages, which book King Philip presented to the pope, according to an inscription on the cover. Next, the original manuscript of the book which King Henry of England wrote against Luther and sent fifty years ago to Pope Leo X. . . . I inspected the library without any difficulty; indeed, anyone may visit it and make what extracts he likes; it is open almost every morning. I was taken to every part thereof by a gentleman, who invited me to make use of it as often as I might desire. . . .

"In the library I saw also a manuscript Virgil in an exceedingly large handwriting, of that long and narrow character which we see in Rome in inscriptions of the age of the emperors somewhere about the reign of Constantine, a character which takes somewhat of Gothic form, and misses that square proportion which the old Latin inscriptions possess. The sight of this Virgil confirmed a belief which I have always held, to wit, that the four lines usually put at the opening of the *Æneid* are borrowed, since this copy has them not. Also a copy of the Acts of the Apostles, written in very fair Greek golden character. The lettering is massive, solid in substance, and raised upon the paper, so that anyone who may pass his finger over the same will detect the thickness thereof. We have, I believe, lost all knowledge of this method."[19]

He took tremendous pleasure in listening to Lenten sermons:

"There were many excellent preachers, for instance the renegade rabbi who preached to the Jews on Saturday evenings in the Church of the Trinità. Here was always a congress of sixty Jews who were bound to be present. This preacher had been a famous doctor among them, and he attacked their beliefs by their own arguments even out of the mouths of their rabbis and from the words of the Bible. He had admirable skill and knowledge of the subject, and of the languages necessary for the elaboration of the same. There was another, who preached before the pope and cardinals, named Padre Toledo, a man of extraordinary ability in depth of learning, in appositeness of expression, and in mustering of his arguments, and a third, who preached at the church of the Jesuits, was distinguished for the beauty of the language he used, the two last being members of the Jesuit society. It is wonderful how great is the part occupied by this college in the Christian economy, and my belief is that never before has there existed any confraternity which has risen to such eminence, or which may sway so powerfully the destinies of the world, supposing that it should be able to prosecute its designs in the future. It occupies well nigh the whole of Christendom; it is a nursery of men distinguished in every department of high affairs and the institution of our church which the heretics of our day have most to fear."[20]

He missed none of the Holy Week ceremonies:

"On the morning of Holy Thursday the pope, in pontifical garb, accompanied by the cardinals, repaired to the second platform of the great portico of St. Peter's bearing a lighted torch in his hand. Then a canon of St. Peter's, who stood on one side of the balcony, read in a loud voice a bull written in Latin by which men of an infinite variety of sorts and conditions were excommunicated; among others the Huguenots were specially named, and all those princes who keep hold on any of the lands of the Church, an article which caused loud laughter from the Cardinals Medici and Carafa, who stood close to the pope. The reading of this bull lasted a good hour; for when the canon had finished reading an article in Latin, the Cardinal Gonzaga, who stood on the opposite side—uncovered like the canon—would repeat the same in Italian. When the reading was done the pope cast the lighted torch down amongst the people; and, whether out of jest or not, Cardinal Gonzaga threw down another, three torches having been kindled. This having fallen amongst the people caused a vast disturbance below, every one scrambling to pick up a fragment of the torch, and giving and taking shrewd blows with fist or cudgel. During the reading of this sentence the balustrade of the portico in front of the pope was covered with a large piece of black taffeta, but, the excommunication having been pronounced, they folded up this black covering and disclosed one of a different color, whereupon the pope gave his public blessing. On these days they exhibit the handkerchief of St. Veronica. This is a countenance wrought in needlework, of a dark and somber tint, and framed after the fashion of a mirror. It is shown with great ceremony from a high pulpit, five or six paces in width, and the priest who holds it wears on his hands red gloves, while two or three other priests assist him in displaying it. No spectacle provokes such great show of reverence as this, the people all prostrate themselves on the ground, the greater part of them weeping and uttering cries of pity. . . . On these same occasions they show to the people likewise with equal ceremonies a lance head enclosed in a crystal vessel. This display is made several times during the day, and the crowd which comes to witness the same is so vast that, as far as the eye can reach from the pulpit aforesaid outside the church, there is nought to be seen but an endless crowd of men and women. Here is the true papal court."[21]

Montaigne was also surprised at the important part which religious confraternities played in Roman life and at the devotion which they exhibited:

"There are more than a hundred confraternities, and there is no distinguished man but belongs to one; there is none for foreigners. Our kings belong to that of the Gonfalcon. Each particular society is wont to exercise, and especially during Lent, certain functions of religious fellowship, and on this special day they walk about in companies clad in linen gowns, each company wearing its particular color, white, red, blue, green, or black, almost all with their faces covered. . . . The whole city, as night approached, seemed to be on fire on account of the procession of these confraternities toward St. Peter's, each one bearing a lighted candle—almost always of white wax—in his hand. I am sure that at least twelve thousand torches must have gone by the place where I stood; for, from eight o'clock till midnight, the street was filled with the procession, marshaled and regulated in such excellent order that, though there were many different companies coming from different places, the ranks were never broken or the progress stayed. Each confraternity had a fine choir of musicians, who sang as they marched. In the midst of the ranks went a file of penitencers to the number of five hundred, who scourged themselves with cords, and left their backs all raw and bloody. This is a riddle which still baffles me, but there is no denying that they were bruised and wounded in cruel fashion, and that this self-torture and flagellation went on without ceasing. Judging by the aspect of their faces, the assurance of their gait, and the steadfastness audible in their discourse and visible in their countenances (for I heard several of them speak, and many uncovered themselves in passing through the street), it would never have suggested itself to me that they were engaged in a painful and irksome task. Among them were youths of twelve or thirteen years of age, and right in front of me was one, very young and fair in seeming, over whose wounds a young woman lamented sore; but the boy, turning toward us, said with a laugh, 'Enough of that; what I do I do for your sins and not for my own.' Not only was there absent all appearance of distress or violence; they even went about their flagellation with an appearance of pleasure, or at least of nonchalance, so marked that they might have been chattering about other matters, laughing, bawling about the street, running and leaping when there was so great a crowd that the procession fell somewhat into confusion. Along with them went certain men carrying wine, which was offered to them now and again, and some of them took a mouthful thereof, and sometimes sweetmeats were given. The winecarriers often took wine in their mouths and then blew it out and moistened therewith the lashes of the scourges, which were of cord, and were wont to become coagulated with the blood drawn to such an extent that it was necessary to moisten them in order to separate the thongs. They also blew the wine over the wounds of some of the victims. The appearance of their shoes and breeches suggested that they were people of mean condition, and that the majority of them had sold themselves to this service. Moreover, I was told that they were wont to grease their shoulders with a certain preparation, but the wounds I saw were so natural, and the scourging was so lengthy, that assuredly no medicament could benumb them to pain. And with regard to those who may have hired them, what profit would they get were this exhibition nought but trickery? Certain other peculiarities of this function may be noticed. When the people in procession arrive at St. Peter's, the only function they attend is the exhibition of *il Viso Santo;* as soon as one company has seen it, it passes on and makes room for another. On this day great liberty is granted to all womankind; for, through the night, the streets are filled with ladies nearly all going on foot. Nevertheless the city has the air of having greatly mended its manners, especially in respect to the relaxation aforesaid, all amorous glances and manifestations being suppressed."

On Holy Saturday, M. de Montaigne went to the Church of St. John Lateran to see the heads of St. Peter and St. Paul. He noted[22] that the relics "have still some flesh upon them, and are colored and bearded as in life. The face of St. Peter is fair, somewhat elongated, with a ruddy, almost sanguine tint on the cheeks, and a forked gray beard, the head being covered with a papal miter. That of St. Paul is dark, broad, and fatter; the head altogether being larger and the beard thick and gray. They are kept high up in a place devised for them, and the exhibition is made in this wise. The people are summoned by the ringing of bells, then a curtain, stretched before the heads, is let down, and they may be seen side by side. They are left visible long enough to let the spectators say an *Ave Maria,* and then the curtain is drawn up again. Afterward they are displayed afresh in the same way, and then for a third time. This exhibition takes place three or four times during the day. The place where they are kept is about the height of a pike from the ground, and a heavy iron grating is in front of them, through which the spectator must peer in order to see them, several candles being lighted outside the grating, but it is difficult to discern clearly the particular features. I saw them three or four times, and found the skin shiny and something like the masks we use."

Montaigne was, it is clear, a confirmed gawker. He loved watching street life, and he had his fill of it in Rome, where "the commonest exercise of the Romans is to walk in the streets . . . and there are streets especially set aside for this purpose. Pretty women, noble men, courtesans—all enchanted him. If he was not under the weather from a purge, he was out and about. On the occasion he saw the public hanging of one Catena, a notorious bandit of the time:

"On January 11, in the morning, as M. de Montaigne was leaving the house on horseback, he met Catena, a famous robber and banditti chief, whom they were taking away from the prison. This man had raised a panic all through Italy, monstrous tales of murder being told about him; notably concerning two Capuchins, whom he forced to deny God, and promised to spare their lives on this condition. But he slew them afterwards without any motive either of gain or of vengeance. M. de Montaigne halted to behold the spectacle. Over and beyond the escort customary in France, they let precede the criminal a huge crucifix draped with black, at the foot of which went a great crowd of men wearing cloaks and masks of cloth, and these were said to be of the chief gentlefolk of Rome, a confraternity sworn to accompany criminals to execution and corpses to the grave. Two of these—or two monks in similar garb—helped the condemned man into the cart and preached to him, one of them letting him kiss continually a picture of Our Lord. This they did so that those in the street might not see the man's face. At the gibbet, which was a beam upon two posts, they held this picture before his face till he was thrown off the ladder. He died as criminals commonly do, without movement or cry; a dark man of thirty or thereabout, and after he was strangled they cut his body in four quarters. It is the custom amongst these people to kill criminals without torture, and after death to subject the body to very barbarous usage. M. de Montaigne remarked that he had written elsewhere how deeply people are moved by the cruelties practiced upon dead bodies, and on this occasion the crowd, who had not felt any pity at the hanging, cried out in lamentation at every stroke of the ax. As soon as he was dead, divers Jesuits or other churchmen went up to a high place and cried to the people on all sides that they should take to heart this example."[23]

On other occasions, this sophisticated traveler was not above indulging in gossip, some of which proved to be edifying as well as entertaining:

"A certain man was with a courtesan, lying in bed and enjoying the full liberty of the situation, when, at the twenty-fourth hour, the *Ave Maria* sounded, and the girl sprang out of bed and knelt down on the floor to say her prayer. Shortly afterward he was with another, when suddenly the good mother (for these girls are always in the hands of some old bawd whom they call mother or aunt) knocked at the door and, having entered in a transport of rage, tore off from the girl's neck a ribbon from which was hanging a little image of Our Lady, so that it might not be contaminated by the sinful act of the wearer. The young girl showed herself exceedingly penitent, in that she had omitted her customary practice of first removing this image from her person."[24]

M. de Montaigne left Rome regretfully, and proceeded by easy stages to Loreto, to which, like everyone else, he made a pilgrimage. He even carried in his baggage, as an offering to the Holy Mother, all the way from La-Motte-Montravel in Guyenne, a picture to which, he tells us "there are four silver figures attached: that of Our Lady, mine, that of my wife, and that of my daughter." Prayers completed, picture set in its place, he traveled north in his accustomed manner, stopping where his heart suggested, as the fancy took him, or as his health dictated. Thus he stopped at the baths of Della Villa, some leagues from Lucca. He enjoyed himself, and gladly submitted to the exigencies of local life. There, the summer visitor who knew how to live owed it to himself to give a ball. M. de Montaigne gladly complied with this charming custom:

"Five or six days before this date I had caused notice of my entertainment to be given in all the neighboring villages, and on the day previous I sent special invitations to all the gentlefolk then sojourning at either of the baths. I bade them come to the ball, and to the supper afterward, and sent to Lucca for the presents, which are usually pretty numerous, so as to avoid the appearance of favoring one lady above all the rest, and to steer clear of jealousy and suspicion. They always give eight or ten to the ladies, and two or three to the gentlemen. Many ventured to jog my memory, one begging me not to forget herself, another her niece, another her daughter.

"On the day previous Messer Giovanni da Vincenzo Saminiati, a good friend of mine, brought me from Lucca, according to my written instructions, a leathern belt and a black cloth cap as presents for the men. For the ladies I provided two aprons of taffeta, one green and the other purple (for it must be known that it is always meet to have certain presents better than the bulk, so as to show special favor where favor seems to be due), two aprons of bombazine, four papers of pins, four pairs of shoes—one pair of which I gave to a pretty girl who did not come to the ball—a pair of slippers, which I put with one of the pairs of shoes to form one prize, three headdresses clear woven, and three netted, which together stood for three prizes, and four small pearl necklaces. Thus I had altogether nineteen gifts for the ladies, the cost of which was six crowns; little enough. I engaged five pipers, giving them their food for the day, and a crown among the lot, a good bargain for me, seeing that they will rarely play here at such a rate. The prizes aforesaid were hung up on a hoop, richly ornamented, and visible to all the company. . . ."

At the appointed hour, the guests arrived and the ball began. M. de Montaigne had recourse to the advice of the most distinguished ladies for the delicate undertaking of choosing the most beautiful young ladies in the gathering and giving them the prizes: "For the distribution of these prizes . . . the girls were called one by one from their places to come before the lady and myself, sitting side by side, whereupon I gave to the signora the gift which seemed appropriate, having first kissed the same. Then the signora, taking it in her hand, gave it to the young girl, and said in friendly fashion, 'This is the gentleman who is giving you this charming present; thank him for it.' I added, 'Nay, rather your thanks are due to the gracious signora who has designated you out of so many others as worthy of reward. I much regret that the offering made to you is not more worthy of such merit as yours.' I spoke somewhat in these terms to each according to her qualifications.

"In sooth it was a rare and charming sight to us Frenchmen to look upon these comely peasants dancing so well in the garb of gentlefolk. They did their best to rival the finest of our lady dancers, albeit in a different style. I invited all to supper, as the meals in Italy are like the lightest of our repasts in France, and on this occasion I only provided a few joints of veal and a pair or two of fowls. . . . I also found a place at table for Divizia, a poor peasant woman who lives about two miles from the baths, unmarried, and with no other support than her handiwork. She is ugly, about thirty-seven years of age, with a swollen throat, and unable either to read or write; but it chanced that in her childhood there came to live in her father's house an uncle who was ever reading aloud in her hearing Ariosto and others of the poets, wherefore she seemed to find a natural delight in poetry, and was soon able, not only to make verses with marvelous readiness, but likewise to weave thereinto the ancient stories, the names of the gods of various countries, of sciences, and of illustrious men, as if she had received a liberal education. She recited divers lines in my honor, which, to speak the truth, were little else than verses and rhymes, but the diction was elegant and spontaneous. I entertained at my ball more than a hundred strangers, albeit the time was inconvenient for them, seeing that they were then in the midst of the silk harvest, their principal crop of the year. At this season they labor, heedless of all feast days, at plucking, morning and evening, the leaves of the mulberry for their silkworms and all my peasant guests were engaged in this work."[25]

M. de Montaigne soon ended this agreeable stay, then loitered again in Central Italy, revisiting Florence and Rome. Finally, with his "stone," his memories, and his journal, he went home.

※ ※ ※

Between a Jean Thénaud and a Michel de Montaigne there can be few points in common, for the two men were separated by a century of upheavals, by a new vision of the universe. But while one watched the sights of the highway with simple heart and the other with critical eye, while one was concerned with praising God and the other with knowing man, they were united by the simple need to go elsewhere, to see the great world. It is a need which the passing of the centuries has not satisfied.

G*

NOTES

IX · Travelers of the Renaissance

1. Beatis, Antonio de, *op. cit.*, p. 255.
2. Erasmus, Desiderius. "Colloquies," in *Erasme, Oeuvres choisies*. Ed. A. Renaudet. Paris, n.d., pp. 193–95.
3. Montaigne, Michel Eyquem de. *Journal of Montaigne's Travels in Italy by Way of Switzerland and Germany in 1580 and 1581*. Translated by W. G. Waters. London, 1903. *Passim*.
4. Bonnaffe, E. *Les arts et les moeurs d'autrefois: Voyages et voyageurs de la Renaissance*. Paris, 1895, p. 11.
5. Beatis, Antonio de, *op. cit.*, p. 174.
6. Thénaud, Jean. *Le voyage d'Outremer*. Ed. C. Schefer. Paris, 1884, pp. 36–37.
7. *Ibid.*, pp. 46–51.
8. *Ibid.*, pp. 53–55.
9. *Ibid.*, pp. 61–71.
10. *Ibid.*, pp. 71–75.
11. *Ibid.*, pp. 89–93.
12. *Ibid.*, pp. 105–6.
13. *Ibid.*, pp. 106–7.
14. Montaigne, Michel Eyquem de, *op. cit.*, pp. 46–53.
15. Montaigne, Michel Eyquem de. *Les Essais*. Ed. M. Rat. Paris, 1958. Livre I, ch. 26, p. 163.
16. Montaigne, Michel Eyquem de. *Journal of Montaigne's Travels* . . . Vol. I, pp. 80–81.
17. *Ibid.*, pp. 86–88.
18. *Ibid.*, pp. 75–77.
19. *Ibid.*, pp. 142–43.
20. *Ibid.*, Vol. II, p. 99–103.
21. *Ibid.*, pp. 118–21.
22. *Ibid.*, p. 121.
23. *Ibid.*, pp. 124–26.
24. *Ibid.*, pp. 290–91.
25. *Ibid.*, Vol. III, pp. 68–73.

PART FOUR

REVOLUTIONS OF THE RENAISSANCE

X · An Age of Discovery

MEDIEVAL Europe at the end of the fifteenth century felt a resurgence of life. The sap of youth rose anew in her tired body and the goods of the world were perceived by her arrayed in a thousand new and seductive ways. A violent desire to possess them gripped her. She had to have them at all costs, even if the old continent did not include them all, even if she must traverse oceans to search for them at the ends of the earth, in countries as yet unknown and at the price of unimaginable perils. Hitherto, her appetite had been whetted by the gold, pearls, perfumes, and spices that came in infinitesimal quantities from those mysterious and distant lands known as "the Indies," through the deserts of Arabia and the perils of the Mediterranean, at the whim of caravans and the caprices of the Grand Turk. The Republic of Venice, superlatively wealthy, had distilled these most precious wares drop by drop, at exorbitant prices.

There were gold for kings and diamonds for their queens. For the noble beauties, perfumes of Tibetan musk or Damascus rose water, emeralds of upper Egypt, rubies of Ceylon, and Persian turquoises. Opium and poppies from the Thebaid, dried fruits from India, camphor from Sumatra, Chinese root from Galaga, gum tragacanth from Asia Minor, cassia from Egypt, manna from Persia—of sovereign healing virtue—filled the pharmacopoeias, either combatting epidemics or more prosaically neutralizing the smell of dirty clothing. For dyeing, there were Armenian scarlet, Coromandel and Bengalese indigo, Levantine saffron and Arabian henna. For cooking one had the five "royal ingredients": black pepper from Malabar and Ceylon, so precious that it could serve as currency; ginger from Arabia crystallized in sugar; nutmegs from the Moluccas, cinnamon from China, and cloves gave sauces that exotic perfume and rare savor necessary to the gourmet. Only these could redeem a diet which basically was tasteless, composed of stews, salt meat, flour, roots, and onions, in times which did not yet possess rice, potatoes, or corn and in which sugar remained an exceptional luxury.

It was known that these treasures, whose quintessence was so costly, existed in prodigious abundance in the Greater Indies, in the Indies of

Cathay and at Cipangu. There, as everyone knew, at the foot of diamond mountains, rose palaces encrusted with gem-stones and tiled with pure gold. The only real problem seemed to be finding an easy route to that Promised Land. It is true that the Mediterranean was forbidden the French by the Turks, and Venetians barred the way. But if the world were round, as people liked to say, then could not Cathay, fabled China, be reached by faring west as well as east? What magnificent wealth awaited those navigators whom a happy fate would bear to the fortune-laden shores of such an El Dorado, who could bring home galleons and carracks laden down with sweet-scented cargoes.

In that adventurous and dynamic century, many were the hardy pioneers ready to launch out on such a quest. Sailing safer vessels, furnished with the mariner's compass, which three centuries of experimentation had rendered practicable, they could set forth—and return, if God preserved them. And the seas were white with sail, and the captains offered their services to the great ones of this world, to the rich and powerful, to those who would provide the financial means they did not possess to equip a few carracks and recruit some good carriers. But only the sovereigns of Spain and Portugal hearkened. In the name of Ferdinand and Isabella, Christopher Columbus discovered in the west the land which would be called America, while Magellan, by his voyage around the world, proved that the earth was round and that, to the southwest, there indeed existed a passage to the Indies. For Manuel the Fortunate, King of Portugal, Vasco da Gama reached the Indies by way of the Indian Ocean after rounding the Cape of Good Hope. As always, to the victor belonged the spoils—in this case, the discovered lands, the trade monopoly. To the Portuguese went the route to the Moluccas by way of the African coast and Indian Ocean, and the lands located three hundred and seventy leagues west of the Cape Verde Islands; that is to say, Brazil. To the Spaniards went Central America and Peru. Naturally, the location of the newly found lands and the means of access to them were carefully kept secret by governments jealous of their rights.

The French clearly had allowed themselves to be outdistanced. Their kings, faithful to the traditional and proved Levantine route to the East, had minimized the importance of these Atlantic adventures at a time when no initiative could succeed without royal patronage. Still, it was perhaps not too late to make amends by exploring that mysterious part of the globe which lies between Europe and Asia, to the north and south of the lands occupied by the Spaniards and Portuguese. Perhaps it was a spur of China, or even a separate continent which would raise, as some feared, a barrier between the two worlds. Or it was perhaps, as others thought, a series of islands separated by straits, which only had to be navigated to reach the journey's goal more rapidly than by the Portuguese route. Thus, because the center of the new countries where Columbus had chanced to land remained out of bounds to the French latecomers, and because they were limited to the search for a passage to India to the northwest, where they would meet no one, so entered into history the search for the famous Northwest Passage. It was a dream which was to haunt merchants and sailors alike from that time onwards, which would absorb their activity and lead them, by the hazard of their undertakings, to results quite different from those expected.

* * *

Armed to the teeth, the holds filled to bursting and manned by a determined crew, the *Marie* or *Humanité* prepared to set sail. Twenty days to Newfoundland, forty to the Canaries, three months to Brazil—if all went well, for no one could count on a safe return to harbor. The perils of the sea were many and varied, and fortunate and few were those who escaped them. It was wiser to confide a life so menaced to the safekeeping of God the Father and to our good mother the Virgin Mary.

> O who would know the ocean's marvels
> Its horrid sound, its bitter perils
> O navigators, O poor sailors
> Who know Great Nature and the rollers
> Of the high seas, with profits vaunted.
> Raise your eyes (in heart undaunted)
> Toward the heavens, and I'll vow to raise,
> To Him who has made it all, my praise.[1]

Besides predictable foul weather and storms, always the sailor's inseparable companions, the tropical waters which the French faced for the first time held new dangers. A Burgundian, Jean de Léry, setting sail for Brazil, recounted his misfortunes:

"The rain which falls under that line and in its neighborhood stinks and smells evilly; it is also so contagious that if it falls on the flesh, it will raise pustules and great blisters there; in addition it marks and spoils the clothing. The sun there is so burning that we endured violent heat and since, apart from the two small meals, we had no fresh water nor any other beverage available, we were hard pressed by thirst. . . . So during these long voyages the sailors wish that the sea would change into fresh water. It will be asked: rather than imitate Tantalus dying of thirst in the midst of water, would it not be possible, in this extremity, to drink, or at least wash out one's mouth with sea water? To this I reply that, unless it is wished to throw guts and bowels immediately out of the body, there can be no question of tasting it, much less of swallowing it, in spite of the alleged recipe for passing it through wax or distilling it otherwise (remembering that the pitching and tossing of vessels afloat at sea are not particularly helpful for making fires or for preventing the bottles getting broken).

"But in that scorching zone our fresh water was so corrupted and appeared so full of worms that, in the simple act of drawing it from the vessels in which it was kept, there was no one who could resist spitting. But what was even worse, in drinking it, it was necessary to hold the cup with one hand and, on account of the stink, hold one's nose with the other."[2]

Another danger, and not the least, was starvation. It haunted the poor mariners and inflicted many, and sometimes fatal, sufferings on them. The ghastly return voyage, which brought back home to their firesides Jean de Léry and his companions, the unfortunate colonists of "antarctic France" (Brazil) who had fled from the tyranny of their commander, the insupportable Villegagnon, cannot be ignored:

"When we were entirely destitute of all victuals, our last meal consisted of the sweepings of the storeroom, that is to say, of the little whitewashed and plastered room where the biscuit is kept aboard ship. We found there more worms and rat droppings than crumbs. Nonetheless, separating it with spoons, we made soup of it; which was as black and bitter as soot, and you can imagine that it was a pleasant meal. Some of us still had monkeys and parrots . . . to teach them a language they did not yet know, they transferred them to the closet of their memory and made them serve as food."[3]

Léry managed to keep his own parrot for a fortnight, but finally he had to sacrifice it on the altar of friendship:

"My parrot was almost as big and fat as a goose, speaking as well as a man, and its plumage was excellent. I had a great desire to save it in order to present it to Admiral de Coligny, and I kept it hidden for five or six days without being able to give it anything to eat. But under pressing necessity, and the fear that it would be taken away from me at night, the same happened to it as the others. I threw away nothing except the feathers, and not only the body but also the entrails, feet, claws, and hooked beak served some of my friends and myself for a meager living for three or four days. And I had even more regrets about it some five days after I had killed it, for then we sighted land. This kind of bird can do well without drinking, and I would have needed only three nuts to feed it all that time.

"Some of the men got the idea of cutting pieces off some rounds made of the skin of the Brazilian animal called Tapiroussou . . . they put them on the coals. When they were fairly roasted they scraped the burnt part with a knife, and this was such a great success that in eating them we thought it was roast crackling. Once we had tried it, whoever had any of the rounds received a lot of attention. They were as hard as dried-out oxhide, but with billhooks and other tools they were all cut up. And those who had some carried the pieces up their sleeves in little canvas bags; they counted them no less carefully than on land the fat moneylenders count the crowns in their full purses. There were some among us who were down to eating their morocco leather collars and the leather of their shoes. The pages and the ship's boys from the press gang were mad with hunger and ate all the horn out of the lanterns (there are always a great number in seagoing vessels) and all the tallow candles they could get hold of. Moreover, notwithstanding our weakness, and at the risk of sinking to the bottom and getting more to drink than we had had to eat, we had to pump out the water without stopping and with great labor, day and night."

Unfortunately the *Tapiroussou*, or tapir, is by no means a giant animal, and the precious rounds were quickly consumed. When leather from any source had completely disappeared from the ship, some other food had to be found. They thought of the rats and mice on board, though they were very skinny, as the hard times had deprived them of their usual crumbs:

"They were pursued with so many sorts of rattraps which each invented that very few, I believe, were left. They had to hide; we looked for them like cats, open-eyed, even at night when they came out in the moonlight. And in fact, when someone had caught a rat he thought more of it than one would have of an ox on land, and I have seen them sold at two, three, or even four crowns apiece. Our barber once took two at a single blow, and one of us made him this offer: if he would sell one, then at the first port we reached he would clothe him from head to foot. But the barber, preferring life to clothing, would not accept. In short, you could have seen mice being boiled in sea water, with their entrails. Those who could get them made more fuss about them than we ordinarily do, on land, about legs of mutton."

Thus pursued, the rodents soon became extinct. The master of the ship, pressed, and perhaps unhinged, by urgent need, was about to kill one of the passengers for food when at last the French coast was sighted. News of pirates off La Rochelle forced them to land at Blavet. They were too exhausted by their privations to think of getting home, and stopped at Hennebont to try to get back a little strength:

"During the two weeks we were there, we had ourselves treated by doctors. But whatever good diet we followed, most of us became swollen from the soles of our feet to the tops of our heads. Myself and two or three others were swollen only from the waist down. And, further, we all had the runs and such upset stomachs that it was impossible to retain anything in the body. We were taught a recipe: that is, juice of *Hereda terrestris* and rice well cooked; when this is taken off the fire, it must be covered in the pot with a lot of old cloths, then take yolks of eggs and mix all together in a dish on a heater. Having, I tell you, eaten this with spoons, like soup, we were suddenly strengthened; and I think that without this means which God gave us this illness would have carried us all off in a few days."

Then, tired of "these Bretons acting like Bretons, whose language they understood less than that of American savages," they reached Nantes with many difficulties, and again there received the care which their state demanded. They ended, like Ulysses, by reaching home.

The fury of the elements, the inaccuracies of the maps, the incompetence of some pilots, plus a thousand and one imponderables were not the only things which compromised a ship's chances of returning safe to harbor. The most fearful dangers were often those springing from the fact that, in this tempestuous sixteenth century, sailors were born pirates. A Portuguese or Spanish ship within range of French culverins was as good as captured. The painful memory of old scores to settle, combined with the bait of rich cargoes, multiplied their native aggressiveness tenfold. They stopped at nothing in the delight of finding an opportunity to jump aboard and fill their pockets at their neighbors' expense. This is how they proceeded:

"He who carries arms and is the strongest wins and lays down the law to his companion. It is true that when these gentlemen mariners strike sail and approach the poor merchant ships, they usually spin them this yarn: that for a long time, owing to storms and calm weather, they have not been able to go ashore or into port and have nothing to eat; they beg them to provide them with some for cash. But if, on this pretext, they succeed in setting foot aboard their neighbors' vessel, do not doubt that to prevent the ship going to the bottom, they will relieve it forthwith of everything they take a fancy to. If they are reproached for this, saying that it is out of order to pillage either friends or enemies in this way, they will not fail to recite the song common among our soldiers ashore: in such a case, they explain that for various reasons it is war and custom."[4]

Even if the outcome was the same as above, the way of broaching the subject was not always quite so courteous; and if the following incident took place on the sacred feast of Christmas, it was, after all, "war and custom":

"December 25, Christmas Day, our sea rovers met a Spanish caravel and fired some musket shots at her. They took her by force thus, and brought her to our ships. It was a fine vessel laden with white salt. This pleased our captains greatly. For some time they had been agreed on splitting a ship between them.... They put all the Spaniards dispossessed of their ship in another caravel and did not leave these poor people a scrap of bisuit, nor any other victuals. What is worse, they rent their sails and even took away their small boat, without which they could neither go on shore nor go on board. So that I think it would have been better (in a manner or speaking) to send them to the bottom of the sea than to leave them in such a state. In fact thus they were at the mercy of the water, and if some ship did not come to their aid, it is certain that either they finally sank or died of hunger. This deed accomplished, to the profound regret of some of us, in the space of four days we took two other caravels, who put up no resistance. The first was Portuguese. Our sailors and principally those who had been in the Spanish caravel which we had brought, were most desirous to loot her. So they fired a few shots with falconets at her. Meanwhile our masters and captains spoke with those on board her, and for some consideration they let them go without taking anything from them. The other caravel belonged to a Spaniard. Wine, biscuit, and other victuals were taken from him. He regretted above all else a hen that was taken, for, he said, she never stopped laying no matter how great the storms, and thus provided him with a fresh egg every day on board his ship."[5]

There were dwellers on land, too, who had a hand in the despoiling of Spanish and Portuguese vessels. One Jean Ango, for example, a Dieppe shipowner, paid very close attention to the overseas expansion of Spain and Portugal and regarded the situation as politically disastrous for France and economically disastrous for Jean Ango. As early as 1520 he had set himself up as the champion of "freedom of the seas," a right which he upheld somewhat obliquely by outfitting, at his own expense, ships intended to rob and destroy those of Spain and Portugal in any part of the world.

The merchants and seamen of France thus were profiting, albeit indirectly, from the riches of the New World long before King Francis I decided that France must participate officially in a transatlantic expedition. In 1534, however, at the urging of his chaplain, Jacques le Veneur, Abbot of Mont-St.-Michel, the king granted subsidies to an expedition "charged with discovering, in the New Found Lands, certain islands and countries where it is said that there is a great quantity of gold," and also a strait which would allow ships to reach China, or Cathay, as it was known, by sailing westward. With the good abbot's advice, Jacques Cartier was placed in command of the expedition.

A native of St. Malo and a burgher of that town, Cartier, for whom life indeed began at forty, had in his youth worked his way up and down the Atlantic coast of America from Newfoundland to Brazil. His experience on the sea had made of him an excellent pilot. Now, accepting the royal commission to find gold and a northwest passage, he made in the king's name three successive voyages, of which he has left accounts.

The first was a simple reconnaissance expedition. The third, which constituted the first French attempt at colonization in the modern sense of the term, ended in failure. Only the second presents special interest and importance; in it Cartier made the most important of his discoveries.

In the course of his first expedition he had followed the route well known to the Basque, Breton, and Norman fishermen who fished for cod as far west as Newfoundland; thence, heading into the unknown, he rounded the cape to the north of these lands and traversed the western part of the great bay which they almost entirely surrounded. Bad weather obliged him to turn back, but the conviction that there was a strait—which he called St. Peter's, because he glimpsed it on that saint's feast day—to north of the island of Assumption, and that that strait was the famous Northwest Passage, leading to China, made him decide to go again in the following year:

"Sunday, day and feast of Pentecost, sixteenth day of May, in the year fifteen hundred and thirty-five, by the command of the captain and by general consent, everyone confessed and we all together received our Creator in the cathedral church of St. Malo. After receiving Him, we all went to the choir of the church, before the reverend Father in God, the Bishop of St. Malo, who gave us his blessing.

"And the following Wednesday, nineteenth day of the month of May, there was a fair and convenient wind, and we set sail with three ships: the *Grande Hermine*, of about a hundred tons, in which were the captain-general, Thomas Fromont, Claude de Pontbriand, son of the Seigneur de Montréal and cupbearer to the dauphin, Charles de la Pommeraye, and other gentlemen. On the second ship, called the *Petite Hermine*, of about sixty tons, the captain, under the orders of Jacques Cartier, was Macé Jalobert, and the master was Guillaume le Marié; and on the third and smallest ship, called the *Hémerillon*, of about forty tons, Guillaume le Breton was captain and Jacques Maingart master."[6]

Because of heavy seas, Cartier reached Newfoundland in just under fifty-seven days instead of in the twenty-four which calm water would have allowed. Following the south coast of Labrador, he arrived at St. Peter's strait and understood, from what two savages, brought back to France on his first voyage, had told him, that this strait led not to China but to countries named Canada and Saguenay. The latter, of which the capital was named Hochelaga, should contain the gold he was seeking. So he entered a wide river, the present St. Lawrence, in which he followed by turns the north and south banks, and was well received by the natives who greeted him with dancing and singing and gave him picturesque presents. He replied to their advances with a gentleness entirely praiseworthy when one thinks of the gratuitous massacres carried out in Central and South America by his Spanish and Portuguese colleagues. He invited them aboard, made the chiefs sit at table with him and proceeded to large distributions of inexpensive wares.

Then, fearing that the St. Lawrence was becoming too shallow for his ships, Cartier left two of them, and the greater part of his equipment, in a haven he called Sainte-Croix, situated not far from Stadaconna, the capital of Canada. He kept with him the gentlemen and twenty-eight sailors, and pursued his way with one ship and some longboats, then with the longboats alone. In spite of various tentative offers of children and other enticements, made for an unknown reason by the King of Canada, Donnaconna, and his subjects in order to turn him from his purpose, Cartier reached the goal of his journey, Hochelaga in Saguenay, of which he has left us this description:

"This town is quite round and enclosed by three rows of palisades, in the form of a pyramid . . . and in height about two lances. It is entered by a single gate which shuts with bars. On this gate and in several places of the enclosure are a kind of galleries, with ladders for reaching them, furnished with rocks and stones for protection and defense. There are about fifty houses each about fifty paces in length, and about twelve to fifteen wide, all in wood and covered and trimmed with large pieces of bark as big as tables . . . and well sewn together in their fashion. These houses have several rooms: in the middle is a big hall where they make their fire and live in community, and all around are rooms where the men retire with their women and children. There are granaries above their houses, where they put their wheat. They make their bread, which they call *carraconny*, in the following way: with the help of flails of wood, like those for flailing hemp, they beat the wheat and reduce it to powder, then make a mass of dough with it; and they make cakes of it, which they put on a wide rock, previously heated, then they cover it all with hot stones. Thus they cook the bread without having an oven. They make many soups of this wheat, as well as of beans and peas of which they have plenty, and big cucumbers and other fruits. They put their fish, eels, and other things into great receptacles; they dry them in smoke in the summer and they live on them in the winter. They sleep on the bark of trees placed on the ground, with wretched covers made of the skins of wild animals, of which they also make their clothing; those of dormice, otters, martins, foxes, wild cats, deer, stags and others; but the majority of them go almost naked.

"The most precious goods which they have in the world are a substance called *esnoguy*, which is white as snow, and comes from squids which they take from the river in the following way: when a man has merited death or when they have taken an enemy in war, they kill him and slash his thighs, legs, arms, and shoulders in great gashes. Then they throw the body to the bottom of the river in the place where the *esnoguy* is to be found, and leave it there ten or twelve hours before pulling it out. They find in the cuts and gashes squids of which they make some sort of necklaces. They use the *esnoguy* as we do gold and silver, and they hold it as the most precious thing in the world. It has the power to stop nosebleeding, as we have experienced. This whole people live by tilling and fishing; they are not interested in the wealth of this world, of which they have no knowledge, and, unlike the inhabitants of Canada, they never move from their country. However, these latter are their subjects, as well as eight or nine river tribes."[7]

The loyal subjects of Hochelaga, perhaps prompted by Cartier's reputation for generosity, gave the Frenchmen a most cordial welcome:

"From the moment we arrived in the town, the inhabitants came in great numbers to meet us and gave us a good reception. They took us to the center of the town, to an almost square place, surrounded by houses and about a stone's throw wide; they signed us to halt there, which we did. And quite suddenly all the women and girls of the town gathered, some with children in their arms; they came to rub our faces, arms and other parts of the body which they could reach, weeping with joy at seeing us, and asking us by signs if we would please touch their children. Then the men sent them away and sat down on the ground around us, as though we would act a mystery play. Soon several women came back, carrying a square mat, a sort of tapestry, which they spread on the ground in the middle of the place and made us sit down on it. The king and lord of the country, whom they call in their language *agouhanna*, was then brought by nine or ten men, on a great buckskin; they put him down on the mats near the captain, while making us signs that it was their king and lord. He was aged about fifty; nothing in his dress distinguished him from the others, except around his head a sort of red circlet, like a crown, of hedgehog spines. This lord was all crippled and ill in his limbs. After having saluted the captain and his people, making clear signs to them that they were most welcome, he showed the captain his arms and legs, and made sign that he would please to touch them, as though he asked for a cure and health. The latter set about rubbing his arms and legs. The *agouhanna* then took the circlet and crown which he had on his head and gave it to him. Soon they brought to the captain the blind, the one-eyed, the lame, the impotent, the very old whose eyelids hung down to their cheeks; they seated them and made them lie down near him, so that he might touch them, to such an extent did they think that God had come down to earth in that place to cure them.

"The captain, seeing this people's faith, recited the gospel of St. John, that is to say, *In principio*, making the sign of the cross over the poor sick people, and praying God that he would give them knowledge of our Holy Faith and of the Passion of our Savior, and the grace to receive Christianity and baptism. Then the captain read aloud the passion of

Our Lord, in such a way that all those present could hear him; and all this poor people made a great silence, and all were marvelously attentive, looking up to heaven and copying the ceremonies which they saw us make.

"After which the captain had the men ranged on one side, the women on another and the children on another, and he gave the chiefs little hatchets, and to others knives, to the women necklaces, and little things to the others; then he threw on the ground, among the children, little rings and *Agnus Deis* of pewter, at which they showed marvelous joy.

"This done, the captain ordered the trumpets sounded and other instruments of music, at which the people were greatly rejoiced. We took leave of them and retired. But the women put themselves before us to halt us and brought us their victuals, fish, soups, beans, bread, and other things which they had prepared with the intention that we should dine in that place. These victuals were not to our taste and, without salt, had no savor; we thanked them and showed them by signs that we needed nothing."[8]

But Cartier cared more about the precious metals which, it was said, were buried in the soil of that country than for the eternal salvation of its inhabitants. According to information he was given there was, farther to the west, a kingdom held by fierce tribes "armed to their fingertips" where the coveted riches were found in abundance. Nevertheless, he was compelled to put off the exploration of these countries till later. Concerned for the situation of his compatriots left at Sainte-Croix in the midst of natives whom he did not trust, and not very eager to challenge savages who had such a fearsome reputation, he preferred to return to his base. At least he was bringing back information which would be useful for a later expedition.

When Cartier reached Sainte-Croix he found his men safe, prosperous, and settled in a fort which they had just completed. Cannon had been carefully placed on the walls, in the event that it became necessary to reinforce the pacific instincts of the natives if ever they should falter. As it was already late in the year, the commander decided to winter in that place. Perhaps he hoped to gather further information from the natives on the different regions of the country; or perhaps he was haunted by his numerical inferiority and by isolation in an alien and potentially hostile country. Soon, however, he had other matters to occupy his mind, for the rigors of the Canadian winter, and an epidemic of scurvy, put his competence and energy to a rugged test[9]:

"In the month of December, we learned that a fatal sickness had descended on the people of Stadaconna, and they assured us there were already more than fifty dead. So we forbade them to come to our fort. Despite this precaution, the sickness spread to us in the most dangerous fashion; some lost their strength, their legs swelled up . . . then the sickness mounted as far as the hips, the thighs, the shoulders, the arms and the neck. The mouth became infected, the gums rotted, the teeth became bare down to the roots and almost all fell out. The sickness made such ravages in our three ships that by mid-February, of the one hundred and ten men we had been, there were not ten left standing; one could not help another, which was pitiful to see, considering the place we were in; for the people of the country came every day before our fort and saw that few of us were standing; already eight were dead, and there were more than fifty whose lives were despaired of."

The situation was tragic. Faced with the magnitude of the disaster, Cartier had his people set to praying and supplication, ordered a procession, and promised a pilgrimage to Our Lady of Rocamadour. There was no reply from heaven. The sickness continued its ravages and carried off a boy of twenty-two, Philippe Rougemont, native of Amboise. Cartier ordered an autopsy:

"Because the malady was unknown, the captain had the corpse opened, to see if it was something we had knowledge of which would allow us to save some of the others. His heart was found to be all white and withered, surrounded by more than a potful of water reddish like dates, the liver good, but the lungs all blackened; the blood had collected over the heart; when it was opened there came out a great quantity of blood, black and noxious. It appeared the spleen was slightly affected for about two fingers, as though it had been rubbed on a rough stone. Then an incision was made in the thigh which was quite black on the outside, but on the inside the flesh was good enough. Then they buried the corpse with as little trouble as possible. May God, by His holy grace, pardon his soul and all the other dead."

Cartier feared the aborigines even more than the scurvy. Should they see the weakness of the French, they would exterminate them. So he concealed the truth from them:

"When they came near to our fort, our captain, whom God had all the time kept on his feet, came before them with two or three men, well more than sick; he pretended he was trying to flog them, and shouting and throwing sticks at them, he sent them aboard and showed by signs . . . that he was making his people work in the ships . . . at making bread and other tasks, and that it was not good that they would come out; which the natives believed. He also ordered the sick to fight and make a noise in the ships with sticks and stones."

Cartier had already lost twenty-five men; forty were dying, and all were infected. Only three or four, of whom he was one, had escaped the epidemic. Then salvation arrived in the person of Don Agaya, one of the natives whom he had taken to France in 1534, after his first voyage:

"One day our captain, seeing the sickness was so acute and his people so stricken, had gone out of the fort and was taking a walk on the ice, when he saw a band of the people of Stadaconna and among them was Don Agaya, whom he had seen ten or twelve days previously very sick with this same illness from which his men were suffering; he had knees the size of those of a child of two years, his teeth were fallen out or decayed, and the gums putrescent and infected. The captain, when he saw Don Agaya whole and healthy, was delighted, hoping to learn from him how he had been cured. Don Agaya answered that it was by the juice and infused leaves of a tree, the only remedy for that illness. The captain asked him if there were not some roundabout, if he would show it him to cure his servant, who had caught the sickness in the house of the Lord Donnaconna, not wishing to reveal how many of his companions were ill. Then Don Agaya sent two women with our captain to look for it; they brought back nine or ten branches of it and showed him how to pound the bark and the leaves and put them all to boil in water; then to drink the water every second day and put the residue of bark and leaves on the inflamed and sore legs. And further, that this tree cured all sicknesses.

"Soon afterward the captain had a brew prepared. None of the sick except one or two would try it. As soon as these had drunk it, they felt better, which was a veritable and evident miracle, for from all the illnesses they were stricken with, after having drunk it two or three times, they recovered their health and were cured . . . and such as had had the pox from five or six years before were completely cured. After having seen this, there was such a crowd that they would have murdered each other to get at the medicine first, so that an enormous tree was used up in less than a week, with such success that if all the doctors of Louvain and Montpellier had been there, with all the medicines of Alexandria, they could not have done as much in a year as the said tree did in a week."

The good weather returned in due course. The ice and snows of winter melted in the spring sun. On the sixth of May, Jacques Cartier left Sainte-Croix, taking on board with him Donnaconna, the chief of Canada, whom he had some trouble in persuading to accompany him:

"He was to describe and tell the King of France the wonders of the world which he had seen in the countries of the west; for this lord has certified that he has been to the land of Sauguenay, where endless gold, rubies, and other wealth are found and of which the inhabitants are whites and dress in woolen cloth. He says he has also seen other countries where the people do not eat at all, have no anus and do not digest; and others where the people have only one leg and other marvels too long to tell."[10]

Jacques Cartier was thus the first to explore the course of the St. Lawrence for six hundred kilometers from its mouth to the Lachine Rapids, and to have established that Newfoundland and Anticosti were islands. But he always remained convinced that the lands he had glimpsed formed the extremity of Asia. His logbook, carefully filled with technical information about navigation in these latitudes, also gives valuable information about the natives of North America and the countries in which they lived. This is his description of the St. Lawrence:

"The banks of the river as far as Hochelaga and beyond are the most beautiful ever seen by man. Quite far away, some mountains are visible from which various rivers run down which form tributaries of its course. Their banks are covered with trees of various species, and with numerous vines, excepting around the villages, where the natives have cleared them to build their houses and lay out their cultivation. Among them are a lot of big stags, hinds, bears, and other animals. We saw the tracks of an animal which has only two feet the size of one's palm and larger; we followed them a long way in the sand and mud. There are many dormice, beavers, martins, foxes, wildcats, rabbits, squirrels, and rats which are surprisingly large and other wild beasts, of which the Indians use the skins for clothing, for they have no other clothes. There are also a great number of birds: cranes, bustards, swans, wild geese, white and gray, ducks and drakes, blackbirds, redwings, ringdoves, goldfinches, siskins, linnets, nightingales, stock doves, turtledoves, and other birds resembling those of France. The St. Lawrence is brim full of fish of every kind. To be found there according to season are almost all species of sea fish and fresh-water fish, many whales, porpoises, sea horses, and *adhotjuys*, a kind of fish previously unknown to us. They are snow-white and as big as porpoises, with the body and head of a greyhound. In June, July, and August, many mackerel, mullets, bass, and big eels can even be found there. In the fall there are smelts as good as in the river Seine, and in the spring plenty of lampreys and salmon. After passing Canada the pike, trout, carp, bream, and other fresh-water fish are abundant. And the people make large catches each in their season, on which they live."[11]

Jacques Cartier's findings were a sure indication that the borders of the back country of the St. Lawrence offered great possibilities for establishing colonial settlements. This notion was so new to the French in 1536 as to be almost unheard of. Francis I perhaps grasped the future possibilities of this idea, for he was patron also of a third expedition the purpose of which was to take possession of these lands in his name— by force if necessary—and to get them going with the help of groups of people from metropolitan France. According to custom, a nobleman was needed to take charge, and the king chose Chevalier Jean-François de la Roque, Seigneur de Roberval—without however excluding Cartier, who held, in the chain of command, the place his birth and merits warranted. Roberval, discouraged by the hardships and difficulties of life in the wilds, returned to France. Cartier had already left, to get evaluations made of the gold and precious stones which he had found on the far side of the Atlantic. His finds proved worthless, and "fake as Canadian diamonds" became a proverb. From then on, the country from which they came, and those who brought them back, lost all credit. The entire enterprise was looked upon as a failure. Cartier had found neither gold nor precious stones, nor even a northwest passage. His work passed into oblivion.

*   *   *

It was only in the second half of the sixteenth century that the crown of France was able to accept the theory, today almost self-evident, of colonial establishment and to seek to apply it, strangely enough, in Brazil.

Brazil had been known since the beginning of the century. A Frenchman, Jean Cousin, had discovered it. Another Frenchman, Paulmier de Gonneville, set foot there honorably in 1505. Thereafter, French mariners frequently visited that country to obtain precious woods, for which they found a ready market in Europe. The French were courteous in their dealings with the natives and were appreciated for the incomparable talents by the lovely Indian women who were clad, quite agreeably to a sailor's eye, in nothing but their tresses. Indeed, it was because of the high esteem in which they were held that the French visitors were not eaten by the natives who, though very friendly, had a disconcerting penchant for cannibalism. The Portuguese, on the other hand, were quick to alienate local populations by their cruelty. Nonetheless, they succeeded in setting up approximately forty administrative districts with only a few losses to the appetite of the natives. The French and Portuguese thus were brought into contact on a somewhat competitive basis, and it is a tribute to the restraint of both parties that their coexistence took on the form only of a minor war and of innumerable acts of piracy on the seas.

Brazil is enormous, its climate delightful, and its land incredibly fertile. Such a country with no recognized master, virgin and remote, could become very profitable—even without gold mines—for anyone who knew how to make it pay. In France, circumstances were about to produce a man who thought he had found a way. Religious controversies were creating an uneasy atmosphere which could hardly fail to degenerate into civil war if something were not quickly done to remedy the situation. Gaspard de Coligny, Admiral of France, conceived a policy the boldness and novelty of which place him in the front rank of great colonial statesmen: he had the idea of making of Brazil, which was going begging, a refuge where those Protestants who had decided on expatriation could practice their observances freely side by side with Catholics. The project, vague until then, took on substance when a gentleman from Provins, the Chevalier de Villegagnon, came forward with an offer of his services to the admiral for founding a colony in Brazil.

Villegagnon was as colorful a personality as the Renaissance could produce. He combined the qualities of a distinguished humanist with those of a valiant soldier, and he had wielded his sword in every part of Europe with that courage which was always characteristic of him. But his impulsive character and the unfortunate incidents provoked by his violent temper obliged him, in order to retain his freedom, to leave France. Such was the man to whom the Admiral de Coligny confided the command of an expedition bound for "antarctic France."

On July 12, 1555, Villegagnon's charge, consisting of three ships carrying six hundred colonists, set sail. On the third of November, after a bad crossing, the ships dropped anchor in Rio de Janeiro Bay. In a short time, the beginnings of a colony had been established and the enterprise looked promising. The next year, the admiral sent to Villegagnon a convoy of Huguenots followed by a minister, and he even contemplated making of the colony a "New France"—with Calvinism, rather than Catholicism, as its official religion.

Villegagnon, however, instead of settling in the country and being occupied in organizing it, shut himself up on an island in the bay and cloistered his men with him. Under the iron rod of his discipline, and compelled to live in total continence, they worked like slaves at the building of Fort Coligny. The severities of the tropical climate, hunger, the lack of water, and bitter religious controversies aggravated the discontent caused by the dictatorial extravagances of the commander. Tempers were short, a rebellion broke out, hangings took place, a few people left, and order was restored. Villegagnon profited by the lull to return to France and look for reinforcements. During his absence, on March 16, 1560, the Portuguese took possession of the "French island." The government, immersed in political problems at home, was not interested, and Villegagnon did not return.

The fall of Fort Coligny to the Portuguese marked the end of French attempts at colonization in Brazil. The country was destined to pass under Portuguese domination. The Jesuits had already embarked on the conversion of the natives. A handful of survivors from the "French island," taking refuge with neighboring tribes and bringing them effective help in their fight for independence, continued the struggle against the common enemy until the beginning of the seventeenth century.

How different might have been the destiny of that century for France if the French Protestants, instead of involving themselves in pointless intermural conflicts, had founded in Brazil the asylum they so ardently desired.

The country so needlessly abandoned was indeed a prize, beautiful and populated by natives of charm and innocence. The young Burgundian pastor, Jean de Léry, a companion of Villegagnon, has left us an interesting account of the land and the people—an account the accuracy of which, it may be noted, has been confirmed in modern times by Claude Levy-Strauss, who took the work with him when he traveled through the same countries recently. Credence may therefore be given to Jean de Léry's account of Brazil and of the tribes in the Bay of Rio, which answered to the picturesque name of Topinambou, as the author knew them in the year of grace 1557[12]:

"If you want to imagine an American savage, picture to yourself a naked man, well fashioned and well proportioned in his limbs, having all the small hairs which grow on him plucked out, his hair clipped almost to the crown of his head and especially in front like a monk's tonsure, behind clipped on the neck, like our majors and those who allow their hair to grow, his lips and cheeks slit, and pointed bones or green stones set into them, his ears pierced with pendants placed in the holes, his body brightly painted, his thighs and legs blackened with dye they make from the fruit of the *genipa*, necklaces hung round his neck, composed of a vast quantity of small pieces of the big sea shell which they call *vignol;* and you see him as he ordinarily is in his country."

Very dandified and vain by nature, the Topinambou was willing to pay any price for feathers of various sorts, with which he decked himself out, white hens feathers first and foremost:

"Either with iron, since they have had it, or formerly with sharp stones, they cut up the down and little feathers, finer than ground meat. They put them to boil and dye them red with brazilwood; then they rub themselves with a certain gum which they have specially for that, and cover their bodies, arms, and legs. In this state they seem to have a downy skin, like pigeons and other birds when newly hatched. . . . As to the ornamentation of their heads . . . they tie and arrange birds' feathers colored crimson, red, and other colors; they make headbands of them quite like the fashion for hair, real or false, which they call rackets or bats. The ladies and young women in France and other countries have for some time looked well enough in this style."

The toucan and ostrich also furnished their plumage:

"That of the toucan is as black as that of a raven everywhere except under the neck, which is all covered with small and subtle yellow feathers, edged with red toward the bottom, for a length of about four fingers, and three wide. They pluck the breast and get a good quantity from it. When they are dry, they attach one of them to each side of their face above the ears, with a wax they call *yra-yetic*. With these two yellow patches on their cheeks one would almost think that they were wearing two gilded copper bosses like those on either side of a horse's bit. . . .

"They also take from their neighbors big ostrich feathers . . . gray in color. They arrange all the quills close together on one side and the rest spread out in a round, like a little canopy or a rose; they make a great plume of it. . . . They tie it with a cotton cord round their waist, the narrow part next the skin, the wide part outward. When they are tricked out with it, you would say they had a chicken coop tied to their backsides."

The Topinambou women were beautiful and went quite naked. They desired no ornament other than their long tresses falling over their shoulders or tied with a red cord:

"The women of these tribes also often paint their bodies, arms, thighs, and legs like the men; they do not cover themselves with featherwork or anything else which grows in their land, and we were never able to get them to dress. . . . Always naked, they excused themselves by their custom, which is this: at each fountain and clear stream which they meet, they squat at the edge or get into it and throw the water over their head with both hands. They wash themselves and dip their whole body, like ducks, and some days more than a dozen times. They say it would be too much trouble to undress so often, which may be a good and pertinent reason. In any case it has to be accepted, for to argue further with these women would be useless and you would get nowhere. . . ."

The Topinambou children are treated like kings. Nothing more charming than a group of these little savages "with their broad backsides, plump and perfect," who run as fast as they can to meet the visitor, in the hope, of course, of a small present. From birth they are the objects of special attention:

"As soon as he has come out from the mother's womb, the father washes him quite clean, then immediately paints him brightly in red and black coloring. Moreover, without swaddling him, he lays him in a cotten bed hung in the air. If it is a boy he makes him a little sword of wood, a little bow, and little arrows as well, feathered with parrot's feathers; then, putting them all near the child, and kissing him with a smiling face, he will say to him: " 'My son, when you have come of age, so that you may avenge yourself on your enemies, be adroit at arms, strong, brave, and a good warrior.' "[13]

If the foreigner who recently landed in Brazil wished to visit these unknown countries profitably, he had to get himself an interpreter and go into the villages. He would be treated as an honored guest, according to the laws of a generous hospitality:

"As soon as the traveler has reached the house of the *moussacat*, that is to say, of the good head of a family who gives food to the passer-by . . . he sits in a bed of cotton hung in the air, and remains there a little while without saying a word. After this the women come around him, squat on the ground on their heels, and hold their two hands over their eyes, and, weeping, wish him welcome in this fashion; they will say a thousand things in praise of him, as for instance: 'You have taken so much trouble to come and see us; you are good; you are brave.' And if it is a Frenchman or any other foreigner from there they add: 'You have brought us so many nice things which we did not have in this country.' In short, as I have said, while shedding big tears they will say various things which seem to be praise or flattery. If, in his turn, the newcomer seated in the bed wished to please them, he puts on a pleasant expression, for his part, and if he does not wish to burst into tears (as I have seen do some of our nation who, hearing the amiability of these women toward them, were such dunces as to go as far as that) at least he must make the pretense, in answering them, of heaving a few sighs."[14]

During this time the *moussacat* pretends not to see anything. After a quarter of an hour, according to custom, he is good enough to notice the noble stranger, and a conversation—almost always the same—takes place between them:

"*Topinambou:* So you have come?
Frenchman: Yes, I have come . . .
T: Have you left your country to live here?
F: Yes.
T: Then come and see the place where you will stay.
F: That's a good idea . . .
T: Have you brought your boxes? (They understand that all the other ships have clothing, which the man may have.)
F: Yes, I have brought them . . .
T: What are the things you have brought in your boxes?
F: Clothes . . .
T: What sort of color?
F: Blue, red, yellow, black, green. Many colors. Dove color. (White is understood to be shirts.)
T: What else?
F: Hats . . .
T: Many?
F: So many you couldn't count.
T: Is that all?
F: No, or, not at all.
T: Tell everything.
F: Wait a bit . . .
T: Did you bring knives?
F: I have brought a lot of them.
T: Are they knives with a cleft handle?

F: With white handles . . . little knives, fishhooks, awls, mirrors, combs, necklaces, or blue bracelets, which are rarely seen. They are the best you ever saw since my people began to come here.
T: Open your box so I that can see your things.
F: I cannot do that. I will show you one day when I come to visit you.
T: Shall I bring you some things one day?
F: What do you want to bring me?
T: I don't know. What do you want?
F: Animals, birds, fish, flour, roots, big beans, oranges, and lemons, anything and everything.
T: What sort of animal do you like to eat?
F: I only want those of this country.
T: Shall I tell you their names?
F: Go ahead.
T: An animal half donkey and half cow; a kind of stag and doe, a boar of the country, a red animal like a piglet three weeks old, an animal as big as a month-old pigling, striped black and white, a kind of hare.
F: Tell me the names of the birds.
T: A bird as big as a capon, the shape of a little guinea fowl, of which there are three sorts. They are of a very good flavor, as much as any other bird. A wild peacock of which there are two kinds, black and gray, with the body the size of a peacock of our country; a sort of big partridge with the body bigger than a capon; a turtledove of the country; another kind of turtledove, smaller.
F: Are there many good fish?
T: There are quite a lot."[15]

This interview finished, the *moussacat* finds out his guest's wishes. Does he want to eat? They put before him fruits, venison, and fish, which the natives eat. Does he want to sleep? They prepare a good white bed for him with little fires around it, the heat of which compensates for the humidity at night. By way of thanks for this generous hospitality, the visitor who knows his way about freely distributes small objects unknown there. The men liked knives, shears, and tweezers; the women, mirrors and combs; the children were delighted with fishhooks.

During his stay the stranger who, like Léry, was interested in his surroundings, would find his attention drawn to one of the most typical customs of these tribes: the making of their usual drink, *caouin*, which fell to the lot of the women exclusively:

"After cutting up the roots of the *aypi* and manioc as small as

A family of Topinambous. From Jean de Léry's *Voyage fait en la terre de Brésil* (1578). Bibliothèque de Grenoble

A visitor is welcomed to a Topinambou household, with the woman of the house crouched at his feet and feigning tears. From Jean de Léry's *Voyage fait en la terre de Brésil* (1578). Bibliothèque de Grenoble

Brazilian cannibals cutting up and smoking their victims. Engravings of 1558, Bibliothèque de Genoble

Oronce Fine, Regius Professor of Mathematics, Bibliothèque de Grenoble

J. Toussaint, Regius Professor of Greek, Bibliothèque de Grenoble

26.

Guillaume Postel, Regius Professor of Greek. Bibliothèque de Grenoble

Erasmus of Rotterdam. Anonymous portrait of the sixteenth century. Musée des Arts Décoratifs, Paris

roots are cut over there for the stew, they boil the pieces in big earthenware pots; when they see that they are tender and soft, they take them off the fire and let them cool a little. This done, several of them squat around these great jars and take these round slices of root thus softened, then without swallowing them they chew them up well and twist them round in their mouth. Then, taking each piece in their hand again one after the other, they put them back into other earthenware vessels which are already on the fire, and they make them boil once more. They stir this mixture ceaselessly with a stick until they consider it is sufficiently cooked, then they take it off the fire a second time, and without pouring or straining it off, they tip everything together into other, bigger containers of glass, each of which would hold about a cask of Burgundy wine. After it has frothed and fermented for a while, they cover these vessels and leave the drink in them until they wish to drink it."[16]

The men were convinced that the *caouin* would be much less good if they meddled with the making of it. Besides, this housewifely occupation was not fitting for them; a very proper sentiment, Léry concluded: ". . . with us we should find it strange, it seems to me, to see those great bare-chested peasants from Bresse and other parts, taking the distaff to spin."

This proceeding having unquestionably aroused some not very amiable reflections regarding the natives, Léry, as a wholehearted defender of transatlantic customs, replied vigorously to the authors of criticisms "touching the mastication and chewing"; let them remember the way wine is made in France:

". . . In the places where the good wines grow, the vineyard laborers at harvest time get into the casks and tubs where, with their fine feet, or even in their shoes, they tread the grapes and they even, as I have seen, splash around again in the presses; there, those people who are disgusted will find a lot of things happening which are no more genteel than that manner of masticating which the American women are accustomed to. And if they say: 'Yes, but the wine, in fermenting and frothing, throws out all this filth,' I answer that our *caouin* clears itself too, and on this point it is the same for the one as the other."[17]

Another practice, equally specific, if not equally innocuous was likely to fill a stranger with lively misgivings for his own security: the *boucan*, or process by which they preserved venison and fish by smoking them on a kind of giant grill. It was a familiar sight of the village to see these *boucans* decorated with haunches of venison, with fish of iridescent colors, and also "thighs, legs, arms, and other big bits of human flesh"—the latter belonging to dead prisoners of war, whose unfortunate destiny was to be eaten smoked.

The prisoner of war of the Topinambou tribes, if one is willing to overlook a cruel death, was well treated. On the day of his death, he was expected to be in perfect physical condition, and he was fed as well as possible, "fattened like pigs at the trough," offered the women he chose—provided they were unmarried, since sexual liberty was allowed in these countries prior to marriage. When he was in prime condition, the date of execution was set, and the neighboring villages were advised. On the appointed day they came in crowds, men, women, and children, and the feast began. A great revel consecrated to dancing and drinking took place, in which the prisoner participated happily before being seized. Then the ceremonies of death began:

"The prisoner is paraded as a trophy for some time in the village. With incredible boldness and assurance he boasts of his past prowess and tells those who hold him bound: 'First of all I myself, brave as I am, bound and tied up your parents!' Then becoming more and more exalted, with an expression to match, he turns from one side to the other and says to one: 'I ate your father,' to another: 'I have killed and smoked your brothers,' and, in brief, he adds 'I have in general eaten so many men and women, and even children, of you Topinambous taken in war that I cannot count them. And besides, do not doubt that to avenge my death the Margaias of the nation from which I come will soon eat as many of you as they can catch,' . . . Or that they bring stones and old broken potsherds or both together . . . and say to him: 'Avenge yourself before you die.' He rushes and flings himself with force and determination on those gathered around, sometimes as many as three or four thousand persons. . . . When the stones and everything he has been able to lay hold of are used up, he who will give the final blow (who has not showed himself all that day until then) emerges from a house. He carries in his hand one of those great wooden swords richly decorated with fine and excellent featherwork, and he has a headdress and other ornaments on his body. He then approaches the prisoner and usually addresses him like this:

"'Are you not of the nation called Margaia which is our enemy, and have you not yourself killed and eaten our relatives and friends?' And he answers, more self-assured than ever, in his language:

"'Yes I am very strong and I have really killed and eaten many.'

"Then, to insult his enemies still further, he puts his hands on his head and cries:

"'O I have not been weak, O how bold I have been in attacking and taking your people, whom I have eaten many a time' and he adds other, similar remarks.

"At that, he who is facing him, ready to put him to death, tells him: 'Now you are in our power and you will be forthwith killed by me, then smoked and eaten by us all.'

" 'Very good,' he answers, as resolved to die for his nation as Regulus was unflinching in enduring death for the Roman republic 'and my relatives will avenge me. . . .' "

"At that proud reply, the prisoner receives on his head a blow from a club which knocks him down dead. He is immediately cut in pieces:

"The women, and principally the old women (for they are more desirous of eating human flesh than the young ones, and constantly solicit those who have prisoners to have them dispatched quickly) come forward with hot water, which they have ready. They rub and scald the corpse in such way that they skin off the outer skin and make it as white as the cooks at home know how to make a suckling pig ready for roasting. After that the master of the prisoner, and others, as they please, take the poor corpse, split it up, and cut it so rapidly in pieces that no butcher in this country can dismember a pig as fast. But more than that, O prodigious cruelty; just as the huntsmen in France after taking a stag, throws the entrails to the hounds, so these barbarians rub the body, the thighs, and the legs of their young children with the blood of their enemies. . . .

"Then all the bits of the body, and even the entrails, are cleaned and forthwith put on the *boucans*. While it is all thus cooking in their fashion, the old women gather round the *boucans* to collect the fat that drips from the poles of the big wooden grills. They exhort the men so to act that they will always have such meat, and, licking their fingers, say: 'It is good.' "[18]

The prisoner is then completely eaten up by the company, with the exception of the brain, the head, which is shrunk, the thigh bones and armbones, of which they make fifes and arrows, and the teeth, of which they make necklaces. And the feast continues for three days and three nights of dancing, eating, and drinking, until the *caouin* is finished and everyone falls, dead drunk, wherever they are.

It was indispensable to know of these customs before traveling among the Topinambous and risking some unpleasant adventures, as happened to Jean de Léry the first time he went among them accompanied by his interpreter, three weeks after landing in Brazil[19]:

"When we came, my interpreter and myself, to the first village, called Yabouraci in the language of the country and Pépin by the French (because of a ship which once loaded there, whose master was so called), which was only two leagues from our fort, I suddenly found myself surrounded by savages. They asked me: 'What is your name?' which at that time I understood no more of their language than High German. And one took my hat which he put on his head, another my sword and belt which he buckled onto his naked body, another my jacket which he put on; they deafened me with their shouts and ran about among their houses with my clothes so that

I thought I had lost everything, and did not know where I was with them."

Léry eventually got his things back and went on to another village. They had just put a prisoner of war to death. Léry, unfamiliar with the local customs, to his horror saw the limbs roasting on the *boucan* and the natives engaged in their customary pastimes. Still in the grip of strong emotion, he was introduced to his host:

"We sat down in a cotton bed hung in the air, the women wept, and the old man who was master of the house made his speech of welcome. The interpreter, for whom these ways were not new and who, apart from that, liked to drink and take *caouin* as much as they did, went off toward the big troop of people dancing, without saying a word to me, nor warning me about anything, and I remained there with a few of them. I was tired, and wished only to rest, and after having eaten a little root flour and other food which they had offered us, I lay down in the cotton bed in which I was sitting. But the noise which the savages made as they danced and whistled all night, while they were eating the prisoner, kept me wide awake; moreover one of them came to me holding in his hand one foot, cooked and smoked, of this prisoner and asked me (as I learned later, for at that moment I did not understand) if I would like to eat some of it. His attitude so frightened me that, need you ask, I lost all taste for sleep. And in fact I really thought that by his gesture in showing me that piece of human flesh he was saying, and wished to make me understand, that I should soon be dispatched in the same way. So, one doubt begetting another, I soon came to the conclusion that the interpreter, on purpose and deliberately, had betrayed, abandoned, and delivered me into the hands of these barbarians. And if I had seen any opportunity to get out of there and run for it, I should not have failed to take it. But, seeing myself surrounded on every side by people whose real intentions I did not know (for as you will see, the last thing they thought was to harm me), I was firmly convinced and was waiting to be eaten forthwith; and that night I called on God in my heart. I leave you to imagine how long it was. So when morning came, my interpreter (who, with these roguish savages had been careening all night long around the other houses of the village) came to look for me. He found me, as he said, not only blenched and downcast in face, but also practically in a fever; so he asked me if I felt ill and had not slept well. At which, still all distraught as I was, I answered, in great fury, that they had completely prevented my sleeping and that he was a scoundrel to have left me in that way among those people whom I could not understand; and, feeling far from reassured, I beseeched him that we should leave at once. But he replied to me that I had no reason to be afraid and that it was not we whom they hated. He had told the savages everything, and they, who, in reality, were delighted at my arrival, and, to be kind to me, had not budged from my side all night, said that they had also been slightly aware that I was afraid of them, and were most concerned about it. My consolation was a broad grin which they gave me (for they are great wags) at having so successfully, though unintentionally, pulled my leg."

So was born, thanks to the Burgundian Jean de Léry, the legend of the Noble Savage, which two centuries later was to enjoy great vogue in France and Europe through the efforts of M. Jean-Jacques Rousseau.

Notwithstanding the failure of Villegagnon's colony in Brazil, the king—now Charles IX—did not abandon hope of succeeding where his predecessors had failed, and Coligny was still to send three expeditions to Florida, directed successively by Jean Ribault, René de Laudonnière, and Dominique de Gourgues, to attack Spain at the most sensitive points of her overseas empire. All three failed, however, and from that moment on France, increasingly occupied with the wars of religion, more or less resigned herself to playing only a token role in the New World.

* * *

The names of Columbus, da Gama, and Magellan evoke today an image of great discoveries and extraordinary courage. They, and many other such captains, were men who dared set out in search of lands, often nonexistent, about which they knew nothing either of the climate or vegetation or of the reception they might find among the natives. Their names have become inextricably associated with the continents of North and South America, the destiny of which would be revealed only by the passing centuries. It was to be a destiny founded not on the gold or jewels so eagerly pursued by the great discoverers, but upon that more modern treasure, "economic potential."

To the mind of the twentieth century, such potential or the lack of it is the element which determines whether or not a goal is worth the effort required for its attainment. For sixteenth-century man, however, for wealth to be "potential" was equivalent to its being nonexistent. He was not interested in cultivating the soil, or in exporting raw materials. His interests and his values were concrete: gold, silver, jewels. And such was the treasure brought back in galleons and caravels from the mines of Mexico and Peru. Precious metals had haunted the imagination of medieval alchemists for a thousand years as they struggled with their stills of brown glass, poured over their irregularly formed multicolored flasks, and sought, without respite, the famous secret of the philosophers' stone, by virtue of which they would be able to multiply a hundredfold the weight of those metals. But where the alchemist had failed the explorer now succeeded. Providence had chosen him to provide Europe with the metals of which it had dreamed so long. But one may wonder whether Providence had foreseen the results of this gift upon the recipient of it. It is true that the arrival of the precious metals awakened the economy, restored exchanges to life, and put new life into commerce and industry. But it also induced profound economic and social upheavals, among them disastrous inflation. Prices had varied but little in the course of the Middle Ages; now, in the space of a hundred years, the monetary stock available for living was multiplied by eight. At first France was not affected by the rise, for Spain jealously guarded her ingots. But when, in 1545, the discovery of the silver mines of Potosí raised silver imports from the New World from ninety to three hundred metric tons, Spain could not control what until then it had tried to conserve. A poor country, producing little, it needed French goods. In 1559, the peace of Le Cateau-Cambrésis activated exchanges that political restrictions no longer forbade and gold and silver poured into France. In the time of Charles IX the high tide was running. The succession of upheavals which came with it fill the pages of political literature, and authors note with dismay the rise in the cost of everything:

"The high cost of everything sold and disbursed in the Kingdom of France is today not only so great, but also so excessive as compared with seventy or eighty years ago, that some things have increased ten times, others four, five, or six times; this is very easy to prove and verify for every article, whether land, houses, estates, vineyards, woods, and pastures, or meat, wool, cloth, fruit, and other goods necessary to the life of man.

"To come to the proof of this and beginning with victuals, it is only necessary to look at what is customary in the French provinces and it will be seen that in most of them the testimony is that the load of *méteil* [a mixed grain of rye, barley, and wheat] is valued and taxed at a lower price than the tenth part is sold for today; and that a fowl, a hen, a goat, and other things due from tenant to lord are evaluated at ten and even fifteen times less than at present. In Anjou, Poitou, La Marche, Champagne, the Bourbonnais, and many other districts customarily put the hen at six deniers, the partridge at fifteen deniers, an ordinary fattened sheep or calf at ten sols [12 deniers= 1 sol], a goat at three sols, a load of wheat at thirty sols, a load of hay weighing fifteen quintals at ten sols, which is ten bales for a sol, the bale weighing fifteen pounds.

"In other places the *sétier* [a measure equal to thirty-four gallons] of wheat is sold at twenty sols, of rye at ten sols, of barley at seven sols, of oats at five sols, a cartload of hay of twelve quintals at ten sols, or taken on the field at five sols; a cartload of wood at twelve deniers, a goose at twelve deniers, a whole sheep without its wool, at three sols six deniers, a fat sheep with its wool at five sols, a kid at eighteen deniers, a hen at six deniers, a rabbit at two deniers, a gosling at six deniers, a calf at five sols, a pig at six deniers, a peacock at two sols, a pigeon at one denier, and a pheasant at twenty deniers. So much for victuals, which today are ten or fifteen times dearer. As for work or days of a laborer, we see by the customs defined, and corrected sixty years ago, that a man's day in summer is valued at six deniers, in winter at four deniers, and with his oxcart at twelve deniers. Recently the day of a man was at twelve deniers, that of a woman at six deniers.

"As to land, the best middling land was valued at only one denier twenty or twenty-five, the fief at one denier thirty, the house at one denier fifty. An *arpent* [approximately one acre] of the best cultivable land in flat country cost only ten or twelve crowns and a vineyard thirty; and today all these things are sold at three and four times as much, even in crowns weighing a tenth less than they weighed three hundred years ago. By that one can see how things have risen in sixty years; which moreover can easily be verified by checking statements, including those of the French treasury, by which it will be seen that the baronies, counties, and duchies annexed to and taken over by the crown are worth as much in revenue as they formerly would have been if sold; and that today one can do no more with six thousand crowns than formerly with one thousand; for what then cost a crown today costs six, eight, ten, and twelve."[20]

The causes of these ruinous prices are the subject of an analysis by France's first economist, a lawyer named Jean Bodin of Angers, one of the most accomplished humanists of the century. He states in his *Réponse aux paradoxes de M. de Malestroit*, that "the principal and almost sole cause of the high cost of living is the abundance of gold and silver which there is today in this kingdom, greater than it ever was four hundred years ago." Thus, he established the first relation between the increase of monetary reserves and the rise in prices. This study is accompanied by a picture of the soaring economy of renaissance France, which is of particular interest because it comes from an unusually well-informed pen[21]:

"But, someone will say, where have so much gold and silver come from? I find that the merchant and artisan who cause the gold and silver to be sold did not work formerly as they do today; for the French, having one of the most fertile countries in the world, gave themselves to tilling the soil and feeding stock which is the prime occupation in France, while the commerce of the Levant came to a standstill for fear of the Berbers who hold the African coast, and of the Arabs whom our fathers called Saracens; who ruled the Mediterranean everywhere, and treated those Christians whom they captured as slaves in chains. And Western commerce was entirely unknown before Spain sailed the sea of the Indies. And to that must be added that the English who held the ports of Guyenne and Normandy, had closed to us the approaches to Spain and the isles. Elsewhere the quarrels of the houses of Anjou and Aragon cut us off from the Italian ports. But for the last sixscore years we have chased out the English, while the Portuguese, girdling another ocean with the aid of the mariner's compass, made themselves masters of the Persian Gulf and part of the Red Sea, and by this means have filled their vessels with the riches of India and fertile Arabia, frustrating the Venetians and the Genoese, who took the merchandise of Egypt and Syria, brought by the Arabian and Persian caravans, to sell us retail at the highest possible prices. At the same time Castile, having got into her power the new lands full of gold and silver, has filled Spain with them and shown our pilots the way to make the journey around Africa marvelously profitable. So it is that the Spaniard who only lives off France, being obliged to get his grain, cloth, textiles, pastel, paper, books, even cabinetmakers' work and all handwork here, has had to seek gold, silver, and spices at the ends of the earth. On the other hand the English, Scots, and all the people of Norway, Sweden, Denmark, and the Baltic coast, who have a great number of mines, seek metal in the bowels of the earth in order to buy our wines, our saffron, our plums, our pastry, and, above all, our salt; which is a manna which God has given us by special grace with little labor; by the lack of warmth for northern peoples above the forty-seventh degree, salt cannot be made there; and below the forty-second the heat is too great and renders the salt corrosive, which harms people and salted things; so that the salt beds of Franche-Comté and the rock salt in Spain and Hungary do not in any way approach the goodness of ours. This results in the English, the Flemish, and the Scots, who make a great business in salted fish, often loading their vessels with sand, for lack of merchandise, to come and buy our salt for good deniers paid in cash.

"There is yet another reason for the wealth of France: the commerce of the Levant, opened up to us by the friendship of the house of France with the house of the Ottomans in the time of King Francis I, so that the French merchants since then have had their shops in Alexandria, Cairo, Beirut, and Tripoli, just as much as have the Venetians and the Genoese. And we have no less credit, as Fez and Morocco, than the Spaniards. This had been open to us since the Jews, driven out of Spain by Ferdinand, retreated to the low country of Languedoc and brought us the habit of trading with Barbary."

In short, the abundance of gold and silver, "of fine ingots, of Portuguese, of rose nobles, of knot nobles, or angels" comes from the richness of the French soil and her agriculture, from the prosperity of her commerce, and of her industry. But it is not the only reason:

"The other reason why so many goods have been coming to us, during the past six or sevenscore years, is the greatness of the population, who have increased in this kingdom, since the civil wars of the house of Orléans and of Burgundy were appeased, which gave us the sweetness of peace and the enjoyment of its fruits for a long period, until the religious troubles; for the foreign wars we have had since those times were but a purgation of the ill humors necessary for the whole body of the republic. Formerly the flat lands and almost the towns themselves were rendered uninhabited by the ravages of civil wars, during which times the English had sacked the towns, burned the villages, murdered, pillaged, and killed a good part of the French people, and gnawed the rest down to the bone; which was the cause of bringing agriculture, commerce, and all the mechanical arts to a halt. But for the last hundred years a vast area of forests and lands has been put in cultivation, many villages have been built and towns populated, so that the greatest benefit to Spain, which really is deserted, comes from the French colonists, who troop off to Spain, chiefly coming from Auvergne and Limousin, to such an extent that in Navarre and Aragon almost all the vineyard workers, laborers, carpenters, masons, cabinetmakers, stonecutters, turners, wheelwrights, carriage makers, *cartwrights*, rope makers, quarrymen, saddlers, and leatherworkers are French, for the Spaniard is astonishingly lazy, apart from the use of arms and commerce; for that reason he likes the active and serviceable Frenchman, as he showed in the enterprise of the Prior of Capua at Valencia where there were ten thousand Frenchmen, servants and artisans, who were in danger for having taken part in the conspiracy against Maximilian, who was then lieutenant general in Spain; but it so happened their masters and the inhabitants of Valencia went bail for them all. There are also a great number of French in Italy."

Bodin enumerates a fourth cause for the inflow of foreign moneys: the trade in silver and the banking operations, which were appearing for the first time and were brought by the Italians to Lyons, that city being a considerable town and international center, with its fairs, its mercantile exchange, its industries, its silk mills and printers, its literary men and poets.

"The last cause of the abundance of gold and silver has been the Bank of Lyons, which was opened, to tell the truth, by King Henry while he was still dauphin, taking ten, then sixteen and up to twenty per cent if necessary. Suddenly the Florentines, Luccans, Genoese, Swiss, and Germans, tempted by the size of the profits, brought a great quantity of gold and silver to France, and many stayed there as much for the gentle air as for the natural goodness of the people and the availability of the country. By the same means the rents constituted on the city of Paris, which amount to fourteen or fifteen thousand pounds every year, have attracted the foreigner who brings his money here to make a profit with it, and finally becomes a resident, which has greatly enriched that city."

And Bodin concludes: "There, sir, are the means which have brought us gold and silver in abundance for the last two hundred years. There is much more of it in Spain and Italy than in France, because the nobility in Italy trade, and the people in Spain have no other occupation. Also everything is dearer in Italy than in France, and even more so in Spain than in Italy; and even service and day labor attracts our people of Auvergne and Limousin to Spain, as I learned from themselves, because they earn three times what they make in France; for the rich, haughty and lazy Spaniard sells his labor very dear, as Clénard testifies who put in his letters in the chapter on expenses, under just one item, to have one's beard trimmed in Portugal is fifteen ducats a year. So it is the abundance of gold and silver which is in part the cause of the high cost of things."

Bodin, not content simply to pass in review the different reasons for the high cost of living, adds, in a positive spirit, the remedies. It is known that the kings of France did their best, by frequent edicts, to stabilize the currency; but it was not until early in the seventeenth century that any appreciable stabilization appears.

Such an inflation could not fail to have substantial social repercussions. Fortunes changed hands rapidly. Those who lived from fixed revenues —landlords, functionaries, and much of the nobility—were already impoverished by the burdens imposed by war and court life, and they watched in despair as their total ruin became daily more imminent. As the nobility sank into genteel poverty, the merchants and entrepreneurs grew wealthy and the moneylenders, bankers, and speculators made fortunes. Eventually, the last-mentioned bought the lands which the ancient nobility could no longer afford to maintain, and assumed not only possession of them but also of the titles of nobility conferred by them. It was a circumstance which was to have far-reaching effects upon the course of freedom in France.

NOTES

X · An Age of Discovery

1. *Le discours de la navigation de Jean et Raoul Parmentier de Dieppe. Voyage de Sumatra en 1529. Description de l'île de Saint-Domingo.* Paris, 1883, pp. 122–23.
2. Léry, J. de. *Journal de bord de Jean de Léry en la terre de Brésil, 1557.* Ed. M. R. Mayeux, Paris, 1957, pp. 82–83.
3. *Ibid.*, pp. 185–99.
4. *Ibid.*, p. 60.
5. *Ibid.*, p. 67.
6. Cartier, J. "Seconde navigation faite par le commandement et vouloir du Très-Chrétien Roy Françoys," in *Les Français en Amérique pendant la première moitié du XVIe siècle.* Ed. Ch.-A. Julien, Paris, 1946, pp. 118–20.
7. *Ibid.*, pp. 146–48.
8. *Ibid.*, pp. 148–51.
9. *Ibid.*, pp. 168–72.
10. *Ibid.*, p. 175.
11. *Ibid.*, pp. 164–66.
12. Léry, J. de, *op. cit.*, pp. 205–19.
13. *Ibid.*, p. 351.
14. *Ibid.*, pp. 364–65.
15. *Ibid.*, pp. 141–46.
16. *Ibid.*, p. 230.
17. *Ibid.*, p. 237.
18. *Ibid.*, pp. 310–15.
19. *Ibid.*, pp. 361–64.
20. *Discours sur les causes de l'extrême cherté qui est aujourd'hui en France et sur les moyens d'y remédier.* Paris, 1574. Ed. Cimber and Danjou, *op. cit.*, t. VI, pp. 423–29.
21. Bodin, J., *Réponse aux paradoxes de M. de Malestroit.* Ed. H. Hauser, Paris, 1932, pp. 12–15.

XI · Schools and Scholars

IF THERE is one characteristic of the Renaissance that can be singled out for particular emphasis, it is the renewal of interest in the civilization and learning of antiquity. The Middle Ages, it is true, had not been unaware of classical Greece and Rome, but medieval man's knowledge, usually garnered from a few unreliable manuscripts, constituted a deformed image, even a travesty of the reality. The Renaissance, convinced that the men of antiquity had held the secret of the art of living, of a wisdom which had vanished with the advent of barbarism in the fifth century, devoted itself to a passionate search for that learning. And it was a search prompted as much by a desire for new life and light as it was by a weariness with the aridity of medieval scholasticism.

As in any search for learning, it was necessary to return to authentic sources. This meant searching for the manuscripts of the ancients, collating them, establishing the authentic texts, and translating and explaining them. Such was the work of the men who came to be called the "humanists"—or, more exactly, the scholars—of the Renaissance. In France, their chief was Guillaume Budé, who was, as we have seen, Grand Master of the Royal Library; their protectors were Francis I and Marguerite of Angoulême; their weapons were the printing presses. And their mortal enemy was the Sorbonne.

The humanists dreamed of Greek and Hebrew, as yet unknown in France, being taught against a setting of lovely gardens, beneath the shade of elegant porticos, in a royal college subsidized by the crown and dedicated exclusively to the study of letters. Such colleges already existed in countries other than France—the College of the Young Greeks in Rome, that of the Three Languages at Louvain, and the University of Alcalá in Spain. To direct this splendid foundation and give it its indispensable luster, they thought naturally of Erasmus, the "prince of humanists," whom Budé approached several times in vain. The king appeared favorable to such projects and promised much, but did little. The debacle at Pavia, captivity, and wars seemed to have robbed him of his interest, when Budé, weary of fifteen years of sterile negotiations, seized the opportunity brought by The Ladies' Peace to force the hand of the Father of Literacy, and thus played a capital and decisive role in the birth of the future Collège de France. Here is the letter which won the adhesion of Francis I:

"Lend, Prince, to the most liberal of professions and the most useful of them all, a share of your solicitude and your munificence. Apply your elevated thought and your generosity to the encouragement of letters and of serious studies. Remember, Prince, what you promised, first following only your own inspiration, later in answer to our importuning. We portrayed philology as a poor but marriageable girl and we begged you to grant her a dowry. You promised us, with that spontaneous natural bounty which is yours, that you would found a school, a nursery garden, so to speak, for men of learning, for renowned scholars. You told us you would adorn your capital with this establishment, which would be a sort of museum for the whole of France. According to your promises, a splendid building should arise, in which the two languages would be taught. In this temple of serious study you would furnish, to those who were prepared to give themselves to it, a suitable maintenance and the necessary leisure; you did not limit in advance the number of members of this community consecrated to Minerva and the Muses; you decided it would be considerable. That is what you promised. Now at the present time they say you have not kept your promises, and as I have stood surety, they blame me for the delay. They laugh at me and call me a liar."[1]

Francis I could no longer hold back. But instead of a royal college endowed with statutes, installed in a setting worthy of the splendid realization so much talked about—and doubtless to avoid provoking the hostility of the denizens of the Sorbonne—the king confined himself to instituting language courses and was careful to avoid giving even this creation the least publicity. He entrusted the language courses to representatives of the new spirit, to five enthusiastic men of letters, who from that time bore the title of "Royal Readers." No statutes, no place in which to teach, an annual pension of fifty pounds, which was paid irregularly (sometimes even four or five years late) and only after repeated demands. Such was the college of the New Learning. But for the newly created Royal Readers, it provided the most precious of all gifts: freedom.

During March 1530, in halls lent sometimes by the College of Cambrai, sometimes by the College of the Lombards or by that of Cardinal Lemoine, the new Readers, Danès and Toussaint, gave their first course in Greek; Vatable and Guidacerio taught Hebrew, while Fine taught mathematics. With no insignia but the cornette (a long band of silk worn around the neck and reaching to the ground), and no obligation to any man, they professed what they pleased, in Latin, for as long as suited them, at whatever hours they pleased, without any program or any regulation imposing constraint upon them. They announced their courses by placards put up on the walls of the neighborhood schools:

"Agathias Guidacerius, Regius Professor, will continue tomorrow at seven at the College of Cambrai his lessons on the Psalms, by the study of the twentieth psalm. On Tuesday at two, one of his young pupils will study the Hebrew alphabet and the grammar of Moses Rinitius. Copies of the latter work are sold at Guillaume Wechel's, at the sign of the Shield of Basle.

"François Vatable, Regius Professor of the Hebrew language, on Monday at one in the afternoon, will continue his interpretation of the Psalms.

"P. Danès, Regius Professor of Greek, the same day at two, will comment at the College of Cambrai on the book of Aristotle. . . . This work, printed as diligently as possible, is sold at Antoine Augerau's, Rue St.-Jacques, at the sign of St. Jacques.

"Paul Paradis, Regius interpreter in the Hebrew language, will resume Monday at ten, beginning with the elements of the grammar of Sanche Pagnini which he has already expounded in the preceding lessons, and at the same hour he will undertake a commentary of the proverbs of Solomon, at the College of the Three Bishops. These works are sold at Gilles Gourmont's."[2]

Passionately devoted to their profession, imbued with the civilizing mission which they believed was theirs, these men were tremendous workers. They lectured for as much as four or five hours a day, on languages, grammar, commentaries, history, geography, studies in civilization, on morals—on all disciplines indispensable to an understanding of the texts they were studying. In this classical world they were bringing back to life, they sought an art of writing, a rule of life, and grounds for hope, interested as they were above all in man, his destiny, and his possibilities for happiness. This was a far cry from the sclerotic teachings of the Sorbonne, which taught how to reason but not how to live, which molded the memory but not the mind, where reigned, to the exclusion of all other philosophers, the all-powerful combination of Aristotle *cum* Scholasticism.

It was not surprising that the Royal Readers quickly assembled a considerable and enthusiastic audience. Paris, the provinces, and soon all Europe, recognized them as masters of thought. Calvin, Ignatius Loyola, Francis Xavier, Rabelais all rubbed shoulders in the borrowed halls. Danès had as pupils those who were to succeed him later: Amyot, Daurat, Guillaume Postel, H. Etienne. Pierre de la Ramée, the eminent lecturer from the time of the last Valois kings, known under the name of Ramus, has thus described the courses of his master, Toussaint:

"Every year Toussaint explained Greek grammar; he brought out the force of each term, the true significance of each word, those that could be used and those that should be avoided; he gave his explanations in an elegant Ciceronian Latin, always clear and comprehensible by those listening. When he could not render a Greek expression by a single Latin term which conveyed all its energy, he used several, wishing to leave nothing obscure, and always anxious to bring light to his hearers' minds. Every day he explained the parts of speech, and some parts of syntax, the better to inculcate the principles and foundations of the language he was teaching. When he had finished his public lessons, he prepared at home compositions in Latin and French, to have them translated into Greek; when he explained an author it was always as a master superior to his subject, but it was also as an able grammarian, who neglected neither special terminology, nor unusual expressions, nor the turn and arrangement of speeches, nor syntax, nor even etymology."[3]

It quickly became the fashion at the court to make an appearance in these classrooms, and in the front row were to be found the great ones of the kingdom, beginning with the king and his sister. Foreign students abounded. They came from Germany, from Flanders, from those countries where, ten years before, the French had gone to look for learning which they did not themselves have. One of the foreign students, Siderander by name, from Strasbourg, in a letter to his family evoked the sense of admiration which the new teachers aroused:

"I wanted to go yesterday to see what was taking place at the Sorbonne. I was already beneath the porch looking at the pictures and statuettes which are sold there when I saw Budé, who was coming out. I at once left the college to follow the illustrious savant and to view him at my ease. I had already been a little while earlier to visit the room of his son, age about fourteen or fifteen. He had in fact asked me several times to come and see his study and check on what he was doing at home. I am now waiting for him to come in his turn and to bring also to see me his younger brother. . . . Both boys are, as I am, following Latomus's courses: the result is that I live with them on a rather familiar footing. The elder, if he continues to work in that way, will certainly be like his father in his knowledge and erudition, as he is like him in face and bearing. They do not live with their father (who lives far from all the colleges) but they have as tutor a certain Fleming, who formerly lived for several years with Budé in Toussaint's company. I questioned the elder brother the other day, to discover what work his father has in preparation, and also what Toussaint and Danès for their part might be preparing. He replied that the latter was living in the country for the moment in company with his bishop, whose preceptor he is in a sort of way, but that he was coming, nevertheless, to give the printers some Commentaries on the two Verrines, of whom Asconius had not treated,

and at the same time the text of this last, corrected and amended. Danès suspended his Greek lessons for the whole of Lent, and he has not recommenced them yet. He expects to be able to begin his discussions again as soon as the king has paid up his salary. So much for Danès. As for his father and Toussaint, my young friend affirmed that they were not preparing, either of them, any new publication."[4]

There is hardly a more worthy interpreter than Rabelais of the enthusiasm engendered among these brilliant minds:

"Now all disciplines are restored, languages are reconstructed: Greek, without which it is a lie for anyone to call himself an educated man; Hebrew; Chaldean; Latin; the printings, so elegant and correct in usage, have been invented in our time by divine inspiration, as has artillery by diabolical suggestion. Everywhere are crowds of learned folk, well-informed teachers, and ample libraries; and I am told that neither in Plato's time nor Cicero's nor Papinian's were there such facilities for study as are to be found now, and there should not be found henceforth either in place or company, anyone not well polished in the offices of Minerva. I see brigands, executioners, adventurers, and grooms of today better informed than were the doctors and divines of my time. What shall I say? Women and girls have aspired to the praise and manna that are good doctrine. There are also, like me, many who at my age have been obliged to learn the Greek alphabet, which I never despised as did Cato, but which I had not had the leisure to understand in my youth; and I gladly delight in reading the Morals of Plutarch, the fine Dialogues of Plato, the Monuments of Pausanias, and the Antiquities of Atheneus, while awaiting the hour when it shall please God my Creator to call me and bid me go forth from this earth."[5]

The Royal Readers lived their finest days. Already the Sorbonne, jealous and uneasy about their success, was preparing to attack, for it was easy to accuse the Readers of being tainted with heresy. Aware of the danger threatening them, Erasmus advised prudence:

"I have looked on it as a favorable omen the fact that, at the moment when the study of languages and that of good literature was being everywhere reborn, classical studies seemed to unite to protest against this progress with so odious a vehemence. It is exactly that way that all the great things begin, those which are assured of a long duration. I was, if not the first, at least among the first in our time, to arouse the whistling of that hydra. I sincerely sympathize with you, my dear Toussaint, who have also been the object of these rude attacks. But it partly depends on us to obtain, in good time, that this jealousy naturally dies down by insinuating ourselves civilly in everyone's good graces, and above all by rendering all possible service. The college founded at Louvain by Busleiden has scarcely been able to subsist, so serious was the conspiracy of those who were persuaded that the progress of these studies would be harmful to their principle. So I gave the professors the advice not to speak the slightest word against the other masters, but to be content with attracting youth by the gentleness of their manners and by their diligence in teaching, and thus to excite the rage of their irreconcilable enemies, for there is nothing more beautiful nor efficacious than this kind of revenge. They obeyed me, and after some months they proved by experience the exactness and excellence of this advice. Thanks to your prudence and to the dignity of your ways, you Parisians have no need of this counsel. Apart from this you will have to engage in a far less violent battle with the Hydra of Lerne, first of all because with you the splendor of a more developed literature has already in great measure dissipated the clouds of an ignorance full of vanity, and also because you have a great prince, not less human and benevolent than powerful, who has not been afraid to admit to being the instigator of this glorious progress. It seems that he has understood that the brilliance of his own glory increases by that much every time he adds something to the advantage of all. . . . The King of France appears to have given further proof of his good sense in assigning salaries only to the professors of the two languages, Greek and Hebrew, for the teaching of the Latin language is already so flourishing that there is no need of a subsidized professor for that study. It is a mark of the royal benevolence to have designated two professors for each language, with a large salary permitting them to acquit themselves of this noble charge with dignity. For this reason, my dear Toussaint, I judge France infinitely happier than if the whole of Italy had been subjugated to her empire. You have received as your portion a magnificent Sparta. It only remains to you to be its ornament, each one in the measure of your power."[6]

Several Readers availed themselves of his advice, for the dark hour was approaching when there would have to be either a choice or silence.

Thus, of this college of which brilliant minds had dreamed, of this asylum where they might, in complete peace, sheltered from the century's preoccupations, have devoted themselves to their studies, for which grandiose projects had been elaborated and magnificent plans drawn, nothing was realized. Does it matter? The essential had been done, not by the king, but by his free subjects. In the great battle of humanism, the Royal Readers, in spite of, or perhaps thanks to, their poverty, were able to endow France with a great free and independent culture. The Modern Collège de France, that house "built of men," is its direct issue.

*   *   *

The lessons of the Royal Readers had borne fruit. Antiquity had been rediscovered in France. The generation of the mid-century took to it with the same enthusiasm as their elders had done. These young people were indeed avid for knowledge, but above all they wished to create works of art; they were less concerned with erudition than with artistic creation. They were young, and they were poets. The school which attracted them was the College of Coqueret, where the principal, the eminent Hellenist Jean Daurat, son of Limousin peasants, guided their passion for study across the vast and hardly explored domain of Greco-Latin poetry. At this new school—which already called itself "the Brigade" before taking, much later, the symbolic name of the Pleiade—the Ronsards, the Du Bellays and the Baïfs, day and night scrutinized the ancient authors whom they recognized as their masters. Books were rare. Time was precious. At two in the morning "Ronsard wakened Baïf, who arose, took his candle and did not let his ardor cool." Their passion for work was unparalleled; "I want to read Homer's Iliad in three days," Ronsard would write.

The enterprise that warranted so many vigils, the muse that inspired these young men, the noble design they pursued were no more nor less than the creation of a new French poetry.

These young people were free from all misgivings—which is not particularly surprising, for they belonged to a century which mistrusted its national past to the point of rejecting it beyond appeal, and regarding it as wholly barbarous. They denied both Villon and the great rhetoricians. They wished to pass over those who, in their time, went so far in their worship of the classical as to write their poems in Latin. "There is no French poetry worthy of the name," they cried, "and we are not unworthy to create one!"

Little by little, through frequent discussions, a doctrine was formulated. The opportunity to affirm it publicly came soon enough, when a certain Thomas Sibilet, a professional writer, published an *Art of Poetry* in which he handed bouquets to Marot, St.-Gelais, and Scève, praising them as equal in talent to the most illustrious classical authors. These sacrilegious opinions unleashed the indignation of the Brigade. Du Bellay replied in its name with a veritable manifesto which appeared in April 1549 under the title of *La deffence et illustration de la langue française*. In it he sets forth ideas which for a long time were looked on as new but which in fact had been borrowed almost word for word from an Italian work by an author named Sperone Speroni. But the unprecedented novelty was that while the Italian whispered, Du Bellay proclaimed from the housetops, with an innovator's enthusiasm, what he regarded as a universal truth. He declared that the defense of the French language had become an absolute necessity. Since the beginning of the century, a whole group of Frenchmen had deserted it for Latin, and, shamelessly plagiarizing Virgil, Horace, Catullus and Ovid, had declared French unsuited to poetic expression. To arrive at a poetry worthy of the name, Du Bellay asserted, one must write in one's mother tongue, as the creators of Italian poetry, Petrarch and Boccaccio had demonstrated:

"Why then are we such great admirers of other people," Du Bellay exclaimed, "why are we so unjust to ourselves? Why do we beg for foreign languages as though we were ashamed of our own? . . . Horace says that when he wrote Greek verses Romulus warned him in a dream not to carry wood to the forest. Which is what those who write in Greek and Latin usually do. . . . When Cicero and Virgil set about writing in Latin, eloquence and poetry were still in their infancy among the Romans and at the height of excellence among the Greeks. If then those whom I have named had despised their own tongue and written in Greek, is it conceivable they would have equaled Homer and Demosthenes? At least they would not have been among the Greeks what they were among the Latins. Apparently Petrarch and Boccaccio, however much they may have written in Latin, that alone would not have sufficed to bring them the great honor they enjoy if they had not written in their own tongue. Knowing which, not a few good minds in our time, in spite of having acquired an uncommon reputation among the Latins, have nevertheless been converted to their mother tongue, even Italians, who have much better reasons to worship Latin than we. I will confine myself to citing the learned Cardinal Pietro Bembo, than whom, I doubt, any man ever imitated Cicero more subtly. I would not be afraid to point to those two French luminaries, Guillaume Budé and Lazare de Baïf. The former has written, and no less amply than learnedly, the *Institution du Prince*. The other has not only translated Sophocles' *Electra* almost line for line, but has further named in our language the epigram and elegy, those beautiful sweet-sour names. . . . It seems to me, reader, friend of the French muses, that following those I have named you should not be ashamed of writing in your own language; but still more should you, if you are a friend of France, and even of yourself, give yourself wholeheartedly to it, with that generous view which prefers to be an Achilles among his own people than a Diomede, and often enough even a Thersites, among strangers."[7]

But, it was argued, French is a poor language, unfitted for poetic creation. It is true, Du Bellay replied, and so are all languages at their beginning. So they must be enriched and illustrated; forgotten words must be sought out, full of savor, in which the tales of chivalry and ancient books of poetry abound, the provincial dialects and trade jargons must be examined, and, if that is not enough, then new words must be coined. The poet, thus having at his disposition a rich language, should make it the rival of Latin by imitating the classics, the only masters. So let him set to work. He will discover, through patient and assiduous study of their writings, the secrets of the masters, and he will quite simply borrow their recipes. He must be aware, too, that he can reach the desired goal only if he breaks with deplorable national traditions and goes back to Greco-Latin purity:

"Then first read and reread, O future poet, turning the pages by day and by night of Greek and Latin examples, leave all that old French poetry to the floral games of Toulouse and to the Puy of Rouen; such as rounds, ballads, lays, royal anthems, songs and other such tripe which corrupts the taste of our tongue and only serves as a witness of our ignorance. Concentrate on those pleasing epigrams . . . imitating Martial or someone else . . . if wantonness does not please you, mix the pleasurable with the profitable. Distill these elegies with a flowing style, following the example of an Ovid, a Tibullus, or a Propertius, mixing in sometimes a few classical fables, no small ornament of poetry. Sing me odes yet unknown to the French Muse with a lute well tuned to the pitch of the Greek and Roman lyres; and let there be no verse in which there does not appear traces of rare and classic tradition. And these will provide you with your material: praise of the Gods and of virtuous men, the vanity of conversation with worldly things, those things that concern young men, such as love, free wine, and all delicate meats. Above all, take care that this type of poem stays away from the vulgar, enriched and illustrated with apt words and not idle epithets, ornamented with weighty sentences and varied with all manner of colorings and poetic ornaments. As for odes, this is not a form of poetry which can enrich us very much, for they are generally concerned with familiar and domestic themes, unless you will make them, like Ovid, in imitation of elegies, or sententious and grave, like Horace. And this goes for satires, too, which the French, for some unknown reason, refer to as *coq-a-l'âne*. Sound for me these fine sonnets, that Italian invention both pleasant and profound. . . . Sing for me, with a resounding pipe and a well-joined flute these pleasant rustic eclogues, after the model of Theocritus or Virgil, and sea chanties after that of Sannazar, gentleman of Naples. . . . Adopt for me too, into the French family, these flowing and neat hendecasyllabics, after Catullus and Pontanus and Secundus. . . . As to comedies and tragedies, if kings and republics wished to restore them to their ancient dignity which farces and morality plays have usurped, I am of the definite opinion that you should work at them, and if you want to make them an ornament of our tongue, you know where you will find the archetypes."[8]

In the course of Du Bellay's *Défense*, he sketches in a portrait of the ideal poet. The poet is no longer the entertainer of yesterday. Now he becomes emotive; his sonnets or his odes, by their sonority, their rhythm, their choice of words, or by the thought they express, should create in their reader a sacred condition of poetic feeling. Keeper of treasures inaccessible to the masses, the poet, inspired by the Muse, is the messenger of the gods and the peer of kings:

"I will not offer him any other precepts, anent the time and place which must be chosen for reflection, than those which his pleasure and disposition dictate. Some like the cool shade of the forest, the sparkling streams softly murmuring among the meadows decked and carpeted with green. Others delight in secret chambers. . . . One must adjust to the season and place. I would well warn you to seek silence and solitude, friends of the Muses (so that you do not let pass those divine transports which sometimes agitate and warm poetic minds and without which one cannot hope to make something which will endure).

"I do not want to forget emendation, surely the most useful part of our studies. Its office is to add, remove, or alter at leisure what this first impetuosity and ardor for writing had not allowed of. That is why it is necessary, lest our writings, like newborn infants flatter us, to lay them aside, review them often, and like bears, by frequent lickings, to give form and fashion to their limbs. . . . But one must not be too superstitious, or incubate one's verses ten years like elephants their young. Above all one should have some wise or faithful companion, or a familiar friend, even three or four, who could be acquainted with our faults. . . . And again I would like to advise you sometimes to frequent not only savants but all sorts of workers and technicians, like sailors, foundrymen, painters, engravers and others, to know their inventions, the names and materials, the tools and the terms used in their arts and trades, to draw on them for fine comparisons and lively descriptions of all things.

"Doesn't it seem to you, gentlemen, you who are such enemies of your own tongue, that our poet thus armed could go campaigning and show himself in the ranks of the brave Greek and Roman squadrons?

"But to conclude these points, know, reader, that he will really be the poet whom I am seeking in our language who will make me rage, subside, rejoice, weep, love, hate, admire, wonder, in brief who will hold rein on my affections, turning me hither and thither at his pleasure. That is the real touchstone, with which you must test all your poetry and in all languages."[9]

This aggressive manifesto, formulated with such fire, could not fail to awaken controversies, but it also rapidly rallied enlightened opinion around itself, and the future Pleiade proved itself by a flowering of masterpieces. Though its members had differing destinies, though Du Bellay, weary of constant reverses, disappeared in the prime of life, though Belleau, Tyard, Baïf, Pelletier, or Jodelle had a lesser renown, Ronsard, the prince of poets, achieved in his lifetime the glory he had summoned with all his desire, for he had rediscovered the secret of touching the heart and giving voice to its free expression.

> Kiss me, Marie. Nay, do not kiss, but with the charms
> Of your sweet breath draw my heart out again
> Nay, do not draw, but rather from each vein
> Suck out my soul diffused within your arms.
> Nay, do not suck. For after I am dead
> What shall I be except a substance vain
> (Forgive me, Pluto) on that shore, where reign
> No loves but shadows, whence all life has fled?
> So, while we're yet alive, let's love, Marie,
> For love rules not the ashen crowds that be
> All withered by a long and iron sleep.
> That Pluto loved Persephone's a jest:
> Such gentle care dwells not in such coarse breast:
> Love dwells on earth; hell never shall it keep.[10]

As luck would have it, two months later, other *avant-garde* artists, architects, and sculptors had recourse in their turn, on the occasion of a public holiday celebrating Henry II's entry into Paris, to a sort of public manifesto of much more extensive circulation.

The coming of this prince was to be celebrated in the history of the fine arts for the important palace revolution it brought about. In the opinion of the new monarch all of the great buildings constructed in the time of his late father, the builder-king Francis I, were completely out of date and, moreover, second-rate, compared to the new residence of Cardinal Du Bellay, the Château de St.-Maur. This building, constructed according to the canon of a new aesthetic, revealed in a most striking way the unquestionable talents of its architect, Philibert Delorme. In the circumstances, it was decided to remove the Superintendence of Royal Buildings from the Italian incumbent, Primaticcio, and to confer it on this French newcomer who was one of the most notable personalities of that young school which was to be known to posterity as the neoclassic.

The leaders of the neoclassic school bore names now illustrious: Pierre Lescot, Sire de Clagny, whom Francis I, shortly before his death, had commissioned to direct the building of the Louvre; Jean Bullant, Jean Goujon, and Pierre Bontemps, all French, all devoted to the classical antiquity of the humanists. They had traveled to Italy to study the Roman monuments and to see with their own eyes the achievements of Bramante, Alberti, and Vignole, who were the first to make a study of classical works. They had read and reread the old and modern theoreticians, Vitruvius and Vignole; they had heard the teachings of Serlio, who had been installed at Fontainebleau since 1541 with a grandiose title but little chance of action. They were a handful of men, convinced and enthusiastic, who made their existence felt. France now had her architects and sculptors. They had already proved themselves. There was no need now to call in Italian artists, as in the late king's time. Let Italy henceforward be content to have begotten the masters before whom she bowed. These had taught them that, since the fall of the Roman Empire, nobody had known how to build. The direct study of the classical models had revealed the secrets of this long-forgotten art: to achieve that harmony which is the very essence of beauty, recourse must be made to divine proportion, symmetry must be sought, regularity, clarity. A plague on Gothic confections, gables, frills, irregular ground plans and deep-cut façades where ornament predominated. Sobriety, spareness, a return to the Doric, Ionic and Corinthian orders—there lay the truth; harmonious rhythm, which achieved a skillful blending of these elements, constituted the most beautiful decoration that could exist.

So the king, without whom nothing could succeed, the king, who was able to consecrate doctrines and talents, gave them their chance by promoting Philibert Delorme. Full of hope, the new men were afire to proclaim their revolutionary doctrine, and—following the first French translation of Vitruvius by the erudite Jean Martin—Jean Goujon published a veritable manifesto, and one written in magnificent language. But he could hope to reach only a limited elite. To reach the great public and to accustom it to the forms he extolled, the new school must find a means of publicity infinitely more effective. Henry II gave them that means in delegating to them the organization of a then traditional ceremony, his entry into Paris as the acceding sovereign.

The entry of the king into a town is an ancient custom, today completely forgotten, by which the town manifests its deference to the great personage visiting it for the first time. Its survival can be found today, and a very pale idea gleaned of it, from the official receptions of heads of state. But how prosaic are these latter in comparison with the past which they imitate. The entry then gave occasion for a veritable public feast, feverishly prepared for months in advance, in which all, rich and poor, played their part. The better to receive the guest who honored it with his visit, the whole town escaped for a few hours, by the all-powerful wish of one of the great ones of this earth, from the monotony of its daily routine, and arrayed itself in enchanting though ephemeral decorations. It offered itself, transfigured, as a spectacle to itself.

Invariably the ceremony began with a procession of the principal organizations of the town from Notre-Dame to the Gate of St.-Denis, there to receive the king. The four great mendicant orders led the procession, followed by the parochial clergy. Then came the tradesmen, richly attired, and the officers of the town, the officers of the king, the magistrates of the Châtelet, and the four autonomous courts: the Court of Moneys, the Court of Aid, the Chamber of Accounts, and the Parliament; and finally came the university.

At the Gate of St.-Denis the king, followed by the court, awaited the procession, and received, along with the citizens' homage, the keys of the city which were offered as a mark of submission. After listening to the inevitable speeches, he took his place under the canopy designed for him, preceded by the Master of the Horse, with drawn sword, and followed by the royal family and the nobility. By the same road along which the procession had come, the king went to Notre-Dame—which he could not enter until he had sworn to respect the liberties of the Church—then he returned to the Palais de la Cité, where a feast was served him.

The décor of these festivities, as one might expect, changed with the centuries and the kings. In the Renaissance, the entry lost its childlike simplicity to become a triumph in classical style, in which the prince, like a victorious Roman emperor, traversed in his chariot a city richly adorned with triumphal arches, obelisks, columns of honor, and also platforms on which were represented, to the delight of the spectators, allegories, pageants, and scenes in mime springing directly from the *Roman de la Rose* or the *Songe due Vergier*. The success of the latter, particularly, relegated the architectural program to the background.

The entry of Henry II in 1549 marked a turning point in this evolution. The artists who organized it, among whom were Philibert Delorme and Jean Goujon, wanted it to be the manifestation of a pure, spare art. They refused to play the role of public entertainers, and dared to prohibit the tricks of the past, the pageants, and mumming so beloved of the public, so as to draw attention to little buildings of light materials erected along the route, the style of which loudly proclaimed the new aesthetics.

Already at the Gate of St.-Denis, the king could judge of their intentions by a triumphal arch, in which harmonious marriage of architecture and sculpture, and a happy choice of symbols, earned it a special success:

"This outer gate, in Tuscan and Doric style, is dedicated to Strength, to indicate that in Paris resides the principal strength of the kingdom . . . At both sides of the piers were two pedestals on which were placed two great colossi clad in rustic garb, taking the place of caryatids, their bases Doric and their capitals entirely covered with gold. They each held in their hands a great crescent of silver, in which was written in black Roman capitals: *Donec totum impleat orbem* [Till he fills the whole world] which is the king's motto. . . .

"Crowning this monument were four personages in profile, larger than life and dressed according to their quality; one, dressed as a bishop, represented the Church; another, bearing classical arms, wearing a scimitar at his side, signified Nobility; the third in a long robe denoted

Counsel; and the fourth, dressed as a winegrower with a hoe in his hand, revealed Labor. All four seemed to be walking with great strides, their hands stretched out to a Hercules of Gaul facing forward in their midst, whose visage bore a singular resemblance to the late King Francis, restorer of the arts and sciences, more eloquent than any king who had reigned in France before him. This Hercules was dressed in a lion skin, its paws being knotted at the bottom of the bust to hide the parts which nature rules, all the rest of the body being naked. In his right hand instead of a club he held a lance entwined with a serpent, covered by a laurel branch, signifying that prudence in war is the occasion of victory. In the left hand he held his bow, and had slung round him a big quiver full of arrows. From his mouth issued four small chains, two of gold and two of silver, which went to the ears of the four above-mentioned persons, but they were so loose that anyone could see they did not serve for constraint but that the four estates found themselves drawn of their own free will by the eloquence of the new Hercules, who had caused to flourish in this kingdom the Hebrew, Greek, and Latin tongues and others, far more than at any previous time.

"At the keystone of this arch hung a tablet with this quatrain written in golden letters on a black ground:

"To my sweet eloquence and goodness royal
Following and honoring was pleasure due
From all; and seeing then my heir ensue
All following honored him, to free will loyal."[11]

Not all the spectators were fully aware of the significance of this Gallic Hercules, founder of Paris, whose power rested on eloquence and not on physical strength, and who was the symbol of the humanist prince, wise and powerful, who held people bound by his word. According to that lover of scandal, Simon Renard, the imperial agent, the simple folk thought that the late king had been depicted eating the four estates.

Henry II admired, in the same street of St.-Denis, the fountain of Ponceau, surmounted by a thundering Jupiter, symbol of royal omnipotence; a second triumphal arch opposite St.-Jacques-de-l'Hôpital, and then, before the Church of the Sepulcher, an obelisk, memorial of Rome and of the Dream of Polyphyles of which the French version was illustrated by Jean Goujon:

"On a richly painted pedestal was the figure of an animal of Ethiopia called rhinoceros, the color of box bark, armored with natural scales, the mortal enemy of the elephant, and who in fact kills it in single combat. . . . Its designer affixed to it, in the middle of its back, a howdah well fixed with two girths, on which this animal seemed to carry a needle, enriched on its three faces with gilded compartments on a background of porphyry. And on the principal face was a great square containing the good wishes of the Parisians in hieroglyphs, which I will quote after first having said that right at the top of this needle on a gilded globe, was placed a France ten feet high, in classical armor, dressed in an imperial blue toga, sown with lilies, making the gesture of sheathing her sword after being victorious over several cruel and wild animals which lay dead beneath the belly of this rhinoceros. . . .

"But, not to forget the hieroglyphs, first there were a lion and a dog full face, both crowned with the French imperial crown, an ancient book closed with a big lock, and in the book a naked sword, piercing right through it, a twisted serpent in form of an adder, a crescent whose horns rested on two swords, a globe surmounted by a foot drawn from nature, a ship's poop and a trident, an open eye, a circle, a poppy, an anchor, two crossed hands on olive branches, a cornucopia on which fell a rain of gold, a stag, a dolphin, a laurel wreath, an antique lamp alight, a horse's bit, and then the helm of a ship. These hieroglyphs signified, addressed to the king, Strength and Vigilance can guard your kingdom. By Counsel, good Speed and Prudence your frontiers will be extended, so that all the round machine of the earth may be in submission to you and that you may rule the sea, having always God to avenge and defend you against your enemies; live, rule, and govern firmly in peace and concord, in plenty of all good things, long and judiciously triumphant.

"On the first face of the obelisk was a tablet on which was written, in letters of gold on a black ground, this quatrain, speaking in the person of France:

> "Long has survived and still will live the name
> Of Hercules who many monsters mewed
> The peoples proud and strong by me, as France, subdued
> Were, are and will be my imperishable fame.

"Such was the dedication of this sacred obelisk to his royal majesty."[12]

Through streets hung with rich tapestries, and watched by the enthusiastic crowds gathered along the route, perched in windows and even on the rooftops, the king continued on his way. He passed before the Fountain of the Innocents, of stone and marble, which Jean Goujon had just completed, and admired, before the Bridge of Notre-Dame, a third triumphal arch where the pilot Typhis, captain of the ship *Argo*, with Castor and Pollux on either side, symbolized the victorious monarch, master of the ship of the republic. He crossed a Bridge of Notre-Dame bordered by thirty-four houses, all inscribed with letters of gold on a red ground and ornamented with sirens in high relief, with Medusa heads, knots, and royal devices: a double H in gold on an azure ground, and silver crescents on a black ground. He then passed yet a fourth arch erected at the other extremity of the bridge, before entering Notre-Dame to be present at divine worship. Then he returned, by way of the Rue de la Calende, to the palace, before which had been raised a final triumphal arch, with a double opening. In the palace itself, a magnificent banquet awaited him.

Henry showed himself well satisfied. At table, comment on the morning's spectacle was continuous and enthusiastic, and everyone lavished praise both on the young artists' accomplishments and on Jean Goujon, particularly, the hero of the hour. But the king did more than praise. Three weeks later, Goujon was commissioned to draw up the design for the façade of the new Louvre, in the same style as the temporary monuments erected for the royal entry into Paris. The splendid result still stands today. And it was the lot of Henry II to initiate a style of architecture that was to flourish for more than three hundred years.

*   *   *

It is worth while to follow briefly the careers of two men who embodied the progress of the New Learning in France. The first of them, Philibert Delorme, "god of the masons," is ranked with Pierre Lescot and Jean Goujon as one of the masters of the neoclassical school, whose existence had just been proclaimed with such brilliance. Unfortunately, time has not been kind to Delorme's works, and only the Chapel of Anet remains intact; the rest have been disfigured by subsequent rearrangement or destroyed by man's stupidity. There are, however, few architects who built as extensively, particularly civil works: the castles of St.-Maur, Anet, St.-Leger-en-Yvelines, Limours, Monceaux, St.-Germain-en-Laye and the Tuileries—without including those already in existence, which he enlarged or completed: Fontainebleau and Villers-Cotterêts, Madrid, and Chenonceaux.

Born in 1510, at Lyons, Philibert was the son and grandson of master masons, whose three hundred workmen he was supervising from the age of fifteen. When he was twenty-three, he made a journey to Rome and for several years passionately studied classical remains in the hope of rediscovering the secret of their beauty. When he returned to France, the building of the Château de St.-Maur brought him into the limelight, and the new king, Henry II, as has already been mentioned, on his accession, named him Superintendent of Buildings. He was all powerful so long as his protector was on the throne; but the jealousies aroused by his rapid rise, the antipathies and even the hatreds engendered by his imperious and difficult temperament, and, above all the prejudices of the royal favorite, resulted in his being dismissed by Catherine de Médicis, who reinstated Primaticcio immediately on the death of Henry

II. This disgrace was the more cruel because, two days later, Philibert and his brother Jean were outrageously insulted by their former subordinates, to the point that their lives were in danger. In the brawl which followed, blood ran, an embroiderer and a painter were killed, and suit was filed against the Delormes by the victims' families. Shortly afterward, the former superintendent was accused of fraudulent administration and embezzlement of funds. He got out of the first affair by paying heavily, and justified himself against accusations impugning on his honesty in a statement addressed, it is thought, to Christophe de Thou, President of the Parliament of Paris. This document brings its author to life and with him the whole context of his life:[13]

"Since several people are saying out loud that I have so much wealth in the Church and in cash, I wish everyone to know the truth, and the services which I have done:

"First, the king gave me the Abbey of Geneston in Brittany, which M. de Rieux did not want because it was worth only three hundred pounds.

"Next, I was given the Abbey of St.-Barthélemy-les-Noyon, which M. de Bayeux had, which was worth only seventeen hundred pounds.

"A year later, the late king gave me the Abbey of Ivry, which was reckoned at thirteen hundred pounds.

"Finally, he gave me the Abbey of St.-Serge d'Angers, which is reckoned at two thousand seven hundred pounds. And that is all the favors the king has done me, which is six thousand pounds, very far from the account to twenty thousand pounds which they say he gave me.

"As to money, I have not had a brass farthing. I was never given, moreover, expense account, wages, pensions, or any other gift whatsoever. I always took with me ten or twelve horses . . . and I kept house wherever I was, as much for the captains, watchmen, controllers, master masons, carpenters, and others. All of them eat at my house, at my own expense, without paying me or making me the smallest present.

"And further, for all the models I had made, both in the king's service and for those around him, nobody paid me a penny, and some I made cost me two or three hundred crowns.

"Besides the great architectural inventions which I worked on every day, I most diligently watched over the king's houses and, but for me, the king, the princes, and other lords would have been crushed and in grave danger of their persons from the beams and floors which often had to be shored up or taken down.

"What profit did I have in Brittany when, in the time of the late King Francis, whose soul is with God, I visited every year and sometimes twice a year, the whole coast and the fortresses and discovered the very large thefts which Captain de la Châtre and Controller Moysant were making, so that the English thought to take Brest, had I not been there. For these gentlemen were arming ships and boats with artillery, powder and other munitions of the king, which they took from the castle, so that there were no munitions, or wheat, or artillery left; one day their ship was taken by the enemy; in this way they knew how the castle was denuded, and decided to come and take it; sixty English ships advanced until they were opposite the castle within cannon shot. By good luck I happened to be at Brest. I took such trouble having the artillery mounted, having sham artillery made to be shown to the enemy upon the ramparts, having powder manufactured, commandeering the populace to bring earth and fagots, to make ramparts and trenches, I gave such orders as these, making the people show themselves with several false standards and a host of pikes. In short, I put up such a good face that the enemy never attacked us at all. Without me the castle at Brest would easily have been taken, and the enemy would have been able to come as far as Nantes with nothing to stop them, on account of the great disorder prevailing in 1546."

Delorme then mentions his exemplary work in Brittany, Normandy, and Picardy and adds:

"And besides all this, have I not rendered many other services, if only by bringing to France good methods of building, got rid of barbarous practices, shown to all how to observe good proportion in architecture, so well that I have made the best workmen there are today, as they themselves admit. Just let people remember what was being done when I began St.-Maur for Monseigneur the Cardinal du Bellay.

"And further, let them consider all I have done; at Fontainebleau, the great ballroom was falling down; has it not been well furnished, both with paneling and with a fireplace and masonry? I do not speak of it; M. de St.-Martin [author's footnote: Primaticcio] knows its value. . . . Besides that I did so many fine works at St.-Germain, St.-Leger, in the forest of Montfort, at Monceaux, at Anet; let them remember the great inventions I produced, not only for the profit of His Majesty, but for all his people, too, as well as the woodwork for the roofs, which can be made of all kinds of wood and of all small pieces.

"And of so many other inventions, so beautiful, discovered by mathematics, that obliged me to spend money daily for models, and I was never paid. That is how I can have a lot of money! And besides five nephews, whose studies I paid and which cost me a lot, I have maintained several learned men who have continually been studying architecture, liberal arts, and mathematics, and I often make myself read from Holy Scripture.

"That is how I have conducted myself, and I have never acquired anything but a white beard, and I have taken as much trouble as any man is capable of starting at fifteen years of age when I began to be in charge. I have served popes, kings, several cardinals and great lords. The late Monseigneur de Langey, Guillaume du Bellay, M. the Cardinal his brother, got me out of the service of Pope Paul, in Rome where I was, and where I had a good post at St.-Martin dello Bosco, to return to France. And for all recompense for having served so well, they have done me all this harm and accused me of numerous shameful actions of which I have been found innocent.

"All I have said above is not for desire for glory on my part, nor from my wish for honor, giving all to God who is the creator and author of all things. I do it on account of the great calumnies and hatreds which they continue to lay at my door, so that all the princes, lords, and men of honor shall know the true facts."

But the queen mother, Catherine de Médicis, had too much taste to dispense forever with the services of such an artist. She recalled Delorme and entrusted great projects to him, including that of the Tuileries. He was to be seen once more at the Louvre, still irascible as always and full of talent. One day he got at odds with Ronsard, whose own nature was no more agreeable. Doubtless he had his reasons. From the first, the poet had manifested the usual arrogance of the noble toward the middle classes, and in addition had sharply attacked Delorme in a biting satire entitled *La truelle croisée*. In the course of this tirade, the imperious Vendômois blamed the king for distributing benefits to his masons, for he had given the Abbey of Livry to Philibert Delorme. The latter, bristling, from then on sought every opportunity for revenge, even the smallest, as is shown by an anecdote reported by Claude Binet, the biographer of Ronsard:

"The Abbot of Livry [i.e., Delorme] one day had the entrance to the Tuileries closed to Ronsard, who was following the queen mother. But Ronsard, who could be quite sharp and biting when he wanted to, immediately had chalked up on the door that the Sieur de Sarlan soon opened for him, these words in capital letters: FORT REVERENT HABE. The queen, on her return, saw this writing and, in the presence of learned men and of the Abbot of Livry himself, asked what it meant. Ronsard was asked to be the interpreter of it, after Delorme had complained that this writing took him to task; and Ronsard said that he agreed that, by a gentle irony, he took this inscription for himself if one read it in French; but that it fitted him still better when it was read in Latin. For in that language the first words were abbreviated from a Latin epigram of Ausonius, which began: *Fortuna reverenter habe*, reminding him to remember his original and lowly rank, and not to shut the door on the Muses. The queen helped Ronsard to his revenge, for she dryly reprimanded the Abbot of Livry after some laughter, and said out loud that the Tuileries was dedicated to the Muses."[14]

Delorme may be considered the first French architect. In the middle of the sixteenth century, the master mason of former times and his counterpart, the Controller of Finance, who together hitherto had ruled the construction works, now had to bow before this newcomer, the architect, who possessed artistic talent as well as the technical knowledge and the common sense of the professional man and of the administrator. Philibert Delorme embodied successfully this personality of modern times. He possessed a very lofty idea of his role, and in his work he delineated the ideal portrait of the good architect, as he should appear to the patron who employs him:

"He should not be unfamiliar with philosophy, with mathematics, or with history, to give reason for what he does, and he should know the origins and progress of everything appertaining to architecture; which includes also portraiture to be able to show by figures and drawings the works he intends to do. Seemingly he should know perspective to make sketches and know how to give clarity to his buildings. Some say that he should also understand medicine, but I do not find the necessity for this, but rather that he should know certain rules of natural philosophy, to know how to discern the nature of sites, the parts of the world, the quality of waters, the regions, and the directions and properties of prevailing winds, the value of woods and sands, the nature of rocks, to draw on them at the proper time and to know which of them are good for making lime or tiles, and how to set everything to work. . . .

"The patron ought to make diligent inquiry about the capacities of the architect; he ought to know which works are his, his modesty, his assurance, his probity, administration, and what fortune attends him in his enterprises, if he is a born manager, and if he is wise. That is of great importance, for if he is foolish, glory-loving, proud, presumptuous, or ingorant, he will undertake a great work which he cannot worthily achieve, and will eat up the patron with charges through ill considering and not foreseeing the necessary things.

"It is a good thing if the architect in his youth has been familiarized with his art, and that he has studied the sciences required in architecture, as, obviously arithmetic, theory and practice, geometry, also in theory, but more in practice, for the features of it which are really useful; as also astrology and philosophy; above all he should well understand the reason of symmetries, to give measure and proportion to everything, façades of houses or every other part of buildings. It will also be a very good thing if he is not unfamiliar with the theory of music, to know how to make use of echoes, and make resonant and audible the spoken word and voice, both from nearby and far away, which is something necessary in temples and churches, for the preaching which takes place there and the psalms and other things which are sung or intoned there. It is the same for auditoriums where pleas are heard, for theaters where comedies, tragedies, historical pieces, and the like are recited and played, so that those who are far off can hear as well as those who are near. The patron, then, having met an architect who has such fine qualities and above all a good heart, can take courage and boldly commit his works to him."[15]

The bad architect, on the other hand, draws down Delorme's wrath, and he has left a picturesque and indignant account of him. Doubtless, he had met a certain number of them along the way:

"In the great undertakings which are done for kings, princes, and great patrons, there is never a lack of men and servants, but usually they are unfaithful in that most of those you see promise that they know how to do everything and are the best conceivable administrators, but most often they know nothing. Truly such people are like the figure of a man whom I show you dressed as a sage, but overheated and out of breath as though he could run with difficulty, and found some desiccated heads of oxen in his road (which signifies a coarse and heavy mind), with several stones which make him stumble, and bushes which catch him and tear his clothes. Such a man has no hands, to indicate that those he represents do not know how to do anything. He also has no eyes in his head to see and know what are good undertakings, no ears to listen to wise men, or a nose to have the scent of a good thing. In short, he has only a mouth for babbling and slandering, and a sage's hat and the dress of the same, to counterfeit a great doctor and keep up a good appearance, so that one may believe he has great worth, and that he possesses some reputation and good opinion among men."[16]

The genius of a man like Philibert Delorme is very diverse. Theoretician of proportions, apostle of classicism, he possessed also an admirable knowledge of the concrete and in his eyes experience was as important as theory. Endowed, in addition, with a remarkable talent for invention, he was the author of a certain number of innovations, of which the most celebrated perhaps consisted in replacing the enormous pieces of wood necessary for the building of very wide roof spans—which were difficult to find on account of their size—by an assembly of small-section timber. That concept was the reason, he tells us, for the publication of his work entitled *Les nouvelles inventions pour bien bâtir:*

"It came to me one day to touch on it in a few words with His Majesty, King Henry, who was at table. But the audience and those present, never having heard speak of such new things and such a great invention, suddenly drew back at what I was saying, as though I had wished to make the king listen to some lies. Seeing them make such a

27. Architect instructing a novice. From Ph. Delorme's *Le Premier Tome de l'Architecture*, Paris, 1567. Bibliothèque Nationale, Paris

An armoire of the French Renaissance, with medallion of Henry II. The Louvre, Paris. Photograph by H. Adant

Armchair of the French Renaissance, with figure of the huntress Diana. The Louvre, Paris. Photograph by H. Adant

28.

A table of the French Renaissance, Dutuit Collection, Petit-Palais. Photograph by H. Adant

swift judgment of what was not yet heard, and that His Majesty did not say a word, I thought it better not to pursue the subject, ordering the building to go on as usual. Some time afterward the queen mother decided to have the tennis court covered in at her Château de Monceaux, to give pleasure and contentment to the king. Seeing that they asked her for such a huge sum of money I spoke again about this invention. The said lady asked me to give it a trial. Which trial turned out so fine and of such great utility that then each one thought how to profit by it, even those who had contradicted it, mocked it, and argued against it. Which thing came to the ears of His Majesty the late king, who had seen and greatly lauded the said invention, and he commanded me to make a book about it to be printed for the decoration of his kingdom so that this way should be intelligible to all."[17]

In 1570, on January 8, three years after the publication of his famous work: *De l'architecture,* in which for the first time in France a professional man confided to a publisher his whole thought and experience, Philibert Delorme, at the height of his career, committed his soul to God. Shortly before, he had designated his last wishes in one of those testaments so precious to the historian, which it was the custom at that time to have notarized[18]:

"In the Name of the Father, the Son and the Holy Ghost, I Philibert Delorme, Abbot of St.-Eloi de Noyon and of St.-Serge d'Angers, Canon of Paris, sane in mind and understanding, knowing that we are all bound infallibly to die, that there is nothing more certain than death, and less certain than the day and the hour of it, not wishing to die intestate, but like a true Christian and Catholic who should order before his death the goods which it has pleased the Divine Bounty to bestow on him, and of which he may freely dispose, I make the present Testament and Ordinance of my last will in the form and manner following:

"And firstly, I recommend, my poor soul departing from this world, to the most blessed Trinity, to the most sacred Virgin Mary, and to all the saints of the celestial choir, and to my good angel, to intercede before God for my said poor soul, and to put and place it among those of his well beloved and elect.

"*Item,* after my said death, forthwith, I wish my body to be attended by two persons, clerics, to pray God without ceasing and alternately for my said poor soul, while waiting for its burial. And to do this I bequeath to each of the said persons the sum of a hundred sols tournois.

"*Item,* I wish my said body to be buried in the church of Paris [author's footnote: the Cathedral of Notre Dame] to which I give and leave the sum of one hundred sun crowns, for there to be done and said there a service and other prayers, and things accustomed after the decease of a canon of the said church and at the interment of such.

"*Item*, and to accompany my body in the said church where it will be buried, I wish such monasteries, communities, and other ecclesiastical persons other than those of the church, and in such number as my executors hereafter named think fit to be called upon.

"In which said executors I confide for arranging the mourning, funeral pomp, obsequies, and burial, to do everything as they shall see fit."

After ordaining anniversary masses for the repose of his soul, the testator comes to his bequests:

"I leave my sister, Jeanne Delorme, my two houses which I have in this city of Paris, the one called the Hotel d'Etampes, giving on to the Rue St.-Antoine, and the other giving on to the Rue de la Cerisaye, and I beg her affectionately to receive and take to her my two natural children, to treat them as her own. . . .

"*Item*, I leave to my brother, Jean Delorme, all my books on architecture, drawings, prints, and portraits, and besides, my place of Plaisance, near Paris, and all its appurtenances, and also that which I acquired at Fontenay from one named Heurtelou. . . .

"*Item*, I leave to Philibert Delorme, my natural son, for his food and keep, two hundred pounds tournois rent a year. For which I wish put in the Town Hall of Paris two thousand four hundred pounds tournois for my said executors in the name of the said Philibert Delorme, which rent, if he dies a minor, I wish and intend it shall return to Jeanne Delorme my sister.

"*Item*, I leave to Charlotte Delorme, my natural daughter, for her food and to help marry her, a hundred and forty pounds tournois of rent a year which I have the right to take on the said town.

"*Item*, I leave to my nephew, Martial Burlet, all my books of theology. . . .

"*Item*, I leave to M. the Premier President of Paris, Messire Christophe de Thou, my houses, place and gardens which I have at St.-Maur-des-Fossés, for which I once refused six thousand pounds tournois, in the assurance that he will have me paid by the king after my death, as he has promised me, the sum of eleven thousand pounds which His Majesty owes me, and it is with the express charge to do this and to oversee it that my present testament is executed. . . .

"*Item*, to M. Tabonneau, Counselor of the King our lord and President of the Office of Accounts of Paris, a covered cup of silver gilt with an ewer, to have some remembrance of me after my death and to help in the execution of this my present testament. . . .

"Before Vincent Maupéru and Jean Lusson, king's notaries in his Châtelet at Paris, was present in person the Reverend Father in God Philibert Delorme, Abbot of St.-Serge and St.-Eloi-les Angers, and canon of the Church of Paris, lying in his bed, ill, nevertheless good and firm of purpose, memory, and understanding, as he said and as he appeared before the said notary by his words, gestures, and bearing. . . . Done and passed, the year 1569, Wednesday the twenty-first day of December."

*   *   *

The second representative of the New Learning in France was Ambroise Paré, whom historians of medicine consider as one of the greatest surgeons of all time. He was born in 1510 at Bourg-Hersent, near Laval, of a family in modest circumstances. It seemed improbable that a glorious destiny awaited the young boy, whose social station and unfavorable early surroundings seemed to stand in the way of the realization of his exceptional gifts. A chaplain, with whom his father had placed his child to be initiated into the mysteries of the humanities, taught him instead all the niceties of gardening; at that point, it seemed an injustice to reproach little Ambroise with his ignorance of the declensions. Nevertheless, his father could not resist that temptation and, furious, made him go to work as scullion for the Countess de Laval. Already, while stirring the sauces, he was reading, they say, Galen, Hippocrates, or Vigo. Absolutely without feeling for his situation as turnspit, Paré succeeded in getting taken on as apprentice by the count's barber. This honorable profession did not stop at haircutting; the doctor, to whom the Middle Ages did not allow the indecent gesture of letting blood, had as his double the modest and illiterate but adroit barber. Minor medical cares fell to him, bloodletting and dressing "boils, bumps, anthrax and carbuncles." Paré's vocation became clear while performing these humble duties, which allowed him glimpses of a world for which he felt he had been made. He did not rest, or allow anyone any peace, until he had gotten to Paris and been admitted to the Hôtel-Dieu.

He could not have found a better school until, a few years later when he left for Italy as surgeon to the armies, he found the school of war. The hospital and the battlefield were the great masters of this self-taught genius, who knew no Latin at a time and in a society which worshiped it, and who scandalously dared to write in his mother tongue treatises about his art. Observation, experience, practice were his masters, instead of the fossilized theories which had brought medieval medical science to a standstill. To these, he wrote, he owed the essentials of his talent:

"In order to see what means I had to make such great experiments, one must know that for the space of three years I lived at the Hôtel-Dieu in Paris, where I had the opportunity to see and to get acquainted with (because of the great diversity of sick people usually lying there) all that can be said and thought about anatomy, as I have often given most sufficient proof, and that publicly at Paris at the medical schools.

"Thus, much was given to me to arrive at a knowledge of the great secrets of surgery. But my fortune made me see even more: for, being called to the service of the kings of our France (of whom I have served four) there was no time or means I did not employ to obtain the graces of the most learned doctors and surgeons, and the most experienced; having the idea that, although their knowledge was great, the soul of the matter is in experience. . . .

"It was not enough to satisfy my curious desire to learn all that could be known of the profession to which I was called, if I had not seen the wars, where they treat the wounded without frills and pampering as they do in towns. For I found myself campaigning, at the battles, skirmishes, assaults, sieges of towns and fortresses, and I also have been shut up in towns with the besieged, being in charge of treatment of the wounded.

"And God knows how much the judgment of a man is perfected in this exercise where, gain being far removed, honor alone is offered you and the friendship of as many brave soldiers as the lives one saves, so that, after God, I should like to boast of having saved an infinite number of them."[19]

It was in the course of these first years passed in Italy at the bedside of the wounded, a prey to the fearful and novel sights which "wounds by harquebuses" made, that he made what he considered one of his most important discoveries: the treatment of wounds inflicted by firearms with softening ointment, instead of cauterizing them with red-hot iron and boiling oil, as was the custom. In 1536, Paré, following the army of the Maréchal de Montéjean, entered Italy. The imperial troops attacked before Susa. The fighting was brutal, and the dead and the wounded were numerous on both sides. A hellish sight awaited the newcomer, however accustomed to the face of death, when he entered the town:

"We passed over the dead; some of them were not yet dead, for we heard them scream under the hoofs of our horses, which stirred great compassion in my heart. In truth, I repented of having left Paris in order to see so pitiful a spectacle. I went into a stable to lodge my horse and that of my servant, and there I found four soldiers dead and three propped up against the wall, their faces entirely disfigured; they could not see, hear or speak, and their uniforms were still sparkling with the gunpowder which had burned them. As I looked at them full of pity, an old soldier came in who asked if there was any means of healing them. I told him no; quickly he drew close to them and cut their throats, gently, without anger. Seeing this great cruelty, I told him he was a wicked man; he answered me, that he prayed to God that were he in the same pass there would be someone who would do as much for him, so that he should not linger miserably."[20]

The surgeons immediately set to work, and Paré, more knowledgeable about therapeutics against the plague than about the wounds of battle, began by imitating them:

"At that time I was a greenhorn; I had never seen wounds made by harquebuses treated by operation. It is true that I had read in Jean Vigo's first book, Chapter 8, "Of Wounds in General," that wounds made by firearms are poisonous because of the powder. To cleanse them he says, they must be cauterized with boiling elderberry syrup, to which a small quantity of theriac has been added. But knowing that such treatment would be extremely painful to the wounded man, I wanted to know, before applying it, how the other surgeons went about this operation; they applied this oil as near boiling as possible to the wounds, and I made bold to do as they did.

"Finally, I ran out of oil, and was obliged to apply in its stead an unguent made of egg yolk, rose oil, and turpentine. At night, I could not sleep soundly, fearing lest, for lack of cauterization, I find the wounded whom I had neglected to treat with this oil dead from poisoning, and I rose very early to visit them. Against all hope, I found those to whom I had applied the unguent feeling little pain; they had slept rather well at night, and their wounds were without inflammation or abscesses. Those who had been treated with the boiling oil I found feverish, in great pain, and with abscesses around the edges of their wounds; therefore I decided never again to burn so cruelly the poor victims of harquebus fire. That is how I learned to treat wounds made by harquebuses; not by books."[21]

Immediately, some claimed that this discovery was actually a regression; for cauterization, however painful, safeguarded to some extent the principles of asepsis, whereas Paré, with his unguents, opened the door to infection. The reply to the objection inaugurated the era of the dirty bandage, which was to last until Velpeau.

There was another discovery, this one of incontestable value, which, since Paré's day, has daily saved the lives of millions. It is Paré whom we must thank for the ligature of arteries, a discovery the more remarkable in that the Renaissance doctor, faithful to classical teaching believed that the arteries did not contain any blood.

Paré tells of one of the first operations where he used this procedure; a poor soldier had received a shot from a harquebus in his left arm; gangrene had set in and threatened the shoulder, even the thorax. His general state was very poor, and the surgeons had declared the wounded man lost when his friends came to find Paré. He came to the dying man's bedside[22]:

"I took the risk, as commanded by our art, of cutting off his arm at the elbow, and, first of all, I tied the arm tightly above the elbow; this done I cut it without a saw, and began the amputation, incising the ligaments which join the bones. One should not be surprised at such an amputation, for Hippocrates, in the fourth book of his Articles, recommends it and says it is very easy to recover from, and sees nothing to fear other than a heart attack, from the pain of the severing of both the tendons and the ligaments. After having made my incision, there was a great flood of blood, in spite of the ligature, because of the blood vessels which are part of the arm; I allowed enough blood to flow to relieve, to lighten, and to ventilate the area and also to prevent gangrene. Then I stopped the blood by immediate cautery, having at that time no other means of doing it; that done, I gently loosened the ligature, and then made several wide and deep incisions in the gangrene, avoiding the inner part of the arm, because of the big veins, arteries, and many nerves which are there. And I at once cauterized some of the incisions, as much to stop the blood as to dry up and consume any poisonous matter present in this part."

The surgeon took great care of the wounded man for more than fifteen days and cured him. "By which" he concluded, "the surgeon must know that he should always be aware that God and Nature bid him never abandon his patients, without always doing his duty, even if he can foresee nothing but death; for Nature often does what to the surgeon seems impossible."

The renown of such a surgeon soon spread to the ears of the mighty. After the death of M. de Montéjean, Paré entered the service of M. de Rohan, and followed him on his various campaigns, during the course of which, at Boulogne, he reduced, with consummate art, the huge wound which François de Guise, Duke of Lorraine, known thereafter as "The Gashed," had received full in the face. After the death of Rohan, the king hastened to attach the former barber to his person as court surgeon. It was in this capacity that he took part in the siege of Metz, of which he has left us his famous account. Catherine de Médicis, after she was widowed, confirmed him in this post and so far recognized his worth as to name him, in 1562, first surgeon to her son, Charles IX. Thenceforward, having to watch over the fragile health of the last kings of the house of Valois, he never again left the court except, when as a last resort, his master consented to allow him to go to the bedside of someone desperately sick.

One of the cures of which Paré was most proud was accomplished in Hainault on the Marquis of Havré. The latter had been suffering for more than eight months from a harquebus shot in his knee, and had been getting steadily worse despite—or perhaps because of—the numerous doctors who were giving him every care[23]:

"As soon as I had arrived, I visited him. He told me he was delighted at my arrival, and that he was extremely obliged to the king for having done him the honor to send me to him. I found him with a high fever, his eyes very sunken, a moribund yellow face, his tongue dry and arid, his whole body very emaciated and thin, his voice low, like that of a man near death; then I found his hip very swollen, full of pus, and ulcerated, oozing with a fetid, greenish liquid. I probed him with a silver probe, by this means I found a cavity near the groin reaching to the middle of the thigh, another around the knee putrid and cunicular, and also some splinters of bone, some detached, others not; the leg was very swollen and full of yellow humor, cold, damp, and windy, so that the natural warmth was being suffocated and extinguished. The said leg was doubled under the hips, the rump ulcerated over an area big as the palm of a hand; and he said he felt a great burning and pain, and the same in his kidneys, to such an extent that he could not rest by day or by night, and had no appetite, but was thirsty. I was told that he often had heart attacks, and sometimes seemed to be epileptic and often wished to vomit, trembling so much that he could not lift his hands to his mouth."

Paré thought the marquis was beyond help. Acutely aware of his human limitations, he retired into the garden and recollected himself, asking that "God would grant him grace to cure him, and that He would bless their hands, and the medicaments they would use, he and the other practitioners at the castle, to cope with so many serious complications." Then he rejoined the others and with them examined the sick man. After having deliberated at length in their company, he made his diagnosis, and explained the therapy he proposed to use:

"I said that it was necessary to cure by contraries, and first of all to ease the pain, making openings in the thigh to evacuate the filth retained there. Secondly, because of the great swelling and coldness of the leg, fearful lest gangrene set in, artificial heat should be applied—thanks to hot bricks on which a decoction made of herbs good for the nerves should be poured, cooked in wine and vinegar, then wrapped in a cloth, and an earthenware bottle filled with the same decoction should be placed at his feet. Hot poultices should also be made and placed on the hip and on the whole leg, made of a decoction of sage, rosemary, thyme, lavender, camomile flowers, and balm, with red roses cooked in white wine and oak leaves, a little vinegar, and half a handful of salt.

"Thirdly, on the ulcer at the base of the back, a plaster made of a desiccating ointment should be placed, to ease the pain and to dry up the ulcer; also a saddle of down should be made which would hold up his pelvis without his weight being on it. Fourthly, to reduce the heat of his kidneys, Galien's refreshing ointment should be applied to them, and over it, fresh water-lily leaves, and a cloth dipped in vinegar and water, to be renewed frequently.

"For the heart attacks, good succulent nourishment should be given, like lightly cooked eggs, Damascus grapes cooked in sugar and wine; also a panada made of the white meat of capon, partridge wings well chopped fine, and other roast meats easy to digest, such as veal, kid, pigeon, young partridges, thrush, and the like. The sauce should be of orange, sorrel juice, sour pomegranates. He might also take broth made of good greens, like sorrel, lettuce, rampion, endive, bugloss, marigold, and similar others. At night he could have pearl barley, with sorrel and water-lily juice, two ounces of each, with four or five grains of opium, and of these four seeds pounded, half an ounce of each, which is a remedy both alimentary and medical, and will induce him to sleep.

"For his severe headache, he should have his hair cut and his head rubbed with tepid oxyrrhodinus; in the same way he should have applied to his forehead a compress of rose oil, water-lily, poppy, a little opium and rose vinegar, with a little camphor, to be renewed from time to time.

"Moreover, he should be made to smell henbane and water-lily flowers crushed with vinegar and rose water, which should be held for a long time under his nose, so that the smell may reach his brain. In the same way, artificial rain should be produced, by running water from someplace into a caldron, in this way the invalid would be induced to sleep."

After this long exposition, Paré went to the patient's bedside, and lavished on him the care he had prescribed:

"I made three openings in his thigh, from which issued a great quantity of filth and blood, and right there I pulled out some splinters of bone, but I did not wish to let out too great an abundance of this blood for fear of weakening him too greatly. Two or three hours later, I had a bed made next his, with fine clean white sheets, then a strong man lifted him into it, and he was glad to have been taken out of his dirty stinking bed. Immediately after he asked to sleep, and did so for almost four hours, which made everyone in the house begin to rejoice. The following days I injected, deep into his ulcers, egyptiac dissolved, sometimes in brandy, sometimes in wine. I applied, to disinfect and dry up the soft and spongy flesh, compresses to the base of the cavities and over all a big plaster. In the same way I bandaged him so skillfully that he had no more pain; once that stopped, his fever rapidly began to fall. Then I made him drink wine diluted half with water, knowing that it restores and revivifies. And all the things that we had decided upon during our consultation were done according to the time and the nature of his pains. The fever gone, he began to mend, and dismissed two of his surgeons and one of his doctors, so that there were only three of us with him. When I saw that he was beginning to get well, I told him he must have violins, and some comedian or buffoon to amuse him, which he did. In a month, we were able to get him to a chair, and he had himself carried around his garden and to the castle gate to see people go by. The villagers for two or three leagues around, learning that he could be seen, came and made merry with singing and dancing, men and women, all together, to show their joy at his good convalescence. . . . He always had them given a gratuity, and they drank heartily to his good health."

All over the country everyone talked of Paré's marvelous cure. He was sent patients, the notables of the town of Mons organized a banquet in his honor "to which they fetched him in two carriages." The marquis' brother invited him to his castle to celebrate both the patient's recovery and his surgeon's talents. The rejoicings lasted several days in the midst of a numerous and joyous assembly. And when Paré bade farewell to the lady of that place, she pulled off her finger a fine diamond worth fifty crowns, and offered it him in gratitude for having taken such good care of her relative. Finally, the master regretfully left him who owed him his life, and who, now convalescent, went where he wished with the aid of crutches. Paré rejoined his sovereign, whose delicate constitution required his constant care.

Henry III was at least able to show his gratitude on the night of the Massacre of St. Bartholomew by spiriting Paré away from his enemies, who, in order to dispose of him, had accused him of heresy.

Ambroise Paré, the barber's apprentice of Laval, died in 1590, heavy with years and with honors. A surgeon of genius, he dominated the practice of medicine in his time. Going far beyond the Italian school, until then the only accepted one, he raised his profession to a respectable and respected place in the world. A strong personality, a sensitive man with courageous mind and skilled hands, he dared give greater credit to the evidence of his eyes than to the theories of books. He was as much an innovator as Philibert Delorme, and his discoveries retain, like the Arnet chapel, all of their importance.

I*

NOTES

XI · Schools and Scholars

1. Lefranc, A. *Histoire du Collège de France depuis ses origines jusqu'à la fin du Premier Empire.* Paris, 1893, pp. 104–5.
2. *Ibid.,* pp. 144–45.
3. *Ibid.,* pp. 174–75.
4. *Ibid.,* pp. 135–37.
5. Rabelais, *Oeuvres complètes.* Ed. J. Boulenger. Paris, 1955, pp. 1226–27.
6. Lefranc, *op. cit.,* p. 118–19.
7. Du Bellay, J. *La deffence et illustration de la langue française.* Ed. H. Chamard. Paris, 1948, pp. 186–94.
8. *Ibid.,* pp. 107–26.
9. *Ibid.,* pp. 169–73, 179–80.
10. Ronsard, P. de. "Le deuxième livre des amours," in *Oeuvres complètes de Ronsard.* Ed. G. Cohen, Paris, 1958. t. I, p. 150.
11. *C'est l'ordre qui a été tenu à la nouvelle et joyeuse entrée que très haut, très excellent et très puissant Prince, le roi très chrétien Henri, deuxième de ce nom, a faite en sa bonne ville et cité de Paris, capitale de son royaume, le seizième jour de juin 1549.* Paris, 1549, ff. 2–3.
12. *Ibid.,* ff. 9–11.
13. De l'Orme, Ph. *Mémoire manuscrit de Philibert de l'Orme sur sa vie et ses oeuvres.* Paris, Bibliothèque Nationale, Portefeuille de Fontette, côté XXXV, A, Bourgogne, généalogie, pp. 204–6 bis. Ed. A. Berty, *Topographie historique du vieux Paris.* Paris, Impr. nationale, 1866–97, Région du Louvre et des Tuileries par A. Berty. Paris, 1866–68. t. II, pp. 179–85.
14. Binet, Cl. *La vie de Pierre de Ronsard, gentilhomme vendômois, 1586.* Ed. P. Laumonnier, Paris, 1910.
15. De l'Orme, Ph., *Le premier tome de l'architecture* . . . Paris, 1567, f. 10.
16. *Ibid.,* f. 280
17. Berty, A., *op. cit.,* t. II, p. 25.
18. De l'Orme, Ph. *Testament.* Ed. Archives de l'Art Français, 2ᵉ série, t. II, pp. 318–30.
19. Paré, Ambroise, *Textes choisis.* Eds. L. Delaruelle et M. Sentrail. Paris, 1953, pp. 73–74.
20. Paré, Ambroise. *Les voyages faits en divers lieux par Ambroise Paré, chirurgien de Laval, racontés par lui-même.* Paris, 1890, p. 234.
21. *Ibid.,* pp. 235–36.
22. Paré, Ambroise, *Textes choisis,* pp. 113–15.
23. Paré, Ambroise, *Les voyages* . . . , pp. 303–9.

XII · The Renaissance of the Soul

IT COULD hardly be expected that so great an eruption of intellectual and emotional energy as the Renaissance would leave untouched that institution which for over a thousand years had been the most important and influential in Europe: the Roman Catholic Church.

The Church, after centuries of unquestioned spiritual and intellectual leadership, was suddenly made to realize in the sixteenth century that she no longer could quell the spiritual unrest of the faithful by the age-honored formulas of devotion. It was an incapacity generated by a variety of causes; perhaps it was the tragedy of the waning of the Middle Ages and, along with it, of the gigantic synthesis which hitherto had provided the believer with a closed circle of security; perhaps it was the great agony of the fifteenth century with the butcheries of the Hundred Years' War and of the plague which decimated the continent. Whatever the cause, the fact was that souls were disquieted by the constant menace of death and, at the same time, lost the certitude of eternal salvation promised by the Church to her faithful servants. An unspeakable anguish gripped Christians at the idea that they must die, and that they knew neither the day nor the hour. And the Church could no longer give peace to those souls obsessed by the agonizing question of salvation, by the uncertainty of the hereafter.

With the failure of traditional sources, there was left for the intellectual elite either the harsh predestination of Ockham, which was perhaps only slightly more discouraging than outright despair, or the effusions of the German mystics. For the masses, who could not attain to such levels, there remained only the refuge of a cut-rate religion, of a pedestrian devotion. And they fell upon it with undisguised relish. They saw in Christ no longer the triumphant and risen Son, but only the Christ of the Passion—the wounds, the blood, the tears, the cross; and to share in the sufferings of the Crucified became the principal preoccupation of popular piety.

The Virgin likewise was the subject of a frenzied cult. Mother of the Savior, infinite tenderness, infinite suffering, for them she was Our Lady of Consolation, the highest resort, she who disarmed the wrath of God. And to win her favor no stone went unturned. The University of Paris declared her to have been conceived without sin, and inaugurated the dogma of the Immaculate Conception. As of old the vassal confirmed his devotion to his lord by the gift of a crown of roses, so now he offered to the lady sovereign of souls the cult of the rosary, a chaplet of prayers, whose originally red, white, and gold roses symbolized the joys, the sorrows, and the glories of Mary. The better to celebrate her merits, he plucked at endless beads in the shadow of oratories, murmured endless litanies, quiet incantations which evoked, through the poetic emblems with which he decked her, all purity: "Hail, Star of the Sea, Window of Heaven, Tower of David, Enclosed Garden, intercede for me; Fountain, Mirror Without Blemish, Rose Without a Thorn, pray for me; Lily of the Valleys, perfumed Nard, protect me."

But the protection of the Queen of Heaven did not suffice these anxious souls. Against the instinctive fear which gripped them, they needed daily, near-to-hand assistance in the form of an everyday friend, familiar and easygoing, to whom it was possible to confide problems big and small without being intimidated by a majestic air. Such a protector was to be found in the person of the patron saint, to whom passionate devotion now was rendered. Doubtless as a reward for an exemplary life, patron saints had obtained from the Lord some spark of His divinity, and they disposed of supernatural powers in favor of all who bore their name. Their statues were everywhere—in churches, naturally, but also on ramparts, on the gates of towns, at the corner of houses—in order that these souls might be protected by the beneficent emanations of their patron saints.

Most popular of all were St. Christopher and St. Barbara—protectors against the most terrible evils, against sudden death, the redoubtable death that carried off the poor sinner into the beyond, without giving him time to be reconciled with God. Then came St. Sebastian, St. Adrian, St. Anthony, and St. Roch, defenders against epidemics and especially against the plague; and these were followed by the cohorts of the other blessed. There were no circumstances in which recourse could not be had to them. In town, they were the patrons of the confraternities founded in their honor by members of a profession whose activities animated urban life. In the country, it was they who made the orchards burst into abundant flower, they who pollinated the cherry blossom when the earth was wet and the spring grass green, on the day when the parishioners in their heavy clogs carried their statues shoulder-high, statues whose role was to shower efficacious virtues on the vines. Later, at the proper time, the peasants would wash the statues' feet with wine. It is not surprising that, on their feast days, the statues of saints were put up for public auction and placed for a few hours in the house of the fortunate bidder to whom this arrangement was supposed to bring luck for an entire year.

France came to be covered with new chapels, with white oratories, into which thronged the crowds whose morbid sensibility gravitated around the twin poles of the pathetic and the tender. On the altars, the Virgin, a simple country girl, nursed her baby and played with Him; the saints with their attributes, the very precious reliquaries, brought comfort to all hearts. On the walls, tortured and bleeding Christs, stations of the cross, recalling the sufferings of Calvary; pictures with such themes as St. Gregory's Mass, the Mystic Wine Press, the instruments of the Passion, extolled the blood shed for sinners; in contiguous chapels, touching entombments drew tears, while in the glory of the sunset sparkling stained-glass windows taught the illiterate the marvels of the Golden Legend; and the tiny, flickering flames of the votive candles reminded the holy patron of the anguished soul that looked to him for protection from the divine thunderbolts.

Simple souls of touching piety thought to achieve their salvation, by themselves, by their own works, thanks to the saints and to the glorious Virgin Mary, almost without God; and to them the rich were indeed blessed, since, by the purchase of indulgences, they could buy the certitude of a place in paradise. This piety, however, could not quench the terror of death, which was everywhere expressed, and which became a theme repeated on frescoes, tombs, castles, door lintels, and even on the pitchers of beer used daily. "I am what you will be, a few ashes." "My body that once was beautiful is now rotted; you who read this will soon be like me." "Think of death, poor fool."

The numerous abuses from which the Church suffered did not suffice to explain the prevailing disquiet. Rather, this new era experienced new spiritual needs, needs which a monolithic, anachronistic religion, encumbered by vain practices, could no longer satisfy. And though the Church was reproached for bad living, she was accused above all of bad faith. Dissatisfied with the old ways of religion, many felt that it was time for a change, for new ways, for a reformation of the Church. That reformation would prove to be, as Lucien Fèbvre called it, "a new way of feeling and of practicing Christianity."

From now on, the burning question of religion occupied the forefront of the European conscience. From Germany arose Luther's powerful voice. To the agonizing question of salvation, he gave the long-awaited reply: man is saved not by his works but by his faith. In France and in the Low Countries, the humanists Lefebvre d'Etaples and Erasmus proclaimed the necessity for a return to Scripture. It was in the reading of the Bible that Christians would find the quieting of their anguish, the long-awaited reply, the solution of their problems, the daily help they needed. It became the very condition of religious life. Thanks to their erudition, these two scholars expurgated from the text later additions, established it, and made it available to all by translating the New

Testament into the vulgar tongue. From these beginnings was born the religious revolution.

In France, the first manifestation of this movement took place within the circle of Meaux, inspired by the bishop of that diocese, William Briçonnet. Briçonnet belonged to the highest social circles. Son of a former favorite of Charles VIII, spiritual director of the king's sister, Marguerite of Angoulême, with whom he kept up a curious correspondence, he had a distinguished and open mind. In 1520 he gathered around him, under the direction of Lefebvre d'Etaples, a small group of clerics—Gerard Roussel, Michel d'Arande, Guillaume Farel, Mazurier, Pauvan—in order to evolve and implement a plan for the reform of the diocese. The idea of a break with the Church did not even occur to them. They wished to reform it from within, without laying hands on the hierarchy; and the only remedy they preached was a return to the pure doctrine of the Gospel. Every Sunday, Briçonnet and his friends preached and spread the Gospel by lectures, commentaries, and printed matter. At the same time, they tried to purify the worship of its excesses and to reduce venality; and they prepared a revision of the liturgy which they wished to translate into French. These attempts aroused the enthusiasm of the masses. At first, it seemed that the reform might be bloodless and painless. Then, Luther's writings began to appear in France. A violent, anti-Roman spirit took hold of people. The circle of the Bishop of Meaux was assimilated to the Lutherans, and thus they were faced with the alternative of breaking either with these violent Germans or with Rome. They did not dare advance along either road and beat a retreat; and with them disappeared all hope of a pacific reform of the Church.

* * *

While the Bishop of Meaux was trying to reform his own diocese according to an established plan, the new ideas spread through the whole country in the usual distorted form. Spontaneous, insidious, without any very definite doctrine, without a leader, the fake message distilled everywhere its corrosive poisons. It was addressed orally to the illiterate crowds, originally by monks and religious preachers of every kind—Franciscans, Augustinians, and secular priests—who went spontaneously from town to town preaching impromptu what they thought was the truth. During their frequent excursions, they came in contact with the like-minded, and by long arguments, in small groups, won them over to their ideas, and after their departure left new converts ready to form other groups in their turn. Nothing is left of these colloquies where the Gospel was commented, where such burning questions as the power of the popes, abuses, the cult of saints, or free will, were argued with vehemence; nothing of the spirited harangues addressed by these preachers to the masses. Everything has been lost except one sermon, given at Grenoble on St. Mark's Day in 1524, by the Dominican Aimé Maigret, a reformer from Lyons:

"What is it to believe in Jesus Christ? Is it to believe that he is God and man, was crucified and died for us, descended into hell, ascended into heaven, is seated at the right hand of God, who will come to judge all mankind? Following the judgment of St. James, I tell you no. What then should be your faith? The faith that you should have is to believe firmly and to hope surely that, because the son of God became man, you, nothing but a poor creature, of no value compared with God, will participate in the divine perfections. Because Jesus Christ has suffered a painful death, your sins will be forgiven you. Because he descended into hell, the devil will have no power over you. Because he rose again, one day we will also, communicating and participating in his immortality, his brightness, his impassibility and the like privileges. Because he went up to heaven, paradise is opened to us, and we will enter it following him. In short, faith in Jesus Christ is to believe that we would never have any part in Paradise except by the virtue of the faith, or by the trust (which is the same thing) that we have in him. . . .

"I do not want now to blame or to say that it is a bad thing to be dressed in a long gray robe, to wear a cord instead of a belt, a dickey instead of a shirt, to have cutaway shoes, a sewn hood and no money in one's purse. I do not say it is a sin to wear a white robe, and, to complete the livery, a black cape over it, a scapular hanging beneath, to eat no meat, drink only from cupped hands, and countless other such external signs. But I say that whoever obliges you to do these, using coercion, ordering you to make such observances under pain of eternal damnation, or, as you say, under pain of mortal sin and other temporal and spiritual pains, is simply sending you back to school."[1]

The theater is a very effective means of publicizing an idea. It was abundantly used during the religious revolution. Without hesitation the argument was carried onto the stage, and there the current state of the Church was violently criticized while the writers' own viewpoint was made clear. *La farce des théologastres* is a specimen typical of this type of polemic. It comes from the pen of a lively gentleman from Picardy, Louis de Berquin, the eminent humanist who gave the French public the first translations into the vernacular of Erasmus and of Luther. Parliament took advantage of the absence of the king, who was protecting de Berquin, to seize the writer's papers, burn his books, and throw him into prison. But Francis I, learning of this affair, hastened to free him, and the students celebrated the happy decision with an allegory whose bold argument did not contribute to reconciling the author and his judges. Faith, assisted by Brothers and Theologasters, respectively incarnated in monks of the Sorbonne or false theologians, complains of a cruel sickness which she declares she owes to theology as practiced in the Sorbonne. But she knows the remedy[2]:

Faith The Scriptures text
Would work good cure on me.

Theologasters It is crude,
Without certitude,
Nor ever saw it we.

Faith How frivolous can you be,
You wise doctors that
Appear so high hat?
Never Scripture text have seen!
St. Paul, where have you been?
These by the Holy Spirit taught,
Know not of godly science aught,
But of Sorbonne cases a fat lot,
All of which are merely rot.
There's no church by any pretext,
Roman, triumphant, militant
Subject or imperious,
That can give me back health.
That can do only the Text.

Brothers We don't know him.
Where's he from? Tell.

Faith Brothers, fratres,
And you, Masters Theologasters,
'Tis in you a great presumption
To discuss my sad consumption
Without knowledge pure
Of the Holy Scripture.
What can you know?

Theologasters Majoris,
And Alexander of Alis,
Durand, Albert, Egidius
And Petrus Reginaldetus,
Bricot, Auget and Tartaret,
Ricquart, Lombard with Meffret,
St. Thomas and de Urbellis.

> *Faith*   Of all their argot I'll have none.
> My cure will never be begun
> By Gerson's Textuary.
> What I need, for 'tis in my nature,
> Is the text itself of Holy Scripture,
> Without *ergo, quod* or *quia*.

At this point, accompanied by Reason, Text, in a sad state, enters, cane in hand, with a bloody face and feeble voice. Both begin a lively discussion with the Theologasters and Brothers on the moral and intellectual indigence from which Christendom is suffering:

> *Text*   Ha, Masters Theologasters,
> And you, brothers opinionasters,
> In a short time you have lost
> Reason, which you sore has cost.
> How come you?
>
> *Theologasters*   Mind what you say: of faith the pillars we.
>
> *Reason*   Roofless pillars; may you not be
> Among those cheats who us deny
> The Gospel? I have heard these
> Saying the Church cannot err.
> Themselves the Church are, they aver.
> Therefore by a neat sleight of hand
> They cannot err, you understand.
>
> *Text*   They have made so dull to me
> Anagogy, Tropology,
> And withal allegory.
> They have cut me up so fine,
> Where I am now I can't divine.
>
> *Brothers*   Listening to you is a pleasure.
> I wonder if God has the leisure?
> Do you think He truly sees
> How many Paris has of fleas?
>
> *Reason*   There's your argot, if you please.

Hearing these cronies exchange their fourfold truth, however, did not cure the sick man. Action was necessary. Therefore Text and Reason decided to go to Germany to seek the advice of Mercury—i.e., de Berquin. This latter declared that he knew the proper remedy and agreed to go to the patient's bedside.

Mercury	Lady, you can truly witness
	To the cause and cure of your sickness.
	You your health for to regain,
	Scripture's text you need, 'tis plain.
	Reason here, without a doubt,
	Must set to work to clean it out,
	Glosses' yeast must wash away,
	If you wish your cure to stay.

Here Reason washes Text, and during this time, Mercury says to the Brothers and the Theologasters:

> Here, good sirs, a sorry farce,
> Compress made from the value of Mass.
> Here's a splendid sticky plaster
> Speculum called, it mirrors disaster.
> In it you can see your head,
> And the Hydras, Sorbonne bred.

Reason	Here is Text, now pure and clear,
	As a cure it has no peer.
Mercury	Kiss him, that he with his breath
	May arouse your faith from death.
	While you to clear Text will cling,
	You'll stay well through everything.
	Some may cavil, but beware
	You don't relapse—take every care.
Brothers	Pray God some evil you befall,
	Evil boy, rude liar tall . . .
Text	I the king of glory pray
	That in his sanctuary he may
	Place Erasmus who the text does scan,
	And Lefebvre that splendid man,
	And you too Mercury, good friend,
	Whom so many oaths do rend
	Of Theologasters and bigots small,
	Full of calumnies, one and all.
Theologasters & Brothers	Discontented, we now depart!
Reason	Let these bigots freely go,
	So I can tell what's on my heart.
	But lest I bring you boredom's woe
	Farewell all . . .

Song was another instrument of propaganda. Marot translated the Psalms into French, and soon everyone was humming them, at court and in town. Simpler couplets were added, more suitable to workers and peasants. Thus, linked to a melody, the new ideas flew from mouth to mouth; and men went singing to the stake, where their tongues were cut out before they were burned alive. As H. Hauser has put it, the Reformation essentially was the heresy of the book. The translations of Luther's works, of the Bible into the vulgar tongue, the books, the pamphlets, the opuscules, containing attacks of every kind against the Church, were purchased at the international fairs of Frankfurt, Lyons, or Medina del Campo, and then distributed by the booksellers. In the first rank of such are the *Colloquies* of Erasmus, where, in dialogues imitating those of Lucian, the great humanist subjects to mordant criticism the exaggerated devotions in which his contemporaries took such delight. First, he lashes out at a practice hallowed by tradition, the religious pilgrimage[3]:

"*Menedemus:* What Novelty is this? Don't I see my old Neighbor Ogygius, that no body has set their Eyes on this six Months? There was a Report he was dead. It is he, or I'm mightily mistaken. I'll go up to him, and give him his Welcome. Welcome Ogygius.

Ogy: And well met, Menedemus.

Men: From what Part of the World came you? For here was a melancholy Report that you had taken a Voyage to the Stygian Shades.

Ogy: Nay, I thank God, I never was better in all my Life, than I have been ever since I saw you last.

Men: And may you live always to confute such vain Reports: But what strange Dress is this? It is all over set off with Shells scollop'd, full of Images of Lead and Tin, and Chains of Straw-work, and the Cuffs are adorned with Snakes Eggs instead of Bracelets.

Ogy: I have been to pay a Visit to St. James at Compostella, and after that to the famous Virgin on the other side of the Water in England; and this was rather a Re-visit; for I had been to see her three Years before.

Men: What? out of Curiosity, I suppose.

Ogy: Nay, upon the Score of Religion.

Men: That Religion, I suppose, the Greek Tongue taught you.

Ogy: My Wife's Mother had bound herself by a Vow, that if her Daughter should be delivered of a live Male Child, I should go to present my Respects to St. James in Person, and thank him for it.

Men: And did you salute the Saint only in your own and your Mother-in-law's Name?

Ogy: Nay, in the Name of the whole Family.

Men: Truly I am persuaded your Family would have been every whit as well, if you had never complimented him at all. But prithee, what Answer did he make you when you thanked him?

Ogy: None at all; but upon tendring my Present he seemed to smile, and gave me a gentle Nod; with this same Scollop Shell.

Men: But why does he rather give those than any thing else?

Ogy: Because he has Plenty of them, the neighbouring Sea furnishing him with them.

Men: O gracious Saint, that is both a Midwife to Women in Labour, and hospitable to Travellers too! But what new Fashion of making Vows is this, that one who does nothing himself, shall make a Vow that another Man shall work? Put the Case that you should tie yourself up by a Vow that I should fast twice a Week, if you should succeed in such and such an Affair, do you think I'd perform what you had vowed?

Ogy: I believe you would not, altho you had made the Vow yourself: For you make a Joke of Fobbing the Saints off. But it was my Mother-in-law that made the Vow, and it was my Duty to be obedient: You know the Temper of Women, and also my own Interest lay at Stake.

Men: If you had not perform'd the Vow, what Risque had you run?

Ogy: I don't believe the Saint could have laid an Action at Law against me; but he might for the future have stopp'd his Ears at my Petitions, or slily have brought some Mischief or other upon my Family: You know the Humour of Great Persons.

Men: Prithee tell me, how does the good Man St. James do, and what was he doing?

Ogy: Why truly, not so well by far as he us'd to be.

Men: What's the Matter? Is he grown old?

Ogy: Trifler! You know Saints never grow old. No, but it is this new Opinion which has been spread abroad through the World, is the Occasion, that he has not so many Visits made to him as he used to have; and those that do come, give him a bare Salute, and either nothing at all, or little or nothing else; they say they can bestow their Money to better Purpose upon those that want it.

Men: An impious Opinion.

Ogy: And this is the Cause, that this great Apostle, that us'd to glitter with Gold and Jewels, now is brought to the very Block that he is made of, and has scarce a Tallow Candle.

Men: If this be true, the rest of the Saints are in danger of coming to the same pass."

The cult of the Virgin in its turn excited Erasmus's sarcasm. He composed a jesting letter, purporting to have been written by St. Mary of the Stone of Basel and left by an angel on the pulpit of the monk

Glaucopute, a disciple of Luther, who was guilty of having revolted against excessive devotion to the Virgin[4]:

". . . Mary the Mother of Jesus to Glaucoplutus sendeth Greeting. This is to let you know, that I take it in good part, and you have much obliged me, in that you have so strenuously followed Luther, and convinced the World, that it is a thing altogether needless to invoke Saints: For, before this time, I was e'en wearied out of my Life with the wicked Importunities of Mortals. Every thing was ask'd of me, as if my Son was always a Child, because he is painted so, and at my Breast, and therefore they take it for granted I have him still at my beck, and that he dares not deny me any thing I ask of him, for fear I should deny him the Bubby when he is thirsty. Nay, and they ask such things from me a Virgin, that a modest young Man would scarce dare to ask of a Bawd, and which I am asham'd to commit to Writing. A Merchant that is going a Voyage to Spain to get Pelf, recommends to me the Chastity of his kept Mistress: And a profess'd Nun, having thrown away her Veil, in order to make her escape, recommends to me the Care of her Reputation, which she at the same time intends to prostitute. The wicked Soldier, who butchers Men for Money, bawls out to me with these Words, O Blessed Virgin! send me rich Plunder. The Gamester calls out to me to give him good Luck, and promises I shall go Snips with him in what he shall win; and if the Dice don't favour, I am rail'd at and curs'd, because I would not be a Confederate in his Wickedness. The Usurer prays, Help me to large Interest for my Money; and if I deny 'em any thing, they cry out, I am no Mother of Mercy. And there is another Sort of People, whose Prayers are not properly so wicked, as they are foolish: The Maid prays, Mary, give me a handsome, rich Husband; the Wife cries, give me fine Children; and the Woman with Child, give me a good Delivery; the old Woman prays to live long without a Cough and Thirst; and the doting old Man, send that I may grow young again: the Philosopher says, give me the Faculty of starting Difficulties never to be resolv'd: the Priest says, give me a fat Benefice: the Bishop cries out for the saving of his Diocess; and the Mariner for a prosperous Voyage: the Magistrate cries out, shew me thy Son before I die: the Courtier, that he may make an effectual Confession when at the Point of Death: the Husbandman calls on me for seasonable Rain; and a Farmer's Wife, to preserve her Sheep and Cattle. If I refuse them any thing, then presently I am hard-hearted. If I refer them to my Son, they cry, if you'll but say the Word, I'm sure he'll do it. How is it possible for me a lone Body, a Woman and a Virgin, to assist Sailors, Soldiers, Merchants, Gamesters, Brides and Bridegrooms, Women in Travail, Princes, Kings, and Peasants? And what I have mentioned is the least part of what I suffer. But I am much less troubled with these

Concerns now than I have been, for which I would give you my hearty Thanks, if this Conveniency did not bring a greater Inconveniency along with it. I have indeed more Leisure, but less Honour and less Money. Before I was saluted Queen of the Heavens, and Lady of the World; but now there are very few, from whom I hear an *Ave-Mary*. Formerly I was adorn'd with Jewels and Gold, and had Abundance of Changes of Apparel, I had Presents made me of Gold and Jewels; but now I have scarce half a Vest to cover me, and that is Mouse-eaten too: And my yearly Revenue is scarce enough to keep alive my poor Sexton, who lights me up a little Wax or Tallow Candle. But all these things might be born with, if you did not tell us, that there were greater things going forward. They say, you aim at this to strip the Altars and Temples of the Saints every where. I advise you again and again to have a care what you do: For other Saints don't want Power to avenge themselves for the Wrong done to them. Peter being turn'd out of his Church, can shut the Gate of the Kingdom of Heaven against you. Paul has a Sword, and St. Bartholomew a Knife. The Monk William has a Coat of Mail under his Habit, and a heavy Lance too. And how will you encounter St. George on Horseback in his Cuirassiers Arms, his Sword, and his Whinyard? Nor is Antony without his Weapon, he has his sacred Fire: And the rest of them have either their Arms, or their Mischiefs, that they can send out against whom they please: And as for my self, although I wear no Weapons, you shall not turn me out, unless you turn my Son out too, whom I hold in my Arms. I won't be pull'd away from him: You shall either throw us both out, or leave us both, unless you have a mind to have a Church without a Christ. These things I would have you know, and consider what Answer to give me; for I have the Matter much at heart.

From our Stone House, the Calends of August, the Year of my Son's Passion 1524. I the Stony Virgin have subscribed this with my own Hand."

The cult of relics and the fabulous riches of the churches equally aroused the indignation of Erasmus. Here he describes the sanctuary of St. Thomas of Canterbury[5]:

". . . The first thing they shew you, is the Skull of the Martyr, as it was bored through; the upper Part is left open to be kiss'd, all the rest is cover'd over with Silver. There also is shewn you a leaden Plate with this Inscription, *Thomas Acrensis*. And there hang up in a dark Place, the Shirts of Hair-cloth, the Girdles, and Breeches, with which this Prelate used to mortify his Flesh, the very Sight of which is enough to strike one with Horrour, and to reproach the Effeminacy and Delicacy of our Age.

Men: Nay, perhaps the Monks themselves.
Ogy: That I can neither affirm nor deny, nor does it signify much to me.
Men: You say right.
Ogy: From hence we return to the Choir. On the North Side they open a private Place. It is incredible what a world of Bones they brought out of it, Skulls, Chins, Teeth, Hands, Fingers, whole Arms, all which we having first adored, kiss'd;
Ogy: ". . . After this we were carried into the Vestry. Good God! What a Pomp of Silk Vestments was there, of Golden Candlesticks! There we saw also St. Thomas's Foot: It look'd like a Reed plated over with Silver; it had but little of Weight, and nothing of Workmanship, and was longer than up to one's Girdle.
Men: Was there ne'er a Cross?
Ogy: I saw none: There was a Gown shewn, it was Silk indeed, but coarse, and without Embroidery or Jewels; and a Handkerchief, still having plain Marks of Sweat and Blood from the Saint's Neck. We readily kiss'd these Monuments of antient Frugality.
Men: Are these shewn to every body?
Ogy: No certainly, my good Friend.
Men: How then did you come to have such Credit with them, that none of their Secrets were conceal'd from you?
Ogy: I had some Acquaintance with the Reverend Prelate William Warham the Archbishop, and he recommended me.
Men: I have heard he was a Man of great Humanity.
Ogy: Nay, if you knew the Man, you would take him for Humanity itself. He was a Man of that Learning, that Candour of Manners, and that Piety of Life, that there was nothing wanting in him to make him a most accomplish'd Prelate. From hence we were conducted up higher; for, behind the high Altar, there is another Ascent, as into another Church. In a certain new Chappel there was shewn to us the whole Face of the good Man set in Gold, and adorn'd with Jewels; and here a certain unexpected Chance had near interrupted all our Felicity.
Men: I want sadly to hear what mischievous Matter this was.
Ogy: My friend Gratian lost himself here extremely. After a short Prayer, he says to the Assistant of him that shew'd us the Reliques, Good Father, is it true, as I have heard, that Thomas, while he liv'd, was very charitable to the Poor? Very true, replies he, and began to relate a great many Instances of his Charity. Then answers Gratian, I don't believe that good Inclination in him is changed, unless it be for the better. The Officer assented. Then says he again, If this holy Man was so liberal to the Poor, when he was a poor Man himself, and stood in need of Charity for the Support of his own Body, don't you think he would take it well now, when he is grown so rich, and wants

nothing, if some poor Woman having a Family of Children at home ready to starve, or Daughters in danger of being under a necessity to prostitute themselves for want of Portions, or a Husband sick in Bed, and destitute of all Comforts; if such a Woman should ask him leave to make bold with some small Portion of these vast Riches, for the Relief of her Family, taking it either as by Consent, or by Gift, or by way of Borrowing? The Assistant making no Answer to this, Gratian being a warm Man, I am fully persuaded, says he, that the good Man would be glad at his heart, that when he is dead he could be able to relieve the Necessities of the Poor with his Wealth. Upon this the Shewer of the Reliques began to frown, and to put out his Lips, and to look upon us as if he would have eaten us up; and I don't doubt but he would have spit in our Faces, and have turn'd us out of the Church by the Neck and Shoulders, but that we had the Archbishop's Recommendation. Indeed I did in some measure pacify him with good Words, telling him, that Gratian did not speak this from his Heart, but had a drolling way with him; and also laid down a little Money.

Men: Indeed I exceedingly approve of your Piety. But I sometimes seriously think on't how they can possibly excuse themselves from being guilty of a Fault, who consume such vast Sums in building, beautifying, and enriching Churches, setting no Bound to their Expences. I allow that there ought to be a Dignity in the sacred Vestments, the Vessels of a Church, agreeable to the solemn Service; and would have the Structure of it to have a certain Air of Majesty. But to what purpose are so many golden Fonts, so many Candlesticks, and so many Images? To what purpose is such a Profusion of Expence upon Organs, as they call them? Nor are we indeed content with one Pair. What signify those Consorts of Musick, hired at so great an Expence; when in the mean time our Brothers and Sisters, Christ's living Temples, are ready to perish for Hunger and Thirst?

Ogy: There is no Man, either of Piety or Wisdom, but would wish for a Moderation in these Matters; but since this Error proceeds from a certain Extreme of Piety, it deserves some Favour, especially when we reflect on the other hand, on the contrary Error of others, who rob Churches rather than build them up. They are commonly endow'd by great Men and Monarchs, who would employ the Money worse in Gaming, or War. And moreover, if you take any thing away from the Church, in the first place it is accounted Sacrilege; and in the second place, it shuts up the Hands of those who had an Inclination to give; and besides, it is a Temptation to Rapine. The Churchmen are rather Guardians of these things than Masters of them. And lastly, I had rather see a Church luxuriant with sacred Furniture, than as some of them are, naked and sordid, more like Stables than Churches.

Men: But we read, that the Bishops of old were commended for selling the sacred Vessels, and relieving the Poor with the Money.

Ogy: And so they are commended at this Day; but they are only commended; for I am o' th' Mind, they neither have the Power, nor the Will, to follow the Example. . . . In the end, we were carried back into the Vestry: There was pull'd out a Chest covered with black Leather; it was set upon the Table, and opened. They all fell down on their Knees, and worshipped.

Men: What was in it?

Ogy: Pieces of Linen Rags, a great many of them retaining still the Marks of the Snot. These were those, they say, that the holy Man used to wipe the Sweat off from his Face and Neck with, the Snot out of his Nose, or any other such sort of Filth which human Bodies are not free from. Here again my Gratian behaved himself in none of the most obliging manners. For the gentle Prior offered to him, being an Englishman, an Acquaintance, and a Man of considerable Authority, one of the Rags for a Present, thinking he had presented him with a very acceptable Gift: But Gratian unthankfully took it squeamishly in his Fingers, and laid it down with an Air of Contempt, making up his Mouth at it, as if he would have smack'd it. For this was his way, if any thing came in his way that he would express his Contempt to. I was both asham'd and afraid. Nevertheless the good Prior, tho not unsensible of the Affront, seem'd to take no notice of it; and, after he had civilly entertain'd us with a Glass of Wine, dismiss'd us. . . .

Ogy: In our Journey to London, not far from Canterbury, there's a narrow, hollow, steep Way, and a cragged, steep Bank on either Side, so that you can't escape it; for there is no other Way to go. Upon the left hand of that Way, there is a little Cottage of old Mendicants. As soon as they espy a Man on horseback coming, one of them runs out, and sprinkles him with holy Water, and then offers him the upper Leather of a Shoe, with a brass Ring to it, in which is a Glass, as if it were some Gem. Having kiss'd it, you give a small Piece of Money.

Men: In such a way, I had rather meet with a Cottage of old Mendicants, than a Gang of lusty Foot-pads.

Ogy: Gratian rode on my left hand, next to this Cottage; he was sprinkled with holy Water, and took it pretty well; but upon presenting the Shoe, he ask'd what was meant by that? This, says the poor Man, was St. Thomas's Shoe. Gratian fell into a Passion, and turning to me, said, What would these Brutes have? Will they make us kiss the Shoes of all that have been good Men? Why do they not as well give us their Spittle, and the other Excrements of their Bodies, to kiss? I pitied the poor old Man, and comforted him being sorrowful, by giving him a little Money.

Men: In my opinion, Gratian was not angry altogether without a Cause. If these Shoes and Slippers were preserv'd as an Argument of Moderation in living, I should not dislike it: But I think it a piece of Impudence, to thrust Slippers, and Shoes, and Stockings, upon any one to be kiss'd. If any one shall do it of their own free Choice, from a great Affection to Piety, I think they deserve to be left to their Liberty."

*   *   *

It was open season not only on institutions but also on men. The "theologasters" and their idle science were the target of the critical darts which verged on satire. Henri Estienne, of the celebrated dynasty of printers, who had settled safely in Geneva, attacked them in a vigorous pamphlet written much later, in the midst of the civil war: *Apologie pour Hérodote*. Although subsequent to our period, the work should be cited here, for its violence links it to the "extremist" publications of 1525:

". . . They took up part of their sermons with questions which were no better than the rest: I mean questions some of which were too inquisitive, but also frivolous and useless, and also, for the most part, stupid and ridiculous. . . . And just what were these questions about? About God, about the divinity and the humanity of Jesus Christ, about the angels. Such as . . . whether God could preach if he so wished . . . whether God could do now all he had done in the past . . . whether God could know something he does not know . . . whether God could take the human nature of a female. But these questions are generally reserved to the most enlightened doctors. Whether God could become incarnate in a woman, a devil, a donkey, a pumpkin, or a pebble. And if he had become incarnate in a pumpkin, how would it have preached, done miracles, how would it have been crucified? They also have very curious questions concerning Jesus Christ and the Virgin Mary, which they take from the doctors they call contemplatives (among whom were Landulph and Bonaventura). For example, did Jesus Christ laugh? Olivier Maillard replies, on Landulph's authority, that he often wept but never laughed. And in the same passage where he says this, he adds several curious things concerning the robe Jesus Christ wore, that it was ash-colored, rounded above as below, in the Jewish fashion, and that this robe was sewn by hand, by the Virgin Mary, and that, as Jesus grew, his robe grew also and never wore out. Also that one year before his passion he was in the habit of wearing another little robe under it. Menot, on the other hand, asserts that Jesus Christ had very tender flesh, so tender in fact that, stubbing his heel against a small stone, he felt more pain than anyone else would have felt in the pupil of his eye. And this is the reason: because his body was made from the very pure blood of the blessed Virgin Mary. Also it was necessary to know which was the greatest pain of all those Jesus Christ suffered, and he found that it was when he entered the garden [Gethsemane] at eleven o'clock and sweated water and blood in such quantity that there was a small stream of it. And how was this known? This was not known from the contemplation of the doctors, as the rest had been, but by a revelation made to a devout woman. . . . Nor is this all: it was desired to know how the whips were made with which Jesus Christ was beaten in the house of Pilate. And also how many strokes . . . And the doctors had so successfully studied this that they had found certain information about all this. In the first place, therefore, in each of the whips was attached a certain sharp instrument like a razor. As to the number of strokes, the revelations did not tally. For according to the revelation of certain doctors there were only five thousand strokes all told, but the revelation of some others gave a thousand more: some said he had five thousand on the body and a thousand on his head. . . .

". . . Moreover their curiosity went even further when they went as far as to ask the following questions: if Jesus Christ had not been crucified, if Judas had not betrayed him . . . if the Virgin Mary would have crucified her son if there had not been found anyone else who would have been willing to do it . . . what conversation was there in Paradise when it was discussed and decided that Jesus Christ should take human flesh in a virgin's womb? What argument had there been between those who offered to go and announce our Savior's resurrection to the Virgin Mary? What did the apostles say to the Virgin Mary, being angry that her son had not kept his promise as to sending them the Holy Spirit? And what argument was there (oh! horrid blasphemy) in Paradise between the Father and the Holy Spirit, who refused to descend to earth for fear that he would be treated in the same manner as Jesus Christ? But why do I call these questions? He tells these and like things with as much assurance as though he had found them in the Holy Scriptures."[6]

In life as in the theater, the Brothers were united in adversity to the Theologasters. Very unpopular because of their ignorance and their lewdness, the monks were taken severely to task. Doubtless, it is correct to see here the revolt of the poor peasant robbed by his clerical overlord, and also the traditional hatred of the Gallican bourgeois for the ultramontane cleric, expressing itself in virulent fashion. This becomes obvious in Henri Estienne, for example, when he violently blames the preachers for having recourse to "sundry nonsense and coarseness" to make their audience laugh.

". . . A Franciscan had a mistress (by dispensation from St. Francis) who told him that, apart from his dress, as to all the rest he pleased her well. 'What dress,' he asked, 'do I need in order to please you completely in everything?' 'A soldier's dress,' said she. 'Then don't miss coming to my sermon tomorrow,' he replied. Next day he mounted the pulpit carrying a sword and dressed completely as a soldier. Then during his preaching he began exhorting the princes to make war on the Saracens and the Turks and the other enemies of the Christian religion, and finally came to say that it was a great pity that no one offered themselves to lead such a praiseworthy enterprise. 'If that is all that is needed,' he said, 'here am I, all ready to cast off this robe of St. Francis to serve you either as a simple soldier or as captain.' And, saying this, he took off his robe and remained preaching for half an hour in a captain's uniform. Having been called on by several cardinals who were friends of his, and asked why he had acted in such a novel fashion, he confessed to them that it had been to please his paramour, as has already been explained.

"Another, near Beauvais, who was preaching in a meadow, after having inveighed against the Lutherans, went on to say to his listeners that he feared there might be some among them who had been infected by their wicked doctrine, and he begged all those in the company who did not feel drawn to them, but were good catholics, to take a mouthful of grass in their mouth in honor of our holy mother the church. Which seeing them do, he said, laughing, "Since the hour when God caused me to be born, I have not seen so many beasts at pasture."

* * *

At the same time as the bookseller, the humble peddler engaged in a tireless activity. Hidden in his bale, in the midst of notions, among combs, mirrors, and ribbons, a short tract, concealed under a harmless title borrowed from the works of Catholic piety, spread the most revolutionary statements. It would be read by candlelight in an isolated barn or in a poor room, by someone who had some instruction, to his less learned companions. Thus, thanks to the peddlers, libels, pamphlets, edifying treatises, alphabets for tiny children where prayers for each part of the day could be found, introduced into the lower classes the ferment of a new religion and there made numerous converts. Crespin's martyrology, in the thirty years from 1515 to 1545, counts only three nobles among its many martyrs. The workingmen, together with the intellectuals, made up the greatest number of victims.

* * *

The history of the town of Bourges in the first half of the sixteenth century illustrates in a typical fashion how the new ideas were able to spread in a provincial town. A fief of Marguerite of Angoulême, Duchess of Berry, and the seat of a university, Bourges offered a ground particularly propitious to the new religion. The first time the town met with them was in 1523, when Michel d'Arande, chaplain of Marguerite of Angoulême, came at her orders to preach the advent sermons. The preacher's eloquence, his personal effulgence attracted crowds, and the cathedral was packed. The archbishop, worried, insisted on his departure, although d'Arande only thought to make the Gospel known to the people in their mother tongue. He left, but he had lit a fire which never went out. Six years later, the university was reorganized. Almost all the professors were favorable to the new current of thought. Numbered among them were such scholars as Alciat, Cujas, Amyot, and Melchior Wolmar. The elite among the youth, among whom were John Calvin and Theodore de Bèze, flocked there and received a progressive education. Around 1533 the regular clergy, with the exception of the Franciscans and the Carmelites, seemed won over to the new reform, rendered still more active by the arrival of refugees from Paris after the Placards affair. Passion ran high, and religious matters came to the forefront of the local scene[7]:

"What caused the study of theology to flourish at that time in this university of Bourges was, among other things, the holy courage of a good old professor called Michel Simon, who, having bested in public dispute a certain Franciscan who had the effrontery to declare that man could be saved by his own natural faculties, from then on ruled the school of theology, to such an extent that it was not allowed to bring up there any argument other than the pure text of Holy Writ. These things did not take place without encountering some resistance: Jean Michel preaching at noon (an unwonted happening) in the parish called Fourchaut, and that to the great regret of the beggars, because as everyone ran to hear him preach, their food got cold. They so arranged matters that one day, the priests, incited by them, began at the same hour to sing their vespers of the dead, thinking by this means to prevent the sermon. This so much aroused the listeners who had already gathered, that they began to proffer indignant cries and to upset their books. The priests, seeing this, ran out of the church in great disorder. This incident did not prevent Michel from starting his sermon over again, and saying the Lord's Prayer in French without adding the Ave Maria, when someone called Bomin, the king's procurer general on the Great Council, but besides that the most ignorant person who ever was, began saying the Ave Maria aloud; but he did not finish it. For suddenly he was so closely pressed by the women, all ready to stun him with their little stools, that he had great difficulty in escaping from their hands and could not prevent the sermon going on to the end. But there was a great row at Bourges. When it had died down a bit, the priests and monks had recourse to Mathieu Ory, a fierce inquisitor who found himself very embarrassed: for those in the parish maintained their preacher was a doctor of theology who had been appointed by their vicar, so that he had no alternative but to come and preach himself. But he did not have such a large congregation, nor did he deserve it, for after beginning his preaching in a low voice, affected and feminine, he suddenly began to bellow in a loud voice like a bull, without any knowledge or doctrine, and he only preached one sermon which he called *Quinque verba Pauli*. So that everyone laughed at him, even the most ignorant of religion. . . . Nevertheless the number of those of the religion grew. It happened then that a man in a hermit's habit, carrying a Bible in his wallet, presented himself on coming out of Marlorat's sermon, and, taking up again the themes of the sermon he had just heard, spoke even more openly than Marlorat against the Roman religion. This was such a success that the schoolboys made him preach later before the great law school, on a high stone where generally the public announcements were made to a trumpet's sound, until, the priests wishing to get hold of him, he was spirited away. . . . Yet he preached learnedly and with great zeal the pure truth, and when any money was put at his feet in alms, he distributed it to the other poor people immediately, contenting himself with some bread."

The reform movement reached its height at Bourges in 1536. Several Sundays in a row, between High Mass and Vespers, the celebrated mystery of the Acts of the Apostles was played, whose violence and outrageous attacks could not leave the upholders of tradition indifferent. Then began the first persecutions, the tortures, the exodus to Geneva of the principal bourgeois, followed by the formation of a regular church. Though it survived somehow the first attacks of the civil war, St. Bartholomew was fatal to it, as to the other communities, and it disappeared for a long time in the storm.

In a country as centralized as France, a Reformation of the Church, even were it desired by the episcopate and the faithful, as a whole had no chance of success unless the king set himself at its head. Now Francis I, brother of Marguerite of Angoulême, friend of Louis de Berquin, who had translated Luther and Erasmus, and of the Hellenist Guillaume Budé, made no secret of the sympathy he felt for the new ideas. No one was unaware that the Gospels had been printed in French by his command. By taste, as by function, he was the promoter of intellectual progress. He was the enemy of Charles V, and it was in his interest to favor the Lutheran heresy in the lands of his adversary, where it gave rise to grave disorders. But he was also the head of the French Church; the Concordat he had just signed at Bologna gave him, in ecclesiastical matters, enormous advantages, and permitted him to profit from the current situation. Even had the Most Christian King of France wished to see religion take a new cause, it was not to his interest to will it, and, whatever might be his tastes or his sympathies, the king was guided in his religious policy by reasons of state. These alone explain the sudden shifts which contemporaries interpreted as changes of mood. For Francis I, the Reformation was only one piece on the European chessboard. A bold opportunist, he supported it where it was to his advantage: in Germany and Switzerland. In his own realm, he tolerated and even approved it, so long as it remained the work of moderates and not of the violent. From the day when it became a matter of disorder and excesses, he was to suppress it without mercy—but only to the extent that exterior considerations, such as his treaties with the German Lutherans, allowed.

Despite the king's forbearance, persecution of heterodox religious belief erupted in France in 1523 and continued thereafter for many years. This Repression, as it was called, was instigated and guided largely as an influential, clever, and determined triumvirate comprising three high-ranking clerics: Cardinal de Lorraine, Cardinal Duprat, and Cardinal de Tournon. With the help of the Sorbonne, which for three centuries had been the watchdog of orthodoxy in France, and of the Parliament of Paris, which was responsible for public order in a society founded on the established religion, and with the support of the Mendicant Orders, the three cardinals fought heresy without mercy. "It is," cried Guillaume Budé, "a conspiracy of audacity, ignorance, and fear!" Obviously, it was necessary to stop forthwith the spread of the new ideas; therefore, nothing must be published without the imprimatur of the Sorbonne, and such books as incurred the least suspicion of heterodoxy must be burned immediately. Humanism, that breeding ground of heresy, must be contained, and not only Luther but also his humanistic supporters, such as Erasmus and Lefebvre, must be attacked, and the study of dead languages must be denounced. In 1530, this triumvirate protested vehemently against the appointment of the famous King's Readers; and in 1536 it demanded the suppression of their printing press.

At the instigation of the trinity of cardinals, investigations were begun, lawsuits were multiplied, and the fires of intolerance were lit all over France. Their first victim was Jean Leclerc, a poor carder of Meaux, "who, for having attached a certain writing against some pardons to the cathedral of the place, was very roughly beaten during three days and then finally branded on the forehead with a red-hot iron. His mother, who had also embraced the Gospel, although her husband was very much against it, seeing her son whipped and branded, kept up his courage by crying out loud, saying 'Long live Jesus and his marks.'"

Six years later, the triumvirate took advantage of Francis I's absence to put his literary protégé, Louis de Berquin, to the torture. In 1534, the king himself was forced to attack his erstwhile friends. Their audacity had overstepped all limits. During the night of December 17–18, they had posted, in several towns of the kingdom, and at Paris, at Fontainebleau, and at Amboise, where the court was, and even in the king's own bedchamber, bills denouncing the Mass. The bill had come from the incendiary pen of a Neuchâtel pastor, Antoine de Marcourt.[8]

"TRUE ARTICLES ON THE HORRIBLE, GREAT, AND IMPORTANT ABUSES OF THE PAPAL MASS INVENTED DIRECTLY AGAINST THE HOLY SUPPER OF OUR LORD, SOLE MEDIATOR AND SOLE SAVIOR, JESUS CHRIST

"I invoke heaven and earth as witnesses to the truth, against this proud and pompous Papal Mass, by which the world (if God does not soon bring help) is and will be wholly laid waste, ruined, lost, and spoiled, because in it Our Lord is so outrageously blasphemed, and the people so seduced and blinded, the which should no longer be suffered and endured. But, in order that the case should be the more easily understood by everyone, it is better to proceed article by article.

"First of all, it is and should be very certain, to every faithful Christian that Our Lord and only Savior Jesus Christ, as great Bishop and Pastor ordained eternally by God, has given his body, his soul, his life, and his blood for our sanctification, in a very perfect sacrifice: which sacrifice cannot and should never be repeated by any visible sacrifice, by anyone unless they wish entirely to renounce this, as though it were without efficacy, insufficient, and imperfect, and as though Jesus Christ had not satisfied the justice of God his father for us, and as though he was not the true Christ, Savior, Priest, Bishop and Mediator; the which thing not merely to say but also to think is a horrible and execrable blasphemy.

"Secondly, in this unfortunate Mass, the entire world has not only been provoked to, but also plunged into and entirely submerged in, public idolatry, by it being given out that under the species of bread and wine, Jesus Christ is contained and hidden corporally, really and personally, in flesh and blood, as fat, big, and perfect, as if he were alive at present. This neither the Holy Scriptures nor our faith teaches us, but is entirely contrary to them, for Jesus Christ after his resurrection went up to heaven and is seated at the right hand of God the Father almighty, from thence he shall come to judge the living and the dead. Also St. Paul wrote thus to the Colossians: 'If you are risen with Christ, seek those things that are on high, where Christ is seated at the right hand of God.' He does not say: seek Christ, who is in the Mass, or in the Sacrament, or in the box, or in the closet, but in heaven. By which it follows certainly that if the body is in heaven, it is not at the same time on earth; and if it is on earth, it is not in heaven. For certainly, a real body is only in one place at any one time, taking up a certain room and a certain place by reason of a certain specified size. By which it cannot be that a man of twenty or thirty years old is hidden in a piece of pastry like a favor.

"Thirdly, these blind sacrificers, to pile error upon error, in their frenzy have furthermore said and taught that after having breathed or spoken over this bread, which they take between their fingers, and over the wine, which they put in a chalice, neither bread nor wine remain; but (as they speak with big and grandiose words) by transubstantiation, Jesus Christ is hid and concealed under the accidents of bread and wine, which is a doctrine of devils, against all truth and against all Scripture. And yet I ask these gross cowl wearers: Where did they find this big word transubstantiation? St. Matthew, St. Mark, St. Luke, St. John, St. Paul, and the ancient Fathers did not speak thus, but when they mentioned the Last Supper of Jesus Christ, they openly and simply called the bread and the wine Bread and Wine.

"Fourthly . . . the true visage of the Last Supper is, first, that we truly participate in the sacrifice of the death and passion of Jesus Christ, and that Jesus Christ should be for us spiritual and eternal good, and that we can be assured, as he declares and assures us by this Blessed Sacrament. The other point is publicly to make protestation of faith and to have current remembrance of the death and of the passion of Jesus Christ, by which we are redeemed from damnation and from eternal perdition; it is also to recall the great charity and affection by which he loved us so greatly that he gave his life for us and washed us by his blood. Thus, by all taking bread and a beverage, we are called to charity and to a great union in which we all, with the same mind, must live and die in Christ Jesus. This, needless to say, rejoices the faithful soul, filling it with divine consolation in all humility, growing in faith from day to day, exercising it gently in all goodness and in amiable charity. But the fruit of the Mass is quite other, as experience has shown us. For by it, all knowledge of Jesus Christ is effaced, the preaching of the Gospel is rejected and prevented, time is taken up with bells, shouts, singing, vain ceremonies, lights, incensings, disguisings, and different sorceries by which the poor world (like sheep or lambs) is miserably deceived, taken in, and taken for a ride and by these ravening wolves, eaten, gnawed, and devoured. And who can relate or imagine the larcenies of these robbers? By this Mass they have seized all, destroyed all, swallowed all. They have disinherited princes and kings, lords, merchants, and everyone alive or dead. Finally, Truth pursues them, Truth terrifies them, the Truth by which their reign will be forever destroyed."

The king was outraged at such audacity; he viewed it as a crime of *lèse-majesté* and resolved to punish it by exemplary measures. He ordered his officers to increase the number of arrests and to bring to justice those guilty of heresy, whose burnings would punctuate like roadside altars the expiatory procession in which he would in person take part:

" . . . The king came to Paris the following January, at the beginning of the year 1535, and ordered for the twenty-ninth of the said month a general procession, in which he himself took part in person, with his three children, on foot, bareheaded, with white burning tapers in hand; during this procession, on the principal places of the town, were very cruelly burned alive six persons, with such tremendous cries from the overwrought populace that they were almost snatched from the hands of the executioners and torn to pieces. What is more, the king, having dined in the great hall of the bishop's palace, where was the whole Court of Parliament in red robes, with a great party of the clergy and the high nobility, together with the ambassadors of several foreign nations, protested before them all with extreme anger that if he had one of his own members infected with this doctrine he would tear it out for fear the rest be corrupted. But if his fury was great, the constancy of the martyrs was still greater. Among others worthy of perpetual remembrances were Barthélemy Milon, whose body was crippled; Nicolas Valeton, the Receiver of Nantes in Brittany; Jean du Bourg, a merchant draper of Paris, living in the Rue St. Denis at the sign of the Black Horse; Étienne de la Forge, of Tournai but who had lived long in Paris, a fine rich man, and not less charitable than rich; a schoolmistress named La Catelle; Antoine Poille, a poor mason from near Meaux."[9]

Crespin has faithfully recorded in his *Histoire des martyrs* the story of their conversion and their suffering. The incredible strength of emotion which emanates from this text, however partial, justifies its quotation. Here to begin with is the history of Milon, the paralytic:

"He was the son of a man named Robert Milon, shoemaker of the town of Paris, a young man crippled in his limbs, except for his arms and his tongue. His conversion is worthy of recounting, to magnify God's mercy toward his own, and to teach us to place all our hope in it. This person had received from the Lord gifts and graces, not only as to his body, but above all, as to his mind. He abused them during his first youth by all sorts of intemperance and dissipation. Health and his body's ability whetted his appetite to go after the things of this world and to commit abominable acts of the flesh: his spirit was also given not only to vanity but also to raillery and to despising the things of God. It happened one day that while engaged in his frolics, he broke several ribs and bruised himself and . . . his body became humpbacked and all misshaped before and behind; the lower parts . . . failed him; in short, the Lord, in order to reform the lost creature, caused a transformation of his body, and from useful made it totally useless . . . leaving him only the use of his arms and his tongue . . . Being in this misery, and aware only of the pain which pressed upon him and the deformity of his body, God gave him an opening to the knowledge of his truth, by means of a believer whom he had mocked when he was passing his father's store. This believer, drawing near to Milon, said: 'Poor man, why do you mock at passers-by? Do you not see that God has bent your body in this fashion in order to straighten your soul?' Milon was astonished at this remark and began to pay attention to this man, who at that moment presented him with a New Testament and said: 'See this book: you can tell me what you think of it.' Milon, after having begun to taste the fruit of reading the New Testament, continued reading it night and day without ceasing and taught his father, family, and those who came to him.

"Such a great and sudden change in this person made many marvel. Those who before had visited him in order to hear songs of music and instruments, which he played with singular grace, were delighted to hear this man speak quite another language from that he had spoken before. For about six years before he suffered death, he was forced to remain in his bed and could not move from it unless four persons lifted him. Being thus bedridden, he taught some young people the art of writing, in which he was without an equal, he engraved on knives, daggers, and swords, and made things for jewelers, and with whatever he gained from this, he fed several poor and needy people who had knowledge of the Gospel. He did not cease instructing and admonishing those who came to see him on account of these exquisite and rare things he made; in short, his room was a real school of piety in which morning and night the glory of God resounded. Therefore during this fury of persecution, he did not escape from being one of the first to be apprehended. . . .

"Morin, foaming with rage, and as though beside himself, thinking only of exercising his cruelty, came into the room where this poor paralytic was lying and said to him, 'You, there, get up.' The paralytic, who was not frightened by the hideous face of this tyrant, said, as if laughing at himself: 'Alas, sir, it would need a greater master than you to make me rise.' He was immediately lifted and carried off by the sergeants, after Morin, in his accustomed manner, had taken the most secret furnishing which he found in the room.

"It would be impossible to tell all the great good and consolation which this person brought to the other prisoners, for he was not more frightened in prison or before the judges than he had been in his bed, even when suffering the roughest treatment. He was condemned to be burned alive by slow fire on the place of the Strand, on the way to which he passed in front of his father's house. The enemies of truth were astonished at the confidence manifested by this admirable servant and witness of the Son of God both in his life and in his death."[10]

Not less moving was the fate of Nicolas Valeton:

". . . Nicolas Valeton, Receiver of Nantes in Brittany, beginning to come to the knowledge of the Gospel by means of good people whom he frequented, and by reading the New Testament in French, seeing the great searches that were being made, and that Morin (with whom he had had a difference) was approaching his house, ordered his wife to move from his room the chest where his books were, and after doing this he went to face the danger. She, terrified on her side, quickly threw the said books into the privies, with other papers that were there, so that the chest was empty. Morin, having come in, sent Valeton to prison and ordered him to be strictly guarded; then, having hunted everywhere and having found nothing, he saw the empty chest. However, he did not tarry at the time, being so anxious to interrogate his prisoner: the which done, and having discovered no charge or information against him, he thought he must proceed more cunningly, for otherwise the receiver would be a man to bear him ill will and give him trouble, for he was a man of mettle and good credit. Having questioned him again about the chest, without avail, he suddenly went to his wife, to whom he put so many questions, so craftily and subtly (in addition he assured her that her husband had confessed that the coffer was the one where he put his books and secret papers), that this ill-advised young woman, trusting the promise and oath of the aforesaid Morin, that her husband would have no trouble (because of money offered and promised by her), she revealed the truth to him. The books were promptly recovered from their hiding-place, and though they were not forbidden, Morin made them seem so bad to the king that he commanded that Valeton be put to death, the more so because having thus ordered his books thrown away, he was suspected of heresy, to which the Court of Parliament willingly agreed. And this person was taken to the Cross of Trahoir, and there burned alive with wood taken in his house. He showed great confidence and strength; which was found admirable by good people, the more so that he had as yet had very little instruction."[11]

The other prisoners suffered deaths just as cruel. Jean du Bourg was burned alive in the Halles, having had his hands cut off in front of the Fountain of the Holy Innocents. Antoine Poille mounted the stake "his tongue pierced and attached by an iron to his cheek which was opened in cruel and horrible spectacle to prevent him from speaking to the people." Etienne de la Forge suffered death by burning in the cemetery St. Jean, and La Catelle was burned in the Rue de la Huchette.

The strong emotions aroused by such a terrible repression had unexpected consequences, in which some doubtless saw the hand of God. To these martyrs, whom, as A. Buisson has said, "their conscience forbade to associate themselves any longer with forms which deprave religion, with practices which materialize it," was given the leader without whom their cause would have been lost in a Europe which, a prey to confusion and equivocation, had become a vast slaughterhouse. As a result of these tortures, John Calvin, of Noyon, in Picardy, who was then a refugee in Strasbourg, felt he could no longer keep silent. He dedicated to the man responsible, to King Francis I, a book where he set forth with precision and clarity the doctrine so long awaited, the famous *Christian Institute*.

"The demoniac," "the impostor of Geneva," "the Anti-Christ," a fisher of souls, a leader of men, the elect of God—so did Calvin appear to his contemporaries, according to their religious convictions. In the light of history, however, Calvin no longer appears in such an equivocal light; he was, above all, a man who came upon the scene at a propitious hour in behalf of a cause which would have been lost without him.

Calvin the man vanishes in his work. And he would have wished it so, for he regarded himself merely as a humble instrument of God. He effaced himself completely, so that not even his grave remains; his body returned to earth in complete anonymity. He is generally portrayed—as in the somber portrait of the Tronchin collection—dressed in black, his face wan, the profile sharp, with a piercing glance darting from under heavy eyelids, the hands argumentative and authoritative. It is an exaggerated image, no doubt; but there are others, more human and more pleasing. His life is known by the partisan accounts both of his detractors and of his disciples—but it is more prudent to rely upon his autobiography. The latter is such a spare work, however, that some preliminary facts are necessary if one is to arrive at a speaking likeness of the Father of the French Reformation.

John Calvin was born in 1509, to a family of tradespeople at Noyon, in the heart of that Vermandois country where the local bishop still ruled as unquestioned lord among those Picardy folk whose name in the Middle Ages had become synonymous with evil thinking. His grandfather was a retired sailor, his uncles were locksmiths; and all were rather harsh personalities, accustomed to fighting, and never yielding when they thought themselves in the right. The entire family seemed, as L. Lefebvre has put it, "to economize, to accumulate means, to gather in some way, penny by penny, a great human capital which they invested whole and entire in one member of the family."

So long as Calvin's mother lived, his childhood was a happy one. She initiated him into the pious practices so highly regarded at that time, and into the popular devotions which he says he enjoyed: the cult of the saints and of the Virgin. He walked in processions in honor of the Mother of God, wove garlands for her, piously lit long tapers of white wax and went to pray to her, a boy of five holding tightly to his mother's hand, in the gloom of nearby chapels. Upon his mother's premature death, Calvin's father, whom he does not seem to have loved, remarried.

The father was a violent, authoritative man, who was to die under excommunication for some financial dealing in which he, the local notary public, had set himself up against the bishop. He had great ambitions for his sons, and above all for John, whose precocious intelligence he sensed. From his earliest years, therefore, John was destined for the priesthood, a calling which Calvin *père* regarded as the only sure way to rise in the social scale. At the age of twelve, John was provided with an ecclesiastical benefice which paid for his studies; at fourteen, he was sent to the schools to acquire that knowledge of theology and law which was the key to the career of which his father dreamed. The young boy spent three years at the Collège Montaigu. There he acquired a solid knowledge of Aristotle and of dialectic—i.e., of the art of reasoning. From Paris, he went to Orléans and to Bourges, where he studied the law and was initiated into literary humanism.

The death of the elder Calvin in 1531 left John free to choose a career consonant with his own tastes. He opted for letters. Already he was burning to make a name for himself. With this in view, he settled in Paris and began to frequent the circles where the new ideas were in ferment, particularly the courses of the first Royal Readers. Then he moved into the circle of the Bishop of Meaux and of Marguerite of Navarre, and soon joined that great intellectual and religious current of reform dominated by Erasmus and Lefebvre d'Etaples. He was soon to compromise himself.

One of his friends, Nicolas Cop, the newly appointed Rector of the University of Paris, pronounced on the day of his inauguration a revolutionary oration. The doctrines of faith and works set out in it smelled strongly of heresy, and there was a great scandal. Rightly or wrongly, Calvin was suspected of having had a hand in the affair, and he and Cop judged it prudent to disappear for a time. Calvin took refuge in Saintonge, with a friend, Canon du Tillet. Doubtless it was there, in the silence of this retreat, that he was converted. Under what influences, following what road, did he come to reject medieval Christianity and to consider as invalid fifteen hundred years of religious practices? Here we touch the great mystery of Calvin's life. No text alludes to the reasons.

From that moment, Calvin abandoned his peaceful sanctuary to become the apostle of the new faith. He resigned his ecclesiastical benefices and went from town to town preaching the Good News to small groups of sympathizers. But it was obvious to him that, unless he wished to be a martyr, he would soon have to leave France.

Before entering upon the new phase of Calvin's life, here is his own description of the part preceding:

"While I was yet a young boy my father intended me for theology. But soon after when he saw that the study of law generally enriched those who pursued it, he was led to change his mind by this hope.

So it happened that I was withdrawn from the study of philosophy and set to learn law, but however much I forced myself to obey my father faithfully, God by his secret Providence finally turned me another way. And firstly, while I was not too firmly addicted to the papist superstitions easily to be drawn out from such deep mire, he subdued me by a sudden conversion and rendered my heart (which, considering my age, was already too rigid about such things) docile. Having thus received some taste and knowledge of true piety, I was suddenly so inflamed with so great a desire to profit from it that, though I did not drop other studies, I no longer had any real feeling for them. I was quite astonished that within a year all who had some desire for the pure doctrine began to come to me to learn it, although I was but a beginner myself. For my part, having always been of a shy and embarrassed nature, I had always loved retirement and tranquillity, now I began to seek some hiding place and means of withdrawing from company. But so little did I get my wish that on the contrary all retreats and hiding places became like public schools. In short, although I always had this wish to live privately without being known, God so moved me and turned me about by different changes that he never left me in peace in whatever place I might be. In spite of my nature, he brought me into the light and made me come forward, as they say."[12]

* * *

Calvin went abroad the better to continue the work he had begun. To preach, yes, but above all to formulate his doctrine; so he sought a shelter where he could devote himself to study. Strasbourg, a town of the empire, seemed to him the proper place. He went there by way of Geneva, which he found in the throes of a revolution. There Farel, the dauphine reformer, asked him for help:

". . . Master William Farel kept me in Geneva, not so much by persuasion and exhortation as by a terrifying imprecation as if God had stretched out his hand from on high to stay me. Because the nearest way to Strasbourg, where I then wished to retire, was closed to me by the wars, I had decided to pass by here briefly without stopping more than one night in the town. Now, a short while earlier, the Papacy had been driven out by means of that good person whom I have just named, and by Master Peter Viret. But things were not yet settled down, and there were divisions, and dangerous and bad factions, among the townspeople. At this point a person, who now has nastily revolted and has returned to the papists, discovered my whereabouts and made it known to others. Upon this Farel (as he was burning with a marvelous zeal to advance the Gospel) made every possible effort to keep me. And after having learned that there were certain special studies to which I wished to reserve myself, when he saw he was getting nowhere by begging, he finally delivered an imprecation, that it would please God to damn my peace and the tranquillity of the studies that I was seeking, in the event that in such a great need I insisted on retiring and refused to give him help and comfort. Which so scared and shook me that I desisted from the voyage I had undertaken."[13]

The two men were chased out of Geneva after eighteen months. At the request of Martin Bucer, Calvin settled at Strasbourg, where he directed the French church there and taught theology. They were happy years, in which he completed his own formation, organized his religious system, and married. But Geneva recalled him:

"Later, when the Lord had pity on this town, and quieted the pernicious trouble and emotion that were prevalent, and by his admirable strength dissipated the many unfortunate counsels as well as the sanguinary efforts of the disturbers of the republic, against my desire and affection the necessity was imposed upon me to return to my first charge. For however much the salvation of this church was as much recommended to me as that one, I would have had no difficulty in abandoning my life had not my timidity given me many reasons for excusing myself from taking upon my shoulders so onerous a burden. But finally the consideration of my duty, which I regarded with reverence and in conscience, won me over and made me condescend to return to the flock from which I had been, as it were, torn; the which I did with sorrow, tears, great anxiety, and distress, as the Lord is my very good witness and as are also several good people who would gladly have seen me out of this pain, had it not been for the fact that what I feared and what had made me consent held them back also and silenced them."[14]

For twenty-three years, from 1541 to his last breath, Calvin reigned over Geneva as a despotic and undisputed master. It was never a love match, and on his deathbed he still dubbed the city a "perverse and wicked nation." At his last farewell to his pastoral colleagues, delivered when he felt his hour was near, one of them took down his last words: "My brothers . . . It would be good to begin with the prayer that God would give me the grace to say everything without ambition, but always with regard to his glory, and also that each person may remember and profit from what will be said. . . .

". . . I have many infirmities, which you have been obliged to endure, and even everything that I have done is worth nothing. The wicked will rejoice in that saying. But I repeat that everything I have done is worth nothing and that I am a miserable creature. But if I can say this, that I have always wished [to say] that my vices have always displeased me and that the root of the fear of God has been in my heart, you can say this too, that my affection has been good and I beg of you that the evil be pardoned me. But if there is any good, I beg that you will conform yourselves to it and follow it.

"As for my doctrine, I have taught faithfully and God gave me the grace to write, the which I have done as faithfully as I knew how. And I have not corrupted a single passage in Holy Scripture nor deformed it, to my knowledge, and although I might have brought to it subtle interpretations, had I given myself to the study of subtlety, I trod all that underfoot and always studied simplicity.

"I have not written anything out of hatred for anyone, but always propounded faithfully that which I thought was to the glory of God. . . . I had forgotten this point: also I pray you change nothing nor innovate (often novelty is asked for), not because I desire for myself out of ambition that what is mine should remain and that it should be kept without trying to improve it. But all changes are dangerous and sometimes do harm."[15]

*   *   *

Calvin did not forge his doctrine all at once. A disciple of Luther, he also borrowed from Zwingli, the Swiss reformer, and from his friend the former Dominican monk, Martin Bucer, who had converted Strasbourg to the new faith.

His unique merit is to have made a synthesis, to have known how to eliminate, clarify, choose, so as to retain only the essentials. He was an inspired architect of the intellect, and formulated a clear, precise, and logical theology, well adapted to the spiritual needs of the French. His accomplishment, responding as it did to so many confused aspirations, to those contradictory tendencies to which the French Reform was a prey, grouped around it those souls in search of a shepherd.

Calvin's doctrine is to be found complete in the *Christian Institute*. He has recounted the circumstances which incited him to write in Latin, then in French, in order that what he wrote should be accessible to all:

". . . But it so happened, while I was staying in Basel, being as it were hidden there and known to few people, that several faithful and holy persons were burned in France, and the news of this having been bruited abroad, these burnings were judged to be very bad by a large part of the Germans, so much so that they conceived a dislike for the perpetrators of such tyranny. To counteract this, certain unfortunate little books full of lies were circulated, relating that Anabaptists and other seditious folk were the only ones to be so cruelly treated. For these by their visions and false ideas upset not only religion but also all political order. Then seeing that these court flunkeys by their disguises tried to make it so that the disgrace of this shedding of innocent blood be buried by false blame and calumnies with which they accused the holy martyrs after their death, but also that by this means they could proceed to the extremity of killing poor faithful people without anyone having compassion for them, it seemed to me that, unless I opposed this procedure virtuously with all that was in me, I could not excuse myself from being found cowardly and disloyal. And this was the reason that drove me to publish my *Institution de la religion chrétienne*. Firstly, in order to reply to these wicked accusations which the others were spreading and to clear my brothers, whose death was precious in the sight of the Lord; then after, in so far as the same cruelties would soon after be perpetrated against many poor people, to ensure that foreign countries would at least be touched with some compassion and solicitude for them."[16]

One of Calvin's essential themes, the very center of his theology, is the necessity for a return to the Bible, the book in which God speaks, the only authority of Protestant Christians. In many of his writings, he proclaims the light of the Gospel:

"Finally, all elements and all creatures gave glory to Jesus Christ. At his command the winds fell, the angry sea was quieted, the fish brought the drachma in its belly, the stones (to give witness to him) were broken, the veil of the temple was rent in twain, the sun was darkened, the tombs opened, and several dead arose. And there was nothing in the sky or on the earth that did not testify that Jesus Christ was their God, Lord, and Master and the Father's great Ambassador sent here below for the salvation of mankind.

"All these things were announced, shown, written, and signed for us in this Testament by which Jesus Christ makes us the inheritors of the kingdom of God his Father and declare his will (like a testator to his heirs) that is to be executed. Now we are all called to this inheritance without distinction of persons, male or female, little and great, servant or lord, master or disciple, cleric or lay, Hebrew or Greek, French or Latin, no one is rejected, everyone who with certain faith will receive what is sent him will embrace what is presented to him, in short, who will recognize Jesus Christ for what he is given by the Father.

"And yet, we all who bear the name of Christians, will we allow this Testament, which so justly belongs to us, be ravished from us, hidden and corrupted? This Testament, without which we cannot pretend to have any right to the kingdom of God, without which we ignore the great benefits and promises which Jesus Christ has made us, the glory and beatitude which he has prepared for us. Without the Gospel we do not know what God has commanded or forbidden, we cannot distinguish good from evil, light from darkness, the commandments of God from the laws of man. Without the Gospel, we are useless and vain, without the Gospel we are not Christians, without the Gospel all riches are poverty, wisdom folly before God, force is feebleness, all human justice is damned by God. But by the knowledge of the Gospel we are made children of God, brothers of Jesus Christ, co-burghers with the saints, citizens of the kingdom of heaven, inheritors of God with Jesus Christ by whom the poor are made rich, the weak strong, fools wise, sinners are justified, the desolate are consoled, doubters convinced, slaves freed. The Gospel is word of life and truth. It is the power of God for the salvation of all believers (Romans, 1, 16) and the key to the knowledge of God which opens the door of the kingdom of God to the faithful, loosing them from their sins, and shuts it on the unbelievers, binding them in their sins. Blessed are they who hear and keep it, for in this wise they show that they are children of God. Unhappy they who will neither hear nor follow it, for they are children of the devil."[17]

The popular devotion dear to the latter part of the fifteenth century had brought heaven down to earth and fashioned a God to the measure of man. With Calvin, the idea of the infinite reappears. The God of whom he speaks is the Creator of Genesis, a God strong and jealous, infinitely good, infinitely just, infinitely strong, of whose kingdom there shall be no end.

"The whole sum of our wisdom, which merits to be called true and certain wisdom, is, as it were, divided into two parts, that is, the knowledge of God and of ourselves. Of which the first must show not only that He is the one sole God, whom all must adore and honor, but also that He is the fount of all truth, wisdom, goodness, justice, mercy, power and holiness, in order that we may learn to wait upon Him and ask for all these things. Morever, that we may recognize them with praise and thanks as proceeding from Him. The second, by showing us our imbecility, misery, vanity, and villainy, brings us to dejection, to mistrust and hatred of ourselves, and after enflames in us a desire to seek God the more since in Him resides all our good, of which we find ourselves bereft and denuded.

". . . for if we look by the light of day upon earth or if we contemplate the things that are around us, it seems to us that indeed we have a very firm and clear view. But when we come to raise our eyes straight to the sun, the strength, that showed itself upon earth, is confused and dazzled by so great a light; so much so that we are obliged to admit that the good view we have with which to see terrene things is very feeble and weak to look upon the sun. And so it is also with our spiritual faculties. For as long as our contemplation does not go beyond the earth, being very well content with our own justice, wisdom, and strength, we flatter ourselves and applaud and are not far from thinking ourselves demigods. But if once we turn our mind to the Lord and recognize the perfection of His justice, wisdom and virtue, by which measure we must judge ourselves, that which before pleased us under the guise of justice appears to be soiled with very great iniquity; that which marvelously deceived us under the cloak of wisdom will be seen as extreme folly; that which had an appearance of strength will manifest itself as miserable weakness; this is how that which seemed to be perfect in us responds to the purity which is in God. From this comes the horror and astonishment which Scripture often tells struck the faithful, every time when they felt the presence of God. . . . For we see how Abraham recognized himself to be earth and dusk the nearer he approached the contemplation of the Lord's glory; how Elias could not wait upon His presence with unveiled face, so fearful was he to look upon Him. And what would man do who is but rottenness and vermin when even the cherubim veil their faces in great fear and reverence? And that is what Isaiah says, that 'then the moon shall be confounded and the sun ashamed when the Lord of hosts shall reign.' "[18]

How can man, in his original misery, be capable by his own unaided force, by his own works, of achieving his salvation? It is clear that faith in Jesus Christ alone can save him:

". . . St. Paul invokes the Psalm's testimony that we are blessed in as much as God does not impute our iniquities to us, but covers and buries them and casts them behind his back in that he does not want to call attention to them. In short, we have three things to note in order to have a certain awareness of our situation. The first is that all our nature is damned and that there is nothing in us but total depravity. And why? Because there is in us only sin and corruption. It is therefore right that God should hate us, that we are so detestable to Him that we cannot come into His sight unless it be to be condemned to eternal death. So much for the first point. The second is, that in spite of all the miseries that are in us, all our felicity abides in the gratuitous mercy of God, in as much as He accepts us and receives us as His children, not imputing our faults to us, but giving us the blood of Our Lord Jesus Christ to wash us in order that we may be as though pure and clean in spite of all the stains and pollutions with which we are soiled. So much for the second point: it is that God draws us from this abyss of misery in which we are plunged by our nature, and that we are blessed in the measure to which he is favorable and propitious to us. Moreover there is a third point, which is that by faith we enjoy this felicity and that we enter into possession of this so precious good. For to the same degree that God offers it by His word and His promises, so must we accept it by faith."[19] From then on the love of God "which passes all understanding" guides and leads man:

". . . If God's providence shines in the heart of the believer, not only will he be delivered from fear and from the distress which formerly weighed upon him, but he will also be relieved of all doubt. For just as we rightly feared our destiny, so also we have good cause to dare confide ourselves trustfully to God. Thus it is a marvelous relief to us to hear that the Lord so completely governs all things by His power, rules all things by His will and moderates all by His patience that nothing can occur save as He has destined. The more so since He has received us into His keeping and has committed us to His angel's charge there is neither water, nor fire, nor sword nor anything that can harm us, except in so far as His good pleasure allows. For so it was said in the Psalm: "Surely He shall deliver thee from the snare of the fowler, and from the noisome pestilence. He shall cover thee with His feathers, and under His wings shalt thou trust: His truth shall be thy shield and buckler. Thou shalt not be afraid for the terror by night nor for the arrow that flieth by day; nor for the pestilence that walketh in darkness, nor for the destruction that wasteth at noonday."[20]

The sinner is reconciled with God. His faith gives meaning to his existence, legitimizes the morality it imposes, removes the fear of death, calls his soul to life, and promises him, in a hereafter it guarantees, eternal felicity. Let the Christian give to the Lord the worship that he owes Him; let him, at the different hours of the day, in order to assume according to his will the humble and difficult duties of daily life, draw his strength from prayer. Thus, this evening prayer:

"Lord God, since Thou has destined night for man's rest as thou has created the day for his work, I ask Thee to grant my body a night of repose and to make my soul rise towards Thee and that my heart to be always filled with Thy love. Teach me, O God, to confide my anxieties to Thee and to remember always Thy mercy, so that my soul, too, can enjoy spiritual repose. Make my slumber not to be excessive, but let it serve to repair my strength, so that I may be the better disposed to serve Thee. May it please Thee also to keep me pure in my body and in my soul, preserving me from all temptations and from all danger so that even my sleep may serve to the glory of Thy name. And since this day has not ended without my having offended Thee in several ways, I who am a poor sinner, may it please Thee, O God, just as now Thou hidest all things in the darkness of the night, so also to bury all my sins, according to Thy mercy, by Jesus Christ my Savior. Amen."[21]

* * *

Catholicism was rejected. The break was complete, and a new church was born. Calvin gave it its doctrine in the *Christian Institute*. At Geneva, he organized, on the model of the primitive Church, a universal church which had Christ for its head and, for ministers, the pastors, who were guardians of the doctrine, they were all equal, a federation—no longer, like the other, a hierarchy. Heir to the true tradition, that of Jesus and his Apostles, the church of Calvin stemmed directly from Christian antiquity and rejected all subsequent alterations; it regarded itself not as heretical, but as uncorrupted and pure. It was the papists who, with their human inventions, had deformed the divine message: "the true church is the one which teaches only the word of God," Calvin said; "the Roman Church has altered this word." And between the ancient and the new Church no transaction was possible. "I am come not to bring peace but the sword."

* * *

Calvin trained martyrs, for, though primarily a theologian and a dogmatist, he was also a leader of men. During the long years in which he imposed on Geneva his inflexible rule, by his inspired intelligence, his tireless activity, the force of his word, and the brilliance of his writings, he forged a race of martyrs ready to die for the honor of their master, the King of Kings.

"The supreme consolation is when we suffer persecution for justice, for we then should remember what an honor the Savior does us in giving us the badges of His soldiery. I call persecution for justice not only what we suffer to defend the Gospel, but also to maintain any just cause. Either to defend God's truth against Satan's lie or to uphold the innocent against the wicked and to prevent their being done harm and injury, we must suffer the hate and the indignation of the world in which we are in danger for our honor, or our fortunes, or our lives, which it cannot harm us to employ for God even to this point. And we should not consider ourselves unfortunate when from His own mouth He calls us blessed. It is quite true that poverty, if taken at its own evaluation, is misery. Equally, exile, despisal, ignominy, prison: finally, death is an extreme calamity. But where God breathes by His favor, there is not one of these things which will not turn for us into happiness and felicity. Let us content ourselves rather with Christ's testimony than with the false opinion of our flesh. From which it will turn out that following the apostle's example we will rejoice every time He finds us worthy to endure contumely in His name. For if, being innocent and of a good conscience, we are stripped of our goods by the malevolence of the wicked, we are made very poor in the sight of men but by this means our true riches increase with God. If we are chased and banished from our country we are the more welcomed into the Lord's family. If we are vexed and molested, we are the more confirmed in our Lord. If we receive opprobrium or ignominy we are the more exalted in the kingdom of God. If we die, the way is opened for us into the blessed life. . . .

"Since Scripture comforts us thus in any ignominy or calamity that we have to endure for the defense of justice, we are too ungrateful unless we bear them patiently and with a gay heart. Especially as this kind of cross is above all other proper to believers and by it Christ wishes to be glorified in them, as St. Peter says."[22]

The palm of the martyr was the supreme glory. "When it is a question of glorifying God, no neutrality can be permitted," wrote Calvin to Madame de Crussol. To defend this honor, to do what God willed the master at Geneva conscripted many knights whose energies he knew how to mobilize. Such were five young men who were burned at Lyons. They were called Martial Alba, from Montauban in Quercy; Pierre Ecrivain, from Boulogne in Gascony; Bernard Seguin, from La Reole in Bazadais; Charles Favre, from Blanzac in Angoumois; Pierre Navihères, of Limoges. They met in Switzerland, where they were making their theological studies and there they decided to return to their country to preach the pure doctrine of the Gospel. As they were going toward Lyons, they traveled for some time with an inhabitant of that city, who asked them to visit him, which they did:

". . . At about two or three o'clock, we all went together to the lodging of this person near Enay, where, after having walked awhile in the garden, we were invited to lunch with him. Having invoked the name of God, as one should, before sitting down to table, we began to use the meats God had given us. While we were seated, and were rejoicing in Godly fashion, suddenly Provost Poulet arrived, his lieutenant, and a great number of sergeants with them. These came into the room where we were. Their president all at once, without a word more, asked each one of us our name, surname, country, profession and other like things that are usually asked. Having done this, and having searched us, we were bound, two by two, and, without our having borne witness or done anything against the king's ordinances; and without showing us any authorization, we were, against all right and justice, taken to the prisons."[23]

They were incarcerated for thirteen long days, not all together but each one in a separate cell "a dark and gloomy hole" from which they only emerged to undergo the interrogations of the ecclesiastical tribunal.

Here are a few fragments of the judicial confession of Pierre Ecrivain, "a man of lively spirit," says Crespin, "to whom the Lord gave a magnificent tongue:"

". . . The *officials* asked me: 'What is your name?' I replied: 'Pierre Ecrivain.'
Question: 'What is your profession?'
Answer: 'I am a student.'
Q: 'From whence come you?'
A: 'From the country of the princes of Berne.'
Q: 'From which town?'
A: 'From the town of Lausanne.'
Q: 'What did you there?'
A: 'I studied the word of God.'
Q: 'What doctrine do they hold at Lausanne?'
A: 'The Word of God.'
Q: 'How do you know that they hold the word of God?'
A: 'As long as I studied there, I attended the sermons, assemblies, and congregations which take place daily and I heard that they preach nothing other than the pure doctrine of God, and I believe it also, for the Holy Spirit assures me of it.'
Then the *official* said: 'Do you then wish to hold and live by their law?'
A: 'Yes, sir, in as much as it is the word of God.' "[24]

The tribunal then inquired as to his opinions on the Last Supper, purgatory, confession, and ceremonies. To all these questions, Ecrivain replied with courage according to his conscience:

"*Q:* 'What say you of the ceremonies of the Church, such as the ringing of bells and other things observed there?'
A: 'As we are surrounded by this flesh, we cannot hear or understand the things of God, as they are, but we have need of help because of our infirmity, also, in the church of the Lord, there must necessarily be ceremonies. . . . I approve those which were instituted by Jesus Christ and observed by the Apostles. As for those of the church of the pope, I reject them absolutely, for they are contrary to the word of God, and turn the poor world away from the true service that we owe Him.'
Q: 'Do you believe that it is necessary to pray to the Virgin Mary, and the saints of Paradise, and that they are our advocates?'
A: 'I believe that there is only one advocate who intercedes and prays for us before God the Father, which is Jesus Christ, in whose name we have the promise that our prayers and petitions will be granted

...erre de Ronsard. Bust at the Priory of Saint-Cosme, ...ar Tours. Photograph by H. Paillasson

John Calvin in his study. Anonymous portrait of the sixteenth century. Bibliothèque du Protestantisme. Photograph by H. Adant

...fèvre d'Etaples. Sixteenth-century woodcut. ...liothèque du Protestantisme, Paris. Photograph ... H. Adant

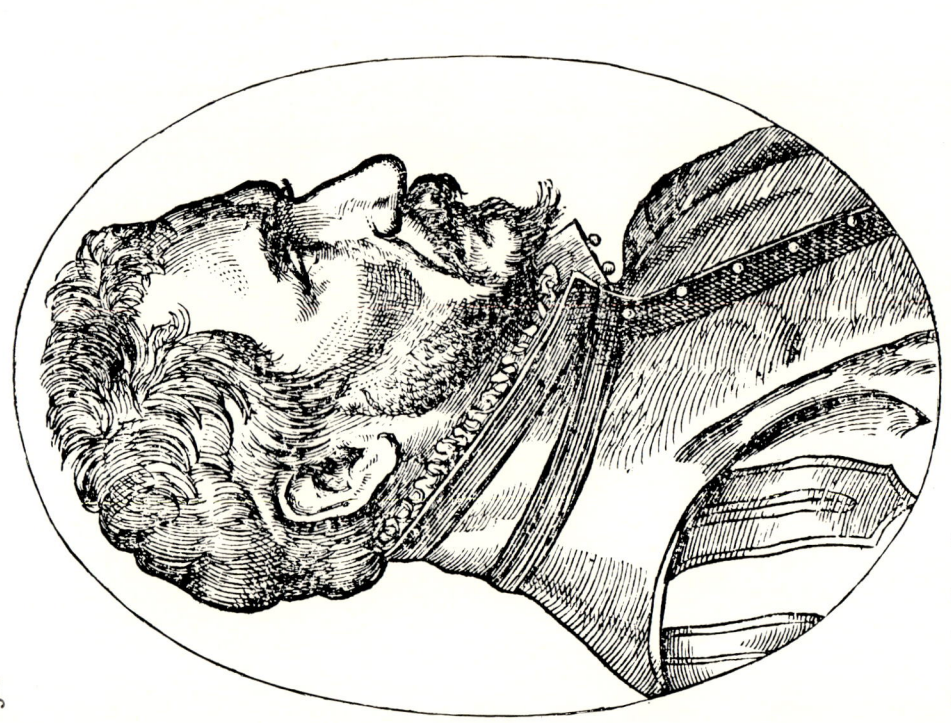

Sixteenth century physician visiting a patient. From a contemporary miniature. Bibliothèque Nationale, Paris

Ambroise Paré, Surgeon to the King, at age 45. Frontispiece to his *Méthode Curative des Plaies et Fractures de la Tête Humaine*, Paris, 1561. Cabinet des Estampes, Bibliothèque Nationale,

An open-air preacher. From a sixteenth-century tapestry of the life of St. Julian. Cathedral of Le Mans. Photograph by B. Arthaud

31.

A sixteenth-century Bible (actual size), called a "chignon Bible" because it was small enough to hide in a chignon. Bibliothèque du Protestantisme, Paris. Photograph by H. Adant

32. Francis I in a procession to atone for the mutilation of a statue of the Virgin. Musée Condé, Chantilly. Photograph by H. Adant

by God our Father. I believe he is our only mediator between God and ourselves. As for the Virgin, I believe she is the happiest among all women, because she believed, and bore Jesus Christ in her womb, being virgin before and after giving birth. And I believe that we should imitate her in her faith, invoking and adoring only one God as she did, as she showed us in her canticle. I also believe that the saints are blessed, that we must imitate them and give God praise in them, because he gave them so many graces, but we must not invoke them, or adore them, because they themselves do not wish it, but on the contrary forbid it.' "[25]

Next day the interrogation went on in the presence of monks. A Jacobite spoke and asked several questions regarding the pope, and on free will:

" . . . 'You say, in your confession, that man has no free will. I will prove you the contrary. It is written in the Gospel, that a man came down from Jerusalem to Jericho, who fell among thieves, and was by them stripped and wounded, but not killed, and left half dead. Now, St. Thomas Aquinas interprets that man as being our free will, saying he had been badly wounded, but not entirely killed. *Ergo,* we still have free will!'
A: 'Firstly, I deny this interpretation.'
Q: 'Are you wiser than St. Thomas?'
A: 'I do not say that I am wiser than he, but I deny that this parable need be so explained; Jesus Christ wishes by it to explain the charity we should have for our neighbor. As for free will, we do not have it at all, for we are entirely dead and not partly so, as St. Paul says. And if we do good, it is God who does it in us by His Holy Spirit. St. Paul also says, that to do good works, it is necessary for God to give us will and perfection: if God gives it, we have therefore not got it.' "[26]

Similar sessions took place the following days. On the fourteenth day, the young men were informed that they were condemned as heretics and schismatics. They appealed. Then began for them a long calvary which they passed in prayers, petitions, pious conversations and correspondence, by which they prepared themselves for death:
"O how that old serpent Satan made great assaults upon us, and with great rage threw burning arrows against us when he showed us the present liberty of our bodies, the goods, riches and honors of the world, the anguish and sorrow our poor parents have for us, and the great joy and happiness they would have from our deliverance. . . . Alas, we are now rejected by the whole earth and esteemed as its dirt and dung.

We see only confusion, cruel torments, and the horrible face of death; we die every day and at all hours for our Lord Jesus Christ and for the hope we have in Him; at the same time we do not lose courage in any way and we are not troubled . . . and we rejoice with an indescribable joy, awaiting with great longing and restful conscience that blessed day when our Savior will appear to gather us into His celestial kingdom, where we shall reign eternally with Him. Have we not much reason to make us rejoice and to glorify us? . . . since our God gives us the great good and honor to receive us into the number of martyrs, we who are nothing but poor earthworms, and to withdraw us from this valley of miseries and misfortunes to take us to His celestial kingdom."[27]

Of the five, perhaps Pierre Navihères endured the most subtle torments. He had to face, from his family, very dear to him but very lacking in understanding, burning reproaches, imperious objurations, and cruel silences, which added to the sufferings of his detention and touched him in the deepest parts of himself. His uncle, Martial Navihères, was the first to take him sharply to task for his ridiculous behavior:

"Pierre, I had not heard and had not expected, in view of what your education had cost me, both at Paris and in that university, that by your lighthearted rashness you would be immediately led astray from sound doctrine, flying toward another which I don't know where you learned. I know well that many who erred with the same obstinacy have been punished by fire, which would have happened to you, if the goodness of God, and of your judge, had not given you the possibility of going back on your crazy ideas. The which I order you to do after reading this letter, without further delay. Do not give more sorrow to your father and mother, nor lack further in the obedience you owe them. By the letters you have written lately, I know that your presumption persuades you to undertake a reform of the state of the church in which we live. This belongs first to God, and then to the magistrate who is appointed to administer it, but not to you, who are nothing but vermin of a proud ignorance. . . . Do not put me to the trouble of writing to you again, nor to others to plead for you, but tell me that your unfortunate words, like those said in a tavern, deserve to be taken back. And recognize the great grace that the officer does you, to be ready to accept you on your repentance. Avoid the shame that you bring and will bring to your friends and relatives; I pray the Lord that He gives you this intelligence. From Poitiers, this fifth of September. From your uncle, if you behave like a good nephew—Martial Navihères."[28]

The young man tried to justify himself and, by frequent letters, to convert his people. In vain, it seems. It is surprising that such writings, composed in distress from the depths of a dungeon, under the threat of the stake and in simple and moving terms, were unable to persuade at least his father and mother:

"My very honored father, I am very grieved at the trouble that is being taken on my behalf, and even more saddened for the annoyance, anguish, and sickness which has come upon you, as upon my mother, because of my captivity. I pray you, in the name of God, to pardon me, since I am the author of all these misfortunes. But reflect that what has happened to me is not without the great foresight of God, who disposes of all things according to his good pleasure and his will . . . and since it is his good pleasure that I should be held captive not as one who swears and blasphemes, a murderer, as lewd, infamous, or a robber, but as a Christian, have you grounds for sorrow or anger? . . . Since it is not for such matters that I have fallen into the hands of men, have you not reason to be glad and to give thanks to Him who has preserved me? For what reasons are you sorrowful?"[29]

This letter remained unanswered, and the pain he felt was poignantly expressed in the last of the missives addressed to his parents:

"The grace and peace of God our Father by Jesus Christ his only Son.

"Although I have not received any letter from you for a long time, nevertheless, I will not cease, by writing, to render you the duty of a son. I do not really know whether I can appropriate to myself what that good and excellent prophet King David says in Psalm 27: 'My father and my mother have abandoned me but the Lord will receive me.' I can certainly say that this good God had not abandoned me, whatever tribulation and affliction I have had, but has always consoled me and consoles me at present, making me rejoice at the honor it pleases Him to do me. But I do not dare truly affirm that you have abandoned me. Could it be that you have come to hate the fruit of your womb, that God gave you? This does not happen even to the brute beasts. You can reply to me that my conduct justifies your attitude, but I cannot see it, since I have done nothing to merit it. . . . If it is because you think that I am a Lutheran, as it is commonly called, you have no reason to hate me, for I am not that, but Christian, believing firmly in what the word of God teaches us . . . and until now, you have not been able clearly to understand what is my faith and my belief in God. I send you now a little book by which you will be able to know it, it is the Apostle's creed, commonly called the *Credo*, which I pray you read with attention, for you will find in it nothing that is not taken from the Holy Scripture."[30]

The arrest of these young men had violently agitated French circles in Geneva. Calvin did not forget his own, and he redoubled his efforts in their favor and dispensed to them freely the spiritual direction which they needed in their trial. Bèze, Viret, and Farel helped him in this task. An abundant correspondence proved to the poor captives how much their masters in Geneva felt at one with them. When Calvin realized that his attempts were futile, and their cause lost, he addressed this last letter to them:

My very dear brothers,

At this hour, necessity exhorts you more than ever to turn all your senses toward heaven. We do not know yet what will be the issue of this affair, but because it seems to me that God wishes to make use of your blood, there is nothing better than to prepare yourselves to this end, praying him to subject you so completely to his good pleasure that nothing will prevent you from following where he calls you. For you know, my brothers, that we must be thus mortified in order to be offered to him in sacrifice. You know that in leaving this world, we do not go off into the unknown and, being assured of the free adoption of your God, you go to it as to your inheritance. What God has ordered for you, Martyrs of his son, is a mark of superabundance for you. Remains the combat, to which the Spirit of God not only exhorts us, but also exhorts us to run toward it. . . . Although your life is in your hands, be ready to leave it at any moment. And, since the Lord uses it for so worthy a cause as witness to the Gospel, do not doubt that it is precious to him. The time is at hand when the earth will make known the blood that has been hidden, and that after having been stripped of these decrepit bodies, we will be wholly restored . . . and gathered together into that eternal kingdom where we will completely enjoy those goods that we only now possess by hope. My brothers, after recommending myself heartily to your prayers . . . I will pray our good Lord to have his hand outspread to preserve you. Your good brother John Calvin.[31]

May 16, 1553, "was the blessed day when the crown of immortality was prepared for them by the Lord after so virtuous a struggle." In the morning they were told they would be burned alive "until their bodies were entirely consumed" at two o'clock on the Place des Terreaux at Lyons. They set themselves then to prayer, calling upon God, quoting Scripture, and singing Psalms. When the moment of execution was near, they were dressed in gray robes and were bound with cords, and hoisted onto a cart which took them to their death. . . . "As they passed on the Place de l'Herberie, at the end of the Saone Bridge, one of them, turning toward the great crowd, said aloud: 'The God of peace, who brought back from the dead the great shepherd of the sheep, Our Lord Jesus Christ, by the blood of the eternal Testament, keep you in all good work to do his will.' Then they began the Apostle's Creed, dividing it by articles, and one following the other, they pronounced it with a holy harmony to show that they had one faith agreeing in all and for all. He whose turn it was to say 'who was conceived of the Holy Spirit, born of the Virgin Mary' raised his voice, in order to let the people know that it was a false calumny of their enemies which made out that they denied this article, and that they had slandered the Virgin Mary.

To the sergeants and their minions who often bothered them, threatening them if they would not keep silence, they twice replied: 'Would you prevent us, who have such a short time to live, from praising and invoking our God?' Having come to the place of execution, they went up with joyous hearts onto the pile of wood that was laid around the stake, the two youngest got up first one after the other, and after having taken off their robes, the executioner attached them to the stake. The last to mount the pile was Martial Alba, the oldest of the five, who was a long time on his knees on the wood praying to the Lord. The executioner, having tied the others, came to take him by the armpits, and wished to make him get down with the others, but he asked Lieutenant Tignac earnestly to accord him the favor . . . to embrace his brothers before dying. The lieutenant allowed it, and then, the aforesaid Martial . . . stooping, kissed the four already tied and bound, saying to each one of them, 'Farewell, farewell my brother.' That done, the said Martial also embraced the executioner and said to him, 'My friend, do not forget my last words.' Then, after he was tied and bound to the same stake, they were all girded with a chain which surrounded the stake. Now the executioner, having received from the judges the order to hasten the death of these five students, put a cord around the neck of each, and the five cords led to a big cord worked by pulleys in order to strangle them more quickly . . . The executioner, after having greased their naked skin, threw on it powdered sulfur, and, having made all these preparations, thought to hasten their death with the aforesaid engine, but the cords were instantly burnt up by the fire, and the five martyrs were heard for some time saying and reiterating aloud these words of exhortation: 'Courage, my brothers, courage.' Those were the last words heard from the midst of the fire which soon consumed the bodies of the five valiant champions and true martyrs of the Lord."[32]

The five students had been given time to recant, but Justice usually was more expeditious in those days. No sooner was a suspect detected than, after having been subjected to some efforts at conversion—generally in vain—he was placed in the executioner's hands. That was the case of many peddlers, such as Macé Moreau:

"Macé Moreau, touched by the fear of God and the desire to be instructed in the true knowledge of the word, retired to Geneva, where, after he had been but a short while, he became, by a change of quality and of his original condition, instead of a vendor of images, a vendor of New Testaments. It so happened that, having taken on a number of these books, he took to the road in France to sell and distribute them. Passing by Troyes in Champagne, he was accosted on coming out from a sermon in the temple of St. Jean in that town, by a certain Nicolas Vaulterin, a hatter commonly called Big Colas, who, realizing more or less of what mind Macé was by the things he said to him, wished only to catch and to ensnare him. And, pretending to be of the religion, he led him, chatting the while, to his house. Macé, full of zeal to advance the glory of God, without knowing anything more about Vaulterin, gave him one of the books he was carrying. Vaulterin immediately seized Macé bodily and took him directly to M. Marc Champy, then the criminal lieutenant of Troyes, who, having interrogated Macé, ordered that his pack of books be brought and searched in his presence; and this done, that Macé should be taken to the royal prisons of Troyes and irons put on his feet. Some time after, this Lieutenant Champy transported himself into the said prisons, where he interrogated Macé on several points concerning the Christian religion, about which the latter replied point by point as he understood it. Then Macé was condemned to be burned alive."[33]

* * *

As has always been the case, the fires burning throughout France did not destroy heretics so much as create martyr-heroes. As the pyres flamed, the new doctrines spread, effectively propagated by the witness of those who died for them. Converts multiplied, and little communities formed around the teachings of one leader, John Calvin. Calvin, for his part, was consumed with the desire to win his native land to his faith. From Geneva there flowed a torrent of counsels, directives, and admonitions; to that city there flowed a stream of the devout, the members of the new churches, who came to be trained for the perilous missions that awaited them. The results of that exchange were soon apparent, and numerous churches began to appear in the city as well as in the country. As soon as there were enough of the faithful to permit it, pastors, elders, and deacons were elected. Thus, in the year 1555, was established the first church of the Reform, that of Paris, in a manner as fortunate as it was fortuitous:

". . . the occasion of the beginning of this church was by the means of a gentleman of Maine, called the Sieur de la Ferrière, who had retired to Paris with his family, in order to be less pursued on account of his religion, and above all, because his wife being pregnant, he did not wish that the child that God would give him should be baptized with the superstitions and accustomed ceremonies of the Roman Church. So then after Jean le Maçon and some others had assembled in the dwelling place of this good gentleman, in a certain place called the Pré-au-Clercs, in order to say their prayers and read the Scriptures there . . . it so happened that the lady being brought to bed, la Ferrière, her husband, asked the assembly not to allow the infant God had given him to be deprived of baptism, for the children of Christians should be consecrated to God, and prayed them to elect a minister who would be able to confer baptism. And because the assembly did not wish to listen to him, he declared he could not, in good conscience, consent to . . . the corruptions of the Roman Church, that it was impossible for him to go to Geneva for this, and that, if the child died without this mark, he would have extreme regret therefrom, and would summon them all before God, if they refused his very just request. This earnest request was the occasion of the first beginnings of the Church of Paris. Jean le Maçon was elected by the assembly . . . and a consistory was established composed of some elders who were deacons, the whole as close as possible to the example of the primitive Church which existed at the time of the Apostles."[34]

The beginnings of the reformed churches in France, as the illustrious potter, Bernard Palissy, a fervent adept of the new religion, recounts them, offered, with few variations, the same characteristics:

". . . There was in this town a certain artisan, poor and indigent . . . who had such a great desire for the advancement of the Gospel that he taught it one day to another artisan as poor as he and as lacking in learning, for both of them had none. Nevertheless, the first showed to the other that, if he wished to employ himself making a few exhortations, it would be the cause of much fruit, and, though the second felt himself totally bereft of knowledge, this gave him courage, and, a few days later, he assembled nine or ten people, and, because he was poorly instructed, he had taken some passages from the Old and the New Testament and had written them down. And when they were assembled, he read them the passages, saying that each one, according to the gifts he had received, should distribute them to others, and that every tree that did not bear fruit would be cut down and cast into the fire. He read another passage from Deuteronomy, saying: "Therefore ye shall teach (these my words) to your children, speaking of them when thou sittest in thy house, and when thou walkest by the way, and when thou liest down, and when thou risest up." He also proposed the parable of the talents to them and a great number of others, in order to achieve two goals: the first, was to show that it pertains to all people to speak of the statutes and ordinances of God . . . the second was to incite certain of his hearers to do the same, for in this same hour they agreed together that six among them would exhort, each one of the six for six weeks, only on Sundays. And because they undertook an affair for which they had never been trained, it was agreed that they would write their exhortations down and would read them before the assembly."[35]

As soon as these communities were sufficiently numerous, they asked Calvin for a pastor. Here is the letter which the church of Vigan wrote on that subject to "its very honored fathers, the ministers of Geneva":

"May mercy, peace, and the charity of our God be multiplied upon you. Very honored Fathers; last October we sent you a man carrying a missive by which we advised you that God, having by his grace driven away a great part of the errors into which we were plunged in the past, had also, by his grace and by the ministers from around about, built, in this town of Vigan, a church numbering up to 1500 persons . . . the which bearer informed us on his return that you had sent him to Lyons to fetch the designated pastor, M. de la Roche, but that he did not find him there, and was obliged to return to you to be furnished with another. But because persecution had broken out in that country since his departure, you had preferred to postpone his coming.

"Now at present, since it has pleased God by his grace to reunite us in as good a state as we were before, we ask you, in God's name, to continue the good that the Lord by your means had begun to do us by providing us with a pastor which you will know is necessary for us. And we promise you to hold him as dear as our own persons, and, to this end, we sent you the present bearer expressly for this purpose.

"He whom you will be pleased to send us must preach publicly, the which he will do in peace, God willing, as have done the ministers who already visited us. It is true that he will have to reply to some argumentative adversaries held back by human prudence, but they are wavering, which gives us the hope of being able to win them.

"We conclude this letter after recommending ourselves to your prayers and petitions."[36]

Before requesting a pastor, the churches had elected elders to ensure discipline, and deacons to administer the common purse, to visit the poor, the prisoners, and the sick, and to teach catechism. Now, provided with pastors, they gathered in secret at night, in attics and cellars and barns, to worship:

"While waiting for all the faithful to arrive, the Scriptures were read in the vulgar tongue. Once all had assembled, the minister prayed to God, all the company kneeling, described the institution of the Last Supper, according to the eleventh chapter of 1 Corinthians, shewed what was the way to celebrate it and how one should present oneself, and excommunicated all seditious persons, the lewd, and those who disobeyed their superiors, forbidding them to approach the holy table. Then those who had been judged worthy to receive this Sacrament, approached the table and received bread and wine from the ministers with these words: 'This is the communication of the body and blood of the Lord . . .' then prayers were said for the king and for the prosperity of his kingdom, for all the afflicted poor, and in general for the whole Church, and a few Psalms were sung."[37]

Under the direction of the pastors and elders, the faithful worked with the fervor of a pristine sect to propagate their beliefs. By 1559, there were over two thousand communities, comprising thirty-four churches, everywhere in France except in Brittany, the eastern provinces, Picardy, and part of the Massif Central. During a synod held in Paris in

May 1559, in the greatest secrecy, the Reformed Church of France was formally constituted according to the directives of John Calvin. The new Church gave itself a confession of faith and a discipline applicable to all its members:

"The occasion of this assembly was that, at the end of the previous year, Antoine de Chandieu, being sent by the Church of Paris to the Church of Poitiers on some business, the Lord's Supper was celebrated there, which was done in a very great assembly, not only of people, but also of the ministers round about. After the celebration of the Supper, the ministers having assembled, they discussed together the doctrine as well as the order and discipline which they observed, then began to apprehend what a good thing it would be if it were to please God that all the churches of France would draw up with one accord a common Confession of Faith and an ecclesiastical Discipline. And, on the contrary, if this were not done, what great evils could arise and divisions, as much in doctrine as in discipline. On breaking up, this little assembly then bade the aforesaid Chandieu to communicate all this to the Church of Paris, to see whether there would be any means of procuring to the churches such a benefit for the future, without which they seemed to be threatened with much confusion. This report having been made to the Church of Paris, after innumerable difficulties had been surmounted, it was concluded that a national synod would be held in Paris, not in order to accord pre-eminence or dignity to that particular church, but because it was the most convenient town to receive in secret numerous ministers and elders."[38]

* * *

King Henry II, a fervent Catholic, was a partisan of merciless repression of the heretics, whom he regarded as no more than simple rebels. His bias, however, had hitherto been tempered by a tendency to minimize the importance of the new churches. But now, events showed that he had underestimated the strength of the "rebels": one night, four hundred of the faithful had been surprised in the Rue St.-Jacques, celebrating their worship; others had had the audacity to come, in great numbers and several days in succession, to chant psalms publicly in the vicinity of St.-Germain. It is likely that these events contributed strongly to the king's decision to conclude the Peace of Le Cateau-Cambrésis with Philip II of Spain, by which he abandoned French claims in Italy. Henry had decided that matters at home required his undivided attention.

Now that peace had been re-established, the warrior-nobles of the realm were free to bring to bear on the adherents of the new religion their strength, their ambitions, the warlike and vengeful spirits which hitherto had found an outlet in the Italian wars. But the faithful, peaceable Christians though they were, were not prepared to allow themselves to be burned without protest, and external pressures quickly made of them a political party and influential faction. The kingdom tensed for action.

Then, as luck would have it, Henry II was killed by a lance splinter which pierced his eye during the celebration of the Le Cateau-Cambrésis treaty. He left a divided kingdom in the hands of a woman, Catherine de Médicis, and minor children.

The wars for the maintenance of the balance of power in Europe had ceased only to make way for other struggles, infinitely more disastrous. Renaissance France was to plunge into the catastrophic civil struggle known as the Wars of Religion (1562-98) and thus to disappear from the European scene for almost forty years. They were years of blood and tears for France.

The new Church, with the vigor of youth, was to hold fast during this terrible trial. Finally, the Edict of Nantes, promulgated by the enigmatic Henry IV in 1598, would proclaim universal freedom and conscience and recognize its right to exist.

For all of the burning zeal of the reformers, Roman Catholicism remained the religion both of the crown and of the vast majority of the people of France. Soon, the Counter Reformation and the ardor of the great Spanish mystics would bring to that ancient institution the spiritual renewal that was essential to her survival. But henceforth, the cherished unity of faith of Christendom belonged to the past.

NOTES
XII · The Renaissance of the Soul

1. Maigret, A. "*Sermon prêché à Grenoble le 25 avril 1524*," from *Le réformateur Aimé Maigret*," by N. Weiss, in *Bulletin de la Société de l'Histoire du Protestantisme Français*, 1890.
2. Berquin, L. de. "*La farce des théologastres*," from *Le théâtre français avant la Renaissaance*, Ed. E. Fournier. Paris, 1872, pp. 418-28.
3. Erasmus, Desiderius. *All the Familiar Colloquies of Desiderius Erasmus of Roterdam*. Translated by N. Bailey. London, 1725. pp. 335-37.
4. *Ibid.*, pp. 338-40.
5. *Ibid.*, pp. 356-61.
6. Estienne, H. *Apologie pour Hérodote*. Ed. J. Ristelhuber. Geneva, 1879. t. II, pp. 217-28, 242-49.
7. Bèze, Th. de. *Histoire ecclésiastique des églises réformées au royaume de France*. Ed. G. Baum et al. Paris, 1883-89. t. I, pp. 74-76.
8. Crespin, J. *Histoire des martyrs persécutés et mis à mort pour la vérité de l'Evangile*. Ed. Daniel Benoît. Toulouse, 1885-89. t. I, pp. 298-302.
9. Bèze, Th. de., *op. cit.*, t. I, p. 34.
10. Crespin, J., *op. cit.*, pp. 302-3.
11. *Ibid.*, p. 304.
12. Calvin, J. "*Commentaires sur de livre des Psaumes*," from *Calvin*. Ed. K. Barth and C. Gagnebin. Paris, 1948, pp. 32-33.
13. *Ibid.*, pp. 35-36.
14. *Ibid.*, pp. 37-38.
15. *Ibid.*, pp. 40-43.
16. *Ibid.*, pp. 33-35.
17. Calvin, J. "*Epîtres à tous amateurs de Jesus-Christ*," *op. cit.*, pp. 85-88.
18. Calvin, J. "*Institution de la religion chrétienne*," *op. cit.*, pp. 47, 49-51.
19. Calvin, J. "*Sermon 10 sur l'harmonie évangelique*," *op. cit.*, pp. 120-21.
20. Calvin, J. "*Institution de la religion chrétienne*," *op. cit.*, pp. 64-65.
21. Calvin, J. "*Catéchisme*," *op. cit.*, pp. 290-91.
22. Calvin, J. "*Institution de la religion chrétienne*," *op. cit.*, pp. 64-65.
23. Crespin, J., *op. cit.*, t. I, p. 586.
24. *Ibid.*, p. 599.
25. *Ibid.*, p. 600.
26. *Ibid.*, pp. 601-2.
27. *Ibid.*, p. 606.
28. *Ibid.*, p. 607.
29. *Ibid.*, pp. 642-43.
30. *Ibid.*, pp. 649-50.
31. *Ibid.*, pp. 658-59.
32. *Ibid.*, pp. 673-74.
33. *Ibid.*, p. 547.
34. *Ibid.*, t. II, p. 537.
35. Palissy, B. *Oeuvres*. Ed. B. Fillon. Paris, 1888, pp. 122-23.
36. "*Lettre de l'Eglise du Vigan*," in *Bulletin de la Société de l'Histoire du Protestantisme Français*, 1868, p. 481.
37. Crespin, J. *op. cit.*, t. II, p. 545.
38. Bèze, Th. de. *op. cit.*, t. I, pp. 199-200.

Epilogue

THE year 1559, as we have seen, was the turning point of the sixteenth century. With it ended the Renaissance in France which had begun in such beauty. That year saw the rupture, perhaps inevitable, which was for many years to destroy the dreams of glory of a spring that had been full of promise for the future. The summer that followed had nothing of the glorious or of the triumphant about it; and the winter of the Wars of Religion has come to epitomize carnage.

What that winter was to be would take another book for the telling. If the reader has found some pleasure in the present volume, he will be able to procure the sequel; for the history of the struggles of the latter part of the century and of the revival of the monarchy which was to end them is one on which another volume is to be written. He will find there the destiny of the widowed Catherine de Médicis, self-effacing until then, confronted, through the misfortunes of the times, with problems and enemies so formidable that they could be overcome only by a monarch of exceptional quality.

Fortunately, the sixteenth century was not to end, as might have been feared, in a national catastrophe. Undoubtedly, the monarchy was deeply shaken; the nobility, decimated; the economy, ruined; the countryside, devastated; the misery, crushing. But France was reborn in the blood of a new dynasty, that of the Bourbons. The Protestant Henry of Navarre, great-nephew of Francis I and closest relative of Henry III, was to be first king of that dynasty. At first, he was refused the throne because of his faith; so, he conquered his kingdom by force of arms, town by town. Paris, however, proud of her orthodoxy, fiercely Catholic, could be captured only by concession; and Henry, opining that "after all, Paris is well worth a Mass," was converted, and crowned as Henry IV.

Realizing that his great-uncle, Francis I, for lack of time and means had not been able to complete his work, Henry took it upon himself to implement the designs of his great forebear. He established, as we have seen, religious liberty. He restored to the monarchy the authority which it had lost during the civil wars. He gave back to an exhausted France the peace and prosperity of yore. And he went on, a quondam renegade, to become the most popular of all the kings of France; it is part of the paradox of his life that, for all that, he was to die under the knife of an assassin. His imperishable image, has passed into folk memory.

With him, the old France ended; the France of the knightly king, of the Pearl of the Valois, of Jacques Cartier, Ronsard, and Jean Goujon. Thereafter the realm, ornamented by the prestige of the Splendid Century, was to advance toward other destinies.

Of the material treasures of the Renaissance in France, little has survived. There are mutilated urns from which hearts, reduced to ashes, were scattered to the winds by heretic or revolutionary hands. There are ruins, where ivy grows and the lizard basks. Time has accomplished its work on this vast canvas of human activity, sparing here and there, capriciously, monuments and paintings from which illustrious faces emerge from oblivion. But, above all, documents remain. Perhaps the most precious of these are those fat, dusty folios, those luxurious gilt-edged quartos specially bound in polychrome calf for the pleasure of the strange M. Grolier and his mysterious friends, those octavos or those tiny sextodecimos covered in shagreen, in olive sheepskin or in warped parchment, with their woodcuts, their illuminated capitals, their vignettes, their booksellers' colophons full of charm and fantasy, and their bindings executed with birds and flourishes. These yield the spirit of the Renaissance, revealing it not only as a time of glory but also of enthusiasm and of joy.

Enthusiasm sent the nobles off to war—especially if that war was in Italy. Enthusiasm went with the navigators and merchants who were off to discover the Gold Route to China. Enthusiasm moved the researchers and the artists in their worship of the mysteries of antiquity and in the labor with which they sought to create, by recreating those mysteries, a truly national art. Enthusiasm sent the Palissys, the Parés, and the Rondelets to search out the secrets of nature. And finally, there was the burning enthusiasm of the soul in search of God.

For the ordinary mortal, there was joy—perhaps the desperate joys of being alive, of fighting, hunting, of violence in games as well as in life. There were the human joys of eating enormous meals, of bursting into great gales of laughter, of wenching, loving, poetizing, of talking at length of the perfect mistress and of the fortunes of love; of learning, of knowing, of traveling, of indulging in every kind of human activity. In short, there was the joy of "assuming as much of humanity as possible." The decay of the race, the anguish of time, boredom—these have no place here. Catherine de Médicis, a survivor of that time of glory, ruled over her decadent sons; and Francis I, the king who counted, was made on the scale of Rabelais and his giants.

Renaissance France had, above all, the face of youth.

GENEALOGICAL TABLE

VALOIS
VALOIS-ORLEANS

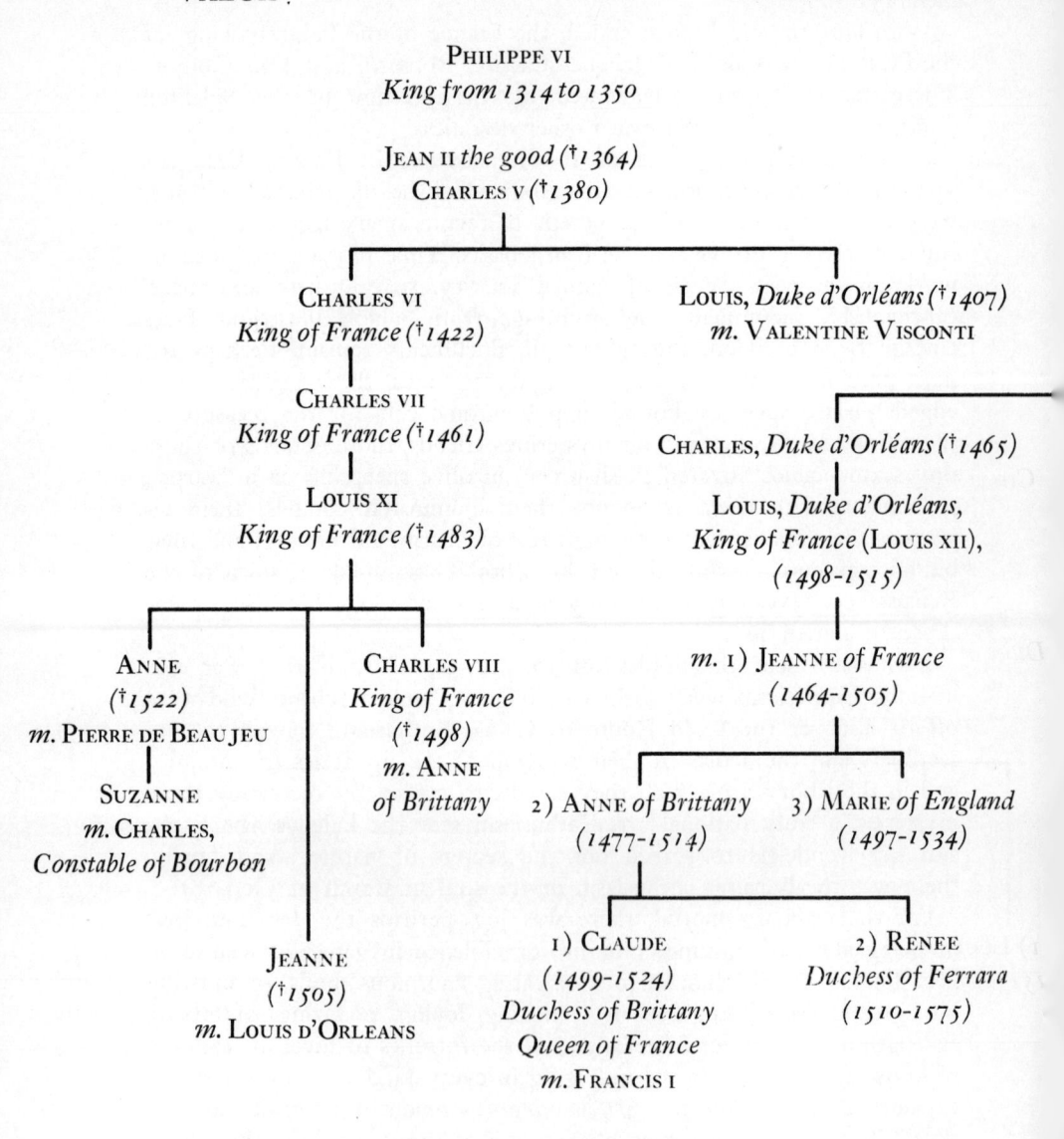

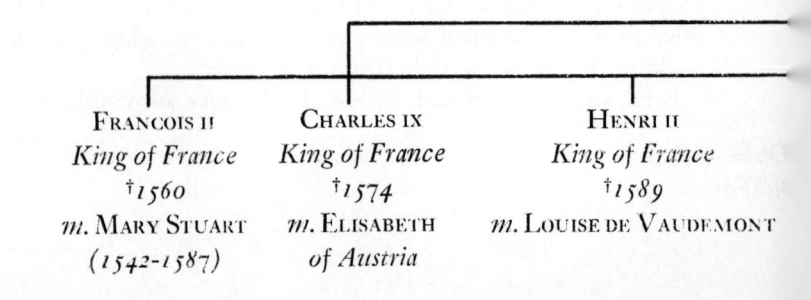

Philippe VI
King from 1314 to 1350

Jean II *the good (†1364)*
Charles V *(†1380)*

Charles VI
King of France (†1422)

Louis, *Duke d'Orléans (†1407)*
m. **Valentine Visconti**

Charles VII
King of France (†1461)

Charles, *Duke d'Orléans (†1465)*

Louis XI
King of France (†1483)

Louis, *Duke d'Orléans,*
King of France (**Louis XII**),
(1498-1515)

Anne
(†1522)
m. **Pierre de Beaujeu**

Charles VIII
King of France
(†1498)
m. **Anne**
of Brittany

m. 1) **Jeanne** *of France*
(1464-1505)

Suzanne
m. **Charles,**
Constable of Bourbon

2) **Anne** *of Brittany*
(1477-1514)

3) **Marie** *of England*
(1497-1534)

Jeanne
(†1505)
m. **Louis d'Orléans**

1) **Claude**
(1499-1524)
Duchess of Brittany
Queen of France
m. **Francis I**

2) **Renee**
Duchess of Ferrara
(1510-1575)

Francois II
King of France
†1560
m. **Mary Stuart**
(1542-1587)

Charles IX
King of France
†1574
m. **Elisabeth**
of Austria

Henri II
King of France
†1589
m. **Louise de Vaudemont**

Index

Abain, M. d', 193
Æneid (Virgil), 195
Agaya, Don, 216–17
Agriculture, 149–53
Agriculture et la maison rustique, L' (Estienne and Liébaut), 149
Alba, Martial, 309
Albanian *estradots* (scouts), 32
Albret, Henri d' (Henry II, King of Navarre), 71, 124
Albret, Jeanne d', 71
Alchemists, 229–30
Alegre, Yves d', 44, 45
Alençon, Duke of, 71, 122–23
Alençon, Marguerite d'. *See* Marguerite of Angoulême
Alexander VI, Pope, 23, 28
Amboise, Charles d', 30
Amboise, George Cardinal d', 20, 27, 50
Amiot, Jacques, 174, 238
Anet, Chapel of, 251
Ango, Jean, 211
Angoulême, Duchess of. *See* Louise of Savoy
Angoulême, Duke of, 68
Angoulême, Marguerite of. *See* Marguerite of Angoulême
Annebaut, Admiral d', 66
Annebaut, M. d' (Marshal of France), 131–32
Anne of Brittany, 28, 39, 69
  marriages of, 15, 24, 27
Anne of Vivonne, 124
Apologie pour Hérodote (Estienne), 282–84
Apprentices in printing, 165, 170, 173
Aquinas, St. Thomas, 195
Aragon, Cardinal of, 17
Arande, Michel d', 285
Architecture
  under Francis I, 101–6, 246
  under Henry II, 246–59
Architecture, De l' (Delorme), 257

Aristides, statue of, 194
Armagnac, Louis d' (Duke of Nemours), 35
Ars, Louis d', 34
Arteries, ligature of, 261–62
Art of Poetry (Sibilet), 242
Ascanio (servant of Cellini), 108
Augsburg, Montaigne's description of, 190–93
Auvergne, Madeleine de la Tour d', 122
Auxerre, Bishop of. *See* Amiot, Jacques
Aventureux, l', 123

Baïf, Lazare de, 242, 243
Ballaguy, 37
Bank of Lyons, 233
Barrès, 23
Bayard Guinegatte de, 36
Bayard, Pierre de, 34, 35–44
  on death of Gaston de Foix, 46–47
  knighting of Francis I by, 48
Bayeaux, M. de, 252
Beatis, Don Antonio de
  on lodgings, 176–77
  on pilgrims, 180
Beaujeu, Anne de, 24
Becquet, Jean, 173
Bellay. *See* Du Bellay
Belleforest, François de, on Fontainebleau, 113
Bembo, Pietro, 37, 243
Berquin, Louis de, 287
  La farce des théologastres, 271–74
Bessarion, Cardinal, 110
Bethlehem, 186–87
Bèze, Theodore de, 285
Bible, 269–70
Bidoux, Prégent de, 54–55
Binet, Claude, on Ronsard and Delorme, 254–55
Birds as weather forecasters, 146–47
Blanche of Savoy (Blanche Paléologus), 37–39

INDEX

Boccaccio, Giovanni, 243
Bodin, Jean, on high cost of living, 231–34
Boileau, Etienne, 165
Boissy, Seigneur de, 135
Bologna, Concordat of, 47
Bomin (king's procurer general), 285
Book of the Courtier, The (Castiglione), 100, 113–15, 119
Book of Trades (Boileau), 165
Borgia, Alexander VI, Pope, 23, 28
Borgia, Caesar (Duke of Valentinois), 28, 50, 57
Borgia, Lucrezia, 37
Boucan (smoking process), 225, 227
Bouillon, Godefroy de, 186
Bourbon, Charles Constable de, 71, 123
  as traitor, 83–86, 88
Bourbon, Duke of, 15
Bourbon, Suzanne de, 84
Bourdeilles, Pierre de (abbé de Brantôme), 25, 84, 113, 124
  on Dauphin Francis, 74
Bourges, new religion in, 284–86
Bramante, 101, 102
Brantôme, abbé de (Pierre de Bourdeilles), 25, 84, 113, 124
  on Dauphin Francis, 74
Brazil
  French settlement in, 219–20
  Jean de Léry's voyage to, 207–10, 221–29
Brescia, sack of, 39
Breviary of St. Gregory, 194–95
Brézé, Pierre de (Grand Seneschal of Normandy), 83
Briçonnet, Guillaume (William), 25, 270
"Brigade, the" (College of Coqueret), 242
Brissac, M. de, 95
Bruges, Louis de, library of, 110
Brusquet (professional fool), 127–29
Bucer, Martin, 296, 297
Budé, Guillaume, 109, 119, 174, 239, 243, 286, 287
  on hunting, 120–22
  royal college and, 236–37
Burchard, Jean, journal of, 56
Burlet, Martial, 258

Cabinet of Curiosities, 112
Cabinet of Paintings, 106–7
Cabinet of Rings, 112

Cairo, description of, 180–82
Calabria, Duke of, 49
Calvin, John, 238, 285, 293–303, 307–8, 310, 311
  doctrine of, 297–302
Cannibalism among Topinambou, 219, 225–28
Caouin (drink), making of, 224–25
Carraconny (bread), making of, 213
Cartier, Jacques, expeditions of, 211–19
Castiglione, Count Baldesar, 100, 113–15, 119
Catena (robber), 198–99
Cavalli, Marino
  on Francis I, 65–67
  on Henry II, 77–78
Cellini, Benvenuto, 107–9
Cemeteries in Cairo, 182
Chabannes, Marshal de, 85, 86
Chambord (palace), 102
Champagne (king at arms), 35
Champy, Marc, 310
Chapel of Anet, 251
Charles (Duke of Savoy), 37
Charles V (Holy Roman Emperor), 29, 67, 68, 70–72, 74, 77, 80–98
  dream of, 80–81
  journey through France of, 133–38
  rivalry between Francis I and, 81–98
Charles VIII (King of France), 51, 101, 104, 110
  death of, 26
  description of, 24–25
  in Italian wars, 22–23, 25–26, 27, 49
  in papal court, 56
Charles IX (King of France), 106, 229, 262
  letter of Catherine de Médicis to, 118–19
Charles of Ghent. *See* Charles V (Holy Roman Emperor)
Charles the Bold (Duke of Lorraine), 15, 80–81
Charlotte (daughter of Francis I), 67, 72
Charlotte of Savoy, 24
Charterhouse at Pavia, 101
Chartreuse de Champmol (mausoleum), 81
Château de Madrid (palace), 102
Château de Monceaux, 257
Château de St.-Maur, 246, 251
Chateaubriand, M. de, 129
Chateaubriant, Françoise de, 113

INDEX

Christ, 187, 267
Christian Institute (Calvin), 293, 297
Cicero, 243
Clagny, Sire de. *See* Lescot, Pierre
"Clattering," 155–56
Claude (Queen of France), 67–68, 69
Clement VII, Pope, 94
Coclès, Barthélemy, description of Charles VIII by, 25
Coligny, Gaspard de, 219–20
College of Coqueret, 242
Colloquies (Erasmus), 176, 177, 275–82
Colonial settlements, 218–20
Columbus, Christopher, 206
Commynes, Philippe de, 32
  verse by, 57–58
Concordat of Bologna, 47
Conversation in court of Francis I, 123–24
Cooking, spices for, 205
Cop, Nicolas, 294
Country houses, 144–46
Country life, 143–63
Courtiers, "perfect," 113–16
Cousin, Jean, 219
Crespin, J.
  on Ecrevain, 304
  on Milon, 290–91
  on Valeton, 291–92

Da Gama, Vasco, 206
Dan, Father, on paintings at Fontainebleau, 104–5, 106–7
Danès, P., 238, 239–40
Daurat (Dorot), Jean, 238, 242
Della Robbia, G., 102
Delorme, Charlotte, 255
Delorme, Jean, 252, 258
Delorme, Jeanne, 258
Delorme, Philibert (father), 246–48, 251–59
  on good and bad architects, 255–56
  will of, 257–59
Delorme, Philibert (son), 258
Del Sarto, Andrea, 104, 107
Discoveries, 205–34
  of Cartier, 211–19
Divizia (peasant woman), 201
Donnaconna (King of Canada), 213, 217
Du Bellay, J., on poetry, 242–45
Du Bourg, Jean, 290, 292
Duboys, Jean, 106
Du Cerceau, Androuet, 102

Du Fail, Noël, 144
  on country life, 146–47, 148–49
Du Plessis-au-Chat, Sieur, 130
Du Tillet, Canon, 294
Dyes, 205

Ecrivain, Pierre, 304–5
Edict of Gaillon (1571), 168, 171
Edict of Nantes (1598), 314
Edward III (King of England), 99
Eleanor of Austria (Queen of France), 67, 68, 83, 93
Embrun, Archbishop of, 90
Erasmus, Desiderius, 236, 240–41, 269
  Colloquies, 176, 177, 275–82
  letter to Charles V of, 92
  on professional fools, 126–27
Esnoguy, 213–14
Estienne, Charles, 144, 149
Estienne, François, 173
Estienne, Henri, *Apologie pour Hérodote*, 282–84
Estissac, M. d', 193, 194
Estradiots (scouts), 32
Etampes, Duchess d', 108–9
Etienne, H., 238

Farce des théologastres, La (Berquin), 271–74
Farel, William, 295–96
Fèbvre, Lucien, 269
Ferdinand of Aragon (King of Spain), 25, 26, 42, 80, 206
Ferrara, Duchess of. *See* Renée of France
Fichet, Guillaume, 167
Field of the Cloth of Gold, 82
Fluxas, Bernadine de, 37–38
Foix, Gaston de (Duke of Nemours), 26, 29, 42–47
Fontainebleau (palace), 102–6, 112–13, 253
  festivities for Charles V at, 133, 134
Fools, professional, 126–29
Foreign mercenaries, 30–32
Fort Coligny (Brazil), 220
Fountain of the Innocents (Paris), 250
France, Paolo de, 56
Francis (Dauphin de Viennois), 93
  baptism of, 122
  death of, 74–76
  imprisonment in Spain of, 93, 95
  proclaimed king by Francis I, 92

Francis I (King of France), 19, 65–78
　children of, 67, 74–78
　court of, 100–35
　　architecture in, 101–6, 246
　　conversation in, 123–26
　　gossip in, 129–33
　　hunting in, 119–22
　　literary art in, 109–12
　　music in, 112
　　painting in, 105–7
　　professional fools in, 126–29
　　sculpture in, 107–9
　　tourneys in, 122–23
　description of, 66–67
　expeditions to new lands and, 211, 218
　general estimate of, 11
　imprisonment of, 86–93
　in Italian wars, 29, 47–48
　marriages of, 67–69, 93
　mother of, 68–72
　religion and, 286–90, 293
　rivalry between Charles V and, 81–98
　royal college and, 236–37
French Park (Paris), 137
Fribourg, Perpetual Peace of, 47
Friburger, Michel, 167
Fromont, Thomas, 212
Fugger family, 191–92

Gaillon, Edict of (1571), 168, 171
Galland, Pierre, on library of Francis I, 111–12
Gama, Vasco da, 206
Genoa
　entry of Louis XII into, 49–52
　rebellion of, 54–55
Genouillac, Galiot de, 47–48
Gering, Ulrich, 167
Gie, Marshal of. *See* Rohan, Pierre de
Gioconda, La (painting), 107
Giocondo, Francisco, 107
Giustiniano, Francisco, on Francis I and Charles V, 81–82
Giustiniano, Marino, 116
Gonneville, Paulmier de, 219
Gonzaga, Cardinal, 196
Gonzaga, Elisabetta, 101
Gonzalvo of Cordova, 33, 34
Gossip in court of Francis I, 129–33
Gouberville, Gilles de, 144
Goujon, Jean, 247, 248, 251
　obelisk illustrated by, 249–50
Gourgues, Dominique de, 229

Granada, Treaty of, 34
Grande Hermine (ship), 212
Gritti, Andrea, 81
Guidacerius, Agathias, 228
Guise, François de (Duke of Lorraine), 262
Guyenne (king-at-arms), 95

Haubourdin (companion of Gaston de Foix), 43
Hauser, H., 275
Hauser, Henri, 165
Havré, Marquis of, 262–65
Hémerillon (ship), 212
Henry VIII (King of England), 28, 69, 70
　in rivalry between Francis I and Charles V, 82–83, 97
Henry II (King of France), 19, 75, 76–78, 97, 233, 313–14
　architecture under, 246–59
　entry into Paris of, 246, 247–51
　imprisonment in Spain of, 93, 95
　marriage to Catherine de Médicis of, 74, 77
Henry III (King of France), 265
Henry IV (King of France), 106, 314, 316–17
Henry II (King of Navarre) (Henri d'Albret), 71, 124
Heptaméron (Marguerite of Angoulême), 124–26
Hérissaie (country house), 144
Histoire des martyrs (Crespin)
　on Ecrivain, 304
　on Milon, 290–91
　on Valeton, 291–92
Hochelaga, Saguenay, Cartier's description of, 213–15
Holy League, 94
Holy Sepulcher, 187
Horace, 243
Hostelries
　French, 176–77
　German, 177–78
　Italian, 178–79
Hôtel-Dieu, 259
Houses, country, 144–46
Hugo, Victor, 65
Humanists, 236–41, 287
Hunting at court of Francis I, 119–22

Immaculate Conception, 268

INDEX

Indies, travel to, 205–6
Infantado, Duke of. *See* Mendoza, Don Diego de
Inflation, 230–34
Isabella (Queen of Spain), 206
Italian wars, 22–59
  battle of Ravenna, 42–46
  battle of Melegnano, 47–48

Jalobert, Macé, 212
Jean II (King of France), 94
Jerusalem, 187
Jesus Christ, 187, 267
Joan of Aragon (Queen of Sicily), portrait of, 107
John II (King of France), 94
Journey of the Cardinal of Aragon (Beatis), 176
Juana the Mad, 80
Julian II, Pope, 28–29, 42
Justiniano, Dmitri, execution of, 55

Kranz, Martin, 167

La Catelle (martyr), 290, 292
La Châtre, Captain de, 252–53
"Ladies' Peace, The," 72, 236
La Ferrière, Sieur de, 310–11
La Forge, Etienne de, 290, 292
La Marche, Robert de, 45
La Matharée (Egypt), 182
Lannoy, General, 86
La Palice, M. de, 33–34
La Pommeraye, Charles de, 212
La Ramée, Pierre de (Ramus), on Toussaint, 238–39
La Roche-sur-Yon, Prince de, 131–33
La Roque, Chevalier Jean-François de, 218
Lascaris, Jean, 110
La Tour d'Auvergne, Madeleine de, 122
Laudonnière, René de, 229
Lautrec, Seigneur de, 46, 48
Le Brêton, Gilles, 102, 103–4
Le Breton, Guillaume, 212
Leclerc, Jean, 287
Lefebvre, L., on Calvin, 293
Lefebvre d'Etaples, Jacques, 269, 270
Le Marié, Guillaume, 212
Lemoine, Cardinal, college of, 18
Le More, Ludovic, 26, 53
Leo X, Pope, 110
Leonardo da Vinci, 104, 107

Le Roy, André, 180
Léry, Jean de, voyage to Brazil by, 207–10, 221–29
Lescot, Pierre (Sire de Clagny), 246
Lescun, M. de, 48
Le Veneur, Jacques, 211
Levy-Strauss, Claude, 221
Liébaut, Jean, 149
Ligny, Sire de, 53–54
Lisieux, Bishop of, 83
Literary art, 109–12
Lives (Plutarch), 174
Lodgings. *See* Hostelries
Lorraine, Duke of. *See* Guise, François de
Lorraine, Jean Cardinal de, on death of dauphin, 74–75
Louis XI (King of France), 23–25, 80
Louis XII (King of France), 16, 42, 67–69, 84, 180
  death of, 28
  entry into Genoa of, 49–52
  in Italian wars, 22, 27–29
  library of, 110
Louis XIV (King of France), 118
Louise (daughter of Francis I), 67
Louise of Savoy (Duchess of Angoulême), 68–71, 76, 84, 123, 124, 180
  letters from Francis I to, 47–48, 87
  poem by, 72
  as regent, 71, 87, 92
Louvre, 19, 246, 251
Loyal Servitor, The (Jacques de Mailles), 35
Loyola, Ignatius, 238
Lusson, Jean, 258
Luther, Martin, 269, 270
Lyons
  Bank of, 233
  description of, 20

Machiavelli, Niccolò, 17, 24
  on Julian II, 29
  on Maximilian of Hapsburg, 26–27
Maçon, Jean de, 310, 311
Madrid, Treaty of (1526), 68, 93, 94
Magellan, Ferdinand, 206
Maheu, Didier, inventory of, 165–66
Maigret, Aimé, sermon by, 271
Mailles, Jacques de, 35
Maingart, Jacques, 212
Mantua, Marquis of, 86

Manuel I the Fortunate (King of Portugal), 206
Marcourt, Antoine de, bill by, 288–89
Marguerite of Angoulême (Queen of Navarre), 71–73, 81, 90, 91, 123, 236, 270, 284, 285
  on Claude of France, 68
  Heptaméron, 124–26
Marguerite of Austria, 72
Marguerite of Navarre. See Marguerite of Angoulême
Marot, Clément, 242, 275
Martin, Jean, 247
Martyrs, 290–92, 303–10
Mary of England (Queen of France), 28, 69
Massacre of St. Bartholomew, 265
Mattois, 160–63
  slang of, 162–63
Maupéru, Vincent, 258
Maximilian of Hapsburg (Holy Roman Emperor), 26–27, 233
Medici, Hippolito Cardinal de, 107
Medicine, 259–65
Médicis, Catherine de, 74, 77, 78, 103, 122, 262, 314, 316, 317
  Delorme and, 251, 254–55
  letter to Charles IX of, 118–19
Melegnano, battle of, 47–48
Mendoza, Don Diego de (Duke of the Infantado), 89
Mercenaries, foreign, 30–32
Mercure (Albanian commander), 32
Mesnil-au-Val (country house), 144
Michel, Jean, 285
Michelet, Jules, 26
Milon, Barthélemy, 290–91
Milon, Robert, 290
Mona Lisa (painting), 107
Monastery of St. Catherine, 184–85
Mondragon, Monseigneur de, 38
Monopolies. See Strikes
Montaigne, Michel Eyquem de, travels of, 178–79, 188–201
Montecucullo, Count Sebastiano de, 74, 76
Montefeltre, Duke Federico di, 100–1
Montefeltre, Guidobado di, 101
Montéjean, Maréchal de, 260, 262
Montespédon, Philippe de (Maréchale de Montéjean), 129–33
Montluc, Blaise de, on Charles de Bourbon, 84

Montmorency, Constable de, 77, 134–35, 137
Montréal, Seigneur de, 212
Moon, sowing and, 152
Moreau, Macé, 309–10
Moysant, Controller, 252–53
Music, 112

Nantes, Edict of (1598), 314
Navarre, King of, 15. See also Henry II (King of Navarre)
Navarre, Count Pedro, 46
Navarre, Queen of. See Marguerite of Angoulême
Navihères, Martial, 306
Navihères, Pierre, 306–7
Nemours, Duke of. See Armagnac, Louis d'; Foix, Gaston de
Nobility, country, 143–63
Northwest Passage, search for, 207, 212
Novi, Paolo de, 54–55

Orleans, Louis d'. See Louis XII (King of France)
Orleans, M. d'. See Henry II (King of France)
Ory, Mathieu, 285–86
Ozillac (country house), 144

Pacheco, Doña Agnes, 74
Painting, 105–7
Paléologus, Blanche (Blanche of Savoy), 37–39
Paléologus, William VI, 37
Palissy, Bernard, on reformed churches, 311
Paradis, Paul, 238
Paré, Ambroise, 259–65
Paris
  description of, 17–19
  first church of the Reform in, 310–11
  Henry II's entry into, 246, 247–51
  reception for Charles V in, 134–38
  thieves' quarter of, 160–63
  University of, 18
Patron saints, 268
Pavia
  battle of, 86
  Charterhouse at, 101
Paz, Captain Pedro de, 43–44
"Pearl of the Valois." See Marguerite of Angoulême
Peasants, 154–60

INDEX

Pellicier, Guillaume, 110–11
Penitencers in Rome, 197–98
Periers, Bonaventure des, 154
Perpetual Peace of Fribourg, 47
Petite Hermine (ship), 212
Petrarch, 243
Pharaoh, desert of, 184
Philip II (King of Spain), 97
Philip the Handsome (Archduke of Austria), 70, 80
Piefort, Jean, 70
Piefort, Pierre, 70
Pilgrims, 179–88
    Erasmus on, 275–76
Pine Grotto, 112
Pirates, 210–11
Platter, Thomas, on Paris, 17–19
Pleiade, 242, 245
Plombières, baths at, 188–90
Plutarch, 174
    Opuscula, 194
Poetry, 242–46
Poille, Antoine, 290, 292
Poitiers, Diane de, 77–78, 83
Pompérant (companion of Bourbon), 85–86
Pontbriand, Claude de, 212
Pope
    audience with, 193–94
    See also specific popes
Posillipo, grotto of, 58–59
Postel, Guillaume, 238
Prices, rise in, 230–34
Primaticcio, Francesco, 103, 104, 107, 108, 112, 246, 251, 253
Printing, 165–74
Prisoners
    of Hochelaga, 213–14
    of Topinambou tribes, 225–28
Pyramids, 182

Rabelais, François, 238, 240
    on printing, 165
Ramus. *See* La Ramée, Pierre de
Raphael, 101, 104, 106–7
Ravenna, battle of, 42–46
Ravestain, Philippe de, 49, 58
Red Sea, 183
Reffuge, Regnault de, 69
Reilhac, François de, 144
Relics, Erasmus on cult of, 278–82
Religion, 267–314
    of Calvin, 285, 293–303, 307–8, 310, 311

    patron saints, 268
    revolution in, 269
Renand, Simon, 249
Renée of France (Duchess of Ferrara), 68
Réponse aux paradoxes de M. de Malestroit (Bodin), 231–34
Ribault, Jean, 229
Rieux, M. de, 252
Robertet, Florimand, 51
Roberval, Seigneur de. *See* La Roque, Chevalier Jean-François de
Rochefort, 69
Rohan, Pierre de (Marshal of Gie), 51, 262
Roman Catholic Church, 267–314
    papal audience, 193–94
    patron saints, 268
    reformation of, 269–314
Romaneaux (country house), 144
Rome, Montaigne in, 193–99
Ronsard, P., 242, 245–46
    disagreement with Delorme of, 254–55
Rosa, Lady, 57
Rosary, cult of, 268
Rosso, Il, 104, 106, 135
Rouen, description of, 19–20
Rougement, Philippe, 216
Rousseau, Jean-Jacques, 229
Royal Readers, 237–41, 287
Rynach, Claude de, 189

Sailors, 207–11
St. Barbara, 268
St. Catherine, tomb of, 185
St. Christopher, 268
St. Eustochia, 186
St.-Gelais, Mellin de, 242
St. Germain (Paris), 19
St. Helen, 186
St. Jacques (Paris), 19
St. Jerome, 183
St. Lawrence River, Cartier's description of, 218
St. Marceau (Paris), 19
St. Michel (Paris), 19
St. Paul, head of, 198
St. Peter, head of, 198
St. Peter's strait, discovery of, 212
Saint-Pol, Constable of, 84
Saints, patron, 268
Saint-Simon, Duke de (Louis de Rouvroy), on tower of Alcázar, 89–90

St. Thomas Aquinas, 195
St. Thomas of Canterbury (sanctuary), Erasmus on, 278–82
St. Veronica, 196
Salerno, Prince of, 49
Saluces, Marquis Jean-Louis de, 129–33
Saminiati, Giovanni da Vincenzo, 200
Sancerre, Count of, 48
Scève, 242
Scholars, 251–65
  poets, 242–46
  Royal Readers, 237–41
Sculpture, 107–9
Selves, President de, on illness of Francis I, 90–91
Seneca, 194
Serlio, Sebastiano, 102, 246
Sforza, Elizabeth, 37
Sforza, Ludovico, 28
Sibilet, Thomas, 242
Siderander (student), letter by, 239–40
Simon, Michel, 285
Slang, Mattois, 162–63
Sluter, Claus, 81
Soldiers, description of, 30–34
Sorbonne, 287
  Royal Readers and, 236, 238, 240
Sowing, month for, 151–52
Speroni, Sperone, 242
Spices, 205
Spinola, Thomasine, 52
Squids, catching in Sagueney of, 213–14
Strikes in printing industry, 168–69
Stromboli, 58
Strozzi, Pierre de, 127–29
Students in Paris, 18
Suleiman ("Emperor of the Turks"), 112
Surgery, 259–65
Suriano, Michael, on situation of France, 15–16

Tabonneau, M., 258
Talmont, Prince of, 48
Tapiroussou (tapir), eating of, 208–9
Taverns. See Hostelries
Terrail, Jeanne, 36, 39
Terrail, Pierre. See Bayard, Pierre de
Theater in religious revolution, 271–74
Thénaud, Brother Jean, pilgrimage of, 180–88
Thomas Aquinas, St., 195
Thou, Christophe de, 252, 258
Titian, 104

Toledo, Padre, 195
Topinambou (Brazilian natives, description of), 221–29
Tourneys, 122–23
Tournon, Françis, Cardinal of, 66, 112
Toussaint, Ramus on, 238–39
Travel Diary (Montaigne), 178–79
Travelers, 176–201
  lodgings for, 176–79
  pilgrims, 179–88
Triboulet (professional fool), 127
Typographers, 168

Ulysses gallery (Fontainebleau), 103
University of Paris, 18
Urbino, court at, 100–1
Urbino, Duke of, 122

Valentinois, Duke of (Caesar Borgia), 28, 50, 57
Valeton, Nicolas, 290–92
Valois family, genealogical table of, 318–19
Vasari, Giorgio, 112
Vatable, François, 238
Vatican Library, 194–95
Vaudray, Claude de, 37
Vaugayres, rebellion in, 53–54
Vaulterin, Nicolas, 309–10
Vendôme, Cardinal de, 70
Vendôme, M. de, 123
Vesc, Etienne de, 25
Vieilleville, Maréchal de, 129–33
Viennois, Dauphin de. See Francis
Vigo, Jean, 261
Villegagnon, Chevalier de, 228
Viret, Peter, 295
Virgil, 195, 243
Virgin Mary, 182, 186, 187
  cult of, 267–68, 276–78
Vitruvius, translation of, 247

Wars. See Italian wars
Weather, birds as forecasters of, 146–47
White Horse Court (Fontainebleau), 103
Women
  of Genoa, 51–52
  Topinambou, 222, 227
  of Valencia, 88–89
Workers (printers), 165–74

Xavier, Francis, 238